9TH FEBRUARY 2010
LINCOLN'S INN

Dear Julian,

Et semel emissum
volat irrevocabile verbum.

Best Wishes,

FIGHTING MONSTERS

Against the backdrop of the British-American law- and war-making of the first decade of the millennium, Fighting Monsters considers how the way we think about law affects the way we make war and how the way we think about war affects the way we make law. The discussion is founded upon four of the martial phenomena (aggressive or 'pre-emptive' war, targeted killings, torture and arbitrary detention) that unsettle our complacent and flabby understandings of what law is to a liberal democracy.

The author argues, first, that force is a quintessential, albeit ambivalent element of any realistic, serviceable and intellectually coherent concept of law. Second, reappraising the classic question at the intersection of martial doctrine and political philosophy in its contemporary context, the author asserts that we need not, in fighting monsters, become monstrous ourselves; that fighting partisans does not entail our own partisanship; and that we can indeed govern without dirtying our hands.

Seeking to ground a total, essentialist and practical theory of legality's sordid relationship with brutality, the book encompasses language and image; war and crime; liberty, security and rationality; amity, enmity and identity; sex, terror and perversion; temporality, spirituality and sublimity; economy and hegemony; parliaments, the press and the public man.

Fighting Monsters

British-American War-making and Law-making

Rory Brown

OXFORD AND PORTLAND, OREGON
2011

Published in the United Kingdom by Hart Publishing Ltd
16C Worcester Place, Oxford, OX1 2JW
Telephone: +44 (0)1865 517530
Fax: +44 (0)1865 510710
E-mail: mail@hartpub.co.uk
Website: http://www.hartpub.co.uk

Published in North America (US and Canada) by
Hart Publishing
c/o International Specialized Book Services
920 NE 58th Avenue, Suite 300
Portland, OR 97213–3786
USA
Tel: +1 503 287 3093 or toll-free: (1) 800 944 6190
Fax: +1 503 280 8832
E-mail: orders@isbs.com
Website: http://www.isbs.com

British Library Cataloguing in Publication Data
Data Available

ISBN: 978–1-84946–093–4

Typeset by Columns Design Ltd, Reading
Printed and bound in Great Britain by
TJ International Ltd, Padstow, Cornwall

To those who make Britain Great.

Preface

This book considers how the way we think about law affects the way we make war and how the way we think about war affects the way we make law. The discussion is grounded by using as cornerstones four of the martial phenomena that challenge law, namely aggressive or 'pre-emptive' war, targeted killings, torture and arbitrary detention. By way of explanatory note, I should say something about the timing and scope of this publication.

I finished writing in early 2009. Rather than updating the text at the proof stage, I preferred to leave it substantially untouched for two reasons. First, as will become clear, the events of the last decade have only been referred to in so far as they help to elaborate a theory of law – to that extent any period of history could have been chosen. Second, it seemed disingenuous to pepper the text with 'wisdom' gained after the event.

At the time of writing, it was my hope (albeit not my belief) that, if and when the time came for publication, what with the changes in British and American leadership, this manuscript would have lost some currency. Lamentably, this is not the case. It is therefore worth taking stock of how the picture has changed (where it has), since Brown (and subsequently David Cameron) and Obama took over from Blair and Bush.

Terrorism is vogue. Violent extremism is a scourge on modern society. Only chance intervened to save a plane full of passengers from being blown up by a London student in Detroit on Christmas Day 2009. Moscow's metro was the target of deadly coordinated suicide bombings in March. The UK threat level has returned to severe. In the United States, a congressionally appointed commission warned a bio-weapon attack would occur in the near future that will 'fundamentally change the character of life for the world's democracies'. Home-grown British- and American-born terrorists are giving their lives in support of various of al-Qaeda's causes around the world. Al-Qaeda itself is a massive, complex and flexible ideological network of independent mobile nodes, capable of low-budget, high impact terrorist attacks. It is also capable of sophisticated missions. In January 2010, for instance, an al-Qaeda double agent, having infiltrated American intelligence, blew himself up in an Afghan base, killing one Jordanian and seven American agents.

Iraq is perilously unstable. Since 30 June 2009, when American troops symbolically withdrew from its streets, the preparations for Iraq's March elections were accompanied by a series of not only sophisticated and spectacular car, truck and suicide bombings but also rocket attacks targeting institutions of the embryonic government and turning the capital into nothing short of a bloodbath. The seeming inability of the two political protagonists, Messrs Maliki and Allawi, to jaw-jaw will do nothing to dampen the sectarian violence that once again threatens to engulf the country. Iran's foray into Iraq's territory and brief occupation of an oil well in the Fakka field betrays its concern about Iraq's ambitious oil production plans. Furthermore, Iran is not the only power interested in Iraq's ongoing instability.

In Britain, the Chilcot inquiry, conducted by a panel selected by the incumbent prime minister including two academics, a former diplomat and a cross-bench peer, seemed less of an inquiry than a platform for those involved to restate their reasons for the Iraq invasion. The proceedings were notable for the absence of lawyers and the predetermination that no fingers would be pointed, matters which broadcast the message that law was irrelevant and that those hoping for some form of accountability would do so in vain. At best then, the inquiry was group therapy for the political class. It will have done little to repair the tattered trust between civilian leadership and armed forces and has done nothing to mend the damaged relationship between those who govern and the governed.

Though there have been modest successes of provincial democracy, we are at war with the Taliban in Afghanistan and Pakistan. The Obama administration's 'new' counter-insurgency strategy of repeated surges, coupled with big cash injections into Pakistan sounds depressingly familiar. In Cuba, Guantánamo Bay's inmates have proven more difficult to dispose of than anticipated by the new President, who has failed to honour his symbolic campaign promise to close the controversial brig. Indeed, rather than drawing a line under the abuses of the outgoing administration, he continues to hold the remaining inmates under the very same, much maligned empowering Act as his predecessor and, to the dismay of the American Civil Liberties community who championed his election, has re-instituted the dubious-sounding Military Commissions to try some of the harder prisoners.

Despite a new 'directive' as to the importance of winning Afghan support by avoiding civilian fatalities and the incoming General McCrystal's request for more boots on the ground to avoid the mortal messiness of aerial warfare, Obama's natural inclination towards a 'take-no-prisoners' approach has led him to prefer local jails, not renowned for their hospitality, as well as the steeply increased use of drone-mounted missile attacks. Though this tactic has had its notable successes, including the killing of Taliban Chief Baitullah Mehsud in August 2009, fatal failures – such as the funeral attack on 3 June 2009, which killed 80 non-combatants – are frequent and disastrously costly. In Pakistan, the frontal in Waziristan has provoked a spate of suicide attacks of unprecedented ferocity conducted by indoctrinated Mehsuds – hundreds of civilians have perished in their explosive ire.

The counter-insurgency abroad is waged against a political backdrop at home of progressively more disturbing revelations about US stewardship of and British complicity in torture of suspected terrorists. In the United Kingdom, in proceedings pertaining to Binyam Mohammed's ordeal at the behest of the US government, purportedly to preserve the sanctity of the British-American intelligence-sharing arrangements, an inordinate amount of judicial time and public money was spent in the government's attempt to suppress several paragraphs of documents detailing his mistreatment and the nature of the United Kingdom's involvement. In the words of the Lord Chief Justice of England and Wales, though the Foreign Secretary did 'everything he lawfully could' to prevent it, 'the publication of the redacted paragraphs would not and could not, of itself, do the slightest damage to the public interest'. Perhaps the most positive aspect of the related proceedings in the United States was that the administration, rather than attempting to bury the perturbing truth, 'did not deny or challenge the accuracy of Mr Mohammed's brutal treatment'. Nevertheless, the prevailing culture of executive secrecy that characterised counter-terrorism operations and policy meant that this book was written squinting in the shadows of our battle against spectral forms within and without our societies. It is no doubt an impaired interpretation of what was, and an idiosyncratic vision of what ought to follow.

With respect to scope, one limiting factor is that the discussion is constructed within the four afore-mentioned jurisprudential cornerstones. Another is that I have concentrated on the British-American alliance against terror. The reasons I have done so are threefold: My limited knowledge of (and access to) other cultures counsels reluctant critique; the British and American administrations took it upon themselves to 'lead' the war on terror – it therefore seems fitting that they bear the brunt of criticism here. That said, though I have no experience of comparative study, I imagine that governments the world over can be expected to grab for similar tools to fix the terror problem – to that extent, it is hoped that this book contains lessons that stretch beyond its parochial frame.

In short, it seems to me that questions not only as to what ought or ought not to be legal – for example 'pre-emptive self-defence', regime change, torture, targeted killings, arbitrary detention – but also as to how the legality or illegality of such extraordinary measures is constituted and determined, have certainly not diminished but might even have increased in importance over the last few years. This book then, is a modest attempt at beginning to address those questions.

It was myself, after all, whom I have betrayed most basely.
Joseph Conrad, *Under Western Eyes*

Acknowledgements

My sincerest thanks go to Francesco Francioni for his mentorship; to Philip Allott, Stephen Holmes, Martin Scheinin, Linda Stone, Adam Stone and Euan MacDonald for their meticulous reading of and helpful comments on an earlier draft; to Matthew Kramer, Neil Walker and George Fletcher for generously sharing their reflections on my work; to Annick Bulckaen, Ben Morris and Ruth Gbikpi for their kind administrative assistance; to the European University Institute in Florence, Columbia University and the Center for Law and Security of NYU in New York City for providing stimulating and scholarly environments in which to think and write; to the British Government and the EUI for funding this research; to my publisher Richard Hart for his enthusiastic backing and to his team for making this a reality; to my friends for their tolerance (particularly Tom, Jack and Thieu), and finally to my family for their unquestioning support.

Responsibility for opinions and errors is the author's alone.

Contents

1

Fighting Monsters

We cannot determine to what height the human species may aspire in their advances towards perfection, but it may safely be presumed, that no people, unless the face of nature is changed, will relapse into their original barbarism.

Edward Gibbon[1]

GIBBON PRESUMES THAT there are invisible shark's teeth, piercing our flesh, preventing our backsliding into a sea of barbarism, and ensuring our onward progression into the warm belly of civilisation. The disciples of human rights have made similar arguments. Now that we have these principles, they say, we will never succumb to the totalitarian tendencies and again commit the gross infractions of human dignity that darkened the last century. Champions of what is called constitutional or liberal democracy say much the same thing. With these immutable, time-honoured restraints on the democratic process, we are told, our societies will protect not the crude right of the majority to impose its will on the totality, but will forever cherish the a priori precepts that underpin and inform democracy, hallowed values like dignity, agency, liberty and equality.

The Anglo-American attempt, during the last eight years, to combat terrorism makes it worth questioning the safety of these comforting presumptions. As Eric Hobsbawm put it, the 'International Red Cross recognises the rising tide of barbarism for it condemns both sides in the Iraq War'.[2] Are there any shark's teeth preventing our backsliding into barbarism? Are human rights anything other than pleasant-sounding platitudes for talking about power? What is there to stop ancient bills of rights being torn up and torched, in an orgy of populism?

Eight years ago, before September 11, many people enjoyed a clear understanding of what was legal and what was not. This clarity has been muddied by a dirty war on terrorism. We were clear that there was to be no punishment without law, and yet people have languished for years in an American prison camp without charge, without access to their families or lawyers, and without, some would say, any prospect of a fair trial. We understood that torture was

[1] E Gibbon, *The History of the Decline and Fall of the Roman Empire* (Alfred Knopf Inc, 1993) 445.

[2] EJ Hobsbawm, *Globalisation, democracy and terrorism* (Little Brown, 2007) 41.

inimical to legality and antithetical to liberal democracy, and yet the torture meted out by American troops on detainees has been so ferocious and unforgiving that men have died in their custody. We thought that the death penalty was so extreme a punishment that it could only follow trial and conviction in a court of law, and yet extra-territorial, extra-judicial executions of suspected terrorists have become a routine counter-terror tactic. We had been given to understand by international elders that the sovereignty of state territory was sacrosanct, and that force could only be used by a state to defend itself from an imminent attack, or pursuant to the authorisation of an international security council, and yet two states have been invaded pursuant to one terrorist attack, and massive force continues to be deployed eight years on, without any such authorisation.

In sum, it could be and has been said that these tactics, adopted by the Anglo-American counter-terror alliance, were more consonant with our understanding of barbarism and brutality than civilisation and legality. New military technology makes killing possible on a larger scale than ever before and has done much to increase the urgency of investigation into these themes. Was *America Online* right to say September 11 was 'The Day We Changed' and do we have to change our laws or our understanding of law to keep up? For many commentators, nothing has changed: the United Kingdom and the United States, by violating the Charter of the United Nations, disregarding the Geneva Conventions, infringing human rights norms and trampling on their own time-honoured constitutional tenets, have simply broken the law. This might be a perfectly reasonable answer but it does not provide an adequate explanation because, at least on a common understanding of criminal justice, law-breakers are punishable for their transgressions. If crimes have been committed by known offenders, and no one can be held accountable, how can we meaningfully say that the law has been broken? Should we not say instead that the law has changed, or that we never really grasped what it was in the first place? Thinking about terrorism takes place in a conceptual morass.

In this discussion, the war on terror is the factual departure point for a jurisprudential inquiry. Without wanting to introduce unnecessary complexity, this statement must be qualified by the assertion that, according to my understanding of law, on which more immediately, it is a social fact; law is very much a result of what people think and do. So, yes, the war on terror is the departure point, but it is also, in a sense, the destination. What follows is an argument about law before it is an argument about terrorism. Nevertheless, I have chosen terrorism, or rather our response thereto, as the subject-matter because it brings into focus an important philosophical or jurisprudential aporia. The following are foremost amongst the questions I wish to address: What is law? How is it constituted? What is the role of force in law? How is legality related to necessity? Is it true, as Napoleon's General Lefevré had it, that '*il faut opérer en partisan partout où il y a des partisans*' ('one must fight like a partisan wherever there are partisans'), and if so, does such fighting belong to the realm of law, war, neither or both?[3]

In the next 300 or so pages, in order to attempt to introduce something approximating clarity where there is presently confusion; to help us avoid adopting measures that are more characteristic of brutality than legality; and to increase our chances of effectively combatting terrorism, it will be suggested that we conceive of law in the following way: 'Law is coercion, approved prior to, subsequent to, or in the absence of its exercise, by power'. This definition of law has certain consequences for conventional legal theory and for traditional understandings of what counts as law. These ramifications will and must be elaborated throughout to explain why I prefer this understanding of law, but here, I would like to give an initial indication of where it might seem unusual, or involve a departure from orthodoxy.

The most obvious feature of my definition is that force is integral to law. To my mind, law without force is like a prison without bars. Law has force to back up its assertions. A norm which does not entail the possibility of its own enforcement, though it might qualify as advice, a moral precept or a social convention, is not, as I see it, law. However, this is not to say that the effect of breaching the law is always punishment or coercion. Many infractions of the law go unpunished. For this reason, I included the words 'in the absence of its exercise' in the definition. An attempt is made herein to set aside conceptions of law as it is commonly understood before (but also by) studying what constitutes law – how it is brought about – in order to understand and reduce it to its essence. I try to capture that essence in the definition proffered immediately above. This is perhaps best elaborated with an example.

If, annoyed by a traffic system, which adds 10 minutes to my morning journey to work, I drive down a one-way street the wrong way, infringing the rules of the road, and I manage to do so unseen, this does not signify that the law does not exist. Rather, by virtue of the fortuitous timing of my offence, I have escaped punishment. If, however, I time my infraction of the rules of the road poorly, and am spotted by an oncoming police officer, who flags me down and gives me a stern ticking off, without applying the strict statutory fine, ascertaining the law becomes, to my mind, more complex.

On one view, we could say I broke the law and the police officer decided the best sentence, which, in his discretion, was a dressing down rather than a fine. On another view, we could say, well, the police officer's discretion was not part of the statutory scheme, so I broke the law, and by letting me off substantially unpunished, the police officer broke the law too. On yet another view we could say that I broke the law, but there was a difference between the law as written

[3] For a jurisprudential discussion of the irregular fighter, see C Schmitt, *The Theory of the Partisan: A Commentary/Remark on the Concept of the Political*, trans AC Goodson (Michigan State University Press, 2004).

and as applied. On another view still we could say, well, if one can, with impunity, drive down that one-way street unpunished, then it is not, in truth, a one-way street, but a two-way street, and there is not really any law against me using it as such, whatever the traffic code might say. Finally, it might be that the *real* law is that it is permissible to drive down the street in both directions, but in the event that one is caught by a police patrol, one must listen to a brief dressing down and, in exchange for a polite, solemn and entirely insincere promise of non-repetition, one can continue with one's onward journey. Notwithstanding its disloyalty to the statute book, should I prefer this last interpretation because it is honest and accurate, and as such, in this example, is best suited to assisting me in choosing my route to work in the morning?

I like this example because the fact that one can list (at least) five different interpretations of the law helps one to learn or recall two essential lessons. First, we cannot ascertain the law, in the sense of rules that will faithfully and, where necessary, forcefully be applied to us by the police and the courts by reading from a statute book. Secondly, law is indeterminate and dynamic to the extent that it depends entirely on what common people – citizenry and officers of the law alike – think and do from time to time. Correspondingly, if a statute on the books falls into disuse, becomes moribund, and is eventually flouted with impunity (prohibitions on marijuana and homosexual practices are salient examples), is it still meaningful to speak of the statute as law, except in a narrow, formal and ultimately inaccurate sense? Law is constant revolution.

My infraction of the traffic rules was a long way from the war on terrorism. Let us take another example, which is closer to the case in point. American infantry arrest, detain, torture and eventually, after establishing that he is not a dangerous terrorist but a peace-loving market-trader, release a citizen of Afghanistan. If that citizen seeks justice in Afghanistan but finds it wanting, attempts to get access to the courts in America, has his application barred by the state secrets rule, but finally succeeds in making an application to, and winning substantial damages against America in the Italian courts, what is the status of that judgment? Let us suppose that America then refuses to recognise Italian civil jurisdiction over acts committed by American soldiers in Afghan territory; that, due to their respect for international rules on state immunity, the Italian authorities refuse to lay claim to American assets in Italy in satisfaction of the judgment; and that, consequently, the damages judgment, though it stands as the pronouncement of a court, cannot be enforced by the victim against the tortfeasor. Is the Italian finding in favour of our wronged market-trader law?

In one sense, it *is* law because it is the decision of a venerable Italian tribunal, pronounced, recorded and solemnised in the usual fashion. In another sense, the unorthodox one I like, it is not law, because it does not have the *force* of law. It cannot be enforced by the ostensible beneficiary of the judgment. Such a Pyrrhic victory might be an effective moral condemnation of American conduct, but 'law' it is not.

A plurality of laws, that is, a situation in which different, conflicting norms regulating one issue are all considered law, is an absurdity. I say that although the law might require elaboration, although it might require testing in the courts, there can only ever be one law governing a situation, at any one time. If it turns out that a rule cannot be enforced, for want of social power backing up the use of coercion – like our Italian damages judgment – in my view, it simply is not law. This approach might be considered unrealistic or crude because it denies a welter of rules, hithertofore considered law, the character of law. On the contrary, I consider it realistic and sophisticated, because it allows us to differentiate law – rules backed by force – from other types of norm, the transgression of which carries consequences such as shame, opprobrium and, crucially, the sort of social pressure that can lead to a change in the law. Incidentally, this hard-edged understanding of law is in no way incompatible with the idea of a complex juridical order (*ordinamento giuridico*) in the sense pioneered by Santi Romano.[4] The law advocated here is simply insistent on the hard or cutting edge of a juridical order. This brings me to another point. That I have said coercion is integral to law does not in any way discount, hide or deny that the vast majority of human interactions guided by law happen outside the obvious instances of law, such as the Parliament, the courtroom, the prison and the police station. A key function of law is its role in normalising behaviour. In Britain and America, when we abide by the law, we rarely encounter its powers, though, and I want to emphasise this point, the law, or more precisely, the very possibility of its coercion, exerts a power on us and we, by acting in accordance with norms we perceive as being part of that law, exert a social power that reciprocally reinforces their binding power. The concept of law proffered herein cheerfully accommodates and indeed depends on the quotidian and humdrum. Most behaviour guided by law is not guided with the aid of a bailiff, a baton or a bullet, but these harder things are at the business end of all rules that can be called law.

I am aware that a reductive definition of law, depending on the possibility of enforcement, excludes many norms thought of as international law from its ambit. Indeed, I am mindful that if torture goes unpunished, or the modern *jus ad bellum* is flouted with impunity, according to my definition, torture and aggressive war-making are legal. As will become clear, I consider this an advantage, not a disadvantage of the definition. Suffice it to say here that, at least in part, it is precisely to provide clarity about what we will and will not accept, what conduct will and will not go unrestrained and unpunished, that we create laws in the first place. Indeed, the point made above about the symbiotic

[4] S Romano, *L'ordinamento giuridico* (Sansoni, 1945). Romano summarises his concept in the following terms: 'L'ordinamento giuridico è un'entità che si muove in parte secondo le norme, ma, soprattutto, muove, quasi come pedine in uno scacchiera, le norme medesime, che cosi rappresentano piuttosto l'oggetto e anche il mezzo della sua attività, che non un elemento della sua struttura' (at 13).

relationship between conduct guided by law (outwith obvious instances of law's coercive quality) and law itself is useful in understanding how this definition of law relates to law as a phenomenon on the international plane.

Put simply, where international rules can be enforced, they enjoy the character of law. A great many international rules can be enforced although their mechanisms of enforcement might in the end rely on governmental powers. In these cases it is perfectly consistent to refer to international rules as law. Furthermore, where governments have accepted limitations on their sovereignty in exchange for the benefits of international community, it is perfectly consistent with the definition offered here to speak of international law.

The *Factortame* litigation, in which a UK rule was set aside by a UK court because of a prior and conflicting European regulation, is an example of this revolution.[5] Irrespective of the theoretical ability of the UK Parliament to secede from the European Union, where domestic and supranational rules clashed, the latter overcame the former. This can be explained in the terms of the definition I have suggested by noting that, when the case was decided, the social power which had accumulated behind the idea of the United Kingdom having accepted a provisionally permanent[6] limitation on its powers was greater than that supporting the notion that the UK Parliament could, in any new legislation, alter its prior European obligations without making that intention express. As a result, the European provision trumped the UK rule. This complex divination took place in judicial minds, but we can observe that the divination undertaken took place against the backdrop of the prevailing political thinking.[7] That thinking determined which rule had the character of law.

International rules which do not enjoy their own enforcement mechanisms or which are not enforceable vicariously by states are not, in my view, law. This would include so-called soft-law, many harmonising measures, conventions lacking enforcement machinery, and unenforceable rules of international public law, such as the hallowed rule prohibiting torture. These rules are better conceived of as guidelines or aspirations and there is nothing stopping their maturing into laws proper. However, there is merit in terms of legal certainty, pragmatism and policy-making in distinguishing between rules which have aggregated the requisite social backing and rules which yet lack that body of public approval, which consequently cannot be considered enforceable. An example of this latter category of rule might be (at least in the UK context) the rulings of the European Court of Human Rights in Strasbourg. A declaration

[5] I grossly simplify the protracted proceedings. See for the revolution, *R v Secretary of State for Transport, ex parte Factortame Ltd (No 1)* [1989] UKHL 1 (18 May 1989); Case C-213/89 *R v Secretary of State for Transport, ex parte Factortame Ltd (No 2)* [1990] ECR I-2433; *R v Secretary of State for Transport ex parte Factortame Ltd (Interim Relief Order)* [1990] UKHL 7 (26 July 1990).

[6] I use this phrase to convey the ambivalence to the European assumption of permanence expressed in the UK courts.

[7] The similarity here with Hart's famous conceptual device, the rule of recognition is intentional: HLA Hart, *The Concept of Law* (1994, Clarendon Press).

from Strasbourg that the United Kingdom is in breach of its commitments under the European Convention on Human Rights requires the United Kingdom (according to international doctrine) to amend its offending laws, but has no effect on the law's quality as such. Similarly, a declaration from a UK court that a statute is incompatible with the government's commitments under the Convention does nothing to strip the statute of its legal character. In both cases, the laws remain on the statute books and enforceable until the UK Parliament in its discretion revises or revokes them, which it might not, with the result that the offending provisions continue to enjoy their legal character. However, what this system of limited external and internal constitutional review achieves is a considerable shift in the social power that goes into law-making in favour of the European and UK judiciaries. Here it is suggested that it is wrong to speak in the UK context of Strasbourg rulings or the Convention as laws. Rather they are better thought of as guidelines; but as guidelines with a prominence reflected in the media they enjoy significant social power and thus contribute, *im Endeffekt*, to the constitution of laws.

A classic question of legal philosophy asks what distinguishes a state from an armed band. The definition of law advocated here comfortably accommodates acts of gross iniquity and therefore clears the ground for the following answer to that classic question: Sometimes, nothing. The point I am driving at is that our thoughts and actions constantly constitute law. If we, by means of our silent acquiescence, or a deadly failure to protest, permit our government to torture in our name, torture, formerly considered the brutal antithesis of legality, becomes legal. The German word, *Gewalt*, perfectly encapsulates the potential of force to oscillate between legal coercion and unapologetic violence. I argue that, in the same way that context imbues *Gewalt* with one of these meanings, we bestow upon force its legality or illegality. Law then, the possibility of coercion which meets with approval, is an expression of and an instantiation of social power. It is not in its nature to rescue us from inequality or injustice: in fact, it can entrench these features of society. Above, I said that, according to the conception of law I favour, a norm need not actually be enforced to be law, but it needs to be enforceable. In this way, we can only discern the true character of a society (and the society of all societies) by identifying the norms backed by force, and approved by power.

These introductory comments are subject to one crucial qualification. In my definition, coercion which is not 'approved by power' – and by power, I mean social power – does not qualify as law. This means that by forcing you to agree with my argument at the point of a gun, I do not thereby become a manifestation or instrument of the law. On the contrary, I have assaulted you by threatening you in this way, and it may be that no social power backs my usage of the threat of force. Indeed, as time goes on, and you inform on me, I might be arrested for my actions. Going back to another example, if leaders or their servants torture with impunity, then a ban on torture is a hollow exhortation; it is not law in the sense I intend. Furthermore, there is great value, particularly in a society claiming to be a democracy and to respect the rule of law (whatever that might be), in a candid admission that practice (systematic torture) does not parry with text (a statutory ban on torture). And yet (here is the internal paradox of law), this does not deprive the assertion that torture is illegal of worth; on the contrary, such assertions are positively required to ensure that the prohibition on torture holds fast. Silence can, according to the circumstances, speak. In plain terms, we can say that there are some laws with which we disagree and against which we protest. Where we protest and our protest is ineffective, this reveals a fundamental condition of a legal order: Laws must be backed by social power. In a democracy, those who protest against majority opinion might find that they are unable to bring about a change in the law. Conversely, without general obedience to rules a legal order cannot persist. The novelty of the definition I have proposed is that we are invited by its essentialism to assess what the true law is, by gauging the social power in favour of particular conduct, irrespective of what we are told by the state and of what might from time to time be written in statute books.

The social power that imbues coercion with the character of law has various sources, which are explained as this argument unfolds. The qualification I want to mention here relates to what I said above about people responding to Anglo-American policy – the invasion of Iraq for instance – by calling it illegal. Such a statement is inadequate as an explanation of what the law actually is, but it is adequate as an exertion of social power. By claiming that something is illegal, depending on the cogency of my claim, I add force to the proposition that it *really* is illegal, and therefore help to imbue the prohibition with the character of law. Description is prescription. Our statements about what the law is cannot sensibly be separated from what the law is. And this, to my mind, is international law's saving grace. Though many of its norms might not be enforceable, they are aspirations, and to that extent, exert the sort of social power that a norm requires before we can assume that it will be actively enforced and not simply honoured in the breach. Here, it is useful to test the definition above with four quick examples, just to understand what it will and will not classify as law. The answers to these puzzles need not be convincing at this stage. The aim here is to show how law is understood here, to set the scene for the following explanation why such an understanding is pragmatic. First, what if a generally well-functioning domestic legal order is flouted by a group of expert criminals, who make a good trade in kidnap and ransom? I have said that to be law a rule needs to be enforceable. If the state has failed to catch these criminals and there is no real chance of them being caught, does this mean that they are above the law, or that the law does not apply to them, or that there is no law? Here, according to the definition I suggest, it is reasonable to speak of a law, which is generally effective but which has been transgressed in an isolated instance by talented law-breakers. Each time the kidnappers break the rule against kidnapping, they risk capture, trial and punishment.

Secondly, what is the effective law in a custody dispute in which the court of one state holds that a child should live with its mother, and the court of another state holds that a child should live with its father? We are left with conflicting judgments. Let us say that, *argumentando*, the child resides with its French father in France, the French court finding for the father, but the English mother of the child won her case in English proceedings. If neither state is willing to forego the decision of its court, and the English government will not enforce its judgment as it would involve a violation of French sovereignty, what is the law? According to the definition of law suggested above, the French ruling is law, for the simple reason that by dint of French territorial sovereignty, the English ruling will not be enforced. Put otherwise, it lacks the character of law because it is unenforceable. The child stays in France.

Thirdly, imagine that, off the shores of a failed state, pirates are boarding ships, taking their crews hostage and demanding ransom monies for their return in breach of international rules against piracy. If there is no international force capable of enforcing them, can we term the international rules prohibiting such conduct 'law'? Though many international lawyers would say that the rules prohibiting piracy are amongst the most important rules of international law, according to the definition of law advocated here, we cannot. For a norm to qualify as law, it must entail the possibility of enforcement. That pirates can ply their trade with impunity makes it unreasonable to speak of law in the sense in which it is described here. This is different to the example of the kidnappers above because in that example, a generally effective domestic police force was failing in an isolated instance to catch skilled criminals. In the pirate scenario, there is no generally effective force and, as a consequence, no law.

Fourthly, in the example given above of my minor traffic violation, if the application of the statutory fine for driving the wrong way up a one-way street depends on a police officer's discretion, pursuant to the definition here, there is a law, as it can be enforced against me, depending on factors such as the police officer's mood and my ability to convince him that I should be granted clemency. If, however, so many people have become accustomed to flouting traffic rules (because of police laziness and/or poor governmental control over the police force, coupled with a general cultural indisposition to following rules) that their enforcement has become impossible, they no longer enjoy the character of law. Again, all that these examples are designed to show at this stage is how the definition of law functions in practice. It is argued throughout that it is sensible to speak of law as a social fact, in the sense that what people think and do from time to time is crucial to a norm's character; for it to be law, it must be vouchsafed by social power.

In an attempt to explain this understanding of law, and its advantages, in a digestible, modern and provocative form, I have used the war on terrorism as a prism. By looking into the prism, we can see the various dynamics influencing the power that drives law and policy. The structure of this prism requires some explanation.

The first thing to say is that the 'war on terrorism' is one that must be fought on many fronts. It certainly cannot be won by militaristic means alone. Moreover, it will be argued herein, that calling it 'war' and using military force is often vastly counter-productive. However, in order to curtail the scope of this inquiry, I have limited my consideration to those responses that are, in my view, jurisprudentially most revealing, namely: indefinite detention; interrogative torture; extra-judicial killings; and war-making. Broadly speaking, these means are most revealing because, first, they seem to run counter to our understanding of legality in a liberal democracy, and secondly, they illuminate the awkward relationship between reluctant bedfellows necessity and legality; war and crime; morality and prudence. Furthermore, these extreme measures are themselves interrelated in interesting ways. For now, it suffices to note that indefinite detention and extra-judicial killings are considered horrific in peacetime but prosaic in wartime, and that when the detention of suspected terrorists becomes subject to judicial oversight, an executive might, perversely, prefer to assassinate them. Furthermore, the usage of torture, though it has been a classic counter-insurgency tactic in the past, has the potential to escalate hostilities by encouraging suicide bombing, making capture and detention more difficult and, as a result, incentivising military pre-emption.[8] Throughout, I shall constantly return to these four themes.

The second thing to say is that the definition of law preferred here is based on the consideration of the afore-mentioned dynamics. These dynamics form the titles of the chapters, and though they may seem expansive, all of the topics are considered only to the extent necessary to make an argument about law. The titles of the chapters correspond to the phenomena that influence or contribute to the constitution of law. The outcome of the aggregation of and interaction between these phenomena is law. This book, then, is concerned with the phenomenology of law. It is a study of the things that, by altering our consciousness, effect law. In order to reflect and explain this way of thinking, each chapter discusses the effects of two or three phenomena that make and mould our laws. The goal is a practical one, to improve our law-making by understanding our law-making. Further, as I endeavour to show, the quality of our law-making powerfully influences our war-making, so by improving our law-making we can reasonably hope to improve our war-making too.

In the chapter on language then, the reader should not anticipate a philosophical treatise on language, but reflections on how it relates to law. In addition, the breadth of the argument is not a foolhardy attempt to evince expertise in many things. Rather it is, and ought to be read as, a tentative effort to liberate the discussion of a problem plaguing all of society from the imbecilic tyranny of

[8] Michael Mukasey, 'Jose Padilla Makes Bad Law: Terror trials hurt the nation even when they lead to convictions', *Wall Street Journal*, 22 August 2007.

genre.[9] We ought not look to the lawyer, or the sociologist, or the economist or the general for a solution to terrorism, and this text does not pretend to offer one. The goal here is far more modest. It is to understand law through our response to terrorism and, along the way, to make some modest suggestions about to how to reduce the incidence of terrorism through prudent lawyering.

In each subsequent chapter before the conclusion, I consider some dynamics that affect how we think about law. Each chapter, excepting the next one, is broken down into three sections: a description of what was, a prescription of what ought to be, and a consideration of how the latter relates to preceding chapters with the aim of incrementally supplementing our understanding of law. The argument can be thought of in terms of the afore-mentioned prism, with sides made up of the following topics: language and image; war and crime; liberty, security and rationality; amity, enmity and identity; sex, terror and perversion; temporality, spirituality and sublimity; economy and hegemony; parliaments, the press and the public man. Wary of this text becoming a jeremiad, though the first part of each chapter – the description – might fairly be said to be maundering, the second part attempts to prescribe how we might better conduct ourselves in this queer conflict – it is forward-looking and constructive.

Before closing this introduction, I shall very briefly introduce the themes of the rest of the argument. In chapter two, I discuss our semantic response to terrorism, the notion of fighting 'terror', the effect had on our actions by our description of the struggle as 'war'; terrorist rhetoric; imagery's ability to ignite warfare; the complex relationship of terrorism to the media; the theatricality of terrorism; mixed up political imagery and depiction of the enemy; and the symbolic resonance of 9/11 itself. How has misdescription led to misfeasance?

Chapter three picks up where two leaves off, taking a look at how the war metaphor has calibrated our actions, and engages with one of the main debates about terrorism: specifically, whether we should have responded as if we were under attack, or as if we had a rather serious problem of social order; that is, whether countering terrorism was war or criminal justice and what the implications of an ongoing global war on terrorism might be. I assess the validity of pre-emptive self-defence, self-defence against terrorism, and the controversial tactic of targeted killings. I then consider the desirability of humanitarian intervention as an exception to the general prohibition on the use of force. Carl Schmitt thought the distinction between war and peace a jurisprudential abyss, over which lawyers build fragile bridges. Can we not put up something sturdier?

The fourth chapter addresses the assertions made by our leaders that, to ensure our security, we would have to accept some restrictions on (other people's) liberty, and that the wars in Afghanistan and Iraq are being fought not only to

[9] André Salmon musing on Picasso's *Guitare* commented that we had been 'liberated from the imbecilic tyranny of genres' as it was unclear, and unimportant whether one classified it as a painting or a sculpture.

make British and American people safer, but also for Afghan and Iraqi freedom. These messages were presented as dictates of rationality, so I test the rationality of these dictates. Chapter four looks at the notion of balancing liberty and security, and the attempt to reconcile military expediency with humanitarian concern. It tries to discern the effect on security of measures taken to improve our security, and gross encroachments on liberty such as detention and torture; finally, I begin to consider whether our reaction to terrorism was driven by reason, or emotion.

Popular conceptions of racial and religious difference are tested in chapter five; the plausibility of the portrayal of the struggle against terrorism as a skirmish in a bigger war, an intractable conflict between Islam and the West, is questioned. This conventional wisdom has exerted a large influence on Anglo-American foreign policy, and no assessment of our war- and law-making since September 11 would be complete without a consideration of it. I consider the effect of racially discriminatory policies on our security; the susceptibility of the human psyche to project baseness on other cultures; the effect of our ideas about identity on law- and policy-making; and the utility of philosophical tools like hospitality, tolerance, plurality and communication.

Chapter six analyses the Bush administration's usage of sexual subjugation in interrogation; the tryst between sex and violence; the opportunistic channelling of young men's frustrations into suicide missions; the condemnation of Western debauchery by Islamist radicals on the one hand, and Western demographic anxiety and the hæmorrhaging of empathy on the other. Six discusses the political spectre of fear; the fantastical roots of that fear; the wisdom of policies of deterrence; and finally, the perversion of torturers, of policies, of politics, of lawyers, of philosophers, and of society and its cherished values. I ask if the detention centres and black sites are simply the physical manifestation of the darker zones of our psyche.

The topics of chapter seven include the obstinate Anglo-American ignorance of the lessons of history; the human ambivalence to eternal time; the effect of mythology on our actions; the assertion that religion is dangerous nonsense; the validity of the contrast between Western rationality and Eastern religiosity; the proper place of spirituality in the state; and the usefulness of the sublime in our understanding of law.

Economy and Hegemony are pondered in chapter eight. What are the merits and demerits of the centrality of money in our ideology? To what extent does capitalism complement democracy? How are our economic goals related to our war plans? What is the nature of American power in the post-colonial world and how intelligently has it been used to combat terrorism? Are al-Qaeda insurgents lightly armed, yet predictably wily, gladiator slaves of a neoteric economic Empire?

A key chapter is nine, as it attempts to determine who is to blame for the degradation of our democracies and the abuse of our laws. It does so by investigating conceptions of guilt, but also by assessing executive stonewalling and secrecy, the sycophantic fawning of Congress and Parliament, the deferential attitude of the judiciary, the complicity of the press and the culpability of the common man.

All these topics have deep implications for how we think about law and the legality of our responses to terrorism. Consequently, the final chapter, on law and justice, gathers the threads of the argument and explains why the particular understanding of law introduced here might well be an invaluable recruit in the ongoing war on terror, precisely because it rejects the necessity of a nexus between legality and moral legitimacy.

This book takes its title from Nietzsche's warning in *Jenseits von Gut und Böse (Beyond Good and Evil)*: '*Wer mit Ungeheuer kämpft, mag zusehn, dass er nicht dabei zum Ungeheuer wird*'.[10] 'He who fights monsters must see to it that he does not thereby become a monster himself'. It is contended throughout that if we are realistic about what the law is, if we stare it in the face, and if we are honest about how it is constituted through and in us, if we self-reflect, we can reduce the incidence of terrorism without adulterating the moral tenets of liberal democracy; that is, we can fight monsters, without ourselves becoming monstrous, without conflating brutality with legality. We can emerge victorious in our confrontation with those unscrupulous terrorists who treat life with such disdain that they kill women and children to promote their aims, whilst ensuring that we treat them with the proper decorum and respect envisaged by our constitutions. In a sense, this entire argument is an attempt to recognise and eliminate the pathologies informing our perception of law and our policies to prevent us from defeating the very thing we wish to protect – the integrity of our societies. This is the challenge, for, as George Kennan once put it, 'there is a little bit of the totalitarian buried somewhere, way down deep, in each and every one of us'.

[10] F Nietzsche, *Jenseits von Gut und Böse* (Naumann, 1886) Aph 146.

2

Language and Image

Watching the pointing hands,
Of country people,
Not knowing their tongue.
Out there in Jutland
In the old man-killing parishes
I will feel lost,
Unhappy and at Home.

Seamus Heaney, *The Tollund Man*

GIVEN THE AIM of understanding our actions in the 'war on terrorism', and how our law-making has effected, affected and been affected by those actions, a consideration of language and image is fundamental. This chapter describes how both have been used and abused by terrorists, politicians, and in popular parlance. Thereafter, it prescribes an approach to language and image to prevent us from allowing such usages and abusages to recur. However, before we pitch up to the battlefield, some clarificatory remarks will be made as to what is intended here by language and image, and, indeed, why they are so important.

Words are bundles of ideas and images, whose meaning although infinitely variable over time is not, at any one time, infinite. Language would be useless if it could not convey particular messages with some precision. So words circumscribe possible thoughts, but thoughts also circumscribe the meaning of words. In *Imaginary Homelands*, Salman Rushdie recalls urging himself not to let zealots make the word 'Muslim' terrifying and to remember a time when it connoted 'family' and 'light'. So words affect what we think but they cannot do so without our input. If they are vessels we are crew.

As individuals, one way we relate our thoughts and identity to others is through words; one way a society generates its identity is through its choice of language. Samuel Huntington observed that 'people rally to those with similar ancestry, religion, language, values and institutions, and distance themselves from those with different ones'.[1] Clearly then, language and identity have an intimate

[1] SP Huntington, The clash of civilizations and the remaking of world order (Simon & Schuster, 1996) 125.

relationship. Martin Heidegger contended that language is the house of being. More recently, George Fletcher went so far as to assert that being oneself 'requires the cultivation of one's native language'.[2] No better illustration of this can be found in history than the linguistic squabbles that characterise the European Union. The English wince at the sound of their language in Continental European mouths; the French jealously guard the place of their language in Europe's collective heritage; and a plethora of peoples vie for the inclusion of their language in the roster of official tongues as if that will verify their independence and equal standing amongst the associating states. Language is the keep of identity and a society will often build a fortress around it. With respect to terrorism, it suffices to note that the appeal of *Euskadi Ta Askatasuna*, the Basque separatist group, was limited by the granting of Basque wishes with respect to language use.[3]

The activity of reading, though it may seem detached, is in fact a close, clandestine form of communication in which the author and reader create new thoughts in the interface between their minds. In this sense, there is not one author of the meaning of a text but two, and naturally, well-written books change minds. So language is a tool that sculpts social reality. And the quality of our perception of reality reflects not only the skill of the sculptor and the sharpness of his tools but also the vision and discernment of his audience. As Rushdie has it, a language reveals the attitudes of the people who use it and shape it.

Language is a constitutive aspect of consciousness, subject to the caveat that the message sent is not necessarily the one received. A word may well carry a different meaning for each person using it. Words, a medium themselves, are refracted in the prism of the mind and, without the mind, there is no nexus between word and meaning, between language and world,[4] and – getting just for a moment ahead of ourselves – between law-as-written and law-as-understood. Nietzsche suggests that we see words in the way we see trees. Their form is clear; at a distance we may even distinguish an oak from a sycamore, but we cannot, unless we concentrate on the detail, make out the bark, leaves and sinews that go to make up the tree. We cannot see its nuance.[5]

Ideas ingrained into a society's identity may clash with others, violently, and these clashes are expressed through language. As Philip Allott tells us, it is 'one of the gravest of all problems in the social history of humanity that societies have tended to incorporate ideas in their identity especially in the struggle with the

[2] GP Fletcher, *Romantics at war: glory and guilt in the age of terrorism* (Princeton University Press, 2002) 32.

[3] Y Alexander, *Combating terrorism: strategies of ten countries* (University of Michigan Press, 2002).

[4] For a similar point, see G Agamben, *State of Exception* (University of Chicago Press, 2005) 40.

[5] FW Nietzsche, *Beyond Good and Evil*, trans J Norman (Cambridge University Press, 2002).

dilemma of the self and the other'.[6] He means to say that a single person may at the same time be a guest and an alien, a president and a pariah, a neighbour and a threat, a journeyman and a gypsy.

This is an appropriate juncture to say that a strict separation between words and images seems unhelpful. Words call to mind images because they contain them. The word 'homeland' conjures a powerful image. In 2008, the mere utterance of the term 'great nation' or 'greatest nation on earth' by the orators of the American Primaries could send a crowd into ecstatic cheering about a partly mythical image. Yet images can transmit precise messages too. Absurdly, a beard or a turban can become an encoded message for suicidal tendencies. The colour of a British Pakistani's skin can alienate him in his own hometown as a security threat. The resonance of images and symbols is enormous. Images invade and dominate our consciousness. In so doing, they can move us to action. In *A Problem from Hell: America and the Age of Genocide*, Samantha Power argues that the reminder of the Holocaust, in pictures from the Bosnian war, partly motivated the creation of a war crimes tribunal for the former Yugoslavia. There are a few contenders for the most potent symbolic images of the early years of this millennium but amongst them must be the destruction of New York City's towering shrines to capital by commercial airliners and the photos from Abu Ghraib that resembled an Auschwitz album.

The influence and invasion of images into our daily space is increasing. Our world is created by media, no longer in a merely figurative sense, but literally – screens bombarding us with imagery seem inescapable, persistent and omnipresent. The 'perspectival optics of life' have wider screens and higher resolution than ever before. Image seems increasingly real, and reality is increasingly conveyed in images, to the extent that some philosophers claim that an event and its portrayal are indistinguishable.[7] Virtuality is monopolising reality. Needless to say, those who control the input of any system exert huge influence on its output. In the modern media, there is a concerning conflation of power and representation. It is worth asking the extent to which the media conceals when it reveals, and how our opinions of world events are coloured by media 'spin' and impoverished by omission. Furthermore, with the necessary incompleteness of the picture available to any one of us at any one time, it is worth remembering that our opinions are based as much on ignorance as they are knowledge, as much on misperception as perception, and as much on misconception as conception. There is a further effect of the streaming of information onto ubiquitous screens. All news received in such a way, intermingled with no less violent fiction, and television of a more trivial nature, takes on an aspect of sameness so that the similarity of the packaging lulls us into the false belief that the content is of equal import. The danger of this blurring of fiction and reality,

[6] P Allott, *Eunomia: new order for a new world* (Oxford University Press, 1990) 73.

[7] Günther Anders argues that *Ereignis* (an event or occurrence) and *Abbild* (portrayal or representation) are no longer distinct in visual media.

and the ease of the choice between them is, apart from mass apathy, that the rules of fiction begin to dictate the presentation of reality, and by extension, that fiction begins to generate reality. This trend can be observed in a cursory glance at Fox News reports or by reflecting how modern politicians must be entertaining and easy-on-the-eye in order to be electable.

Moving away from the media now, words have incredible power to shape and even foreclose debate. Consider the following extract from a trial of aircraft hijackers in Berlin. Judge Stern is responding to the Prosecutor's assertion that a court should be slow to interfere in foreign relations, classically the preserve of the executive:

> When was it that judges were supposed to worry about that in deciding what the law is? ... in construing the rights of human beings? And when did it become permissible for lawyers in a courtroom or a litigant to tell the Judge that the piece of litigation is so important to the litigant that the Judge is ordered to find a certain way? What system of justice are you referring to? ... What Judge would do it for you? ... That's a vile thing for a Judge to listen to. He can't be a Judge if he listens to that.[8]

Rightly or wrongly, this powerful, indignant rhetoric, which was supplemented with a reference to the potent image of similar claims made earlier in that very city by the Nazi executive to shield its misfeasances, has the effect of curtailing the range of acceptable responses. In short, it would be a brave advocate who would stand up against such a tirade.

The next point to make (by unceremoniously upending Hobbes) is that swords without covenants are but metal. Though people might well take up arms under duress for want of a better option, it is ideas, expressed through language, that best mobilise – 'das Wort ist tatsächlich ein Molotov Cocktail'.[9] Allott is unambiguous on this point: 'We live and die for words; we create and kill for words; we build and destroy for words; wars and revolutions are made for words'.[10] It is trite to say that words can incite, but seemingly innocuous ideas can radicalise when juxtaposed with other seemingly innocuous ideas; it does not, for instance, take much spin to present self-determination and plurality as mortally irreconcilable enemies. Language can be used to mediate in the classic sense of the word, but also to mediate between ideas and action; to draw battle lines in the sand of semantics. So, in considering the effects of violence on language (and by extension law), it is important to grasp the effect of language on violence.

First, an explanatory note: though the concern here is violence, and law's relation thereto, the action *proprio* is of no interest. Rather, the focus is on the causes of the violence, and of violence done to the law, if you will. If historians

[8] Quoted in a useful article by JJ Paust, 'Judicial Power to Determine the Status and Rights of Persons Detained Without Trial' (2003) 44(2) *Harvard Law Review* 503, 525.

[9] 'The word is actually a "molotov cocktail"'.

[10] P Allott, *Eunomia: new order for a new world* (Oxford University Press, 1990) 5.

can be charged with concentrating on describing acts of violence rather than explaining their causes, the modern media is similarly condemnable. Of preponderant importance are the underlying conditions that bring about violence. These conditions always involve an evolution of ideas. Consequently, hardly any time will be spent with graphic descriptions of our reaction to terrorism; rather, the concern here is with causality. I ask how we should understand law in order better to comprehend our forceful, ill-conceived reactions to terrorism.

Returning briefly to images, before considering what the foregoing means for law, it is worth noting how we *imagine* versions of ourselves, our societies, other societies and the world. Echoing Allott, Rushdie argues:

> Waking as well as sleeping, our response to the world is essentially imaginative, that is, picture-making. We live in our pictures, our ideas. I mean this literally. We first construct pictures of the world and then we step inside the frames. We come to equate the picture with the world, so that, in certain circumstances, we will even go to war because we find someone else's picture less pleasing than our own.[11]

Perhaps we can sharpen that picture. To the extent that our imagery is borrowed from the media, our world is imposed. We do not live in the world, an imaginary world lives in us – it pervades us. The inference to be drawn here is that modernity does not cure our propensity to go to war for imposed ideas and borrowed boundaries – on the contrary, it may worsen that condition. The contagious nature of communicable ideas and the power of rhetoric and description should not be underestimated. A superb illustration of this is Joseph Conrad's melancholy confession that, in the composition of his book, *The Secret Agent*, there had been moments where he was an extreme revolutionist. In sum, writing and speech and image have enormous sway over the human mind. The potential violence, or rather, *Gewalt* in the ideas they communicate is limitless.

What does all this mean for law? Well, rather than description and prescription being hermeneutically separate (and hermetically sealed off) from one another, it is argued here that to describe is always to prescribe. In legalistic terms, to determine the register is to delimit the range of rules that may be selected. Judge Stern's tirade was one example of such foreclosure, but this semantic narrowing of the focus can take place on a larger scale. Colm Campbell explains that 'in many conflict situations (including Northern Ireland), there is not only a violent conflict, there is also a '"meta-conflict" – a "conflict about the conflict"'.[12] Moreover, when states assert that a certain set of rules (the criminal law or the laws of war) should apply to a situation, they are making a claim about what that situation is (civil disobedience or armed conflict), normally because they want to legitimise a particular response to the crisis (criminal charges or infantry charges). These assertions partially determine people's and states'

[11] S Rushdie, *Imaginary Homelands* (Granta Books, 1991) 378.

[12] C Campbell, 'Wars on Terror' and vicarious hegemons: The UK, International Law and the Northern Ireland Conflict' (2005) 54 *International & Comparative Law Quarterly* 321 325.

reactions to the situation, and can influence not only perceptions but, through influencing perceptions, can affect the outcome of the conflict itself. The choice of register or rules may change over time according to how actors wish to respond to a conflict and it should come as no surprise when opposing forces have dramatically different versions of events. The best modern example of this can be found in the Gaza Strip. The narratives used by Palestinians and Israelis to describe and consequently justify their various actions and reactions are mirror images. Depending on the narrator, Israel is at the same time an illegitimate occupying force terrorising the ousted rightful inhabitants and a legitimate democracy weathering repeated, illegal, terrorist attacks.

In the context of terrorist attacks, the language used can paralyse the normal processes of rights enforcement. As fear shocks a body into paralysis, terror freezes the body politic. The terms 'crisis' and 'emergency' suggest the extraordinary nature of the situation, one which cannot be coped with without undermining normal guarantees of civil liberties.[13] (The distinction between emergency and normality will be discussed in greater detail the next chapter.)

The final preliminary point to make about the relationship of semantics and symbols to law is that theatre is central to the latter. The social presence of law, its image and therefore its prestige, depend on the rituals of the instances and agents of government. In the English courts, barristers bow on entering a court, which rises on the entry of the judge, who proceeds, robed, to sit atop an elevated bench. So powerful is this mysticism that a chancery judge might tell an advocate appearing without a waistcoat that *he cannot be seen* or one without a wig that *he cannot be heard*. These terms are more than mere euphemisms for the English legal community's costume fetish. The theatricality in the phenomenology of law is of great import, not because it is right that we retain our comical ways, but merely because we ought to be cognisant of the effect theatrical trickery can have on our impression of the law. As Jeremy Bentham has it,

> [s]eated in a chair in the character of a justice of the peace with common language in his mouth, a common coat upon his back and no hair upon his head, Solomon himself would not gain the praise of wisdom. Seated on a woolsack, Bartholon would pass muster while talking about entering appearances and filing common bail, clothed in purple and fine linen, artificial hair and ermine.[14]

Similarly, the arts have tremendous power to convey and create authority. Even a cursory survey of music, painting, sculpture and architecture will testify to art's capacity to put the pomp in power.

Having introduced language and image and touched upon their effect on law, it is time to study their roles in the 'war on terrorism'. This section criticises our semantic response to terrorism by looking at political language, media coverage

[13] FN Aoláin, 'The Individual Right of Access to Justice in Times of Crisis' in F Francioni (ed), *Access to Justice as a Human Right* (2007).

[14] *The Works of Jeremy Bentham*, John Bowring (ed), (1838–43) vol 7, 282.

and popular imagery. It may be said that political talk has descended into a paroxysm of misdescription which betrays an underlying paralysis of political morality. In this section, several of the key phrases in the war on terrorism are discussed.

In the name of freedom, American and British political leaders promise us that they will lead the fight against terror(ism). We are grateful for this. Less terror is what we need. But this oath is worse than meaningless – it is dangerous. Fighting 'terrorism' is like fighting 'judo'. One can physically fight a terror*ist* just as one can physically fight a practitioner of judo (however inadvisable that may be) but to speak of fighting judo, or combatting the 'judo' in society is an obvious misnomer. Notwithstanding the ethical codes which pervade the individual martial arts, the point is that judo, like terrorism, is a technique more than an ideology – confusion between the two can be costly. There is a definite coincidence between the complete ambiguity of our enemy, the obnubilation of the social phenomena that culminate in terrorism, the imprecision of our military programmes, and our wanton squandering of defence expenditure. Terrorism can be a misleading and costly synecdoche. For those who argue that we must fight terror to defend freedom, the answer is this: I am not more free if I fight terrorism, in the same way that I am not freer if I elect to spend my time fighting judo. On the contrary, I am a time-wasting, menacing lunatic, who should be straightjacketed to prevent me harming myself and those in my violent vicinity. In a battle against a badly drawn enemy we risk harming innocent others with the result that the ambiguous adversary takes shape, becomes formidable and very real.

For anyone reading the papers, the analogy will be obvious. In Afghanistan and Iraq, American forces indulged in dangerously untrammelled aggression. The pin-the-tail-on-the-donkey bombing of wedding parties, villages and mosques has maimed, terrified and terrorised communities. This caused bitterness, radicalisation, and worse, unification. Families, friends and sympathisers of victims are now returning that imprecise aggression and can be expected so to do for the foreseeable future. As Osama bin Laden has it, so long as Muslims are not permitted to enjoy security, the West will not enjoy it either.[15] Western Muslims are uncomfortably caught in the middle.

It might well be that the ambiguity of the rhetoric reflects the fact that we do not know who to blame. It is frightening when boys from England's North commit suicide bombings in the South, when the children of Leeds kill the commuters of London. How can we fight terrorists if they come from our own societies? The answer is that we cannot fight them, not with conventional means, so we chose enemies we (thought we) could beat. First the Taliban, and then an off-balance dictator. Thus, we fight (our sense of) terror, with terror. We fight monsters monstrously, hoping to frighten them and scare off their friends. In the

[15] B Lawrence (ed), *Messages to the World: The Statements of Osama bin Laden* (Verso, 2005).

logic of Paul Wolfowitz, terrorists and tyrants must be in collusion anyway; all monsters must be friends by virtue of shared monstrosity. The generality of this approach is immediately apparent. When Murder, the King of terrors, stormed into the peaceful forecourt of the metropolitan mundane, the response of our leaders was general where it needed to be surgical and reckless when it required careful planning.

What does not help is the setting of surreal targets, like 'winning the war on terror', or worse, 'winning it within five years'. Robert Redford's Senator, played by Tom Cruise in the film *Lions for Lambs*, cries, 'Do you want to win the war on terror? That is the defining question of our times'. Aside from the foolhardy notion of fighting terror, noted above, this question is preposterous. As Stephen Holmes correctly observes,

> [t]he conditions that make Islamic radicalism dangerous to the West are ineradicable features of the modern world. They include global systems of transportation, communication, and banking, rivers of petrodollars, and the gradual spread of nuclear know-how.[16]

This is not to say that we cannot reduce the incidence of terrorism around the world. Of course we can. But to aim to eradicate it completely, with war, is to set ourselves an unrealistic, moving target, which operates to justify inappropriate, escalating levels of military expenditure and mobilisation. The first brave step towards achieving security must be realising its impossibility. A world without violence is a dream, it is an ideal, a worthy ideal to boot but, in real terms, so long as there is dynamite, disenfranchisement and despair, there will be sporadic outbursts of violence in society. As Grenville Byford has it,

> [w]ars have typically been fought against proper nouns (Germany, say) for the good reason that proper nouns can surrender and promise not to do it again. Wars against common nouns (poverty, crime, drugs) have been less successful. Such opponents never give up. The war on terrorism, unfortunately, falls into the second category. Victory is possible only if the United States confines itself to fighting individual terrorists rather than the tactic of terrorism itself.[17]

There is a further problem with fighting terrorism. As Adrian Guelke has it, even by 'the 1990s, the concept of terrorism had become so elastic that there seemed to be virtually no limit to what could be described as terrorism'.[18] Tareq and Jacqueline Ismael argue that, in the vernacular of the Bush administration, terrorism 'means Muslim terrorism and refers to virtually any act of violence,

[16] S Holmes, *The Matador's Cape: America's Reckless Response to Terror* (Cambridge University Press, 2007) 203.

[17] G Byford, 'The Wrong War' (2002) *Foreign Affairs*, Vol 81(4) 34.

[18] A Guelke, *The Age of Terrorism* (Tuaris, 1995) 1.

protest, or resistance in the Muslim world'.[19] But it is difficult for political leaders to resist the temptation to call their enemies 'terrorists'. Tomis Kapitan observes that the usage of the term,

— discredits any group to which it is applied;
— dehumanises them;
— places them outside the norms of acceptable social and political behaviour;
— portrays them as people impervious to reason and therefore disincentivises negotiation;
— erases any incentive people might have to understand their motivations;
— deflects attention from policies that might have contributed to their grievances;
— paves the way for the use of force; and
— provokes fear.[20]

Aggregated, these effects succeed in unhelpfully funnelling our emotions about those labelled 'terrorists' towards violence and away from understanding, towards a military reaction and away from criminal and social justice, towards annihilation and away from reconciliation. Referring to Ariel Sharon's brutal assault on the Jenin refugee camp, Kapitan notes that Sharon's usage of the rhetoric of fighting terror garnered the support of the Israeli public and the American press, allowing Sharon to continue with his violent campaign, whilst further aggravating the sense of injustice and outrage felt by the Palestinians and those sympathetic to their cause. Consequently, Kapitan asserts that the rhetoric of terror can actually prolong and intensify internecine conflict.

Former President George W Bush took the final step in making the phrase 'terrorist' almost entirely useless, except to clear the ground for a disproportionate (and ongoing) military response to September 11, when he said that 'you are either with us, or with the terrorists'.[21] In the time it takes to say a sentence, countless Europeans decided they would rather, given such a stark choice, put up with splinters.

Having discussed 'terrorism', we can now move onto the 'war' that is being waged against it. Presented with the choice of being with Bush or with the terrorists, one could be forgiven for feeling that these were claustrophobically narrow days. Of that which we cannot speak, thereof we must remain silent. Perhaps this was an example of Newspeak, the Orwellian language pursuant to

[19] TY Ismael and JS Ismael, 'September 11 and American policy in the Middle East' in J Strawson (ed), *Law after Ground Zero* (London, 2002) 158.

[20] T Kapitan, 'The Terrorism of "Terrorism"' in JP Sterba (ed), *Terrorism and International Justice* (Oxford University Press, 2003) 52.

[21] President Bush speaking with President Chirac, 6 November 2001, White House.

which the range of possible thought diminishes with the systematically diminishing range of possible expression. The perfect President for perpetuating a reckless war on terrorism would be one with a limited set of unsophisticated conceptual categories at his disposal.

Particularly troubling is the pervasiveness of the war metaphor and the consistency with which political leaders have adopted it when speaking of the response to terrorism. In a contribution to a book on *Terrorism and International Relations*, Emílio Rui Vilar, President of the Calouste Gulbenkian Foundation, incongruously laced his pacific message with fighting talk – even when referring to promoting conciliatory dialogue, his language was of conflict.[22] Conrad was acutely aware of the dangers of such trends. In *Under Western Eyes*, the narrator laments the demise of imagination, 'smothered out of existence a long time ago under a wilderness of words … the great foes of reality'.[23] We need not share Conrad's angst to understand how a word misapplied can obscure fact.

But is the declaration of 'war' on things just a harmless metaphor, or does it have deleterious effects? Philip Heymann argues that,

> what we face is a very prolonged series of contests with opponents that do not have the powers of a state, or hope to defeat our armies, or destroy our powerful economy, or threaten to occupy our territory – the dangerous characteristics we have traditionally associated with war.[24]

The designation of the campaign against terrorism as war is imprudent, as it foregrounds military responses whilst obfuscating more effective tactics, such as intelligence gathering, police work, precision arrests and prosecutions.

Furthermore, it is not necessarily wise to frame a response to terrorism in the terminology of war because this can have the effect of elevating terrorists to the (more) honourable status of soldiers, and, in so doing, losing the negative connotations associated with terrorist criminality. In Northern Ireland, being classified as 'prisoners of war' with the kudos that brings, rather than criminals, was a matter of such importance to detained members of the Irish Republican Army that in protest at their designation they starved themselves.

Heymann makes the further point that, in the current struggle against al-Qaeda, the frame 'war' promotes that organisation to a status of political parity with the state it most despises. This is free propaganda for terrorists.[25] However, the other side of this coin is that if a war has popular support, which in the aftermath of September 11, Afghanistan did, a President who goes to war can expect their popularity to soar. Contrariwise, a President who struggles to keep a lid on domestic crime, and it should not be forgotten that September 11,

[22] DS Hamilton, *Terrorism and international relations* (Calouste Gulbenkian Foundation; Center for Transatlantic Relations, Paul H Nitze School of Advanced International Studies, Johns Hopkins University, 2006).

[23] J Conrad, *Under Western Eyes* (Courier Dover Publications, 2003) 3.

[24] PB Heymann, *Terrorism, Freedom and Security* (The MIT Press, 2003) 161.

[25] ibid, 28.

was a domestic crime, can expect their ratings to plummet. As Elaine May points out, former President Bush, who was elected despite widespread concern that more people had voted for his opponent, watched his ratings skyrocket as his foreign policy became more aggressive in the aftermath of September's calamities.[26]

The terms used by Bush to prepare the ground for his enthusiastic foreign policy were Manichean – on September 12, he predicted a 'monumental struggle between absolute good and evil'. Andrew Norris points out that acknowledging America's own use of terror, for instance, the World War II bombing of Japanese cities, 'would automatically make it impossible to rally the nation to fight "evil" in the name of "the war on terror"'.[27] Norris wants us to eschew 'moralistic oversimplifications' in our categorisation of conflicts. This sounds sensible, but better still would to be avoid such blatant hypocrisy that the word 'terrorism' becomes reversely pejorative, tainting not its subject, but the speaker. Another function of Manichean interpretations of conflict is that such language completes the process of dehumanisation noted by Kapitan, which begins by calling an enemy absolutely evil, is fought, as we know from Carl Schmitt, using any means; and ends not merely with repulsion but total extermination.

What of terrorist rhetoric? The most dramatic hijacking in recent years was not of commercial airliners but of the notion of jihad. Thanks to bin Laden and Ayman al-Zawahiri's borrowed and twisted hermeneutics, jihad – every Muslim's duty – is a holy war; to many Westerners it is now synonymous with murderous Islamic terrorism. This couldn't be further from the terms origins. Jihad derives from the Arabic term *jhd*, 'which has the root meaning of "using, or exerting, one's utmost power, efforts, endeavours, or ability, in contending with an object of disapprobation"'.[28] As Abdullah Saeed explains, this struggle 'can exist at several levels: to free oneself from sin, bad deeds, thoughts and words, or to purify oneself spiritually (*jihad al-nafs*). A person making such an effort is considered to be engaged in a Jihad'.[29] Jihad is an overwhelmingly peaceable notion. It is necessary to engage in sustained jihad for the pursuit of 'piety, knowledge, health, beauty, truth and justice'.[30] This is different only in name to similar Western, Christian ideals of active love being hard work on oneself and in the community.

[26] ET May, 'Echoes of the Cold War' in ML Dudziak (ed), *September 11 in History: A Watershed Moment?* (Duke University Press, 2003).

[27] A Norris, '"Us" and "Them"' in T Rockmore, J Margolis and AT Marsoobian (eds), *The Philosophical Challenge of September 11* (Blackwell Publishing, 2005) 27.

[28] A Saeed, 'Jihad and Violence: Changing Understanding of Jihad Among Muslims' in T Coady and M O'Keefe (eds), *Terrorism and Justice: Moral Argument in a Threatened World* (Melbourne University Publishing, 2002) 73.

[29] *ibid*, 73.

[30] KAA Fadl, '9/11 and the Muslim Transformation' in ML Dudziak (ed), *September 11 in History: A Watershed Moment?* (Duke University Press, 2003).

It is important to note that both the Qu'ran and Islamic law prohibit conflict except in the face of acts of aggression. In seemingly intractable conflicts, particularly in Darfur and Israel, it is all too easy to forget that if only everyone adhered to this rule, there would be no violence except in error or insanity. Defence is pointless without the possibility of attack. And yet, instead of refuting and ridiculing the notion of aggressive jihad, the Western media has thoughtlessly peddled and propagated the idea that we are engaged in a holy war. At this juncture, it is worth considering the force of bin Laden's rhetoric, not only to get the measure of what politicians are up against but because he is not as widely read in the Western academy as he is on the web.[31] That his statements were a mirror image of the Bush administration's bulletins goes without saying but I shall mention five features in particular.

First, not wasting the opportunity to refer to the Bush depiction of the Afghanistan war as a 'crusade', bin Laden asserted that the conflict was 'fundamentally religious' in nature. This has several notable effects. First, it expands the categories of aggressors to include all Christians and their allies whilst also functioning as a call to arms to all those of the Islamic faith. Second, it draws on the deeply negative connotations of the crusades to galvanise Muslims. Third, it cosmifies the conflict, appealing to ideals that go beyond earthly advantage – I will say more on this in the chapter on sublimity. Accordingly, bin Laden's rhetoric is dressed up in religious terms. This is not to say that he does not appeal to other registers, such as morality, and politics.

Second, aside from taking every chance to refer to the questionable policies of the United States, bin Laden incorporates references to the moral turpitude of American society, and, addressing the American people directly, he beseeched them to 'reject the immoral acts of fornication, homosexuality, intoxicants, gambling and usury'.[32] This sort of appeal has great resonance amongst the more pious Americans, but an even stronger, broader appeal is to simple fairness: 'We will not cease our raids until you leave our fields'.[33] This is bin Laden's essential, most powerful message; it is a straight appeal to equity, the ideal of security and respect for sovereignty: When he is accused of organising and inciting terrorism, he readily points to Israeli bombings of refugee camps and American bombing of mosques, casting his actions as legitimate 'self-defence' or 'reactive terror'. When lambasted for killing innocents, he simply alludes to the infant mortality caused by United Nations sanctions on Iraq. A UNICEF report of 1998 found that sanctions had resulted in the deaths of an extra 90,000 Iraqi children a year since 1991.

Third, bin Laden does not shy away from speaking with 'thunder and heavenly fireworks to feeble and dormant senses'.[34] He is well aware that

[31] B Lawrence (ed), *Messages to the World: The Statements of Osama bin Laden* (Verso, 2005).
[32] *ibid*, in 'To the Americans', of 6 October 2006.
[33] *ibid*, in his address of 26 December 2001.
[34] FW Nietzsche, *Thus Spoke Zarathustra*, RJ Hollingdale (Penguin Classics, 1961 [1883]) 117.

ordinary people, whatever their living conditions, might well be slow to approve of his incendiary injunctions. Consequently, he attempts to consolidate his support by appeals to a romantic interpretive framework for modern events, for instance that, after the Cold War, America has escalated its campaign to try to 'get rid of Islam itself'.[35] This proposition is patently untenable, but it might well ring true for families of those in arbitrary detention or amongst innocent Afghan villagers being bombed from on high.

Fourth, notwithstanding the weightiness of his themes, and his fire and brimstone approach, bin Laden manages to inject the occasional dash of humour, mocking the disparity between the magnitude of America's spending on its 'intelligence services', its inability to capture him, and the paucity of evidence furnished by those services that he is responsible for terrorist atrocities. Prefiguring Holmes's book, *The Matador's Cape*, which criticises America's reckless, self-defeating response to terrorism, bin Laden jokes that it was easy for al-Qaeda 'to provoke this administration and lure it into perdition' and that 'to some analysts and diplomats, it seems as if we and the White House are on the same team'.[36] Quite.

Fifth, he is also acutely aware of the public concerns about the conflicts of interest between the Bush cabal *qua* government and the Bush cartel *qua* shareholders: 'The White House leadership, which is so keen to open up war fronts for its various corporations whether in the field of arms, oil, or construction, has also contributed to these remarkable results for al Qaeda'.[37] For now, it is worth noting bin Laden's attention to the detail of the issues that divide his audience; a more searching look at the dynamics of the military-commercial complex and of the relationship between public and private interest follows in due course.

The relationship of terrorists like bin Laden to the media is complex. At the offset, it is worth noting two points: First, the news media is under increasing pressure to cater for the needs of an audience accustomed, thanks to new forms of entertainment, to excitement, action and the extreme. Put simply, coverage of terrorism ups ratings. Second, terrorism relies, for its effect, on the media. The definition of terrorism is discussed below, but an obvious aim of terrorism is to instill fear – terrorism needs coverage to sustain a support base.

Bearing in mind this unsettling tryst, it is clear that words contain great power and can trigger violence, particularly when they are accompanied by images and mainlined into our collective consciousness. The media absorbs and redistributes violence. In a way, then it monopolises violence, which was the traditional role of the state. Russell Farnen puts it in the following terms, 'what we know as terrorism is actually a media creation: mass media define, delimit, delegitimise

[35] B Lawrence (ed), *Messages to the World: The Statements of Osama bin Laden* (Verso, 2005), in an interview in *Nida'ul Islam* in November 1996.

[36] *ibid*, in his address of 29 October 2004.

[37] *ibid*.

and discredit events that we have not actually seen'.[38] With the prescriptive effect of description in mind, it is worth remembering the tremendous power of the media to crown and crucify, to sully or sanctify: Was he a suicide bomber or a courageous martyr?

The relationship of terrorism and the media can be that of fire to oxygen; it cannot be denied that publicity creates constituencies for terrorist causes. Alex Houen, in a thorough book on modern terrorism and literature, remarks that, after the hijacking of TWA Flight 847 in 1985, the 'exposure of the hostages' ordeal intensified the domestic pressure on the government to capitulate, which it did, convincing Israel to release 766 imprisoned Shi'ites in return for the hostages' release'.[39] A Palestinian spokesman is said to have commented that the infamous Munich operation was like 'painting the name of Palestine on the top of a mountain that can be seen from the four corners of the earth'.[40] For terrorists, coverage is leverage.

Coverage is also a macabre harbinger. It is worth questioning what it is that perpetuates terror. Is it the bombing or the broadcasting? Houen quotes Sergei Kravchinsky, the exiled Russian nihilist, who complained that 'it is the sensational journalism which deserves the palm for its efforts in spreading and protracting the dynamite epidemics'.[41] It is the report of the gun rather than the gun itself that puts the fear up us. And the event itself is not that which occurs but that which can be narrated;[42] the suicide bombing, the assassination, and the roadside bomb all are soft clay on the editor's wheel until jiggered, jolleyed and spun. People 'murdered' upset us more than people 'killed' and 'fences' are more 'neighbourly' than 'walls'.

It would be remiss not to mention the effect of the repetition of images. This process, particularly marked in the American *modus* for dealing with the World Trade Center tragedy, of converting of brutality into banality, has not only a soothing, rehabilitative effect, but can desensitise and dehumanise. One would be forgiven for thinking that the CNN newsreel at the bottom of screens in city offices has something of the drip feed or the soporific lullaby about it. '28 die in Baghdad car bomb' we are told in a conveyor-belt snippet beneath a screen dominated by the markets. It is as if our weakly felt moral duty to pay attention to the global carnage precipitated by wars ostensibly waged to preserve our way of life can be discharged by the two second flicker of attention, on the way up to our desks, to absorb that daily dosage of death and destruction. For the conscience then, *quia est in eo virtus dormitiva*,[43] whilst for the nerves, well those it

[38] Quoted in A Houen, *Terrorism and modern literature, from Joseph Conrad to Ciaran Carson* (Oxford University Press, 2002) 11.

[39] *ibid*, 12.

[40] D Hirst, *The Gun and the Olive Branch* (Nation Books, 1977) 311.

[41] A Houen, *Terrorism and modern literature, from Joseph Conrad to Ciaran Carson* (Oxford University Press, 2002) 74.

[42] See generally, A Feldman, *Formations of Violence* (Chicago University Press, 1991).

[43] FW Nietzsche, *Beyond Good and Evil*, trans J Norman (Cambridge University Press, 2002).

keeps on edge. Repetition ad nauseam of people hurling themselves from skyscrapers was in the common interest of terrorists and those in the Bush administration who wanted the sense of ire and injustice to be strong enough to bridge the evidential gap between Saudi suicides and Saddam Hussein.[44]

To say, with Farnen, that the media call the shots, or to argue to the contrary, with John Bowyer Bell, that it is the media who are vulnerable to capture by the terrorists, is to err. We do not read or watch what the papers print or the television transmits; rather, the papers print and the television transmits what we will read and watch. Further, the suppression of free speech is a classic feature of governmental responses to terrorism (discussion of which here is postponed until the chapter on the public man). It should not be thought that the take here on the media is entirely negative. In these times of executive secrets, stonewalling and cynicism, much of what we do know is testimony to the bravery, enterprise and doggedness of the media, many of whom have given their lives to give us the news. At the time of writing, according to the Committee to Protect Journalists, 179 journalists and media workers have died since the beginning of the Iraq war.[45] To put this in context, the BBC reported that the number of UK troop deaths in Iraq has reached 176.[46]

Moving from the packaging to the content, the 'war on terrorism' has been a war of words and images as much as it has been actual, internecine fighting. Given that terrorists want to maximise publicity for their cause, they are expert not only in attracting attention but also in conveying messages through symbols. The following passage is a classic terrorist statement involving iconography and narrative:

> The September 11 attacks were not targeted at women and children. The real targets were America's *icons* of military and economic power. America was struck by God Almighty in one of its vital organs, so that its greatest buildings are destroyed … Thanks be to God that what America is tasting now is only a *copy* of what we have tasted.[47]

Bin Laden's redescription has several purposes. First, it is intended to humanise the atrocities of September 11, by denying that the targets were women and children. (We can assume this is scant consolation to the victims' families and friends.) Second, it romanticises the event, by incorporating it into a cosmic battle, led by God against the sins of a contemporary Gomorrah. Third, it attempts to accentuate and personify America's vulnerability by referring to the damage to its 'vital organs'. Fourth, it casts the attack in the historical context of

[44] See for a similar view, J Habermas and J Derrida, *Philosophy in a time of terror: dialogues with Jürgen Habermas and Jacques Derrida* (University of Chicago Press, 2003) 108.

[45] 'Press Deaths in Iraq', *Committee to Protect the Press*, available at: www.cpj.org.

[46] 'UK Troop Deaths in Iraq', *BBC*, available at: news.bbc.co.uk/2/hi/uk_news/3847051.stm.

[47] B Lawrence (ed), *Messages to the World: The Statements of Osama bin Laden* (Verso, 2005), statement of 7 October 2001.

American meddling in the Middle East whilst simultaneously diminishing its importance, calling September 11 a mere 'copy'.

The romanticisation of the attacks requires a little more explication. When we think of a society, we think not only of persons but of its conceptual contours. In other words, societies are as much ideas as they are folk. Perhaps more precisely, a society is the idea it has of itself.[48] One way to assail a society, therefore, is to destroy its icons. The targets of September 11, including the Pentagon, the World Trade Center and, presumably, the White House were, respectively, the (aggressive) military, the (usurious) economy and the (impious) liberal democracy.

Notwithstanding the harsh reality of the events of that day, the twisted steel and charred corpses, they fell on only one of the battlegrounds. They are symbols or signifiers. Equally potent events took place on the plane of iconography, in the theatre of ideas. The opportunity to parry in the battle of ideas was not lost on Colin Powell, who told us that this was not an assault on America, but an attack on 'democracy', 'civilization' and the '21st Century'. His exhortations remind us of the need for extreme caution. Though this theme will be returned to in the chapter on the public man, suffice it to observe for now that expansionist interpretations of events are all too easily deployed to provoke (per bin Laden) but also to justify responses out of all proportion to the magnitude of the terrorism (per Powell). In the same vein, Houen draws attention to the mythical quality of Bloody Sunday, Bloody Friday and the Enniskillen and Omagh bombings in the minds of the paramilitary and civilian community of Northern Ireland. He is correct to highlight the dangers of what he calls 'discursive overdeterminations of terrorist events'.[49]

Another point worth elaborating briefly is the notion of the terrorist attack being a copy, or the layered theatricality of terrorism. In this sense, September 11 was very similar to the arson attack of 22 May 1967 by radicals on an American department store at the outset of a celebration of US fashion in Belgium. Those who died were representational victims, experiencing, per Ulrike Meinhof, that 'crackling Vietnam feeling'. But they were also guilty of indulging in, and buying into the American aggressors' cultural wares. Modernly, much of bin Laden's rhetoric centres on this idea of giving the West a taste of its own medicine, whilst emphasising that it is but a taste, and that the real oppression is of Muslims. But further, he paints a picture of all Americans and their allies aiding and abetting, or at least acquiescing in, the unjust, inequitable structures of the United Nations, global capitalism and oil-rich oligarchies in the Middle East. Those who died in New York were, to bin Laden, at the same time, real victims, representational victims and criminals by electoral association.

[48] This is, in essence, the view espoused by P Allott, *Eunomia: new order for a new world* (Oxford University Press, 1990) 240.

[49] A Houen, *Terrorism and modern literature, from Joseph Conrad to Ciaran Carson* (Oxford University Press, 2002) 267.

The power of terrorist imagery is formidable. It has been suggested, not without grounds, that the terrorist 'combines in himself the two sublimities of human grandeur: the martyr and the hero'.[50] Terrorists are also well aware that their popularity is inversely indexed to the cruelty with which they are treated and the severity with which the state curtails civil liberties in reaction to terrorism. To make this point, Houen quotes from Sergius Stepniak's novel, *The Career of a Nihilist*:

> If we have to suffer – so much the better! Our sufferings will be a new weapon for us. Let them hang us, let them shoot us, let them kill us in their underground cells. The more fiercely we are dealt with, the greater will be our following. I wish I could make them tear my body to pieces …[51]

Given the depravity of their means, terrorists are always keen to emphasise the piety of their ends, the quasi-legal justification for their actions, and their selfless service of sacred ideals. Bin Laden features in his videos not only with a Kalashnikov, but also in a rustic setting, clothed in the loose-fitting robes of that modest poverty characteristic of religious men, against the backdrop of a library filled with weighty, authoritative texts of the Islamic jurisprudential tradition. According to the head of the Central Intelligence Agency unit responsible for hunting bin Laden, he 'is seen by millions of his co-religionists – because of his defense of Islam, personal piety, physical bravery, integrity and generosity – as an Islamic hero, as that faith's ideal type, and almost as a modern-day Saladin'.[52]

All those who wish to lead attempt to associate themselves, and yet transcend themselves with a supreme cause, be it a nation or a notion.[53] These are not mere squabbles about semantic preferences. A freedom fighter enjoys a kudos and legal status unavailable to the terrorist. In a case in point, a Milanese judge, Clementina Forleo, rejected the characterisation of Islamic militant activists as terrorists, preferring to think of them as supporters of insurgents in Iraq and, consequently, acquitted them of the crime of international terrorism: 'Chi compie attentati in un contesto bellico, se non coinvolge civili, non è un terrorista'. ('In conflict, a combatant who does not target civilians is not a terrorist'.) Though the Appeal Court, diplomatically, did not align itself with Forleo's bold statement, it affirmed the absolution of the indicted men, doubting the cogency of the prosecution evidence.[54]

[50] S Kravchinsky and S Stepniak, *Underground Russia* (C Scribner's Sons, 1883) 44.

[51] A Houen, *Terrorism and modern literature, from Joseph Conrad to Ciaran Carson* (Oxford University Press, 2002) 288.

[52] M Scheuer, *Imperial Hubris* (Brassey's, 2004) 104.

[53] R Eatwell, 'Reflections on Fascism and Religion' in L Weinberg and A Pedahzur (eds), *Religious Fundamentalism and Political Extremism* (Frank Cass, 2004).

[54] For a summary of the decisions, see the report in *La Repubblica*, of the 29 November 2005, '*I tre Islamistici non sono terroristi a Milano assoluzione e polemiche*' (available at: ricerca.repubblica.it/repubblica/archivio/repubblica/2005/11/29/tre-islamici-non-sono-terroristi-milano.html).

From a symbolic standpoint, the bombing of property and buildings are both particularly effective. The British Suffragettes bombed what they saw as man's God – property – in order to stir him into action on behalf of the non-enfranchised women of the country, and to throw into relief the elision of possessions and women. The bombing of buildings is highly suggestive, as it symbolises the destruction of existing establishments whilst provoking thought about how to rebuild society. This is potent stuff, but the even stronger symbolism of cosmic justice and clashing civilisations must be considered later in the chapters on the sublime and enmity.

Naturally, not only terrorists resort to the usage of theatricality. States have a considerable repertoire and no small amount of expertise in putting on a show for the collective psyche. In this final part of the descriptive section of this chapter, I shall consider some of the tactics used, for better or worse, by states in the symbolic battle with terrorists.

One of the more dubious strategies of the Bush Administration was the intellectually incoherent conflation of the terrorist with the tyrant: Apparently, you 'can't distinguish between al Qaeda and Saddam when you talk about the war on terror'.[55] As Holmes puts it, 'the swivel of the cannon from Osama to Saddam was accompanied by the blurred image of the enemy as a terrorist-tyrant'.[56] It may well be true that terrorists and tyrants have a similar characteristics, pathologies and aims,[57] but that is hardly a sound basis for artificially aligning them together in a new, ad hoc 'axis of evil'. We should not be tempted to think that Bush is incapable of distinguishing the leader of a country from the leader of an underground terrorist movement, but as an assumption upon which to ground foreign policy, let alone military strategy, the assertion that Osama and Saddam are some sort of 'bicephalous monster' or part of the same problem, is deeply troubling. If this was the ambiguous target at which our leaders took aim and fired, the spectacular imprecision of the wars in Afghanistan and Iraq becomes easier to comprehend. A further pernicious (and foreseeable) consequence of the impressionist sketch of the enemy was the inflammation of latent racial hatred: In America, 'Muslims became the targets of hostility, threats, racist slurs, assaults and even murder'.[58] The ubiquity of bin Laden's face, and the insistence of the association of him with 'everything loathsome and hateful to the collective imagination'[59] gradually meant that anyone bearing a passing resemblance (a turban or a darker shade of skin would do) to a stereotyped Muslim was tarred and feathered with the brush of sexism, barbaric cruelty and religious

[55] GW Bush, discussing terrorism with Columbia President (The Oval Office 2002).

[56] S Holmes, *The Matador's Cape: America's Reckless Response to Terror* (Cambridge University Press, 2007) 302.

[57] Apologists for overzealous American foreign policy tend to make these arguments. For a good example, see P Berman, *Terror and Liberalism* (WW Norton & Company, Inc, 2003).

[58] ET May, 'Echoes of the Cold War' in ML Dudziak (ed), *September 11 in History: A Watershed Moment?* (Duke University Press, 2003).

[59] E Said, 'Islam and the West are Inadequate Banners ', *The Observer*, 16 September 2001.

fanaticism. This state of affairs was compounded by the irresponsible depictions in the popular media of an 'immensely homogenised Islamic Arab "world" devoid of the humane, enlightened and magnanimous societal achievements of Western – more specifically American – civilisation'.[60]

The next, familiar, tactic used by the Western alliance was to depict the enemy as irrational, implacable and fanatical. In September 2004, in the Des Moines Town Hall, in Iowa, a place that is probably towards the bottom of al-Qaeda's list of targets, Dick Cheney told his avid listeners that America's foes 'know no restraint';[61] on 6 October 2005, former President Bush told us we were facing 'a radical ideology with inalterable objectives'. These are cowardly calumniations. But it is not only in the United States that this sort of obfuscation is peddled. Vilar, clearly a diligent student of the grievances propping up al-Qaeda's support base, commented that today's 'terrorism is nihilist terrorism, it is destruction for destruction's sake, more violent and more lethal'.[62] Naturally, terrorists are equal to this challenge and respond in kind: America, say both al-Zawahiri and bin Laden, 'only understands the logic of power and war'[63] and Bush 'has a heart that knows no words'.[64] Sadly, the excessively militaristic reaction of America and the United Kingdom to September 11 increased the relative credibility of the terrorists in some quarters: On 27 January 2002, in the *New York Times*, Elaine Sciolino reported that '95% of well-educated Saudis support Bin Laden's causes'.

A further tactic, mentioned earlier, has been to say that terrorism is pitted against democracy, or in the parlance of the Bush administration, that terrorists 'hate freedom'. Kofi Annan claimed that 'terrorism represents a global threat to democracy, the rule of law, human rights and stability'. We might well suspect that Annan's *real* concern was that exaggerated, iron-fisted state responses to terrorism represent a global threat to democracy, the rule of law, human rights and stability. For it remains completely unclear to more stoic observers how terrorism presents a threat to democracy. Even in the event of a massive series of nuclear strikes by terrorists, in the aftermath, those of us remaining can still, and probably would, vote on what to do (or rather for whom is to decide what to do). In the same way that the wars in Afghanistan and Iraq cannot exterminate Islam – a religion survives its individual adherents – terrorist attacks can never overturn or upset democracy. Democracy may lose currency but that will be due to its failure to deliver results, its futility against the capitalist system, or because of the apathy endemic in mass society, not because someone flies a plane into a building

60 TY Ismael and JS Ismael, 'September 11 and American policy in the Middle East' in J Strawson (ed), *Law after Ground Zero* (London, 2002).

61 Remarks, Town Hall Meeting, 7 September 2004, Des Moines, Iowa.

62 DS Hamilton, *Terrorism and international relations* (Calouste Gulbenkian Foundation, Center for Transatlantic Relations, Paul H Nitze School of Advanced International Studies, Johns Hopkins University, 2006) xi.

63 B Lawrence (ed), *Messages to the World: The Statements of Osama bin Laden* (Verso, 2005), in his statement of 25 August 2002.

64 *ibid*, 57.

or releases gas into a subway. Unlike people, ideas and dreams do not die.[65] To this effect, Lord Hoffman commented that there 'may be some nations too fragile or fissiparous to withstand a serious act of violence. But that is not the case in the United Kingdom'.[66]

In this connection it is worth noting the granular attention paid to the image of statesmen, in the attempt to curry support amongst the electorate. Michael Byers argues that

> the stereotypical middle-class American is a hardworking, gun-owning, 'handyman', who lives in a large wooden house in a far-flung suburb and drives a four-ton SUV. After 11th September, the then President's use of such expressions as 'dead or alive', 'let's roll', and 'smoking out of holes' resonated in the US, helping him achieve dizzying heights in the polls; in November 2004, it helped him win re-election.[67]

On a darker note, William Pfaff made one of the more disturbing suggestions about the Bush administration's ferocious publicity campaign. He suggests that it is not torturing prisoners because the information procured (euphemistically called 'human intelligence') is useful, but because of 'symbolism'. Paradoxically enough, it might well be thought that a liberal democracy prepared to torture will stop at nothing including tyranny, brutality and hypocrisy, in order to protect what it holds dear, namely liberty, civility and legality. This might sound far-fetched, but such symbolism is by no means foreign to American military strategists, or to their civilian leaders, as this excerpt from a paper penned by Air Force General Charles Horner shows. Tellingly, it was forwarded to US General Tommy Franks by Donald Rumsfeld, in December 2001.

> In the end, if we are going to lead, then we must be considered the madmen of the world, capable of any action, willing to risk anything to achieve our national interests ... If we are to achieve noble purposes we must be prepared to act in the most ignoble manner.[68]

As Holmes points out, 'this is how terrorists and tyrants think'.[69] More importantly for my inquiry, this is an unambiguous statement that when fighting monsters, we do not have to take care, according to Nietzsche's injunction, that we do not become monstrous. Rather, Horner tells us that to win, we must show that we are even more monstrous than the monsters we face. Three vital questions are thrown up by this attitude. First, is Horner's thinking, according to which ignoble means are justified by the noble ends, compatible with the notion of legality in a liberal democracy? Second, is it possible, contrary to Horner's

[65] People who embody mass ideological movements tend to be killed in public ceremonies, and some, like Mussolini are killed twice, once privately, and once ritually.

[66] *A v Secretary of State for the Home Department* [2004] UKHL 56, para 95.

[67] M Byers, *War law: international law and armed conflict* (Atlantic Books, 2005) 152.

[68] C Horner, 'How and Where to Apply Shock and Awe'.

[69] S Holmes, *The Matador's Cape: America's Reckless Response to Terror* (Cambridge University Press, 2007) 91.

assertion, to lead nobly rather than ignobly; is it possible to rule with clean hands? Third, can we properly lay claim to nobility and legitimacy if our means are ignoble and illicit? I shall return to this theme where it is more apt, in the chapters on rationality and perversion.

Images mobilise and unite. Statemen have very rarely been artists. Winston Churchill was an amateur painter and his rhetorical flair is legendary. Adolf Hitler was obsessed with aesthetics, though his career as an artist was as inconsequential as his career as a statesman was infamous. Indeed, his fascination with the perfect form presaged his disastrous shortcomings as a leader. The evocative power of images should not be underestimated. Walter Abish asks whether it is possible 'for anyone in Germany, nowadays, to raise his right hand, for whatever the reason, and not be flooded by the memory of a dream to end all dreams?'[70] Thus, the smallest gesture can call forth images of the greatest magnitude. Houen illuminates the point that 'political ontology can become entangled in everydayness'.[71] For present purposes, it is worth noting that in America, the flag consumerism, the purchase of countless standard-bearing paraphanalia, sales of which increased exponentially after September 11, is at the same time an expression of solidarity, nationality and adherence to the nebulous ideal of liberty.[72]

Mohandas Gandhi was perhaps the paradigmatic statesman artist, a man who, on 5 April 1930, catalysed the dissolution of British rule over India like salt-water in his hands. September 11 was described by Karlheinz Stockhausen, who felt humbled by the suicide bombers, as 'the greatest work of art that exists for the whole cosmos'. The impropriety of this description is obvious. What can be said is that, for a man wanting to galvanise the *umma*, to turn legions of Muslims into religious warriors, no better way to convince his followers of God's support – no better way to prove to the downtrodden that indeed they could injure the seemingly omnipotent superpower – could have been chosen than to destroy the symbols of America's economic and military power, with nothing but instruments of that power. This was David and Goliath writ large. Art it was not; powerful theatricality it was.

There are several features of the symbolism of suicide terrorism that are particularly potent. I shall mention only two. The first is that, at least to Western eyes, it involves the ultimate sacrifice. Someone prepared to lay down their life for an idea commands our attention. Second, the randomness of the attack is terrifying. More people are killed in farming accidents in the United States every year than are killed by terrorism; the number of homicides, where Americans kill

[70] Quoted in A Houen, *Terrorism and modern literature, from Joseph Conrad to Ciaran Carson* (Oxford University Press, 2002) 230.

[71] *ibid*, 232

[72] On flag consumerism, see M Dudziak, 'Remembering September 11' in ML Dudziak (ed), *September 11 in History: A Watershed Moment?* (Duke University Press, 2003).

Americans, is of course, far higher.[73] What distinguishes suicide terrorism in the popular imagination is that it can strike anyone, anywhere. Notwithstanding the infinitesimally small possibility of dying in a suicide bombing in the American or English countryside, the total disregard for any and all human life shown by suicide terrorists is deeply unsettling for us all.

What I would like to convey now is that images or the symbols that represent them are also, in and of themselves, events. A map, for example, when it is published, is, aside from being a political statement, necessarily retrospective. It is an attempt to draw boundaries as they are and is, therefore, condemned to being out-of-date. But a map is also prospective. Its intention is to help us find our way, both in the sense of getting from A to B but also politically, to stop us from straying out of our jurisdiction. Popular maps in Argentina carry the parenthetical (Arg) next to *Las Islas Malvinas.* In a crucial way, to which I will return in the discussion of temporality, maps exist everywhere but the present.

Though images can be events, events can be described with images. Jacques Derrida argues, rightly or wrongly, as follows:

> September 11, *le 11 septembre*, September 11. The brevity of the appellation (September 11, 9/11) stems not only from an economic or rhetorical necessity. The telegram of this metonymy – a name, a number points out the unqualifiable by recognizing that we do not recognize or even cognize, that we do not yet know how to qualify, that we do not know what we are talking about.[74]

Is it not more likely that the blandness of the appellation '9/11' helps us swallow the otherwise indigestible tragedy; that the simple number somehow neutralises the otherwise nauseatingly high loss of life? Or is September 11 not really that difficult to understand? Unless you subscribe to inside-job conspiracy theories or think that God struck America, what happened is that some very angry men flew planes into buildings. It was a crime (against humanity) and a legally tidy one at that because most of the perpetrators disposed of themselves. The use of the ambiguous title, 9/11, allows the event to escape classification as a crime of very angry men, and remain unfathomable and authentic. The ambiguity, coupled with the connotation of emergency of the numbers 911, grants the government a blank canvass. A unique attack demands a unique defence. But it is tempting to say that we have witnessed a humanly inconceivable reaction to a humanly unthinkable action. This is not just philosophy: the refusal precisely to categorise what happened on September 11 is the fundamental reason for the incoherent manner in which we have responded.

Before moving onto how we might think about language and image in a manner that preserves our credibility, the integrity of our governments, and the

[73] The US Department of Justice estimates that the number of homicides in the US was 16,039 in 2001, the statistics are available at www.ojp.usdoj.gov/bjs/homicide/homtrnd.htm.

[74] J Habermas and J Derrida, *Philosophy in a time of terror: dialogues with Jürgen Habermas and Jacques Derrida* (University of Chicago Press, 2003) 87.

respectability of our laws, it is worth noting one of the strangest features of the governmental rhetoric. I think it can be stated plainly: The obsessive emphasis on security has contributed to creating a climate of insecurity. At first blush, the words 'homeland security' conjure up notions of family, living in an ancestral dwelling-place, perhaps built of solid stone with a hearth, located in a community patrolled by loyal policemen, and safe from external aggressors. The homeland is a tremendously powerful image of well-being and, for that reason, has an odious and hateful history. Its invocation by politicians often presages the 'unscrupulous use of the sense of home, roots and history to justify and legitimise xenophobia, tyranny and the dread syntax of ethnic purity'.[75] The notion of the *Heimat* is not merely the sanctuary of arrogance as Uncle Adam told Zygmunt in Siegfried Lenz's novel, *The Heritage*, but it is a refuge for that skulking, poisonous orderly of the racist credo, Ignorance.

A feature of the American heritage and homeland prior to September 11 was that it tended to be either spiritual or elsewhere or both. The Bush administration changed all that. An attack on the vital organs of America, in America, was seen as a not-to-be-squandered opportunity to relocate the homeland not only geographically, but also ideologically. A homeland, like the idyllic Shire in JRR Tolkien's *Lord of the Rings*, a story conceived of in the First World War and penned in the Second, is a place threatened by an external aggressor, which you must defend from invasion.[76] This notion of expulsion or repulsion can make life tremendously difficult for immigrants and members of ethnic minorities. Second- and third-generation Pakistanis in London, that last colony of the Empire, have experienced alienation in British society, despite being an integral part of that society, and irrespective of the fact that they consider themselves more British than Pakistani. German Jews experienced a similar alienation after assimilation prior to their mass extermination. The diarist Victor Klemperer, son of a Rabbi, fought, like Hitler, in the Bavarian troops in World War I. He married a German girl, became Professor of Language and Literature at Dresden, and converted to Protestantism. Indeed, he considered the 'Jewish nation' a comedy, and the Nazis 'unGerman'. The widespread and inextricable assimilation of Jews into the fabric of German society has led Niall Ferguson to suggest that 'the anti-Semitism of the Nazis is best understood as a reaction to the very success of the German-Jewish assimilation'.[77] Is British Islamophobia similar in this respect? Or has Britain's embrace of ethnic minorities always been limp, cold and half-hearted? These questions, though research-worthy are beyond the scope of this book.

Returning to the present day, and shifting our focus across the Atlantic, the upheaval in the topography of the American identity was to result in xenophobia

[75] S Rushdie, *Imaginary Homelands* (Granta Books, 1991).

[76] A Kaplan, 'Homeland Insecurities: Transformations of Language and Space' in ML Dudziak (ed), *September 11 in History: A Watershed Moment?* (Duke University Press, 2003) 63.

[77] N Ferguson, *The War of the World* (Allen Lane, 2006) 252.

where there had been hospitality, purity where there had been plurality, and aggression where there had been toleration. Was the Bush administration's invocation of the notion of the homeland, and its creation of the Department of Homeland Security, anything other than reckless, instrumental and incendiary scaremongering? The transformation or revelation of the ferocious nationalism of American society was unambiguous in the ecstatic cheering that followed the rhetorical references to 'the greatest nation on earth' or 'in history' in the speeches of the candidates in the 2008 Electoral Primaries. Even the victorious Democratic candidate who had opposed the Iraq war stooped to such oratorical lows. The objective observer would be forgiven for an absence of audacious hope.

I have been describing and admonishing the manner in which the state and society responded to terrorism through language and image. In the remainder of this chapter, the aim is to prescribe how we might think about language and image so as to better equip ourselves to fight terrorism in a manner consistent with preserving the principle of legality and upholding the integrity of liberal democracy.

Above, I made much of the – at best mindlessly careless and at worst, deliberately deceptive – use of language by politicians. In essence, I suggested that to bastardise and maltreat language is to orphan the law and molest society.

Terrorism requires a concerted, variegated, forceful response, but to call that response 'war', and in so doing, obscure the complexity of the problem, obfuscate the correct answer and narrow the range of conceivable options, is foolhardy in the extreme.[78] The public must refine their lexical palate. It will not do for people to swallow the gross misdescriptions cooked up by politicians and dished up by the media. To take just one example, the very usage of the semantically-loaded terminology of the homeland should have provoked a public gag reflex. We should be slow to endorse or acquiesce in such unstable nomenclature as a platform for policy. James White says that language obtrudes into our consciousness only when it is vague or imperfect, otherwise it disappears from view.[79] This is a cute point, but it fails to capture the effect of language on a sloth public mind. The only thing that disappeared from view when vagueness (think of 'civilisation under attack') and imperfection (think of 'the war on terrorism') diluviated political and media declarations was our taste for critique. Public obsequiousness is considered in detail in due course.

For now, we can admit how rough sketches or characterisations of the enemy lead to poorly tailored policies. The example I gave above was of the depiction of the enemy as implacable, nihilistic and responsive only to the language of force. The famous philosopher Jürgen Habermas, for example, has said that al-Qaeda 'do not pursue a program that goes beyond the engineering of destruction and

[78] PB Heymann, *Terrorism, Freedom and Security* (The MIT Press, 2003).

[79] JB White, 'What Can a Lawyer Learn From Literature? (Review of *Law and Literature: A Misunderstood Relation* by Richard Posner)' (1988–89) 102 *Harvard Law Review* 2014, 2015.

insecurity'.[80] This is flummery. Al-Qaeda is not a social club for the violently disposed. Yes, those of a violent disposition will find an outlet in its ample fold, but the organisation has, precisely because of its 'program', deep support in communities and its leadership have realistic aims. On 23 February 1998, the World Islamic Front for Jihad Against the Jews and the Crusaders, declared three clear goals:

— the withdrawal of US troops from Saudi Arabia;
— an end to sanctions against Iraq; and
— Islamic control over Muslim holy sites in Jerusalem.[81]

These goals are not radical, fanatical or nihilistic, nor for that matter are they particularly objectionable. They are certainly feasible and it would take a stubborn diplomat to call them unreasonable. All three pertain to self-determination, the freedom that terrorists apparently loathe, territorial sovereignty and autonomy. The latter is religious in nature but it can hardly be described as fanatical. Habermas confuses these aims with al-Qaeda's means, which, of course are the engineering of destruction and insecurity. Aware of the 'benefits' of this roughly sketched enemy, America and the United Kingdom paid scant attention to the actual demands of the terrorists and concealed them from the public.

More than it should be an armed conflict, the campaign against terrorism should be one of ideas conducted with words. The wise campaigner will use words made from an amalgam of sound ideas and fact. We should seriously question whether those who wield words recklessly are fit to govern, to legislate and to influence our thought. Our descriptions are prescriptions; yet, though they can narrow a field of inquiry, though they can incarcerate, they can also liberate and inspire. Words that subjugate are constantly embattled by words that liberate. Somewhat infatuated by poetry and its purported resistance to power, Raoul Vaneigem, a Belgian Philospher, wrote that there is an 'ill-defined and shifting frontier where language captured by power (conditioning) and free language (poetry) fight out their infinitely complex war'.[82] In a parallel conflict, words can be enlisted in the service of both state terrorism and militancy.

Images can also be conscripted, and we learned above, with the help of Houen's searching analysis, that terrorism must be fought with words but also with 'phenomenality'. The manner in which states respond to terrorist acts, words and images reverberates symbolically. In court, after a barrister has made a case for the civil claimant, her opponent presents the case for the defence, at

[80] J Habermas and J Derrida, *Philosophy in a time of terror: dialogues with Jürgen Habermas and Jacques Derrida* (University of Chicago Press, 2003) 29.

[81] JM Schwartz, 'Misreading Islamist Terrorism' in J Margolis, T Rockmore and AT Marsoobian (eds), *The Philosophical Challenge of September 11* (Blackwell Publishing, 2005) 43.

[82] R Vaneigem, 'Basic Banalities II' in K Knabb (ed), *Situationist International Anthology* (Berkeley CA, Bureau of Public Secrets, 2007) 123.

which point counsel for the claimant has a right of reply. Not to avail herself of that right is a show of confidence in the integrity of her convictions, and, moreover, belief that the tribunal, given the choice, will plump for her arguments. Of late, politicians have thought fit to respond, albeit sometimes indirectly, to the statements issued by bin Laden. Granted, the behaviour of America and Britain has been so reprehensible that bin Laden may have one or two points. However, bin Laden advocates the murder by all Muslims of all Americans, Jews and their allies. Such an individual is clearly not to be countenanced. A liberal democracy need not dignify the utterances of an advocate of mass murder with a response. To respond directly or indirectly to such an absurd enjoinder is, unlike the confident barrister, to show doubt about the rightness of one's cause but also to display a lack of faith that the tribunal, which in a democracy is the public, can choose between the tenets of a liberal democracy and those of a ruthless terrorist. As for the media, though they must report terrorist statements and acts, and trust, like the government that the public will neither indulge the whims of murderers, nor become enraptured by their violent propaganda, they must always be mindful of fear-mongering and eschew reporting for the sole sake of entertaining.

Without getting ahead of ourselves, it can be noted here that both terrorism and law are coercive and discursive in that both employ force and both create narratives. As with terrorism, force is intrinsic to law itself. It is our belief in its coercive quality that makes it law. And, like the reporting of law, the reporting of terrorism is inseparable from terrorism itself. The report is the voice of the law as it is the voice of the gun. The report has its own powers, both retrospective (defining the past) and prospective (prescribing the future). Descriptions and figurations of both law and terrorism, to borrow a phrase from Houen, have their own performativity. These points should be borne in mind going forward along with the recollection that history has witnessed terrorists become lawmakers. We might discover that the relationship between law and terror is more intimate than might initially have been presumed. And, if so, it is imperative, if we want to live by law and not in terror, to discover the nature of their dealings.

Events and images, words and ideas are all performative, sometimes in competition, sometimes in concert. Having asserted that the report of an event determines the event, the simpler proposition that events produce reports should not be neglected. It suffices to recall Campbell's analysis of the meta-conflict attending every conflict to realise that the dynamic relationship between narration and action should be understood if we want to respond intelligently to terrorism. Here, legislation and cartography are not dissimilar. Both are descriptive prescriptions. Both are events and representations. Both are products of human imagination; both operate retrospectively to (re)define history and prospectively to influence the future. Legislation and cartography conspired in Guantánamo Bay, to broadcast an unambiguous message to the world. Instead of American decency, 'Gitmo', as it is affectionately known, showcased its depravity; the treatment of its uncharged, undressed, sleep-deprived, underfed detainees did not smack of legality but of cruelty; it was characterised by duress not due process; its very existence demonstrated American hypocrisy not transparency; such a place, being the very hall-mark of tyranny is inimical to liberal democracy. Guantánamo Bay is the black heart of the American homeland. The irony was not lost on Holmes:

> The most infamous penal colony in a Communist country is now located at Guantanamo Bay Naval Base. We have come a long way since Solzhenitsyn. To Cuba, it turns out, the US has spread not the blessings of liberty but the rule of manacles, stress positions, cages and hoods.[83]

Armed with words and images, the power exerted by the state through its determinations of events is considerable. That power can be amplified or neutralised by the media. In its ideal form, the press constitutes a fourth branch of government, a watchdog hounding maladministration, a lamp of truth, a mirror for society, and a marketplace of ideas. In order for people to make informed decisions, it is of the imperative that the press is free – independent of government. This may sound obvious but balanced reporting about, for example, why Palestinian mothers send their sons to suicide missions, is almost entirely absent from the American and British news. Nationalist press is as good as no press; it is a mere delegate, vassal, or echo of the rulers. The press does, however, require the support of the state, for a press dependent on profit becomes a subset of the entertainment media. What if we enjoy being scared, for example? The press should not have to conform to the strictures of screenwriting or the economy, but rather of incisive, investigative and accurate reporting.

Given the power of the press, it would seem that it must counter rather than exacerbate popular racist stereotypes. It is not acceptable to show the carnage of suicide bombing and then cut to a scene of prayer in a mosque, artificially creating a link between the Islamic faith and a propensity for blowing oneself up.[84] The media has enormous power to influence our prejudices but also our priorities. Martha Nussbaum comments that:

> Floods, earthquakes, cyclones – and the daily deaths of thousands from preventable malnutrition and disease – none of these makes the American world come to a standstill, none elicits a tremendous outpouring of grief and compassion. At most we get what [Adam] Smith so trenchantly described: a momentary flicker of feeling, quickly dissipated by more pressing concerns close to home.[85]

[83] S Holmes, *The Matador's Cape: America's Reckless Response to Terror* (Cambridge University Press, 2007) 258.

[84] For evidence countering the stereotype that suicidal proclivities flow from the Islamic faith, see RA Pape, 'The Strategic Logic of Suicide Terrorism' (2003) 97(3) *American Political Science Review* 343.

[85] MC Nussbaum, 'Compassion and Terror' in JP Sterba (ed), *Terrorism and International Justice* (Oxford University Press, 2003) 233.

And yet, the shrinkage of the world due to telephony, email, video-chat, skype-ing, twittering and international broadcasting, means that the human race has an historically unprecedented opportunity to learn about the plight of those on the other side of the world; the modern media have the ability to broaden the horizons of the significant human capacity for empathy. This is subject to an important caveat, to which I will return later: to assert that the media control our agenda, that they sort and rank the things that should be of interest is true only to the extent that we are happy to deny that we are free to choose between media. Again, we do not read what the papers print; the papers print what we will read. The media might well be more important than ever before, and, in the investigation of the role of parliaments, the press and the public man, the suggestion is made that editorial integrity steers congressional morality, which guides the public mores that drive editorial integrity.

Having written 30 pages on the usage of words, my own semantic choices require some explanation. Until this point, in order to plunge directly into the muddied terminological waters, I have delayed defining some of the pivotal terms in this debate. It would be remiss of me to proceed without stating what I understand by the words I have already begun to use. It is uncontentious that fighting terrorism requires definitional clarity. That said, given that this entire discussion is intended to suggest a way of thinking about law, the definitions here will be fleshed out as I proceed, and are only fully explained in the final chapter. The 'what' follows immediately. The 'why' follows by increments.

In choosing our words and acquiescing in the nomenclature selected by others, we describe our (partly imagined) present and prescribe our future. More than that, in mutually clarifying terms, we permit communication.[86] It is an author's prerogative to set the terms of the debate, but an attempt has been made here, so far as is possible, to use language in a common-sense way. A restriction of the possible meaning of a term facilitates discussion. I have chosen to write about this theme in a manner that is consciously between what White characterised as the academic and literary methods; that is, I issue invitations into cordoned off terrain.[87] That said, there is nothing artificial about the definitions herein. On the frequent occasions of doubt, the Oxford English Dictionary definition was preferred to contrived lawyerly constructions.

The first problematic term is, of course, 'terrorism' but before coming to that, it is worth setting out what is understood here by 'brutality', which will be applied throughout to objects of disapprobation. By brutality, I mean mindless or seemingly mindless, arbitrary or excessive violence or savagery. Brutality will consistently be compared with legality in order to bring out the tension between force meted out arbitrarily, something alien to civilisation, and force that enjoys the quality of civility, exerted in the defence of defensible ideas. An example of

[86] This is the fundamental message of J Habermas in *Faktizitaet und Geltung* (Suhrkamp, 1998).

[87] JB White, 'Thinking About Our Language' (1986–87) 96 *Yale Law Journal* 1960.

the former is the torture with impunity of a member of a suspected terrorist's family to ascertain their whereabouts, and an example of the latter is punishment of a person, subsequent to a jury trial establishing beyond reasonable doubt their transgression of a previously, duly, publicly promulgated law.

How then, are we to define terrorism? An entire thesis could be written on this topic. Debates on the definition of terrorism tend to be heated and clouded by the fallout from the latest attack. The United Nations have failed to settle on a definition, and though there are 13 international conventions on its various manifestations, such as hijacking and hostage-taking, no overarching multilateral treaty complete with a definition of the phenomenon exists.[88] In the *United Nations Global Counter-Terrorism Strategy*, adopted on 8 September 2006, the member states reaffirmed their determination (ie, admitted their abject failure) to conclude a comprehensive convention on terrorism and to resolve the outstanding issues related to its definition.[89] My preferred approach is not to list the now innumerable suggested definitions, but to take one and strip it down to its essentials. The 1983 US State Department Definition of Terrorism reads: 'Terrorism is premeditated, politically motivated *violence* perpetrated against noncombatant *targets* by *subnational groups or clandestine agents*, usually intended to influence an audience'.

There are several problems with this definition, some glaring, some less so. I have italicised the glaring problems. First, by stating that terrorism can only be committed by *subnational groups or clandestine agents*, America impliedly reserves the right to commit premeditated, politically motivated violence against noncombatant targets to influence an audience. The hypocrisy is obvious so I need not labour this point. Suffice it to say that it is unclear why the indiscriminate killing of civilians by a democratically elected (or any other type of) government is any less reprehensible than the indiscriminate killing of civilians by anyone else. A definition that excludes state massacres (or threats of force) is too skinny.

Second, I prefer the term 'aggression' to 'violence' for the simple reason that violence undertaken in self-defence should not be considered terrorism. Those who take up arms to repel an aggressor should not be confused with terrorists. Relatedly, 'aggression' has to stay. However useful it might be in terms of explaining why people turn from discourse to force, a definition that includes

[88] The existing international instruments include the following (short titles used): 1963 Aircraft Convention; 1970 Unlawful Seizure of Aircraft Convention; 1971 Civil Aviation Convention; 1973 Diplomatic Agents Convention; 1979 Hostages Convention; 1980 Nuclear Materials Convention; 1988 Airport Protocol; 1988 Maritime Convention; 1988 Fixed Platform Protocol; 1991 Plastic Explosives Convention; 1997 Terrorist Bombing Convention; 1999 Terrorist Financing Convention; 2005 Nuclear Terrorism Convention. All are available at: www.un.org/terrorism/instruments.shtml.

[89] The text is available at: www.un.org/terrorism/strategy-counter-terrorism.shtml#resolution. The accompanying strategy bears the reference A/RES/60/288. This is a good place to start for anyone interested in the protracted debate about the definition, which began in earnest after the attack on the Olympic village in Munich.

non-violent coercion or what could be referred to as 'structural violence' is too flabby for legal purposes. For example, Joseph Margolis's inclusion of economic or political control causing disparity might well capture socially objectionable policies, but it is of no use to us in striving for a serviceable legal term.[90] It should be noted at this stage that 'aggression' has a specific meaning in international law. Pursuant to Article 39 of the Charter of the United Nations, it is now the job of the United Nations Security Council to determine acts of aggression, which it should do (according to the General Assembly's Resolution 3314) by reference to the following definition of aggression: 'Aggression is the use of armed force by a State [or group of States] against sovereignty, territory or political independence of another State, or in any other manner inconsistent with the Charter, as set out in this definition'.[91] The Resolution then goes on to list manifestations of aggression, including naval, air and military sorties or deployments; the placing of state territory at the disposition of another state for such sorties or deployments; blockades; and the enlisting of mercenaries or irregulars. Importantly, no consideration of whatever nature may serve as a justification for aggression, be it political, economic, military or otherwise. Aggression is not used here in this specific state-orientated sense, but is intended to carry the meaning it has in plain English. Naturally, that meaning contains all of the above, but also extends to more classical terrorist acts.

Third, it is not clear why killing one person cannot be terrorism. For instance, few would doubt that Gavrilo Princip's deadly act of 1914 qualified. In fact, as Ferguson observes, the assassination of Archduke Francis Ferdinand was probably the most effective piece of terrorism in recorded history, given that it set into motion a chain of events that destroyed the Austro-Hungarian Empire and transformed Bosnia Herzegovina from a colony to part of an independent state, an end result which would have gratified Princip.[92] But that is beside the point. Having removed those three glaring problems, the US State Department's definition reads: 'Terrorism is premeditated, politically motivated aggression perpetrated against a non-combatant or non-combatants, usually intended to influence an audience'.

One of the less glaring problems is why terrorism has to be 'politically motivated'. What about the Harvard maths graduate and former assistant Professor at Berkley, better known as the 'Unabomber', Theodore Kaczynski? Convinced of man's increasing slavery to technology, he sent bombs to universities and airlines.[93] Were his actions murder and vandalism but not terrorism? Is

[90] See generally, J Margolis, 'Terrorism and New Forms of War' in J Margolis, T Rockmore and AT Marsoobian (eds), *The Philosophical Challenge of September 11* (Blackwell Publishing, 2005).

[91] This Resolution is available at: daccessdds.un.org/doc/RESOLUTION/GEN/NR0/739/16/IMG/NR073916.pdf?OpenElement. The ICC has had difficulty defining aggression for the purposes of international criminal law. The definition above is by no means undisputed.

[92] N Ferguson, *The War of the World* (Allen Lane, 2006) 72.

[93] These worries informed the films Bladerunner and I-Robot, neither of which I recommend.

the increasing encroachment of technology into our lives not a political issue? I see no reason to acquit our paranoid, murdering mathematician of terrorism.

What about a violently pious preacher who uses a sniper rifle to kill scantily clad strippers as they exit 'Gentlemen's Clubs', convinced that the sale of sexuality is the root of society's moral degradation? Our zealous priest would probably say his was a religious or moral rather than a political conviction, yet I see no reason to spare him from being denounced as a terrorist. Is such a sniper not terrorising members of the nocturnal workforce? I will leave in the words 'politically motivated' for the simple reason, elaborated upon later, that I find it very difficult to point at any issue and say it is not political.

Next, the term 'non-combatant', though it throws up its own set of questions we shall have to answer, can stay. But it might be preferable to remove the word 'usually' from the phrase 'usually intended to influence an audience'. The definition, disabused of duplicity, excess and incoherence, now reads: 'Terrorism is premeditated, politically motivated aggression perpetrated against a non-combatant or non-combatants, intended to influence an audience'. The reasons for keeping 'non-combatant' and jettisoning 'usually' are as follows: The *core moral objectionability of terrorism is twofold.* We instinctively abhor attacks on people who have elected not to fight. That includes revulsion for indiscriminate or excessive use of violence and force deployed irrespective of the identity or history of the victims. Next, we instinctively disapprove of attempts to influence people with fear.[94] The 'fear factor' is what distinguishes terror from murder, for instance.[95] If, enraged, a man kills his wife on finding out about her affair with his gardener, he does not wish to terrorise other adulterous spouses, but merely wishes to dispose of his own. These twin objections undergird central tenets of the law of war and domestic criminal codes,[96] and the centrality of both facets was approved by the Trial Chamber for the International Tribunal for the Former Yugoslavia in the *Milošević* judgment:

> No-one knew whether they might be the next victim … Terror is … the intentional deprivation of a sense of security … And it's not just … the fear that comes from being nearby the combat. This is a fear calculated to demoralise, to disrupt, to take away any sense of security from a body of people who have nothing … to do with the combat.[97]

[94] V Lowe, '"Clear and Present Danger": Responses to Terrorism' (2005) 54 *International & Comparative Law Quarterly* 185

[95] It was held, in *Prosecutor v Milošević* ICTY (2007) Case No IT-98–29/1-T, para 953, that 'the crime of terror shares the same elements with the crime of unlawful attacks against civilians, except for the additional requirement that to constitute terror it must be established that the acts were committed with the primary purpose of spreading terror among the civilian population'.

[96] R Dworkin, 'Terror and the Attack on Civil Liberties' in T Rockmore, J Margolis and AT Marsoobian (eds), *The Philosophical Challenge of September 11* (Blackwell Publishing, 2005) 92.

[97] *Prosecutor v Milošević* ICTY (2007) Case No IT-98–29/1-T, paras 885–6.

The definition of terrorism proffered above has the added advantage of consistency with the relevant passages of the Qur'an on the law of war.[98] Crucially, a neutral definition that focuses on prohibited *means* without concern for the *ends* is far more likely to generate widespread assent.

This emphasis on means introduces a fundamental point, which I will build on later. Aggression as a means, has its own logic and momentum. Consequently, where blows are exchanged, blood is spilled and violence becomes cyclic, aggression can override, overshadow and usurp ends. Many deaths in the troubles in Northern Ireland were explicable on the basis of family feuds, revenge killings and tribal honour rather than the politics of devolution. Notwithstanding what I said above about the absurdity of a 'war on terrorism', what we should aim to eradicate from human behaviour is the resort to immoral means. In so doing we remove the potential for force's self-justifying self-propulsion not as the *continuation of* politics but as the *replacement for* politics. Though it is refuted that terrorism is an ideology – rather it is a tactic – our battle *is*, in this limited sense, against terrorism, against certain unacceptable means, because of aggression's potential to infiltrate, misappropriate and perpetuate conflicts.

Having once again jumped the gun, I should briefly note that 'force' is meant in the sense of physical strength or power exerted on a subject, but also to refer more particularly to the deployment of military, aerial and naval capacities. The latter is normally distinguished from the former by calling it 'the use of force' as opposed to 'force' *simpliciter*.

Another central term to which I will refer throughout is 'power'. Power here is not intended as a synonym for force, rather it refers to three things which again, are cursorily treated here, in the anticipation of spending more time on them shortly. First, it denotes the influence that derives from knowledge of an adversary's physical or military superiority. For brevity's sake, I will call this 'awe'. This may take the form of respect or fear. Perhaps the most laconic statement of the latter is Chairman Mao Tse-tung's assertion that political power grows out of the barrel of a gun. Second, power signifies the influence of a conviction, reason or an 'idea'. An example of this kind of power is the influence exerted on us by ideas such as democracy, or fairness, or utility. It is power that grows out of political accord. Finally, power designates the persuasive effect of 'aesthetics'. This is meant in the broadest possible sense; it would, for instance, include the effect of great beauty. In *The Siren*, by Elizabeth Meade, Vera brags: 'I could name twenty, thirty men who would die for me, I could even mention women who would go that length of devotion'.[99]

[98] A useful summary of these sections can be found in A Saeed, 'Jihad and Violence: Changing Understanding of Jihad Among Muslims' in T Coady and M O'Keefe (eds), *Terrorism and Justice: Moral Argument in a Threatened World* (Melbourne University Publishing, 2002).

[99] E Meade, *The Siren* (White, 1898) 95.

The alert reader will have realised that these three types of power are not watertight, instead they flow in and out of one another. For example, the sounds and lines of a fighter jet might produce an aesthetic arrest additional to the terror evoked by the knowledge of its immense destructive potential – its power is its terrible beauty. Moreover, an idea such as distributive justice may have an aesthetic quality to add to its conceptual appeal – justice is a beautiful thought. That said, occasionally, it will help us to distinguish between the power latent in aesthetics, awe and ideas. We might, for instance, instinctively think that ethnic purity is a beautiful idea, we may even be arrested by the appeal of homogeneity, but our reason may oust those initial urges, and the idea of ethnic plurality, the dialectics of miscegenation may eventually hold sway. On a lighter note, the prospect of international law has tremendous aesthetic appeal as a form of power over power; a form of social order beyond the state; an instantiation of people's rights over raw governmental might; and as a standing invitation to governmental self-limitation and betterment.

The final and fundamental term I would like to iterate before the end of this chapter is 'law'. It was hopefully clear from the above comparison of brutality and legality that it is not argued here that force is somehow external, antithetical or inimical to law. On the contrary, force is an integral part of law. Given that the entire argument in this book is geared towards understanding law's relation to force through the prism of terrorism, each chapter can be considered an enlargement on our understanding of law. This notwithstanding, it is worth repeating the definition of law I prefer: 'Law is coercion, approved of prior to, subsequent to, or in the absence of its exercise by power'.

The steps taken thus far were necessarily careful but the pace quickens in the subsequent chapter as we enter contested territory – the no man's land of war and crime.

3

War and Crime

I can no more be persuaded that the Government can take no strong measures in time of rebellion, because it can be shown that the same could not be lawfully taken in time of peace, than I can be persuaded that a particular drug is not good medicine for a sick man, because it can be shown not to be good food for a well one.

Abraham Lincoln, Letter to Erastus Corning and others, 12 June 1863.

AT THE TIME of writing, the BBC website carried a report of yet another fatal mistake in the Afghanistan campaign. On 6 July 2008, in Nangarhar, whilst travelling through a mountain pass separating the villages of a bride and groom, a wedding party was obliterated by US aerial bombing. Afghan authorities reported that 47 people died. One man lost 14 members of his family. The bride, having narrowly escaped two bombs, ran down the hill but was killed by a third. US spokeswoman Lt Col Rumi Nelson-Green commented that, on the 6th, the army had information that a large militant group was on the move in the Nangarhar mountains. She called any civilian loss of life tragic and assured the interviewer that the United States never targets non-combatants.[1] Was the bombing crime, war, neither or both?

As in the last chapter, I shall briefly describe the concepts in play, namely, war, crime, war crimes and terrorism. Naturally, the borders of these categories are contested but we can at least trace those borders by recalling common understandings of the terms. The concern of the whole argument here being to find ways to respond to terrorism whilst preserving some notion of legality; without contradicting our sense of the integrity of liberal democracy, the particular aporia of this discussion is how terrorism should be thought of in relation to the two paradigmatic exercises of state power, the prosecution of war and crime.

Criminal justice bespeaks the code and procedures set up by society in order to deter, punish and rehabilitate those who transgress agreed upon standards of socially acceptable behaviour. Amongst other punishments, criminals can be detained subsequent to a finding of their guilt by a tribunal of their peers. Incarceration is correctly considered to be one of the more draconian exhibitions of society's collective power. Consequently, a plethora of procedural rules have

[1] 'US kills Afghans in Strike', *BBC News Online*, 13 July 2008, available at: news.bbc.co.uk/2/hi/south_asia/7504607.stm.

been developed to ensure that only the guilty are so detained – amongst the better-known of those norms are the prohibition of hearsay and the standard of proof, according to which a person may only be found guilty if the jury are sure beyond reasonable doubt that he committed the crime charged. Substantive rules also pervade the criminal law's cautious approach to the exercise of its great power. An example is the principle, commonly traced back to *Ezekiel* 18:20 (contradicted elsewhere in the Bible), that the son shall not bear the iniquity of the father. The reasoning behind this is human agency. The son, particularly prior to being conceived, had no influence on his father's actions and did not choose the family into which he was born. That said, the notion that someone might have good or bad qualities resulting from their ancestry is foreign to neither British nor American society. 'Good chap', so we say, 'I knew his old man. He comes from good stock'. Much of our criminal law, for instance the ban on hearsay evidence, or the individuation of guilt, runs counter to such sentiment.

War is different to crime[2]. Activities considered illegal and morally reprehensible in peacetime, such as killing or the destruction of property, are considered both legal and praiseworthy in wartime.[3] This is not to say that vice and virtue are inverted, or that virtue is absent from war; rather, the rules would appear to be different. That there are any rules in war is of course disputed by some, for example, Admiral John Fisher, who revolutionised the Royal Navy, and fathered the battleship HMS Dreadnought, and who tells us that 'the essence of war is violence. Moderation in war is imbecility. Hit first, hit hard, and hit everywhere'. One wonders how he might have responded to the news of the wedding party obliterated in the hills. Is that an example of hitting everywhere or is it better understood as the erroneous targeting of people with whom the United States is not actually at war?

Prisoners of war are dissimilar to prisoners of peace. Notwithstanding the horrendous treatment of countless captured soldiers in World War II, the purpose of such detention is not punishment, or deterrence or rehabilitation. It is pure prevention. Prisoners can no longer fight. After hostilities cease, they are (to be) released. It makes as much sense (at least in the comfort of a library) to speak of the murder of a prisoner in peacetime as it does the murder of a prisoner in wartime. However, guilt is very different in war. An enemy soldier may have committed no crime but he should be considered part of a collective entity threatening to the state. Though the subject of collective responsibility is considered later, it suffices for this introduction to say that guilt in war is not individual. One is targeted because of adherence to a perceived group, not because of personal misdeeds.

[2] For one of the most readable accounts of the history of warfare, see J Keegan, *A history of warfare* (Pimlico, 1993).

[3] GP Fletcher, *Romantics at war: glory and guilt in the age of terrorism* (Princeton University Press, 2002) 47.

What is a war crime then? The very existence of this category is tribute to human aspiration; some actions are beyond the pale of acceptable human conduct even in the hell of war. Again, the inversion of vice and virtue in wartime is not total. It is not enough to say *inter armes silent leges* because there is *jus in bello*. It suffices to note the tenets of Bushido or the treatment of collateral damage in the Qur'an to realise that the idea of honourable conduct of warfare is one of some antiquity. Modern variants are found in the 1899, 1907 and 1954 Hague Conventions; the 1949 Geneva Conventions; the 1977 Additional Protocols; and in the jurisprudence of international tribunals. The law of war, sometimes referred to as international humanitarian law is 'designed to regulate the conduct of hostilities'.[4]

It is an irony of modern times that these principles of *jus in bello* implicitly disregard the position that war should permit of no rules, that we should embrace its glorious atrocity so that we avoid it at all costs; and yet the assurance of shared atrocities was, in essence, the 'MAD' logic behind the Cold War preservation of power – the brinkmanship of mutually assured destruction. Irony aside, if both civilians and soldiers can be criminals, these two categories cannot be watertight in the human imagination. But that human imagination is fogged.

With respect to the Kosovo campaign, General Clark euphemistically lamented that 'we could not present an unambiguous and clear warning to Milosevic' because of 'legal issues'.[5] Those legal issues included the *jus ad bellum*, a British wish to procure permission for the war from the Security Council, and the *jus in bello*, for instance, the 'squeamishness' of Canadian pilots – apparently not shared by their American counterparts – about responding to fire from schools or hospitals. Terrorism agitates the fissures between war and crime. We would instinctively agree that terrorists are criminals but would hesitate to call them 'soldiers' or even 'war criminals'. And yet, we might more readily agree to the proposition that September 11 bore witness to a crime against humanity, according to the common-sense use of these words, than we would to the assertion that it was an act of war.

The aspirations of international criminal justice are almost uniformly unmatched by reality. In 2005, with respect to the attempts to bring alleged war criminals to justice, Michael Byers lamented as follows: that Radovan Karadzic and Ratko Mladic 'remain at liberty … is chilling evidence of the transitory and opportunistic character of most international efforts to prevent or punish international crimes'.[6] Byers does not deny that there have been successes. September 1998 saw the former Prime Minister of Rwanda, Jean Kambanda, and a former mayor, Jean-Paul Akayesu, convicted of genocide by the International Criminal Tribunal for Rwanda. The former had advocated the extermination of the Tutsis

[4] *Legality of the Threat or Use of Nuclear Weapons, Request for an Advisory Opinion by the United Nations General Assembly* (1996) 110 ILR 163.

[5] M Byers, *War law: international law and armed conflict* (Atlantic Books, 2005) 122–3.

[6] *ibid*, 23.

and the latter had incited the systematic rape of their women. Indeed, Karadzic, who had adopted a fake identity as a mystic healer, and drank in a bar underneath a picture of his former self, has now been captured and faces trial.

But international justice is plagued with inconsistencies. As the Karadzic example proves, men tumbling from high trees often have enough influence effectively to disappear into the foliage without hitting the ground. One fears that some are so powerful they will never stand trial for their crimes. Further, international justice means different things for different people.

Many, without any apparent sense of irony, argued that Saddam Hussein, the former leader of Iraq, should be hanged 'in the name of human rights'. George Bush was one: 'He is a torturer, a murderer, and they had rape rooms, and this is a disgusting tyrant who deserves justice, the ultimate justice'.[7] Many others should perhaps be forgiven for failing to grasp the distinction between Saddam's torture chambers and those at Abu Ghraib, between systematic torture and a policy of water-boarding, between targeted killing and cold-blooded murder. According to the doctrine of command responsibility, a war crime is committed by a commander-in-chief if he knows or has reason to know that his subordinates are violating the laws of war, and if he fails to do anything to prevent the same.

The 'trial' of Saddam suffered from several shortcomings. First, he remained, at all times up to his hanging, in the custody of those who had toppled his regime. Second, no lawyers for the defence accompanied Saddam on his first appearance in the courtroom. Third, though the trial was filmed and broadcast by Al-Jazeera and CNN, Saddam's voice was denied to eager viewers. Fourth, the trial was conducted in Iraq, by Iraqis who had, if there was any truth in the allegations against Saddam, suffered greatly under his heavy hand. Does this have the look of impartiality or bias, justice or a victor's fiat, fair trial or an 'election-year show trial'?[8]

Human ambition does not stop at regulating the conduct of war, but extends to regulating the commencement of conflicts. In essence, unsatisfied with the crude justice of greater force, some have attempted to distinguish between legal and illegal wars. By way of introduction to the issues that are considered later in this chapter, I shall briefly summarise the position here. The Charter of the United Nations, arguably the closest thing we have to a constitution for the world, mandates in the third and fourth parts of its second Article, as follows:

3. All Members shall settle their international disputes by peaceful means in such a manner that international peace and security, and justice, are not endangered.

[7] 'Bush calls for Saddam Execution', *BBC News*, 17 December 2003, available at: news.bbc.co.uk/2/hi/americas/3326311.stm.

[8] The phrase is Byers'.

4. All Members shall refrain in their international relations from the threat or use of force against the territorial integrity or political independence of any state, or in any other manner inconsistent with the Purposes of the United Nations.

Further, Chapter VII (Article 39) of the Charter authorises the Security Council of the United Nations to 'determine the existence of any threat to the peace, breach of the peace, or act of aggression' and should the Security Council consider that non-military measures 'would be inadequate or have proved to be inadequate', it may use such force 'as may be necessary to maintain or restore international peace and security' (Article 42). The first time this power was exercised in relation to a humanitarian crisis was Somalia in 1992.

The prohibition on the threat or use of force might have *three exceptions*. I will touch on them here by way of introduction. First, states have not relinquished what is called the inherent right to self-defence. Obviously, this right grows out of the basic human instinct of self-preservation, but it is considered, in international jurisprudence, to originate in the pre-emptive strike by the British Navy on the *SS Caroline* during the 1837 quelling of a rebellion in Canada. In rather spectacular fashion, the steamship was torched and sent over the Niagara Falls. The Canadian rebels had received American support and the burning of the boat sparked a diplomatic furore. The manner in which that furore was resolved led to the modern law of self-defence. The Secretary of State, Daniel Webster, commented that the use of force is permitted only where the necessity of self-defence is 'instant, overwhelming, leaving no choice of means, and no moment of deliberation'. He prudently added that nothing unreasonable or excessive could be considered self-defence. Now, Article 51 of the Charter further restricts the right of self-defence to situations where a state faces an international armed attack. It also mandates that acts of self-defence be reported immediately to the Security Council and ordains that the right to respond would terminate as soon as the same took action.

The second possible exception is that the prohibition on the use of force might not apply to humanitarian intervention, where the Security Council does not act.[9] The March 1999 NATO bombing of Kosovo, absent a Security Council mandate, was not considered legal by many international lawyers, but few actually took the step of denouncing it – one theorist who adopted this 'schizophrenic position' was Martii Koskenniemi.[10]

Third, some would argue that there is a nascent right to intervene in a country to promote democracy, forming an exception to the ban on the use of force.[11]

[9] See for a discussion of this, F Francioni, 'Balancing the Prohibition of Force with the Need to Protect Human Rights: A Methodological Approach' in E Cannizzaro and P Palchetti (eds), *Customary International Law on the Use of Force* (Martinus Nijhoff, 2005); and F Francioni, 'Of War, Humanity and Justice: International Law after Kosovo' (2000) 4 *Max Planck Yearbook of UN Law* 107.

[10] M Koskenniemi, 'The Lady Doth Protest Too Much' (2002) 65 *Michigan Law Review* 159.

[11] M Byers, *War law: international law and armed conflict* (Atlantic Books, 2005).

Naturally, the Security Council could authorise such action, but what is in dispute is the unilaterally invoked right of a state to intervene in another country to promote democracy. (All these purported exceptions are returned to in due course.) For now, it is perhaps worth registering that the pro-democratic intervention argument was one of the revolving justifications for the Iraq war, albeit one that was not mentioned at the outset.

Before moving on, a discrete point should be made about the prohibition on the use of force. The UN Charter only forbids international armed attack – a cross-border assault. Now, as a matter of internal state law, it might be legal for the military to be deployed in response to a purely domestic emergency. Nevertheless, the Charter's restriction seems a little unwieldy in an age where the distinction between the native criminal and the foreign enemy is fast disintegrating.

The meaning of terrorism was dealt with in the preceding chapter and will not be rehearsed here. But, equipped with that definition, we can now move on to explore where terrorism stands in relation to the categories of war and crime. Again, I shall consider how the narratives of war and crime have coloured the response to terrorism before suggesting how they might otherwise be useful in tailoring a suitable semantic straightjacket for modern terrorism. That it is better to think terrorism's objectionable feature is its methodology, not its putative end, is argued throughout. This realisation should inform our response to terrorism, for to ignore this lesson is to risk fighting fire with fire – quite literally in some cases: the Allied fire-bombing of Japanese cities is one such example.[12]

The first observation to make is that the dogmatic incantation of the phrase 'war on terrorism' has led to illegal, immoral and deeply imprudent responses to terrorism.[13] And, though it was immediately apparent to Dick Cheney and Paul Wolfowitz, less nimble thinkers craved a more convincing explication of why we elected to go to 'war with terrorism', when the historically preferred strategy was to treat such attacks as crime. There was no necessarily foreign aspect to September 11; indeed, 'nineteen people living in the US hijacked American airplanes from American airports to destroy buildings and murder thousands of people in the US'.[14] As Elaine Tyler May recalls, the responses to the attack on the *USS Cole*, the Oklahoma City bombing, the Unabomber,[15] and even the previous attempt by radical Islamists to destroy the World Trade Center, were all considered crimes and the perpetrators were treated as criminals. So why was the criminal paradigm lost? Fletcher claims that Americans 'are more sensitive to

[12] M Ignatieff, *The lesser evil: political ethics in an age of terror* (Edinburgh University Press, 2003) 163.

[13] This argument began in the last chapter. It is supplemented throughout.

[14] CL Eisgruber and LG Sager, 'Civil Liberties in the Dragon's Domain' in ML Dudziak (ed), *September 11 in History: A Watershed Moment?* (Duke University Press, 2003).

[15] See ch 2 above, text to fn 93.

national honor than we are inclined to admit. To sit back and suffer attack, without responding in kind, is to accept a form of national humiliation'.[16]

Could it be that the assault on Afghanistan was an emotional rather than a rational reaction to September 11; a way of both venting rage and vindicating honour? And what of Iraq? How could the invasion of yet another sovereign state be conducted under the umbrella of a war on terror, particularly given the spurious nature of the apparent links between al-Qaeda and Saddam? Holmes's list of the reasons for the Iraq invasion is worth quoting in full:

> An invasion of Iraq was embraced as a means serving the following disjointed ends: to frighten any group or state that might feel emboldened to replicate or outdo 9/11; to offer solace to American voters traumatized by 9/11 by letting them see US military supremacy in action; to increase the power of the executive branch and shrink the power of Congress and the courts; to show that the US was still responding aggressively to 9/11 even after 'running out of targets' in Afghanistan, and thereby to improve the Republican Party's electoral prospects in 2004; to 'get it right this time' that is, to finish a job that George H.W. Bush had left undone; to avenge Saddam's 1993 attempt to assassinate the first President Bush; to establish OSD primacy in the war on terror and, in the process, field-test Rumsfeld's proposals for military reform; to break OPEC by increasing output of Iraqi crude, perhaps via sweetheart deals with American oil companies; to evacuate troops from Saudi Arabia, thereby removing a focal point of anti-American rage, but nevertheless keeping US forces within striking distance of the Saudi Oil fields in case a fundamentalist revolution toppled the monarchy; to destroy an important regional threat to Israel; to make sure that Saddam would not acquire the capacity for nuclear blackmail after France, Germany, and other countries dismantled the UN embargo; to express America's self-love by offering to replicate American political institutions abroad; to counter 'moral relativism' by revealing that the world really is divided between good and evil.[17]

What can be said of these reasons? In September 2004, Secretary-General Kofi Annan told us from the platform of the BBC World Service that the Iraq war was illegal because it was the Security Council's role to decide what measures should be taken in the event of Iraq's non-compliance with a previous Security Council resolution. Let us put aside for the moment that none of these reasons can be disguised as self-defence and that the war was denounced as criminal by the leader of the United Nations, in order to deal with the other reasons in turn: Solace for the American people and revenge for a familial vendetta are emotional reactions of questionable utility in the crafting of a foreign policy.[18] It goes without saying that both are ethically repugnant, particularly in a country of purportedly Christian persuasion. The advancement of American national interest, whether it be strategic, territorial or economic is a morally invalid reason

[16] GP Fletcher, *Romantics at war: glory and guilt in the age of terrorism* (Princeton University Press, 2002) 13.

[17] S Holmes, *The Matador's Cape: America's Reckless Response to Terror* (Cambridge University Press, 2007) 126.

[18] M Byers, *War law: international law and armed conflict* (Atlantic Books, 2005).

to launch an aggressive war. The same can be said for internal political dynamics. The usage of war abroad as political leverage at home is perhaps the ultimate cynicism; that it works is an indictment of both America's leaders and its people.[19] It is hard to know whether the pooling of executive power is a consequence of a counter-terrorism campaign or whether a counter-terrorism campaign is a consequence of the pooling of executive power. This matter is investigated in chapter nine. The display of military power to frighten copycat criminals is nothing short of terrorism. Holmes's point about self-love will be dealt with in more detail later as it is suggestive of some of the base motivations undergirding the seemingly shameless display of political self-interest that has embarrassed the law. We might find that a heady cocktail of self-love and self-loathing intoxicated the American people in the wake of September 11.

In order to look at the reasons for the Iraq invasion in the round, I deferred the consideration of self-defence above, but it does warrant separate treatment – debate about self-defence is as if a portal for the darker urges. It will be argued here that pre-emptive self-defence is at worst an excuse for imperialism and at best a euphemism for attack. It is, in any event, an unabashed catachresis.

On 7 June 1981, Israeli F-16A fighter planes bombed a nuclear reactor being constructed outside Baghdad, at Osirak. Israel had contended that Iraq, armed with nuclear weapons, would constitute an unacceptable threat in light of Saddam's enmity for Israel. Operation Opera, as the Osirak strike was called, was couched in the terms of pre-emptive self-defence. France lost a national and was appalled. America, along with the rest of the United Nations Security Council, condemned the attack as an illegal violation of the Charter.

It is illuminating to compare America's condemnatory stance then, with what has come be known as the Bush doctrine, thought up 20 years after Operation Opera:

> 'If we wait for threats to fully materialize, we will have waited too long,' the president said, speaking at the commencement of the 204th graduating class of West Point, the nation's oldest military academy. 'We must take the battle to the enemy, disrupt his plans and confront the worst threats before they emerge'.[20]

It did not take long for more discerning listeners to realise that this doctrine, if that is the right word, would give all states discretion to pick off potential enemies as, or before, they arise. This sounded like a good idea to the then Australian Prime Minister John Howard, who thought that the Charter of the United Nations should be amended to include a right of pre-emptive self-defence. Frankly, such an amendment would have been tantamount to tearing up the

[19] The British are by no means immune to the effects of a 'good war'. Former Prime Minister Thatcher's 1982 Falklands (Islas Malvinas) war no doubt helped her to secure a decisive election victory in 1983.

[20] 'US must act first to battle terror', *New York Times*, 2 June 2002, available at: query.nytimes.com/gst/fullpage.html?res=9904E4DC123AF931A35755C0A9649C8B63.

Charter. Realising that the tide, particularly in the Middle East and South-East Asia was against the 'confronting imaginary threats' approach, the Bush doctrine was amended and became the National Security Strategy of 2002:

> For centuries, international law recognized that nations need not suffer an attack before they can lawfully take action to defend themselves against forces that present an imminent danger of attack ... most often a visible mobilization of armies, navies, and airforces preparing to attack. We must adapt the concept of imminent threat to the capabilities and objectives of today's adversaries.

This sounds more like the *SS Caroline*, but it is the last sentence which is of the greatest import. The implication here is that 'today's adversaries' might use nuclear weaponry 'that can be easily concealed, delivered covertly, and used without warning', causing mass destruction and death. Consequently, this is not a different product to the Bush doctrine, but different packaging. Like clockwork, on the radio on 28 September 2002, former President GW Bush said that the 'danger to our country is grave, and it is growing'; Saddam Hussein 'could launch a biological or chemical attack in as little as 45 minutes'. In the meantime, MI6 had received similar intelligence. Lord Butler said the 45-minute report 'came "third hand" through a main, well-established source via a second link in the reporting chain and originally an Iraqi military source'.[21] Four days before the Bush radio address, the British government produced their September Dossier, with a foreword by Tony Blair stating that 'military planning allows for some of the WMD to be ready within 45 minutes of an order to use them'.[22] Blair carrolled in accompaniment to the American drums of war. In case there was any doubt, the *Sun* newspaper clarified that the Brits were '45 minutes from doom'.

That this was a case of adapting threats to foreign policy rather than adapting foreign policy to threats has long since been demonstrated, but this recent history demonstrates the dangers of any interpretive room for manoeuvre in the definition of self-defence. It is worth reflecting on whether the Bush doctrine, or the Bush doctrine-lite espoused in the National Security Strategy, are conducive not to creating a more peaceful, safer world, but to validating cyclic conflicts and whitewashing aggression. The Namibian foreign minister, Hidipo Hamutenya, appreciated this danger, noting in the 58th session of the United Nations General Assembly in September 2003 that

> the central theme, that runs through nearly all the speeches at this session is the call for a return to multilateral dialogue, persuasion and collective action, as the only appropriate approach to resolving many conflicts facing the international community.

[21] '45 minutes', *BBC News*, 13 October 2004, available at: news.bbc.co.uk/2/hi/uk_news/politics/3466005.stm.

[22] British Government, 'September Dossier' (September 2002).

This is easy to say, but what should be done if a state, like America or the United Kingdom, feels (rightly or wrongly) threatened by an allegedly volatile dictator with nuclear weapons? The High Level Panel on Threats, Challenges and Change addressed precisely this query:

> The short answer is that if there are good arguments for preventive military action, with good evidence to support them, they should be put to the Security Council, which can authorize such action if it chooses to. If it does not so choose, there will be, by definition, time to pursue other strategies, including persuasion, negotiation, deterrence and containment – and to visit again the military option.

The panel was alive to the objection that the powers that be might consider there is no time for UN red tape:

> For those impatient with such a response, the answer must be that, in a world full of perceived threats, the risk to the global order and the norm of non-intervention on which it continues to be based is simply too great for the legality of unilateral preventive action, as distinct from collectively endorsed action, to be accepted. Allowing one to so act is to allow all.

There is no doubt that the UN Security Council suffers from institutional sclerosis. Furthermore, its authorisation for military action can never equal moral correctness just as the moral correctness of military action will never guarantee authorisation. These excerpts carry enormous authority, not least because they brought together 16 former prime ministers and ambassadors; Brent Sowcroft, National Security Advisor to former Presidents Gerald Ford and George Bush Senior was one. For present purposes, the Panel's findings are useful not only because they shed some light on the ætiology of aggression, the fear of 'perceived threats', but also because they present a vision of how liberal democracies, or at least, sovereign states might deal with such threats, in a process of mutual reassurance and agreement. That process, properly adhered to, would greatly reduce the threats confronting the international community.

Low intensity conflicts do present challenges for states. To justify the Osirak strike, Israel also described itself, in a manner now familiar, as being in a permanent state of war. But where an armed attack has occurred and the immediate threat has passed, any action by the victim against the attacker is a new attack or reprisal, illegal pursuant to the nascent norms of international law, and only 'justifiable' by reference to non-legal notions of revenge. Reprisals cannot be interpreted as self-defence without self-deception. Deterrence is not defence but attack for the purposes of defence. Part of the great achievement of modern liberal democracies was the individualisation and 'appropriation' of guilt by the state, so that perpetrators are punished impartially and individually. This was a movement away from private revenge and victim's justice. Now, it might be argued that it is more difficult for a state to turn the other cheek than it is for a citizen because the latter can rely on a police force and a criminal justice system to apprehend and punish his assailant. But this is no real argument for allowing states to exact 'private' revenge. A person enjoys the benefits of the police and judiciary because the society, of which he forms part, set up and sustains those institutions. It stands to reason that states ought to do the same on the international plane. Here is the crucial point: aggression is not a mere personal assault; it is a refutation of the notion of there being any society in the first place. Revenge or reprisals compound this refutation. Aggregated, they destroy our belief in the possibility of peaceable communal living – domestically and internationally.

What about self-defence against terrorism? Several cases are now examined to see how the United States has responded in the past. This is by no means an exhaustive account. On 26 June 1993, America fired 23 Tomahawk missiles at Iraqi Military Intelligence Headquarters in Baghdad, killing seven people. William Clinton, the Democratic President, called this a 'firm and commensurate response' to an attempt, two months earlier, to assassinate former President George HW Bush in Kuwait in a car bombing. The then British Prime Minister, John Major, supported the missile attack. The late President Saddam Hussein, who denied Iraqi involvement in the assassination attempt, denounced the attack as vile cowardice. Clinton explained in his televised address: 'we could not and have not let such action against our nation go unanswered'. Madeleine Albright, then American Ambassador to the United Nations, after presenting evidence of Iraq's involvement, echoed this message, calling the bungled car bomb 'a direct attack on the US', and claiming that retaliation was permitted under Article 51 of the UN Charter. Clinton's 'do not tread on us' message was an unambiguous endorsement of Hamas rules, honour killings, and of the sort of 'primitive reciprocity' recommended by Henry Kissinger.[23] Japan seemed to understand this primitive reciprocity, calling the response 'unavoidable' but the Arab League affirmed the orthodox position – America should have obtained Security Council authorisation. Notwithstanding Albright's attempt, which strains legal and linguistic credulity, to use the language of self-defence, Clinton's more candidly stated goals were to protect by punishment and deterrence.

Reprisals have been illegal in international law at least since the adoption of the UN Charter in 1945. The Security Council clarified the position in no uncertain terms in 1964 – in response to a British air attack on Yemeni territory – condemning armed reprisals as 'incompatible with the purposes and principles of the UN'. Perhaps to prevent self-interested actions or actions blinded by nationalist fury, it would be better for the Security Council to be the arbiters of both the cogency of evidence and the suitability of an armed response.

On 7 August 1998, simultaneous car bombs exploded outside American embassies in Africa, killing over 200 people. 12 were Americans. The attacks were attributed to bin Laden, who said that the sites were targeted due to the invasion of Somalia and American involvement in both a planned partitioning of

[23] B Woodward, *State of Denial* (Simon and Schuster, 2006) 408.

Sudan and Rwandan genocide. Two weeks after the bombings, on 20 August, President Clinton addressed the nation at prime time to report his orders to launch 79 Tomahawk cruise missiles at sites in Afghanistan and Sudan. (Political cynics might be gratified to recall that on 17 August, President Clinton testified before a Grand Jury as to the nature his relationship with Monica Lewinsky – she gave her evidence on the day of the launch.)

The missile attack in Sudan attracted particular controversy because its target was a pharmaceuticals factory, which, alleged Clinton, produced a nerve agent, VX, and had ties to bin Laden. On 26 April 2006, David Cloud of the *New York Times* reported that 'Clinton administration officials conceded that the hardest evidence used to justify striking the plant was a single soil sample that seemed to indicate the presence of a chemical used in making VX gas'.[24] Germany's Ambassador to Sudan affirmed Noam Chomsky's view that the bombing of the pharmaceuticals plant caused a medicine shortage and, as a consequence, the deaths of tens of thousands. The National Security Advisor, Sandy Berger, in a comment that might have left grammarians and international lawyers slightly fuddled, said: 'I think it is appropriate, under Article 51 of the UN Charter, for protecting the self-defense of the US … for us to try and disrupt and destroy those kinds of military terrorist [sic] targets'. Though Cuba and Pakistan objected, the affair was not considered by the Security Council. Byers argues that the broad lack of international condemnation of this action contributed to 'obfuscating the limits of self-defence, if not to changing the law as it governs recourse to force against countries that harbour or otherwise support international terrorists'.[25] Given the industry with which America seeks approval when it wishes to take an action which is illegal in international law, it is vital that other states contemporaneously express their opinions on transgressions. Silent bystanders cannot be annoyed that the law has changed without their voices being counted.

Constituency-building was a prelude to the American attempt to pave the way for the response to September 11 2001. But it sought support informally – the US government did not request Security Council authorisation to invade Afghanistan. However, international sympathy, and what Security Council members stood to gain in their own battles, was so marked, that permission would probably have been forthcoming. Again, it is a shame that the exact parameters of the right of self-defence were not thrashed out in public debate. Terrorists had developed bases in London and Hamburg, and it is certainly arguable that the *travaux preparatoires* for September 11 had more connection to these countries than Afghanistan, but did this mean that America could send its agents into England and Germany in violation of territorial sovereignty?

[24] D Cloud, 'Colleagues say CIA Analyst played by the rules', *New York Times*, 26 April 2006, available at: www.nytimes.com/2006/04/23/washington/23mccarthy.html?_r=1&oref=slogin.

[25] M Byers, *War law: international law and armed conflict* (Atlantic Books, 2005) 63.

Byers concludes that where terrorists have attacked a country, its 'right of self-defence now includes military responses against countries that willingly harbour or support terrorist groups'. This distinguishes 'Londonistan' from Afghanistan, for whilst Westminster condemned September 11, the Taliban adopted the precarious position of hosting the man considered responsible, whilst entreating America for restraint.[26] Furthermore, it would not appear to be necessary to trigger the right to ferret out terrorists abroad, that the attack on the respondent state was on its territory; that is to say, an attack on its interests or nationals abroad might suffice. How then, can a state respond? It is part of any sensible understanding of self-defence that the acts taken in response to an attack must not be excessive or unreasonable. Given that those who perpetrated September 11 killed themselves in the attack, and that the American concern, at least ostensibly, was to get at the organisers (at the time of writing, bin Laden remains at liberty), no time will be wasted on arguing that the Afghanistan and Iraq wars were unreasonable or excessive. Similarly, it is not worth discussing whether the strike on the pharmaceuticals factory was a proper response to an attempt on the former President's life.

What is perhaps more interesting, particularly given that it reveals the strains in the Anglo-American counter-terror partnership, is the case of targeted killings. By way of illustration, Israel has operated a policy of targeted 'frustration', which aims to pre-empt or stem the flow of the suicide bombings that claimed over a thousand Israeli lives in the five years preceding 2005. Two of the more salient return strikes took place in 2004, where successive Hamas leaders, Sheikh Ahmad Yassin and Abdel-Aziz al-Rantissi, were killed by Israeli hellfire missiles fired from helicopters. The former was killed, along with nine bystanders, as he left a mosque, the latter in his car, along with a bodyguard, his son, a woman and her daughter. The British Foreign Secretary, Jack Straw, affirmed that 'the British government has made it repeatedly clear that so-called "targeted assassinations" of this kind are unlawful, unjustified and counter-productive'; Israel said the attacks were legitimate measures of self-defence taken in response to ongoing suicide bombings targeted at its citizens; the Spokesman for the White House said that 'we have repeatedly made clear, Israel has the right to defend itself from terrorist attacks'.

When it considered the legality of the policy of targeted killings, in a comprehensive judgment, the Israeli Supreme Court held that it cannot be determined in advance that targeted killing is always lawful or unlawful.[27] Its legality will depend on the number of bystanders slaughtered or maimed by the assassination; the perceived military benefit; whether or not there was another,

[26] 'After the Attacks', *New York Times*, 13 September 2001, available at: query.nytimes.com/gst/fullpage.html?res=9A0DE0D61338F930A2575AC0A9679C8B63&scp=31&sq=taliban%209/11&st=cse.

[27] *Public Committee against Torture in Israel and Palestinian Society for the Protection of Human Rights and the Environment v Government of Israel et al* (2006) HCJ 769/02.

less drastic, way to eliminate the threat; the quality of the planning and conduct of the operation; and the respectability of any ex post inquiry into the killing. Such are the predilections of the academy that the literature on this tactic is voluminous. In keeping with the nature of this text, rather than trawling through the law and the many opinions in the literature on this subject, I will summarise the arguments for and against a policy of assassinating suspected terrorists. It is worth recalling here that we are concerned not so much with what the law is, but what it should be. In this case, as in many, though I oversimplify, the opposing points of view pivot around one legal point. That fulcrum, immediately recognisable to international lawyers, is as follows: In no circumstances shall civilians be the objects of attack, 'unless and for such time as they take a direct part in hostilities'.[28]

Broadly speaking, the proponents of targeted killings advance arguments to the following effect: First, the instigators, masterminds and planners of waves of suicide bombings cannot sensibly be considered civilians because they intentionally kill innocents. They are better considered military commanders, and thus, proper military targets in the war on terrorism. Suicide bombing is a deadly, cost-effective military tactic against which a state should be permitted to defend itself.

Second (it is argued), even if those who plan and conduct suicide bombings are technically considered civilians, they forfeit their immunity from attack by engaging in the planning and conduct of hostilities. They become unlawful combatants; they take part in fighting without incurring the reciprocal risk entailed by wearing uniform, and openly bearing arms and insignia.[29] Cowardice and the endangerment of civilians should not be rewarded with immunity.

Third, the requirement that a civilian who takes a direct part in hostilities can be harmed only during such time that he is actually engaged in hostile activity is not part of customary international law. To insist on a rigid interpretation of this

[28] Protocol Additional to the Geneva Conventions of 12 August 1949, and Relating to the Protection of Victims of International Armed Conflicts, 15 August 1977, Arts 51(1) and 51(3). Armed forces of a Party, as defined in Art 43 of the 1st Additional Protocol to the Geneva Conventions, 'consist of all organized armed forces, groups and units which are under a command responsible to that Party for the conduct of its subordinates, even if that Party is represented by a government or an authority not recognized by an adverse Party … Members of armed forces are combatants'.

[29] Geneva Convention relative to the treatment of Prisoners of War, 1949, Art 4. See also Art 43 of the 1st Additional Protocol to the Geneva Conventions (above n 28); and Art 44(3) of the same, which mandates: 'In order to promote the protection of the civilian population from the effects of hostilities, combatants are obliged to distinguish themselves from the civilian population while they are engaged in an attack or in a military operation preparatory to an attack. Recognizing, however, that there are situations in armed conflicts where, owing to the nature of the hostilities an armed combatant cannot so distinguish himself, he shall retain his status as a combatant, provided that in such situations, he carries his arms openly: (a) During each military engagement, and (b) During such time as he is visible to the adversary while he is engaged in a military deployment preceding the launching of an attack in which he is to participate'.

rule would create an unacceptable zone of immunity for those who choose to be warlords in secret and worshippers in public. This can be described as the 'revolving door' whereby a terrorist is a legitimate target whilst on an operation but enjoys immunity between sorties.

Fourth, the targeted killing of terrorist masterminds is resorted to only where a state has exhaustively considered all other options, including arrest. Assassinating terrorists is the only way to stop the droves of deadly suicide bombers. Where suicide bombings are planned and launched from outside the state's territory, there is nothing the state can reasonably be expected to do to prevent the attacks, except for pre-emptive strikes.

Fifth, though targeted killings, especially where air-to-ground missiles are used, often result in the deaths of innocent bystanders, a state should not be prevented from protecting itself merely because terrorists customarily surround themselves with human shields. The deaths of a few innocent bystanders are justified by the pre-emptive rescue of innocent victims of waves of suicide bombings orchestrated by terrorist leaders.

Now, the opponents of targeted killings argue, more or less vociferously, as follows: First, for the safety of civilians, until proven otherwise, it must be assumed that people who neither carry arms, nor bear insignia, nor wear uniform are non-combatants entitled to be shielded from the carnage of war. Since the decision to undertake a targeted killing is made in secret and the victim has no opportunity to refute the assertion that they are a terrorist, targeted killing is nothing other than transnational tyranny.

Second, although a civilian suspected of planning a terrorist attack might be engaging in criminal activity, it does not follow that the state enjoys the right extra-territorially to assassinate him as if he were an enemy soldier. If all states had such a right, territorial sovereignty would be meaningless. A suspected terrorist must remain immune until taking up arms; otherwise we risk destabilising the international system with anarchic, cyclic violence. Prima facie, it is unclear why a state should be able to kill the citizen of another country charged with inciting murder when it cannot in this manner kill its own citizen. Indeed, if a state may not extra-judicially kill a murder suspect who is a subject, a fortiori, it should not be permitted extra-judicially to kill a murder suspect who is both a foreign national and outside its jurisdiction. To do so would be to exercise a power abroad greater than that enjoyed at home.

Third, and further, even if the state is allowed, under customary international law to attack a civilian who is a part-time, or sporadic contributor to a war effort, it may only do so where the threat from that civilian is imminent. Any other rule would explode the crucial distinction between combatants and non-combatants set up to insulate the non-military population from the lethal violence of war. The 'revolving door' argument, that a terrorist may not enjoy immunity from attack between operations is misconceived. Where a person is involved or reasonably suspected to be engaged in an attack or conducting hostilities, he is a legitimate military target, but where he is suspected to be planning an attack, he is a mere suspect, and not a legitimate target.

Fourth, it is a convenient myth that targeted killing is an option of last resort. Political consensus on what constitutes terrorism would facilitate punishment or extradition of terrorists. Short of that, the process of arrest, detention and trial is a less extreme option than extra-judicial assassination. Though the military argues that arrest attempts in hostile territory would pose an unacceptable threat to soldiers, this threat pales into insignificance compared with the jeopardy to the public created by a policy of targeted frustration. Moreover, it is part of a soldier's job description to risk their life for military advantage; consequently, risks to soldiers cannot count for as much as risks to civilians, whatever their nationality.

Fifth, particularly when missiles are launched from helicopters or unmanned predator drones, the risk to innocent bystanders can be intolerably high. Terrorists may unscrupulously mingle with the public but this does not white-wash the immorality of killing scores of innocents to eliminate one terrorist.

The Israeli Supreme Court judgment is both understandable and admirable, but it might respectfully be suggested that it suffers from one shortcoming – its simplistic approach to the relationship between liberty and security, military advantage and morality. The decision seems to be informed by the notion that liberty and security must be balanced, or that a trade-off must be made between military expediency and humanitarian considerations.

Now, it would be harsh to attribute this error to the judges alone because the images of balance and trade-offs are all-pervasive as well as being insufficiently examined in the literature. Take the following excerpt, relied on by the Court, as an example:

> International humanitarian law in armed conflicts is a compromise between military and humanitarian requirements. Its rules comply with both military necessity and the dictates of humanity. Considerations of military necessity cannot, therefore, justify departing from the rules of humanitarian law in armed conflicts to seek a military advantage using forbidden means.[30]

In the next chapter, I shall investigate the utility of the imagery of the balance or trade-off between military expediency and the dictates of humanity in more detail. Suffice it for now to say that the use of 'forbidden means' does not always redound to the advantage of the military campaign. In other words, it is at best facile and at worst genocidal to assert that moral concerns always hamper military progress. For example, in the context of terrorism, the end goal of the military is, we must assume, the reduction of the incidence of terrorist attacks and the creation and sustenance of a secure environment, not the annihilation of the cultural group to which the terrorists belong.

[30] C Greenwood 'Historical Development and Legal Basis' in D Fleck (ed), *The Handbook of Humanitarian Law in Armed Conflicts* (Oxford University Press, 1995) 132.

In the recent Israeli context then, the overriding aims of the military would be to help stem the flow of suicide bombings against Israeli targets and to promote a peaceful accord with the Palestinian population. The stemming of the flow of suicide bombings and the achievement of a secure environment for Israelis and Palestinians are humanitarian aims. They are moral aims. The aims of the military, therefore, *are* moral, not solely prudential, or at least, are moral as well as prudential. Targeted killing then (particularly when it is imprecise and causes collateral damage), whilst it might kill terrorists, risks creating even more terrorists. Imprecise attacks such as those on the popular figures Sheikh Ahmad Yassin and Abdel-Aziz al-Rantissi risk further radicalisation, inflicting on terrorism a Medusa's death. We can conclude that killing terrorists not engaged in an attack, would be a military strategy of little promise. Where the threat is not imminent a more prudent tactic would be to incapacitate, incarcerate and indict terrorists.

To summarise, the best criticism of targeted frustration, which is almost absent from legal commentary is that, precisely because extra-judicial assassinations are so messy and immoral, they are of questionable military utility. Moreover, a fairly good case can be made that targeted frustration is, by reducing the conflict to an internecine blood feud, prolonging the antagonism between Israeli and Palestinian peoples. If that is true, the policy is counter-productive in the campaign against terrorism and therefore imprudent in the extreme. If, on the other hand, a state's real military aim is genocidal, that is to kill as many suspected foreign terrorists as possible, along with members of their family and co-religionists, all under the camouflage of a legitimate military campaign, targeted killing is a brilliant tactic.

Perhaps more taxing still, than the case of targeted killings, is that of humanitarian intervention. Afghanistan was, albeit retrospectively, said to be a war for women's rights, and Iraq, to rescue citizens from Saddam's torturous regime. These were convenient flags to hoist over both campaigns but had precious little to do with the intentions of the interveners, whose humanitarian talk was brazen instrumentalism. Since humanitarian intervention, however unbelievably, could have been but was not used to justify either war at the outset, its relevance here is limited. Nevertheless, humanitarian intervention *proper* does help complete our picture, and tends, it is suggested, to lend some coherence to the proposals made below about the only legitimate use of force. As any serious student of international law or relations will know, it is tremendously difficult, and probably inadvisable to study in isolation the individual exceptions to the prohibition on the use of force. There is no place, or need, here to list the possible historical candidates for humanitarian intervention or for a fact-heavy dissection of the issues. Thus, instead of wasting time on spurious after-the-event claims made by America and the United Kingdom that they in some way wanted to help the wretched inhabitants of the Middle Eastern fronts of the war on terror, I will look at a single past instance of humanitarian intervention, with the aim of laying the foundations for a suggestion later in this chapter, for how I think the defence of others fits into this discussion.

The death of the British Empire gave birth to political upheaval. In 1947, misshapen twins were born of a 'Caesarean section' of India. Though physically separated at birth by over a thousand miles, and speaking different tongues, the twins were politically conjoined, their identities entwined. In reaction to increasingly strong attempts by East Pakistan to free itself of its sister, culminating in a declaration of independence on 26 March 1971, General Khan of West Pakistan sent his army into Dhaka in an express attempt literally to reduce the majority in favour of separation into a minority. All the symptoms of ethnic enmity were present. Systematic rape, pillage, torture and massacre characterised the campaign. India's support for East Pakistan incurred the wrath of the West Pakistani military, war ensued, and in December, India occupied East Pakistan and declared her the independent sovereign state of Bangladesh. As Byers observes, most countries were in opposition to India's surgical intervention, stopping the genocide, and not a single country endorsed it, but perhaps most tellingly of all, 'even Bangladesh, the beneficiary of India's 1971 invasion of East Pakistan, reaffirmed the principle of non-intervention in domestic affairs'.[31] As I said above, this example is not intended as a statement of the law on humanitarian intervention;[32] rather, the aim is to highlight the lukewarm attitude towards humanitarian intervention amongst states, including that of a victim-cum-beneficiary. How the defence of others fits into the legal jigsaw is addressed below.

Though they are gradually permeating the collective consciousness, the post-9/11 mindset was obstinately impervious to the implications of the war paradigm. If counter-terrorism is war; and the war is endless in duration and, like terrorism, global in ambit, limited government is antiquated; martial law at home and abroad is the brave new formula for rule; and we live in an empire of threat.[33] Extraordinary rendition, targeted killings, and massive encroachments on the sovereign rights of other states (let alone the individual rights of their citizens) become the rule, not the exception. And it would be a mistake to assume that these changes only affect others – the Bush administration attempted to jettison the time-honoured principle of habeas corpus, even for American citizens. It is odd in a country which fought off monarchical prerogative in a bloody war of liberation, where a statue to liberty greets you as you enter its most famous harbour, that freedom from detention dangled for a time on the thin thread of presidential say-so.

[31] M Byers, *War law: international law and armed conflict* (Atlantic Books, 2005) 95.

[32] There is a welter of literature on this topic, a good starting point is F Francioni, 'Balancing the Prohibition of Force with the Need to Protect Human Rights: A Methodological Approach' in E Cannizzaro and P Palchetti (eds), *Customary International Law on the Use of Force* (Martinus Nijhoff, 2005).

[33] D Golove and S Holmes, 'Terrorism and Accountability: Why Checks and Balances Apply Even in "The War on Terrorism"' (2004) 2 *NYU Review of Law & Security* 2–7.

We have questioned the suitability of the war paradigm for responding to terrorism, but is the crime paradigm any better? As mentioned earlier, detention is a feature of both war and peacetime. Its usage therefore provides us with a Rosetta stone for decrypting state counter-terrorism policies. The litigation on Guantánamo Bay was in the international spotlight throughout the Bush administration's 'war on terror'. The latest holding of the highest American judicial instance, at the time of writing, was to the effect that foreign detainees at the Cuban base had the right, pursuant to the Constitution of the United States of America, to challenge their designation as 'enemy combatants' before the civilian courts in petitions for habeas corpus.[34] In contradistinction to Abraham Lincoln's emergency medicine analogy, which introduced this chapter, stands Anthony Kennedy J's holding:

> The laws and Constitution are designed to survive, and remain in force, in extraordinary times. Liberty and security can be reconciled; and in our system they are reconciled within the framework of the law. The Framers decided that *habeas corpus*, a right of first importance, must be a part of that framework, a part of that law.[35]

It was only by a vote of one that Kennedy's view on the reconciliation of security and liberty prevailed. Recalling the importance of symbolism in understanding our reactions to terrorism, it is no exaggeration to say that America is divided as to what it stands for; this could not be made clearer than by quoting from Scalia J's dissent:

> It breaks a chain of precedent as old as the common law that prohibits judicial inquiry into detentions of aliens abroad absent statutory authorization. And, most tragically, it sets our military commanders the impossible task of proving to a civilian court, under whatever standards this Court devises in the future, that evidence supports the confinement of each and every enemy prisoner.
>
> The Nation will live to regret what the Court has done today. I dissent.[36]

Though more will be said on the interaction between the branches of government, it is worth flagging up that former President Bush, in a comment as predictable as it was telling, referred to the decision as an 'opinion' with which he did not 'have to agree', and, though the effect of the decision was to declare unconstitutional the Detainee Treatment Act of 2005, Bush said he would 'consider new legislation'. Whilst the American organs of power flirt with one another, maligned detainees languish in a notoriously cruel brig. The distinction between war and crime permeates these judicial opinions; or, to put it more precisely, the interpretation of what the 'war on terror' *is* divides the judges.

[34] *Boumediene v Bush, President of the United States; Al Odah v United States* Nos 06–1195 and 06–1196, 553 US 723 (2008).

[35] *ibid*, 70.

[36] *ibid*, dissenting opinion, at 25.

It has not escaped the attention of commentators that if the executive is left free to define the nature of the enemy; the level of the threat posed by that enemy; the fronts and ambit of the war; and the methods for arrest, detention and trial of the enemy; without any form of judicial oversight, then that power is nothing short of tyrannical. Christopher Eisgruber and Lawrence Sager observe that 'the Bush administration has created a third track for detention of suspected terrorists and enemy agents, one that features neither the protections of the ordinary criminal process nor the protections of ordinary prisoner of war status'.[37] Holmes and Golove argue that this executive 'paradigm-shopping' results not from confusion as to how to respond to terrorism, but from 'the administration's one consistent aim, the desire to limit accountability and oversight'.[38] In a rare political move, Lord Steyn asserted that the 'purpose of holding the prisoners at Guantánamo Bay was and is to put them beyond the rule of law, beyond the protection of any courts, and at the mercy of the victors'.[39] Does this mean that the seemingly elusive nature of terrorism has more to do with governmental cynicism than conceptual fogginess? Has history repeated itself in that a heinous *crime* has drawn us into a *war*?

This line between crime and war was drawn by Chief Justice Harlan Fiske Stone in his opinion in the 1942 'German saboteurs' affair. I say affair rather than case because his verdict on the guilt of the defendants, who had arrived undercover on the Eastern Seaboard during the Second World War to sabotage American economic sites, was written several months after their execution. Stone's line was drawn between lawful and unlawful combatants. The distinction between combatants and non-combatants exists to protect civilians; the argument for outlawing certain guerrillas or insurgents is that they enjoy the benefits of fighting undercover without exposing themselves to the risk of wearing uniform and insignia.[40] In this fashion, they also endanger the civilian population by becoming indistinguishable from non-combatants. Modernly, the same 'dirty tactics' criticism is rightly levelled at terrorists.

These arguments make sense in the abstract but the reciprocal risk argument is increasingly absurd where warfare in Afghanistan is conducted by high-flying predator drones, controlled by officers sitting in front of computer screens in Middle America. It is certainly arguable that such practices invalidate any reciprocal risk argument. Further, although this will vary with circumstance, the danger to civilians is arguably increased more by high-altitude bombers than it is

37 CL Eisgruber and LG Sager, 'Civil Liberties in the Dragon's Domain' in ML Dudziak (ed), *September 11 in History: A Watershed Moment?* (Duke University Press, 2003) 172.

38 D Golove and S Holmes, 'Terrorism and Accountability: Why Checks and Balances Apply Even in "The War on Terrorism"' (2004) 2 *NYU Review of Law & Security* 2–7.

39 J Steyn, 'Guantanamo Bay: The Legal Blackhole' (2004) 53 *International & Comparative Law Quarterly* 1, 8.

40 GP Fletcher, *Romantics at war: glory and guilt in the age of terrorism* (Princeton University Press, 2002).

by camouflaged combatants, lawful or otherwise. The tragic killing of the wedding party in Nangarhar is just one such anecdotal piece of evidence in support of this proposition.

At this point we can pause to note that there is something sinister in the detachment of pilots from the human cost of what they are doing. World War II bombers described an eerie surreality during the ruthless fire-bombing of German cities. Disturbingly, the pilot of an unmanned predator drone, sitting at a screen showing a satellite image in varying hues of green, who need not be on the same continent as the target, has an experience that is arguably less real and human than many new virtual reality, high-definition computer games. If there must be war, should it not at least be up close and personal, so that its gruesome reality is inescapable for the perpetrators?

If the campaign against terrorism is war, after we have achieved a victory (a possibility implicit in some of the more preposterous of politicians' promises), should we repatriate captured terrorists without punishment or trial as required by the norms of war? The answer to that must be 'no' because, if it is proved that a person is a terrorist, and therefore an enemy of all humankind, they should be punished. Conversely, as Fletcher points out, no one cared about the Japanese pilots who returned safely from the attack on Pearl Harbor.[41]

If the fight against terrorism is crime, Guantánamo Bay will come to represent one of the most flagrant denials of due process in recorded history. To take just one example, Mr Huzaifa Parhat, a Chinese fruit vendor, sent a message to his wife imploring her to remarry, because he regarded his seven-year Gitmo detention, on what the United States Court of Appeals called 'bare and unverifiable evidence', a de facto death.[42] If the fight is crime, the usage of predator drones, for instance on 3 November 2002, to kill suspected members of al-Qaeda in Yemen, is not only extra-judicial assassination – a long phrase for murder – it is also a grave violation of territorial sovereignty and international law. As a result of these considerations, it has been argued that terrorism necessitates a 'third model' that fits neither the criminal law, nor the war paradigm, but that does not dispense with the moral principles informing both.[43] 'Criminal procedure places restraints on executive power that, although acceptable in ordinary circumstances, become suicidal in the face of a terrorist conspiracy, say, to smuggle a nuclear suitcase into an American city'.[44] Naturally,

[41] *ibid.*

[42] W Glaberson, 'Evidence Faulted in Detainee Case', *New York Times*, 1 July 2008, at: www.nytimes.com/2008/07/01/washington/01gitmo.html?_r=1&scp=3&sq=muslim%20guantanamo%202008&st=cse&oref=slogin.

[43] R Dworkin, 'Terror and the Attack on Civil Liberties' in T Rockmore, J Margolis and AT Marsoobian (eds), *The Philosophical Challenge of September 11* (Blackwell Publishing, 2005); D Golove and S Holmes, 'Terrorism and Accountability: Why Checks and Balances Apply Even in "The War on Terrorism"' (2004) 2 *NYU Review of Law & Security* 2.

[44] D Golove and S Holmes, 'Terrorism and Accountability: Why Checks and Balances Apply Even in "The War on Terrorism"' (2004) 2 *NYU Review of Law & Security* 2, 3.

terrorists should be prevented and punished. But our aims must be to prevent terrorist attacks – predominantly the role of the international and domestic police and intelligence communities, and punish offenders – the job of the criminal justice system. Alan Vaughan Lowe points out two very weighty reasons for eschewing the 'war' in favour of the 'crime' paradigm. First, there is a risk inherent in calling the fight 'war', that a group of perceived 'enemy nationals' is created along racial and religious lines, creating societal schisms. Second, 'the primary and defining characteristic of terrorism is precisely that terrorist attacks are directed at the innocent'. Consequently, Lowe argues as follows: 'Terrorism is completely antithetical to the rule of law: and *all* States should be free, and indeed obliged, to cooperate in its repression. For that, the appropriate framework is that of international criminal cooperation'.[45]

We are crippled, at least for now, by the inadequacy of international criminal justice, which, in turn, is hamstrung by the reluctance of states to relinquish that choice tool of international relations, double-standards. It is perhaps pertinent to mention what has become affectionately termed the 'Hague Invasion Act'. In 2002, unsatisfied with having rejected the jurisdiction of the International Criminal Court in case American activities fell within the definition of international war crimes, such as torture, or the indiscriminate killing of civilians, or terrorism, Congress passed the 'American Service-Members Protection Act', which authorises the President 'to use all means necessary and appropriate to bring about the release' of American military personnel.[46] In case the implication was not clear, this means that US duplicity is backed by the full force of its military. More will be said on this later.

In the immediately foregoing, I described how states have categorised terrorism; in what follows, some suggestions can be made as to how it ought to be classified. The hypothesis underlying the rest of this chapter is that aggression is the quintessence of all crime. On that note, a preliminary point to make is that the existence of war always betrays or follows a failure of human imagination and compassion. It is in this sense that Allott claims that war is 'made nowhere else than in the world of consciousness'.[47] Such a failure is endemic to assertions, like that of Joseph Margolis, that the realities of modern warfare make a confinement of the effects of 'admissible military strikes' to combatant populations or installations unfeasible.[48] The reality is not that modern warfare makes 'collateral damage' unavoidable. The reality is that 'collateral damage' is simply considered part of the acceptable cost of warfare. Were it not for geopolitical

[45] V Lowe, '"Clear and Present Danger": Responses to Terrorism' (2005) 54 *International & Comparative Law Quarterly* 185, 190.

[46] American Service Members Protection Act, 2002, available at: www.state.gov/t/pm/rls/othr/misc/23425.htm.

[47] P Allott, *Eunomia: new order for a new world* (Oxford University Press, 1990) 264.

[48] J Margolis, 'Terrorism and New Forms of War' in J Margolis, T Rockmore and AT Marsoobian (eds), *The Philosophical Challenge of September 11* (Blackwell Publishing, 2005) 196.

factors, cowardice and cynical attempts to secure strategic advantages, armies could meet one another on battlefields far from civilian populations, or not at all.

Here, it is worth briefly considering the relationship of politics to war. The pithiest explication is that of Carl von Clausewitz. He considered war to be the continuation of politics by other means.[49] This phrase, though deceptively matter-of-fact, is, with respect, deeply pernicious, for it clothes war in the drab daily garb of politics. What I am driving at here, as argued in the preceding chapter, is that his description is prescriptive. It includes war in a roster of political options, inexplicably excluding the possibility that war is inimical to politics, or the failure of politics. Allott, for example, suggests that the resort to war can be phased out of the options available to the human consciousness. He wills it that 'where there was *use of force* there will be the exercise of social power under the law'.[50] In the course of this argument, much more will be said on this theme, but for now, we can pose a question: Is it not better to think of war as the denial of society and the antithesis of politics, rather than being an extension of politics? Is not war what happens when politics fail? Is the suffix of *Machtpolitik* redundant?

To develop this line of thought, to discover whether war is part of politics, we can refer to the romantic and the rational. George Fletcher has written a helpful study of how these two broad schools of thought relate to terrorism. His depiction is neatly encapsulated in the following short excerpt.

> Kant is the leading Enlightenment expositor of faith in reason. Reason, a quality shared by all human beings, illuminates the path to objective truth. The slightest contamination of reason by sensual impulses destroys reason's impartiality. Kant fled from sensuality in order to embrace reason as the path to truth, while the Romantics embraced nature, sensual impulses, the inner world of feeling as the lamp of truth.[51]

The quandary is that if we base all our responses on reason, we lose our humanity. We forsake our best qualities, such as the capacity for mercy or unconditional love. (This avowal achieved popular acclaim in the character of the amusingly dispassionate Mr Spock of television's *Star Trek*.) Yet, if we base all our responses on our emotions, we are indistinguishable from beasts, and we waste the gift of reason, the usage of which, if we follow writers like Jean-Jacques Rousseau, elevates us from barbarity into civility. Could we not argue that true humanity lies at a point equidistant from reason and passion, somewhere between brain and blood? Can we arrive at self-understanding, and therefore by extension, selflessness, without a long voyage into the darker realms of human nature? The answer would seem to be that unless we explore, map, and finally cordon off our totalitarian, perverse tendencies, unless we stare our imperfection

[49] C von Clausewitz and B Pochhammer, *Vom Kriege* (Vier Falken Verl, 1940).

[50] P Allott, *Eunomia: new order for a new world* (Oxford University Press, 1990) 268.

[51] GP Fletcher, *Romantics at war: glory and guilt in the age of terrorism* (Princeton University Press, 2002) 19.

in the face, the human project is doomed to perpetual warfare. It is through frank self-expression and honest reflection on our propensity to vanity, avarice and intolerance that this wisdom inures, enabling us to plot a safer course through the stormier waters of human experience. I will enlarge on this later.

This quick sketching of a philosophical backdrop allows us to situate reprisals cast as self-defence in their proper place. As Oliver Wendell Holmes Jr said, 'the life of the law has not been logic but experience'. Punishment is frequently conceived of as a concession to human vengeance or societal solidarity with the victim.[52] But might we not accept that revanchist voices should have no say in punishment? Such a stance would seem to be more consistent with the prevalent international understanding of war law than Clinton's afore-mentioned 'don't tread on us' policy. A strong reassertion of the norms of acceptable political conduct is only possible if we dispense with primitive notions relating to the purposes of punishment. Allott has a point when he argues that aggressive war or revenge attacks are the international instantiation of behaviour considered criminal domestically.

Perhaps we could conceive of punishment as rehabilitation, of both the offender and society. Punishment asserts society's threshold of legal conduct and can be understood as the rehabilitation of a criminal falling short of that threshold. Where the system works fairly and effectively, the criminal is encouraged to and does understand their punishment as an external manifestation of their guilt. In this way, punishment purges guilt. Avengement is not properly part of punishment. In my view, avengement contains aggression, the afore-mentioned quintessence of crime. Why should justice accommodate aggression as defined here? Though it will be discussed in a little more detail later, here we can suggest an oft-overlooked distinction between the passions and love. The passions can be regarded as partial, limited and conditional, whereas love, like reason, can be thought of as impartial, unlimited and unconditional.

Sometimes punishment for crimes as serious as murder is difficult to justify. The best example of this comes from the law of provocation. Much Western law rests on the idea of reasonableness, but, when applied to reality, this idea disintegrates like a spacecraft re-entering the atmosphere on the wrong trajectory. Judges began by asking: Would a reasonable man have reacted violently to this provocation? They then faced cases of women and boys who had been provoked, sometimes with systematic violence and buggery. These judges asked whether a reasonable person would have acted violently if he had shared the characteristics of the defendant, including age, sex, vulnerability, and so forth. Reasonableness, that objective pillar of the law, crumbles under the weight of sympathetic subjectivity. Where, for example, a boy beat a man to death with a pan after the man had sodomised him, did a punishment far worse than the boy would deserve for murder not precede the crime?

[52] *ibid.*

These cases demonstrate that our punishment is inherently arbitrary. The proposition upon which the criminal law is built – 'I, Mr Reasonable Man, would never have done that' – is a fiction, for we have a staggered start in life and different disabilities. Nonetheless, the fiction is necessary. Our justice is bound to be arbitrary but the impossibility of its perfection does not excuse or incapacitate law-makers from attempting to instantiate it any more than the indeterminacy of π excuses or incapacitates artists from drawing circles.

The relevance of all this to terrorism is patent to Fletcher. He recalls how the Unabomber, Ted Kaczynski, who took to terrorism in good faith to stem the evil, inexorable flow of technology into our lives, instructed his lawyer to plead his 'guiltless sincerity'. As Fletcher recognises, the 'argument was correctly rejected but the impulse to excuse on the grounds of sincerity made itself felt'.[53] Naturally, anarchy would prevail if we did not set basic limits on behaviour, but those limits must include a ban on revenge, for, if punishment for crime is hard to justify, punishment without proof of crime, like in the case of Mr Parhat, is pure ire, and risks incurring ire in return. Obviously, any punishment can deter, but only just punishment is curative. Unjust punishment might incite, ostracise and radicalise. Bin Laden was quick to capitalise on the foolhardy arbitrariness of Allied knee-jerk reactions to terrorism: 'The US does not have solid evidence against us, just some threads and indications. To begin bombing on the basis of such guesswork is injustice'.[54] The flaw in General Horner's strategy of convincing the world that Americans are 'madmen' is, well, that the world might just begin to think they are. Such a strategy purchases damaging notoriety at the price of a valuable reputation for propriety. It denigrates American democratic government.

Above, mention was made of the goals of preventing and punishing terrorism. Neither of these goals requires a departure from the crime paradigm, though both necessitate international agreement on prohibited means. The easiest way to secure that intercultural consensus is to agree, first, to live by the standards we expect of other societies. Given that terrorism is presently ineradicable, societies have time aplenty to consider how to deal with it. Congress, parliaments, police forces, the media, intelligence agencies, civil service, judiciary and civil liberties organisations can act in concert to design the most effective measures. Of preponderant import when tailoring a response to the threat are proportionality and precision – both of which inform the present laws of crime and war.

The challenge then, according to the hard-edged conception of law in this thesis, explained later, is to turn this code into law by backing it up with force. This might not require a formal pooling of military power by states but it certainly requires that states finally renounce aggression and avengement as tools of foreign policy. Furthermore, where states do succumb to the temptations of

[53] *ibid.*

[54] B Lawrence (ed), *Messages to the World: The Statements of Osama bin Laden* (Verso, 2005), statement of 12 November 2001.

these means, the rest of the international community should be steadfast in its denunciations. Any unilateral aggression or avengement dressed up as pre-emptive self-defence must be exposed for what it is, vigilante violence.

With respect to the nascent international criminal order, agreement on prohibited behaviour would facilitate international, rather than victors' justice. Perhaps the most powerful endorsement of this comes not from a jurist but from the architect of the Vietnam War, former Secretary of State for Defense of the United States of America, Robert McNamara. The condemnation that would proceed from the international criminal punishment of terrorists would contribute to building the constituency of disgust at prohibited methods necessary to discourage the resort to terrorism.[55] In contrast, swashbuckling reprisals encourage that resort. Domestic or victors' justice cannot compete with unified, international condemnation. Indeed, the more deadly the terrorist attack – the more lives claimed – the more reason there is to submit the trial of the perpetrators to an international court.[56]

Here, a distinction should be drawn between global or international justice and international jurisdiction. Though small-scale domestic terrorism can quite aptly be dealt with by national courts, the practice of trying terrorists in domestic courts is dangerously susceptible to political abuse.[57] States should not be allowed to dispose of their enemies in show trials. This is the main, though by no means the only shortcoming of the Military Commissions at Guantánamo Bay. An international court would not be susceptible to abuse in this way, and could reasonably be expected to preside over the trial in an impartial manner, something we would be foolish to expect of domestic courts claiming international jurisdiction. Nonetheless, states can, by expressing their opinions on the illegality of the behaviour of world leaders, begin to create a culture in which world leaders face opprobrium and eventually punishment for failing to prevent their troops committing war crimes.

Hans Kelsen said that the punishment of war criminals should be an act of international justice, not the satisfaction of a thirst for revenge. Similarly, there would seem to be a strong argument for considering terrorist bombings crimes against humanity. The provision for their trial and punishment in an international court would help prevent societies yielding to the temptation to commit equally despicable crimes in return.

America's failure to support or defer to the International Criminal Court is a clear signal of its unwillingness to renounce 'don't tread on us' foreign policy and an obvious embrace of duplicity as a national policy.[58] Though Article 29 of the

[55] LR Helfer, 'Transforming International Law after the 9/11 Attacks' in ML Dudziak (ed), *September 11 in History: A Watershed Moment?* (Duke University Press, 2003).

[56] M Byers, *War law: international law and armed conflict* (Atlantic Books, 2005).

[57] GP Fletcher, *Romantics at war: glory and guilt in the age of terrorism* (Princeton University Press, 2002).

[58] PB Heymann, *Terrorism, Freedom and Security* (MIT Press, 2003) 128.

Rome Statute invalidates norms such as the American Service-Members Protection Act for the purposes of the ICC, it is important that states begin to protest against attempts by heads of state to erect immunities protecting their actions, enshrining their duplicity whilst in office. Before this happens, of course, agreement must be forged on what means are prohibited. It would be appalling if such consensus faltered because states wanted to reserve for their commanders immunity for the intentional bombing or sundry terrorisation of civilian populations.

International criminal law should provide for punishment for all those who aim to terrorise, displaying a flagrant disregard for human life and the notion of proportionality. The law, to stand any chance of adherence, must be colourless. That means it must apply to banned means, whatever the ends, and whoever the perpetrator, whether they rally under the Knight's Banner like al-Qaeda, under a nation's flag like the military or the secret services, or simply work for private military corporations.[59]

Above, I touched on the distinction between lawful and unlawful combatants. It is submitted that there are several important considerations here. A uniform represents accountability but it also makes it easier to protect civilians, such as aid workers, the press, and unfortunates simply caught up in a war zone. Fighters who wear uniform are also protecting themselves in the event they are captured. If persons engaging in conflict wish to be treated as soldiers – lawful combatants – rather than spies or terrorists, they would be well advised to wear uniform, carry their weapons openly, bear an insignia of their organisation, act in a chain of command, and conduct themselves in accordance with the laws of war. States capturing such persons should then extend to them the rights enshrined in the Geneva Conventions for prisoners of war. After the conflict, they should be returned to their homeland without prejudice.

That said, we might have serious reservations about whether it is legitimate for states to treat captured terrorists, understood to be combatants who use unlawful means, with any less decorum. Suspected terrorists are indubitably suspected criminals and status as a suspected criminal, at least in areas where police are well behaved, does not entail a loss of rights. Rights are not deposited with valuables at the jailhouse door. It is difficult to see why states should be able to dispense with the Geneva Convention's guarantees, and those of sundry human rights conventions, merely by asserting that a combatant was unlawful, ie a terrorist. If a state suspects that a person in their custody is a terrorist, they should turn that person over to an international authority competent to try such persons in adversarial hearings with all the features of domestic criminal justice. More on this later.

[59] S Holmes, *The Matador's Cape: America's Reckless Response to Terror* (Cambridge University Press, 2007).

A good deal was said above on the incoherently expansive approach to self-defence characterising the Anglo-American response to the perceived terrorist threat. In what follows, an attempt will be made to delimit the circumstances in which a state might resort to the use of force.

Law aside, it would seem that proportionate force resorted to in self-defence and/or defence of others from imminent or ongoing attack is the only acceptable justification for force. I want to be clear that this does not rule out a first strike where an attack is imminent, for example, where troops have amassed on a border, or long-range missiles have been fired, or where a terrorist is poised to detonate a bomb. However, what should be equally clear is that such a notion of imminence should not be stretched to cover an attack on a state that might *one day* pose a threat.[60] At the time of writing, Prime Minister Gordon Brown had called the Iranian President Mahmoud Ahmadinejad's purported injunction that Israel be wiped off the map abhorrent and reiterated his determination to hinder the Iranian nuclear programme. (Israel apparently responded by tabling the option of kidnapping the outspoken Iranian leader.)[61] According to the suggestion here, however, even in the sorry event that Iran armed itself with nuclear warheads capable of being fired at Israeli territory, and even if its President continued to rant about the impropriety of Israel's existence, in the absence of a manifest intention imminently to attack Israel, no right of self-defence would inure. A repeat of Operation Opera in Iran would be highly regrettable, and, with the 45-minute claim fresh in our memories, an Iranian sequel to the Iraq invasion would be unforgiveable. It is hoped that nuclear war is not necessary before all states accept a principle limiting them to defend themselves only in the case of an imminent attack. The mere possibility of future attack is not enough to justify attack, particularly where unaccountable politicians are disingenuous about the threats we face. The alternative is gazing into the cloudy crystal ball installed by Bush into the Oval Office in order to respond to threats before they materialise.

In domestic criminal law, if a celebrity were aware that a stalker was plotting his demise, the celebrity would not be excused for killing the stalker in 'pre-emptive self-defence'. Such an action would constitute murder. The criminal law operates on the basis that allowing one person to take justice into their own hands would be to permit anarchy. Consequently, the only legal route available to the prospective celebrity victim would be to inform the police of the stalker's evil plot and have them deal with it accordingly. On the international plane, it is the lack of an effective police force that, for some, legitimises American policing of

[60] For an example of this view, see T Rockmore, 'On the So-called War on Terrorism' in T Rockmore, J Margolis and AT Marsoobian (eds), *The Philosophical Challenge of September 11* (Blackwell Publishing, 2005).

[61] 'Israel could kidnap Ahmadinejad', *BBC Online*, 8 September 2008, available at: news.bbc.co.uk/2/hi/middle_east/7605852.stm

the world.[62] Nevertheless, aside from the fact that few states would acquiesce in such a role for the ailing superpower, it is hard to argue against the position that respect for the UN Charter rules would greatly reduce the incidence of transnational terrorism and war between states, obviating the need for one militarily powerful state sentry to overwatch borders from above the law. As the High Level Panel on Threats, Challenges and Change recognised, the reasons for denying citizens the right to take justice into their own hands apply with equal, if not greater, force to states.

The notion of self-defence suggested here is not new, it is a restatement of the *SS Caroline* rule. It is, however, worth further explication, not in terms of international law, which was set out at sufficient length above, but in philosophical and practical terms. John Stuart Mill argued that 'the only purpose for which power can be rightfully exercised over any member of a civilised community, against his will, is to prevent harm to others'.[63] In a civilised international community, therefore, this principle might also apply, and has some chance of achieving universal assent. The obverse of this Millian coin is that harming innocents is always morally reprehensible (even if in extreme circumstances it might be a lesser evil).[64] The term 'innocent' here should not be understood in a religious or criminal sense, indeed, there may be virtuous soldiers and blameworthy civilians, rather it refers to the status of combatant and non-combatant mentioned earlier.[65] A person may not use force in self-defence if they are not about to be attacked themselves. Similarly, they may not defend another person, unless that other person is about to be attacked.

This is an uncluttered, colourless doctrine. By *uncluttered*, I mean that the motive for the attack is irrelevant (unless, of course, it is itself self-defence) and by *colourless*, I mean that the identity of the attacker is irrelevant. To explain this odd terminology, an example will be helpful. If a policeman shoots me in the leg whilst I am jogging, this is illegal in the same way that it would be illegal for my girlfriend to shoot me in the leg whilst I am jogging. But if I happen to be jogging towards her whilst she is stood on the edge of a cliff and I intend to kick her over that edge, she enjoys the same justification for shooting me in my leg as the policeman, namely, to defend her(self) from an untimely death. The use of force by states and terrorists is no different. The legitimacy of defensive force derives not from the identity of the user; rather it is a function of circumstance, and circumstance alone.

[62] For the one of the best, though by no means watertight, expositions of the position that international American policing is necessary, see R Kagan, *Of paradise and power: America and Europe in the new world order*, 1st edn (Alfred A Knopf: Distributed by Random House, 2003).

[63] JS Mill, *On Liberty* (Broadview Press, 1869) 51.

[64] GP Fletcher, *Romantics at war: glory and guilt in the age of terrorism* (Princeton University Press, 2002) 154.

[65] See R Fullinwider, 'Terrorism innocence and War' (2001) 21(4) *Philosophy & Public Policy Quarterly* 9.

Even more clutter can be cleared away from the law on self-defence. According to the UN Charter, for the right of self-defence to accrue, an 'armed attack' must occur. The International Court of Justice has provided some guidance on what this means. It has indicated that an attack must be 'most grave' in order to trigger the right of self-defence.[66] So, in the context of terrorism, a suicide attack by a general aviation craft (a small plane) might not reach that threshold.[67] This seems to be an unnecessarily restrictive approach to the notion of 'armed attack'. The natural meaning of the concept seems to have equal resonance in the spheres of war and crime. It is submitted that the problem is *not* the size or severity of the attack: A man hitting me with a stick is an armed attacker, and I consider his attack grave. Yoram Dinstein has argued persuasively along similar lines: 'In reality there is no cause to remove small scale armed attacks from the spectrum of armed attacks'.[68]

I would submit that the size of the attack is relevant only to the proportionality of the response. Returning to my assailant and his stick, it might be a proportionate response for me to raise my arm to block the blow before pushing him away to repel the attack. It might not, however, be a proportionate reaction for me, having repelled the attack, to punch his onlooking friend in the face. Similarly, it might be a proportionate response for a state to shoot a hijacked aircraft out of the sky if there is cogent evidence that it will imminently be used in a suicide attack on a nuclear installation. It would not be a proportionate reaction for the state to go on to fire missiles at the country most closely affiliated with the hijackers. Thus, the need for self-defence to be proportionate is common to criminal and international law. In light of the stakes involved, it is far more important to the latter.

Clearly then, the source of the problem (and the solution) lies in the proportionality of the response and in the distinction between crime and war, a distinction which grows out of the statal ordering of the international system – the external and internal dominion over peoples of the concept of sovereignty. The validation of the use of force carries with it the image of a state sending bombers, cavalry or infantry to a foreign territory. In the fight against terrorism, this type of reaction is patently inappropriate. If a state officer could prevent a murder by shooting a dagger from the hand of a madman, he would do so, and his action would be legal as (extended) self-defence. Exactly the same is true of a terrorist who can be shot before he detonates a bomb in a tube station or of a sniper who can be killed before he pulls the trigger on a gun aimed at the head of

[66] *Nicaragua v United States of America* [1986] ICJ Rep 103.

[67] D Huskisson, 'The Air Bridge Denial Program and the Shootdown of Civil Aircraft under International Law' (2005) 56 *Air Force Law Review* 109, 145

[68] Y Dinstein, *War, Aggression, and Self-defence* (Cambridge University Press, 1994) 173; J Hargrove, 'The Nicaragua Judgment and the Future of the Law of Force and Self-defense' (1987) 81 *American Journal of International Law* 135, 139; E Cannizzaro and P Palchetti (eds), *Customary International Law on the Use of Force* (Martinus Nijhoff, 2005); A Cassesse, *The Current Legal Regulation of the Use of Force: Current Legal Regulation* (Martinus Nijhoff, 1986).

a head-of-state. If the notion of 'state' self-defence is unshackled from the image of military incursion in foreign lands, the conclusion that the state can defend itself, using force against terrorist attacks becomes more palatable. That acceptability derives from the tailoring of the state response to the level of threat or aggression. Unhelpful legal detritus such as the notion of the gravity or severity of an attack is better thrown out. Correctly, in the afore-mentioned Israeli Supreme Court decision on the policy of targeted frustration, the tribunal easily concluded that waves of pro-Palestinian suicide bombings constituted an armed attack. This brings us to the issue of whether a liberal democracy ought to resort to assassinating terrorist leaders.

Above, I set out the arguments advanced by the proponents and opponents of the tactic of targeted killing. Here, I would like to look at two imaginary extra-judicial killings in order to assess how well they sit with the precepts of liberal democracy. These hypothetical, though conceivable scenarios are set in the modern world; Israel's well-publicised 'war on terrorism' can serve as a very rough *mise-en-scène* for ease of exposition. I shall assess each killing on three overlapping bases: expediency, morality and legality.[69]

In the first scenario, based on intelligence from a trusted informer, Israeli security officers suspect that two Palestinian terrorists, known to the authorities, are approaching a busy marketplace in Haifa intending to detonate suicide bombs to slaughter scores of traders. The state officers rush to the square and begin to scour it for the suspects. A sniper with a semi-automatic rifle is installed on the roof of a bar. The intelligence seems to be confirmed by on-the-spot surveillance of the appearance and movements of two men in a car. As officers are about to descend on the vehicle to attempt an arrest, the duo exit the car, exchange glances and proceed towards the bustling square. The officers retreat and the director of field operations gives a command to the sniper to take out both of the suspects. With two shots, he kills both before they reach the crowd.

How can we assess this operation? At first sight, it seems expedient. Shooting into a town square obviously increases the risk to civilians, but the sniper was able to take out the suspects with surgical precision before they reached the crowd. Moreover, if it turns out that the suspects were strapped up with explosives, the morality of the operation is hard to question because the two bombers posed an imminent threat to the lives of innocents. The notion of innocence here is of course not absolute but is intended in the narrow sense of persons who are not taking part in hostilities – the market traders and members of the public. This operation can be thought of as a police action to rescue people going about their daily lives from criminal aggression. Nevertheless, the lawfulness of the operation turns in part on the reasonableness of the state's belief in the threat. If their intelligence is wanting, they might have killed two peaceable traders. Clearly, the

[69] At the outset, it should be noted that I wish to postpone full consideration of the detention of terrorists until a little later, for what follows in the next chapter is logically prior thereto.

less time is available to the state officers to decide how to react to a purported suicide bombing, the greater the risk of fatal error. The legality of a counter-terrorist operation depends entirely on the quality of its planning and conduct.

Where, as in the situation depicted above, there is reasonable belief in an imminent threat to the life of innocents, 'waiting to see' is not an option for a state that takes seriously its responsibility to protect the citizenry. But using a sniper in this fashion ought not be considered legal if the escalation of events could have been avoided by earlier intervention and arrest of the suspects. It seems that three factors are of immense importance here. First, the sourcing and evaluation of intelligence should be expert. Where human life is concerned, where a state risks killing an innocent, acting on a shoddy survey or an unreliable source is unacceptable. Second, that expert intelligence must be accompanied by expert legal advice. Turf wars between security officers and legal officials are literally deadly – cohesion is paramount. State officials should be equipped to intervene as soon as the investigation reaches a point where enough evidence has amassed against the alleged perpetrators that they can be arrested and tried for an attempted terrorist attack. To allow a terrorist plot to proceed beyond this point, to a situation in which the only way to stop the attack is the resort to lethal force, is nothing other than negligence. For instance, in a case concerning the shooting by British security officers of members of a suspected terrorist cell in a public square in Gibraltar, the Strasbourg Court held that

> the use of lethal force would be rendered disproportionate if the authorities failed, whether deliberately or through lack of proper care, to take steps which would have avoided the deprivation of life of the suspects without putting the lives of others at risk.[70]

Furthermore, and this is the third commonly overlooked factor of immense importance, flexibility in sentencing for acts preparatory to terrorist crimes facilitates early intervention. Where state officers know that they can secure sentences for budding bombers and cautious conspirators, they will be under much less pressure to await near-completed attempts whilst the danger to the public escalates. Frequently, negligence leading to unnecessary risk to civilians, including the suspected terrorists, will not be the negligence of the officers on the ground, but negligence in briefing, communication of information, teamwork, or the setting of protocol.[71]

Finally, there is no way to assess the reasonableness of the operation without an independent ex post public inquiry. Wherever the state resorts to extra-judicial killing, a body, independent of the police force, military and security services should be appointed to investigate the quality of their efforts. The innocence or otherwise of the deceased suspected bombers, though an emotive factor, is

[70] *McCann v United Kingdom* Series A No 324 (1995) 21 EHRR 97, para 235.

[71] Independent Police Complaints Commission, 'Investigation into the shooting of Jean Charles de Menezes' (2005).

actually irrelevant to the legality of the operation, which depends entirely on the reasonableness of the officers' belief in the imminence of a threat to the lives of the public. This is not a 'no harm, no foul' situation. It ought to be understood that independent scrutiny in cases of official killings should be of the strictest variety. That said, we might anticipate a more forgiving standard of review the closer the killing is in time and place to the theatre of combat.

In a second scenario, we can imagine the same two aspirant suicide bombers, discussing their plans the day before with a third man, the alleged operational mastermind in a hideout in contested territory; that is, in lands claimed by Palestinian groups and over which the state of Israel has no stable governmental control. The Israeli military has intelligence about this clandestine meeting, decides that an attempted arrest or ambush of the suspected terrorists would present an unacceptable risk to its personnel, so instead plumps for launching air-to-ground missiles from a helicopter, obliterating the hideout and a nearby bar, killing the alleged terrorists and three innocent bystanders, maiming three more, and causing minor injuries to seven.

May a liberal democracy resort to such heavy-handed measures? In terms of expediency, though the attack was effective in terms of eliminating the suspected terrorists, several factors militate against the prudence of such an operation. First, the usage of missiles destroys not only buildings but also any chance of conclusively proving the guilt of the victims – using a missile instead of a sniper is like opening a door with a wrecking ball instead of a key. This is politically inexpedient, as it is far easier for a state to demonise terrorists in a court of law than it is when a state opts to kill them without trial. Moreover, the imprecision of the attack and the likelihood of collateral damage entail the demonisation of that state. The state sells its legitimacy in exchange for terrorist scalps – this is a bad bargain because no army can enduringly control territory without the support of the local population. Second, the military expediency of such an assault is questionable. Killing one terrorist is of little use if the injury, maiming and slaughter of innocent bystanders galvanises support for terrorist causes and methods.

The military might protest that the targeted killing was a measure of last resort because arrest would have been too risky. However, such a protest simply betrays the fact that the military values the lives of its operatives over those of non-combatants endangered by the missile attack. Again, this is a substandard public relations exercise. In purely moral terms, this operation is hard to justify because, apart from the fact that the state is exerting ultimate power over the lives of people outside of its jurisdiction, no attack is imminent (though it is a future possibility). The risk to civilians, the questionable military utility of such an attack in a campaign against terrorism, and the fact that the state sentences the suspects and those around them to the maximum penalty without even a gesture towards legal process, makes this sort of assault difficult to reconcile with any notion of legality. Furthermore, no independent public inquiry will be possible where the state has no control over the territory in question, so it is hard to see how the military's decisions can meaningfully be scrutinised.

It is worth reflecting at this juncture that, if a state had intelligence that a similar criminal meeting were in progress inside its territory, there would be no suggestion of destroying the building with missiles. Rather, interception and arrest would be the only option. If the summary execution of suspected conspirators on home territory is not an option for a liberal democracy, it is difficult to comprehend why it would permit itself summarily to execute suspected conspirators on contested or foreign soil. Unless one draws a very strict and ultimately unsatisfactory distinction between liberal democracy *qua* principled law enforcer and liberal democracy *qua* unprincipled prosecutor of war, it is difficult to understand how a government would display obedient subservience to the precepts of legality internally and yet manifest flagrantly untrammelled discretion in its foreign affairs. Perhaps surprisingly, such unscrupulousness is endorsed by some experts, in theories discussed in due course.

Holmes has contended, in a different context, that an executive might exhibit the same pathology as a man with a hammer, who sees every problem as a nail. A similar observation can be made here. A state that equips itself with a policy of targeted killings might well overlook other, more clinical, and eventually more durable solutions to the blight of terrorism. Arrest, extradition, reconciliation, and the creation of interstate consensus as to 'forbidden means' are all options that might well fail to occur to a beleaguered democracy if the quick, messy and temporary fix is within its reach. Indeed, just as an injudiciously used hammer can render a job more difficult, so a poorly conceived policy can hamper attempts to generate the necessary unified international front to counter terrorism.

On 12 August 2008, in the Pakistani territory of South Waziristan, four missiles struck a camp linked to Afghan warlord Gulbuddin Hekmatyar, whose foot-soldiers are understood to be engaging US forces in Afghanistan. The strike killed a reported nine people. Pakistan condemns the violation of its sovereignty. First Lieutenant Nathan Perry, spokesman for the US army, denies American military involvement.[72] Naturally, he does not speak for the CIA, which does not speak at all but has conducted strikes with predator drones in the past.[73] It is very difficult for America to justify a policy of targeted killings of suspected terrorists (as distinct from known military foes), given its military ascendancy and political leverage, and because of the dangers involved in such a policy of exacerbating

[72] 'Officials: Missiles kill nine in Pakistan', *Washington Post*, 14 August 2008, available at: www.washingtonpost.com/wp-dyn/content/article/2008/08/13/AR2008081300469_2.html.

[73] 'Pakistan shuns CIA build up sought by US', *New York Times*, 27 January 2008, available at: www.nytimes.com/2008/01/27/world/asia/27pakistan.html?scp=2&sq=predator%20cia&st=cse.

rather than extinguishing the terrorist threat.[74] Nevertheless, the BBC reported that between August 2008 and July 2009, 450 people had been killed in almost 50 drone strikes in Pakistan.[75] The United States is the only country believed to have the capacity to conduct these attacks. President Obama is consulting Pakistan on the policy of drone attacks in the region and has given no indication that he intends to renounce this means.

In defending ourselves, we must do what we can to take into account the aggressor's standpoint. If the aggressor is under the impression it is defending itself, there is a clear danger of escalation in the event that the respondent reacts with force. The present situation in Israel and its Palestinian surrounds is the paradigm example of this sort of descent into cyclic, internecine conflict. Today, Israel claims it wants to 'eliminate members of Hamas' but that Palestinian civilians are not targets; that its aim is to prevent further rocket attacks on Israeli soil. At the time of writing, over 250 civilian women and children have been killed in the conflict, galvanising Palestinian rage and lending credibility to Hamas' propaganda about the genocidal intentions of their Jewish neighbours. Israel's war can be criticised on moral and legal grounds but, to my mind, one of the most powerful criticisms is that the war was borderline imbecilic. With such crude tactics, Israel is not only bound to fail in its stated aims, but the manner of its war-making is almost certain to defeat the objects it cited for making war in the first place.

In the approach endorsed here, both self-defence and defence of others from imminent attack justify the use of force. However, the defence of others, in the guise of humanitarian intervention, involves complex issues. Though a complete survey is not possible here, I shall try to address some issues thrown up by the war on terrorism, as it has been fought. First, when purporting to defend others, it is important, where possible, that they are consulted, or at least, that some attempt is made to understand their perception of the predicament, particularly given the risks and uncertainties involved in any intervention. In light of the recent history of Iraq, it is unnecessary for me to labour the point that, rather than helping, intervention can worsen the plight of a people. Richard Miller expressed this well:

> Afghans could justly fight against the Taliban, hoping for larger gains in justice and imposing grave risks on compatriots whom they ask to join their struggle. They could reasonably take the offense to their own dignity of submission to Taliban rule to be unacceptable. But whether outsiders, not suffering the injustice of the Taliban, may rightly impose such dangers is another matter.[76]

[74] Cf M Ignatieff, *The lesser evil: political ethics in an age of terror* (Edinburgh University Press, 2003) 133.

[75] 'Drones kill dozens in Pakistan', *BBC Online*, 8 July 2009, available at: news.bbc.co.uk/2/hi/south_asia/8139739.stm.

[76] RW Miller, 'Terrorism, War, and Empire' in JP Sterba (ed), *Terrorism and International Justice* (Oxford University Press, 2003) 193.

In the context of Vietnam's involvement in Cambodia, the French Representative to the United Nations said this of the doctrine of humanitarian intervention:

> The notion that because a regime is detestable foreign intervention is justified and forcible overthrow is legitimate is extremely dangerous. That could ultimately jeopardize the very maintenance of international law and order and make the continued existence of various regimes dependent on the judgement of their neighbours.[77]

This sort of view can be fruitfully be compared with that of Francesco Francioni, Professor of International Law at the European University Institute, who, contrary to the French concern with jeopardising the prevailing order, sees a role for the breach of existing international law:

> [I]t seems that the correct methodological approach to the question under discussion is to ask whether a technically illegal act of use of force committed by a state or a group of states to stop gross violations of human rights in another society may be justifiable, not for the simple moral necessity of saving human lives, but in view of the *legal necessity of breaching the law in order to gradually transform it and make it more coherent with fundamental principles of justice and human rights.*[78] (emphasis added)

He is by no means blind to the risks of abuse inherent in such a doctrine. For Francioni, the US-led intervention in Iraq cannot 'be characterized as a limited use of force intended to stop large scale violations of human rights'; rather it is better thought of as 'the pursuit of an hegemonic design of power politics' under the false flag of democracy.[79]

Francioni is right in a sense. Morality needs no counsel – an able-bodied passer-by witnessing a rape in progress needs no authorisation or second opinion to intervene. But the behaviour of states is such that it is very hard to find cases in international law of selfless intervention. The interest in the prevention of unilateralist, moralist, hegemonic foreign policy is so great, our expectations of states are so low, and the risks of intervention are so high, that it is difficult to see why states should be permitted to 'go it alone', particularly when a perfectly workable mechanism exists for the ex post authorisation of force. Morality then, due to the practicalities of the international order, needs the Security Council.

In 2001, the International Commission on Intervention and State Sovereignty suggested a change of focus:

> This Commission strongly believes that the responsibility to protect implies an accompanying responsibility to prevent. And we think that it is more than high time for the international community to be doing more to close the gap between rhetorical support for prevention and tangible commitment. The need to do much better on

[77] UN Document S/PV.2109, at 4

[78] F Francioni, 'Balancing the Prohibition of Force with the Need to Protect Human Rights: A Methodological Approach' in E Cannizzaro and P Palchetti (eds), *Customary International Law on the Use of Force* (Martinus Nijhoff, 2005) 279.

[79] *ibid*, 291.

> prevention, and to exhaust prevention options before rushing to embrace intervention, were constantly recurring themes in our worldwide consultations, and ones which we wholeheartedly endorse.[80]

Citing the great disparity between military spending and charitable spending, Byers argues that 'proponents of the responsibility to protect who focus on military intervention are participating in a terrible charade'.[81]

The recent empowerment of Iran, the ironic result of the disempowerment of an Iraq so worrisome to Western powers, might go some way towards convincing political leaders that it will take enduring, concerted, and honest efforts to relinquish the duplicities that have characterised the use of force in the war on terrorism. When a criminal culture based on the threat of force becomes so entrenched in the mindset of a community, brave efforts are required of its members to flush it out, because it is in the interests of none to renounce aggression as a political tool unless all do so.

The 'take-home' message of this chapter is that aggression is the quintessence of all crime. It degrades victim, aggressor and all humanity.[82] Those who resort to force other than in the repulsion of an imminent attack must be regarded as *communis hostis omnium*. In this way, one man's terrorist will be another man's terrorist, and clear lines can be drawn as to when it is acceptable for states to resort to force. That force may be used only to repel an imminent attack seems to me to be the only point on which stylised foes may still be able to agree. Let us put aside preposterous self-deceptions about pre-emptive self-defence, actions which in ordinary language are called 'attack'. Apart from being morally repugnant, semantically tortuous and deeply imprudent, they catalyse interminable cyclic conflicts.

The *semantic* incoherence of the expansive version of pre-emptive self-defence brings us to a consideration of how the issues discussed here relate to those of the previous chapter. Three observations immediately spring to mind. First, an international definition of terrorism would significantly improve our understanding of and ability to combat the phenomenon. If the nascent world community can agree that certain methods are never legal, it might have the beginnings of an international criminal code. The debate on the definition of terrorism, a terminological debate, contains the key which can unlock the door to international criminal law, and ultimately bar the practice of indiscriminate killing of civilians for political ends.

Second, the rhetorical and symbolic designation of terror as war foreclosed or obfuscated suitable options whilst foregrounding less prudent methods. Expansive, romantic, and ultimately chimerical interpretations of September 11 as an

[80] International Commission on Intervention and State Sovereignty, 'Responsibility to Protect' (2001) 19.

[81] M Byers, *War law: international law and armed conflict* (Atlantic Books, 2005) 111.

[82] See, for the notion of crime against humanity, *Prosecutor v Erdemovic, Sentencing Judgment* (1996) 108 ILR 180.

attack on 'democracy' and 'civilisation' had a very real effect on Western responses. In this vein, it is worth considering whether a state's right to self-defence is a claim to anything other than metaphorical validity. Would it not be more accurate to say that a state has the right to protect its people and only then, by extension, the institutions and conventions that are set up in order to fulfil that task? Charles Fried said that individuals come first: 'Whoever says otherwise is trading in metaphors'.[83] To say that a state has a right to defend itself does seem a dangerously elastic figuration. Indeed, that figurative elasticity has helped catapult America and the United Kingdom into offensive wars for oil and soil with huge costs in blood and treasure (leave alone moral standing). It is perhaps better to conceptualise a state's right of self-defence as a mere outgrowth of the right we all have to defend ourselves and others from aggression.

Third, the power of images to bring about war is underestimated at our peril. The dramatic images of September 11, coupled with the 45-minute claim (derived from a piece of 'third-hand' intelligence) called to mind the apocalyptic image of a British Hiroshima or a New York Nagasaki. Though it would be unfair to say there were no protests against the Afghanistan and Iraq invasion, this end-of-life-as-we-know-it imagery was enough to subdue critical analysis of facts, oust evidential considerations, and in the end, benumb basic popular morality. The political rationalisation of both wars was, and is, that they are being fought for our security and the liberty of Afghanis and Iraqis. It is to liberty, security and rationality that the discussion now wends.

[83] C Fried, *Modern liberty and the limits of government*, 1st edn (WW Norton & Co, 2007) 19.

4

Liberty, Security and Rationality

O superbi Christian, miseri lassi,
Che, de la vista de la mente infermi,
Fidanza avete ne' retrosi passi,
Non v'accorgete che noi siam vermi,
Nati a formar l'angelica farfalla,
Che vola alla giustizia sanza schermi,
Di che l'animo vostro in alto galla,
poi siete quasi antomata in difetto,
sì come vermo in cui formazion falla?

Dante Alghieri, *La divina commedia,* Purgatorio, Canto X, Lines 121–9

LIKE MONARCHS, LIBERTY, Security and Rationality sit on the thrones of Western political culture. Their relation to the war on terror needs no introduction but the uncertainty of their lineage necessitates some preliminary words on each.

In a deceptively simple phrase, Fried tells us that 'liberty is individuality made normative'.[1] His reverence for liberty extends beyond its usefulness for procuring the goods or pleasures we seek. Liberty, for Fried, 'is worth more than just the sum of the goods we are not prevented from attaining'.[2] To deprive a person of their power of choice is to infantilise but also to dehumanise them; but restrictions on choice are not intrinsically inhuman – what matters is that choice is not limited arbitrarily, but by our consent or silent assent. But to what extent will we assent to the deprivation of our liberty? The two-pronged answer would seem to be: to the extent that it benefits us without harming others. This brings us to Mill's work, mentioned earlier in the context of self-defence. He argues that 'the sole end for which mankind are warranted, individually or collectively, in interfering with the liberty of action of any of their number, is self-protection'.[3] Enter security.

As security takes the stage as a natural curtailment of liberty, equality also begins to feature. The notion that we are entitled to the maximum amount of liberty compatible with the enjoyment of that same amount by everyone else has

[1] C Fried, *Modern liberty and the limits of government*, 1st edn (WW Norton & Co, 2007) 22.
[2] *ibid*, 49.
[3] JS Mill, *On Liberty* (Broadview Press, 1869).

enormous sway in Western society. This is the Speaker's Corner at which liberty and equality convene, and frequently debate the meaning of social and distributive justice. What if Mahmoud, born to Pakistani professors in Britain, enjoys more liberty than Mohammed, his cousin, born to Pakistani refugees in Bangladesh? What if children born in Parisian ghettos are more likely to end up in jail than in college? Some very modest headway is made into these questions in the chapter on the economy. For now it suffices to bear them in mind.

In civilised societies, an attempt is made to set limits on liberty using the criminal law. We attempt, together, to facilitate our individual and collective flourishing by choosing which behaviours are to be abnegated in order to promote those which we decide, together, are more praiseworthy pursuits. Our freedom is in chains but, in a healthy society, we turn the keys in our own shackles, and in a constitutional democracy, by means of rules restricting changes in the law, we hurl the keys out of the reach of the temptations of short-term populism. As noted in the last chapter, although criminal codes can be fantastically detailed, much of the criminal law is based on the nebulous concept of reasonableness. We must have reference to some benchmark in order to prevent anarchy. To put it as briefly as possible, if we want to live in a society tolerably free of aggressive encroachments into space we consider our own, we can but try. Criminal codes in most liberal states are more or less sensible rules intended to promote social cohesion by imposing minor constraints on conduct. Laws contain instructions for good behaviour. The men of England's towns, for instance, should not assume consent to their unsolicited, amorous gropings on the dance-floor, however attractive they might appear to themselves during a night out on the tiles. These rules are designed to protect minimum spheres of freedom, enjoyed by all, in this case, a woman's freedom to dance uninhibited by unwelcome solicitations.

As this example demonstrates, liberty would be meaningless without others who threaten to encroach thereupon. It is a social not an individual notion and my liberty is limited precisely to the extent that my sphere collides or threatens to collide with another's. Any realistic notion of liberty therefore *entails* security. Thus, per Mill (et al) we accept reduced liberty in exchange for increased security. By virtue of our shared inhabitation of a limited space (for pragmatists), or our shared humanity (for natural lawyers), we have entitlements as against one another even in the absence of state apparatus. That said, as Edmund Burke might have put it, rights in the abstract are worth precious little to people dealing with the vicissitudes of life in the real world.[4]

Western theorists have concluded, rightly or wrongly, that only the liberal democratic state can protect our entitlements in a manner that does not favour the strong, the rich and the cunning over the weak, the poor and the biddable. Through law, the state governs the relationship between liberty and security.

[4] E Burke, *Reflections on the revolution in France* (Yale University Press, 2003) eg 152.

Through the apparatus of a good state, we govern this law. We find it irksome when a bad state mismanages this relationship, fails to protect us, oppresses us or detracts from our liberty without appreciable gains in security. James Nickel puts this in the following colourful terms:

> Greedy or hungry neighbors who will raid, kill, steal, dispossess, kidnap, and rape pose what I call the *First Problem of Insecurity*. To protect ourselves from them we create government and legal protections of personal security, liberty, and possessions. We enact criminal laws, create courts and jails, and proceed to convict and punish offenders. We thereby solve – or at least ameliorate – the First Problem. The system of law and government is dangerous, however, and we still have reason to be fearful, but now our fear is of the government's predations, corruption, and ineptitude. This is the *Second Problem of Insecurity*.[5]

Anyone reading the newspapers will be aware that both the first and second problems of insecurity loom large in the war on terrorism. Indeed, efforts honestly or ostensibly taken to resolve the first problem of insecurity – the threat from aggressive others – frequently turn out to worsen the second problem of insecurity. Apropos in the context of the Bush administration's war on terrorism is the understanding that, although the subordination of the few to the will of the many might rightly enrage a libertarian, more tyrannical still would be the subjugation of the (peaceable) many to the will of the (belligerent) few. More will be said on this later in the examination of presidential powers.

Aside from liberty and security, this chapter looks at what I have elected to call rationality. By rationality, I refer simply to the prudent or pragmatic thing to do, that which common sense dictates; the strictures of science not spirits, enlightenment rather than enchantment. Rationality, or prudence is often contrasted with morality, particularly where governments seek to justify actions by reference to security: they might say, for instance, 'ethnic profiling might not be moral but if more terrorists come from certain communities, then it is an acceptable policy, justified by rationality'. This contrast between prudence and morality will be tested below. It is included in this chapter because, it will be argued, the oversimplistic oppositions between liberty and security, and between prudence and morality contrive to contribute to imprudent policies making us less secure. The failure to recognise these deceptive oppositions is a failure of rationality.

The regal Statue of Liberty greets you when you enter New York Harbour. On entering Camp Delta at Guantánamo Bay Naval Station – itself an unequivocal expression of the freedom to contract, held as it is on lease by the US pursuant to a contract with Cuba that can be terminated only on the agreement of both parties – a sign welcomes you: 'Honor bound to defend Freedom'. Inside, it is a different story, and one that has been documented so well now that it need not be rehearsed here. Suffice it to say that 'Gitmo', rather than being a symbol for the

[5] JW Nickel, 'Due Process Rights and Terrorist Emergencies' (2007) 1 *European Journal of Legal Studies* available at www.ejls.eu.

American belief in freedom, has become synonymous with the two preferred techniques of tyranny, arbitrary detention and torture.

Such was the intense focus on the stripping, slapping, punching, kicking, electrocuting, cross-dressing, water-boarding and occasional murdering of detainees that it is all too easy to forget that many of the men in American detention, whose innocence has never been tested in adversarial proceedings (and might never be), have been there for a period of time equivalent to the sentence reserved for the most serious of criminals.[6] Further, if a convicted criminal, serving his sentence, were subjected by prison guards to the inhuman treatment endured by the men in Camp Delta, we would be outraged, the guards would be stripped of their office and convicted, and the criminal would be handsomely compensated. Incredulity and numbness characterise human reactions to Gitmo. We struggle to respond appropriately because what is happening in Cuba is, frankly, off the chart.[7]

One would be forgiven for thinking that a person's liberty, as described above, was limited by every other person's liberty. This might be called liberty's modesty. The Chief Justice of the US Supreme Court opined that civil liberty means a citizen's liberty, not liberty in an abstract state of nature. However, Guantánamo Bay has nothing to do with this modest variety of liberty. Officers at Delta Camp are 'honor bound' to protect a different brand of liberty, American freedom, and to the measures that may be taken in defence of that absolute liberty, there are, it seems, no limits. It does not appear to matter to Americans who acquiesce in the existence of places like Guantánamo that the security of American liberty is bought at the price of the security of foreigners' liberty. Jeremy Waldron observed this dynamic: 'If security-gains for most people are being balanced against liberty-losses for a few, then we need to pay attention to the few/most dimension of the balance, not just the liberty/security dimension'.[8]

We also need to pay attention to whether or not secret and secretive prisons, which eliminate the liberty of strangers, actually improve our security in any meaningful way. There are very strong arguments to the contrary. The easy-to-grasp, oversimplified image of balancing liberty and security has not only hampered public understanding of the choices made by governments in combatting terrorism but has also weakened our grip on why terrorism happens in the first place.

[6] A Taguba, 'US Army Report on Conditions in Detention' (2004, available at: www.npr.org/iraq/2004/prison_abuse_report.pdf).

[7] For a selection of reports, see 'Three die in Guantánamo Suicide Pact', *Sunday Times*, 11 June 2006, available at: www.timesonline.co.uk/tol/news/world/article673738.ece; Committee Against Torture, 'Consideration of reports submitted by states parties under Article 19 of the Convention CAT/C/USA/CO/2' (18 May 2006); A Lewis, 'Guantánamo's Long Shadow', *New York Times*, 21 June 2005, available at: www.nytimes.com/2005/06/21/opinion/21lewis.html?_r=1&th&emc=th&oref=slogin.

[8] J Waldron, 'Security and Liberty: The Image of Balance' (2003) 11 *Journal of Political Philosophy* 191, 203

The assertion that 'the very nature of democracy makes the fight against terrorism very difficult' is bandied around as if self-evidently true.[9] This is as if to say, as former President Bush once tellingly did, that it would be easier to clamp down on terrorists in a dictatorship than it is for a democracy fight terrorism with the proverbial one hand behind its back. There is truth in the statement that, since the free market makes it easy to procure goods for making bombs, and civil liberties to some extent make it difficult for security services to hound potential bomb-makers, it will be hard entirely to eradicate violence from liberal society. However, to say that liberal democracy is somehow ill-equipped to counter terrorism might well be foolhardy defeatism. A rarer assertion, and one more attentive to human nature, is this:

> Just and moderate governments are everywhere quiet, everywhere safe; but oppression raises ferments and makes men struggle to cast off an uneasy and tyrannical yoke ... Some enter into company for trade and profit, others for want of business have their clubs for claret. Neighbourhood joins some, and religion others. But there is only one thing which gathers people into seditious commotions, and that is oppression.[10]

Here John Locke indicates the manifest advantages to a government of just and liberal disposition. Terrorists understand this perfectly well. They know that heavy-handed executive responses to security threats undermine support for the government of the day and lend credence to their claims of oppression. Terrorists know that it is 'the response to terrorism not terrorism itself that does democracy most harm'.[11] The obverse of what Locke is saying is that where a government safeguards political and personal empowerment, it removes the incentive for violent expression. According to Locke then, contrary to the fallacious image of balance, meddling with liberties can *increase* insecurity. Of course, some reconciliation of the concepts is needed, but heightened security does not, without more, necessarily result from curtailments of liberty.

Since 2004, evidence has piled up not only that the Bush administration operated a systematic, global programme of extraordinary rendition and torture, but also that this regime was approved at the highest levels.[12] The argument for torture is that, by sacrificing the liberty and dignity of one, we might ensure the

[9] DS Hamilton, *Terrorism and international relations* (Calouste Gulbenkian Foundation; Center for Transatlantic Relations, Paul H Nitze School of Advanced International Studies, Johns Hopkins University, 2006) 221 (Fernando Gil).

[10] J Locke, 'A letter concerning toleration' (1689).

[11] M Ignatieff, *The lesser evil: political ethics in an age of terror* (Edinburgh University Press, 2003) 61.

[12] Anyone interested in a history of the series of leaks, memos, and admissions should consult backcopies of the *New York Times* or search online at: www.newyorktimes.com. See also *El-Masri v US* (Fourth Circuit Opinion) 4: 'Stephen Macpherson Watt, a human rights adviser to the American Civil Liberties Union, filed a sworn declaration in the District Court, dated April 7, 2006, in which he asserted that Secretary of State Condoleeza Rice, White House Press Secretary Scott McClellan, and [CIA] Directors Tenet and Goss had publicly acknowledged the US had conducted renditions'.

security of many: In the words of John Yoo, legal acolyte of the former President, 'any harm that might occur during an interrogation would pale to insignificance compared to the harm avoided by preventing such an attack, which could take hundreds or thousands of lives'.[13] Again, the image of a balance floats before our eyes with liberty (of one nameless Afghan) in one pan and the security (of our close friends and family) in the other. But how reliable is this image?

In Alex Gibney's documentary, *Taxi to the Dark Side*, a British survivor of Guantánamo Bay recounts how people react to the story of his detention: 'if you weren't a terrorist when you went in, after what they put you through, you would have good reason to be one now'. Far from being a useful tool for preventing terrorism, torturing a person, apart from shattering any trust they have in government or belief in its fairness, also has the potential to stir in them the sort of anger that drives terrorism.

Marcus Tullius Cicero questioned the utility of torture on other grounds.

> The course of examination under torture is steered by pain, is controlled by individual qualities of mind and body, is directed by the president of the court, is diverted by caprice, tainted by hope, invalidated by fear, and the result is that in all these straits there is not room left for the truth.[14]

When Cicero made his complaint, torture was part of judicial procedure, but even where it is conducted today, 'outside' the law in times of apparent emergency, it is unclear that torture, a great sacrifice in terms of liberty, yields any benefits in terms of security. Michael Rolince, FBI Counter Terrorism Agent, said that 'torture and coercion gets you, in the vast majority of cases, wrong information that takes you off on wild goose chases'.[15] In the now infamous ticking bomb scenario, where an agent chooses to torture under the pressure of saving thousands from imminent disaster, wild goose chases are something that he can little afford. Again, the explanation that we must accept limitations on liberty to increase our security seems to be less cogent than the metaphor of balance suggests. A further prudent reason to uphold the ban on torture is that terrorists are more likely to opt for deadly suicide attacks if they risk being tortured on capture. The use of torture thus increases the risk of suicide bombing.

Notwithstanding the hubris that informs the view that 'the US can go it alone', most commentators would agree that states are safer if they have powerful allies. Canada has put America on a list of countries where prisoners are at risk of

[13] J Yoo, 'Memorandum for Alberto R Gonzales Counsel to the President' in KJ Greenberg and JL Dratel (eds), *The Torture Papers: The Road to Abu Ghraib* (Cambridge University Press, 2005) 208–9.

[14] Quoted in S Holmes, 'The Curious Debate' in K Greenberg (ed), *The Torture Debate in America* (Cambridge University Press, 2005) 121.

[15] P Bergen, 'War of Error', *The New Republic*, 22 October 2007.

being tortured.[16] A Foreign Affairs Committee Report in the United Kingdom stated that, due to the rather peculiar definition of torture in the United States, 'the UK can no longer rely on US assurances that it does not use torture'.[17] These statements do not terminate the alliance with the United States, but the Canadians and British are distancing themselves from the United States, not without considerable hypocrisy in light of the Canadian complicity in interrogations in Guantánamo Bay and the United Kingdom's opening of its runways for American rendition flights.

Liberty has been hijacked in the war on terrorism. Allied troops, in the process of deposing dictators and despotic governments in order to install democratic governments either side of Iran, marched under a flag of freedom. In the official rhetoric, these were wars of liberation, the stuff of Oliver 'Ironsides' Cromwell and the American Revolution; they were wars fought against oppressive tyrants and terrorists for human rights. Yet, pro-democratic intervention is inherently problematic because the notion of a foreign power imposing a democracy, rather than a people fighting for its own democratic rights (should it want to claim them), contradicts the fundamental premise underlying democracy, that of self-determination, according to which a people should be free to choose how it is governed, or in other words, how it governs itself. Consequently, this purported exception to the use of force has had an icy reception in international law.[18] In the case of both Iraq and Afghanistan, the claim of pro-democratic intervention is even more unconvincing because it came as an afterthought, and, by any measure, far too late to mask the recondite motives of the Anglo-American alliance.

According to international law, pursuant to its UN Charter, Chapter VII powers, the Security Council could authorise military intervention to restore or establish a democratic government. Notwithstanding the rhetoric of Tony Blair and George Bush, in international law as it is generally understood, it remains unambiguously illegal, under the Charter of the United Nations, for a sovereign state or states to invade another sovereign state in order to effect a change in its government. Similarly illegal, as affirmed by the International Court of Justice in the *Nicaragua* case, is the financing or supplying of usurping forces.[19] It is perhaps one of the ironies of modernity that, in the United Nations General Assembly, a majority of states 'deeply deplored' a 1983 American operation to replace military rulers in Grenada with a democratic government. In short, the majority *voted* against democracy. Indeed, call them what you will, despots, dictators,

[16] 'Canada puts US on torture list', *BBC*, 18 January 2008, available at: news.bbc.co.uk/2/hi/americas/7195276.stm.

[17] Foreign Affairs Select Committee, 'Foreign Affairs Ninth Report' (20 July 2008).

[18] Examples of purported democratic intervention are Grenada in 1983, the Panama invasion of 1989, and Haiti in 1994. The latter was arguably authorised by the Security Council. Byers offers a good summary of state attitudes towards pro-democratic intervention: M Byers, *War law: international law and armed conflict* (Atlantic Books, 2005) ch 7.

[19] *Nicaragua v United States of America* [1986] ICJ Rep 103.

tyrants, *juntas*, oligarchs and autocrats, all rely on some degree of popular support, apathy or obedience to stay in power. To ignore that acquiescence and barge into a sovereign state brandishing a blueprint for a bill of rights is, at worst, anti-democratic, and at best, an emasculation of the citizenry. In one of his more profound observations, Nietzsche maintained that, so long as defence of community is the only factor dictating moral judgements, there can be no development of 'love for thy neighbour'.[20] Given the persisting importance of sovereignty in international law, the argument that a coalition of the willing can invade a country, murder its leader, and install democracy therein is as unconvincing as the contention that a mob can break into my house, throw me out on the street, and install another occupier. The bounds of my liberty within my home are restricted. I cannot, for example, physically abuse my wife, and in such a situation the police can intervene. A passer-by may also enter my house and intervene to prevent me committing horrible crimes against my family, if there is no time to alert the police. The difference in international society is that the stakes and the risks of abuse are higher. If a government is perpetrating horrendous human rights abuses against its own people, of course the international community has an obligation to intervene. The system set up for facilitating humanitarian intervention *proper*, namely the UN Security Council and its founding Charter, is infinitely preferable to ad hoc coalitions of the willing. It is regrettable that the UN route was bypassed by states which were instrumental in its design.

Aside from the highly questionable legitimacy of pro-democratic intervention and its self-contradictory nature, there are real practical problems facing democratic crusaders. Democracy is a habit of mind that must germinate in the collective psyche – it is difficult to implant. In his book on America's war on terror, Holmes poked fun at the American neo-conservative fantasy that legitimacy could be 'delivered on the back of an Abrams tank'.[21] Despite the weighty evidence of the historical trials and tribulations of peoples attempting to change from autocracy to democracy, Jeanne Kirkpatrick tells us that 'no idea holds greater sway in the mind of educated Americans than the belief that it is possible to democratise governments anytime, anywhere, under any circumstances'.[22] It seems that few modern American neo-conservatives are able clearly to see these facts due to their welling up at the romantic notion of emancipating thankful farmhands and downtrodden women from backward regimes. In a critique of the Carter administration, but one that could equally be levelled at the naïve romanticising of the Bush clique, Kirkpatrick noted that:

> Many of the wisest political scientists of this and previous centuries agree that democratic institutions are especially difficult to establish and maintain – because they

[20] FW Nietzsche, *Beyond Good and Evil*, J Norman (Cambridge University Press, 2002) 88.

[21] S Holmes, *The Matador's Cape: America's Reckless Response to Terror* (Cambridge University Press, 2007).

[22] JJ Kirkpatrick, 'Dictatorships and Double Standards: Rationalism and Reason in Politics' (1979) Commentary.

make heavy demands on all portions of a population and because they depend on complex social, cultural and economic conditions.[23]

Kirkpatrick is right, of course, but as the child of a bloody, prolonged revolution itself,[24] and having suffered the pubescent upheavals of civil war, it is odd that America has so little appreciation for the difficulties of establishing and maintaining democracy. We have lived through times where sovereignty, self-determination, human dignity, and liberty itself, have been sacrificed on the altar of liberty. These are dangerous precedents and, though the Afghanistan and Iraq wars are ongoing tragedies, they should teach future generations that although liberty may be a prerequisite for the achievement of anything, and though choice may be intrinsically worthwhile, liberty, this 'individuality made normative', is not more than the blank canvass of man.

Turning our attention from liberty to security, we might begin by noting the failure of the promise of the new world order of security after the erosion of empires and the solemn formation of the United Nations. Leaving aside the fact that the end of the Second World War heralded the beginning of multiple conflicts in the Third World, in the so-called developed world, common understandings of actions beyond the pale of executive competence made possible by the horrors of the Holocaust, reciprocal deference of the five permanent members of the Security Council, and unprecedented levels of intercontinental trade were envisioned as stakes in the earth propping up global security.[25]

How fragile that security seems. For Margaret Thatcher's Britain, security was threatened by allowing the voice of the leader of Sinn Féin, accused of being a terrorist leader, to be heard on television. Apparently, it was safer for an actor to read a transcript of the words of the Irish Republican politician.[26] Similarly, for the Russians and Chinese, critical journalism endangered security.[27] As the Americans under Bush understood it, security was jeopardised by allowing detainees to communicate with their families or lawyers. These attitudes did not seem coherent with Lockean liberality. The suppression of dissent seems inadvertently to verify the criticism. The banning of Gerry Adams' voice arguably increased his prominence and that of his cause. Savvy authors will contrive to have the publication of their books banned to increase circulation.

Misconceived measures taken to increase security have a tendency to increase insecurity. In a world where scientists can be bought and plans stolen, history has demonstrated that a sure way to provide our arch-enemies with weaponry to destroy us is to design it ourselves. One of the best demonstrations of this was the Chechen usage of Soviet-made air defence missiles, procured on the collapse of

23 *ibid.*

24 EJ Hobsbawm, *Globalisation, democracy and terrorism* (Little Brown, 2007) 60.

25 M Byers, *War law: international law and armed conflict* (Atlantic Books, 2005) 26.

26 *Brind and others v Home Secretary* [1991] All ER 720.

27 GP Fletcher, *Romantics at war: glory and guilt in the age of terrorism* (Princeton University Press, 2002) 132.

the Soviet Union, to shoot down Russian helicopters and aircraft.[28] Again, measures taken to increase security exacerbated insecurity.

On the global plane, it seems that the modern instantiation of the idea that trade between neighbours could be substituted for war between neighbours coincided, immediately after World War II, with a dramatic increase in the destructive potential of weaponry. From the AK-47 to the A-bomb, it seemed that you got more bang for your buck. The trading neighbours also realised the lucrative nature of the arms trade; that you got more buck for your bang. The result of this has been that 'most effective states have lost the absolute monopoly of coercive force, not least thanks to the flood of new, small, portable instruments of destruction, now easily accessible to small dissident groups, and the extreme vulnerability of modern life to sudden disruption, however slight'.[29] Again, due to insufficient prudence, and a comforting suspicion in the arms trade, from manufacturer to vendor to buyer to user, that someone else was to blame, measures taken to increase security, actually increased insecurity.

Another example of how ostensible efforts to improve security might in fact result in insecurity is the usage of immigration regulations to deport, detain, or otherwise pester minority communities. What is odd about such measures is that though they originated in federal echelons, their use has been resisted in local communities by police officers who understand that such haranguing and harassment is more likely to antagonise minorities and erode support for the police officers, making their job more trying.[30] Again, security measures can endanger communities and provoke violence. In the North of England, for example, it would be imprudent in the extreme further to alienate Muslims, pushing them towards the resentment that turns, by shades, into reactionary radicalism.

The issue of nuclear terrorism is a helpful bridge between the topics of security and rationality. Earlier, I noted the imagery of a New York Nagasaki or a British Hiroshima, used to drive the military incursions into the Middle East. At the apex of his unpopularity, former Prime Minister Tony Blair said it was not 'utterly fanciful' to 'imagine states sponsoring nuclear terrorism from their soil'.[31] This may well be the case, but the posturing of UK and US governments has sent the message that it is safer for states to have, than it is for them not to have, nuclear weapons. Iran seems to have compared the accommodating allied treatment of North Korea, a nuclear power, with the aggressive approach to Iraq and Afghanistan, both non-nuclear powers, and come to the perfectly reasonable

[28] M Kramer, 'The Perils of Counterinsurgency – Russia's War in Chechnya' (2004) I *Security* 4, 32.

[29] E J Hobsbawm, *Globalisation, democracy and terrorism* (Little Brown, 2007) 102.

[30] CL Eisgruber and LG Sager, 'Civil Liberties in the Dragon's Domain' in ML Dudziak (ed), *September 11 in History: A Watershed Moment?* (Duke University Press, 2003) 166.

[31] 'UK Nuclear Plans', *BBC*, 4 December 2006, available at: news.bbc.co.uk/2/hi/uk_news/politics/6205174.stm.

conclusion, based on the evidence to hand, that the best way to ensure its own security is to develop nuclear capabilities.[32] Holmes argues that nuclear weapons are factors of destruction – they are Western contributions to Western insecurity.[33] We must acknowledge, however frightening it might be, 'that only a tiny proportion of the millions of cargo containers arriving each year in the world's ports will ever be opened for inspection'.[34]

Neither the United Kingdom nor the United States has taken steps to reduce their nuclear capacities. The United Kingdom is updating its submarines and Trident weapons systems. The United States is developing battlefield nuclear weapons. Furthermore, if Bush and Blair were genuinely concerned about nuclear weapons ending up in the hands of terrorists, it is unclear why they permitted the ransacking of Iraq's largest nuclear research facility at al-Tuwaitha.[35] The research centre was thought to contain hundreds of tons of natural uranium and nearly two tons of low-enriched uranium, which could be further processed for arms use.[36] The failure to secure the site was either spectacular negligence or persuasive proof of the insincerity of their concerns to prevent nuclear terrorism becoming a reality.[37]

As a matter of fact, the prospect of nuclear terrorism, however improbable, *is* terrifying.[38] Terrorists do not have a fixed abode, and what does seem 'fanciful' is that any state would openly sponsor a first strike, making retaliation a highly dangerous game of chance. To stay in power, governments promise us security. To admit their near defencelessness against this threat would be considered electoral suicide. When fear is mixed with pride, a normal human reaction is to attack – even if it means making an enemy – to conceal our vulnerability.[39] There are circumstances in which this might work but it is fair to say that Western threats of force, heavy-handed use of the armed forces, arbitrary detention, and bloated rhetoric have strengthened, not diminished, sympathy for

[32] JM Schwartz, 'Misreading Islamist Terrorism' in J Margolis, T Rockmore and AT Marsoobian (eds), *The Philosophical Challenge of September 11* (Blackwell Publishing, 2005) 66.

[33] S Holmes, *The Matador's Cape: America's Reckless Response to Terror* (Cambridge University Press, 2007) 331.

[34] In DS Hamilton, *Terrorism and international relations* (Calouste Gulbenkian Foundation; Center for Transatlantic Relations, Paul H Nitze School of Advanced International Studies, Johns Hopkins University, 2006), Gareth Evans 152.

[35] S Holmes, *The Matador's Cape: America's Reckless Response to Terror* (Cambridge University Press, 2007) 115.

[36] 'After the War: Nuclear Fuel', *New York Times*, 24 July 2008 available at: query.nytimes.com/gst/fullpage.html?res=9D01E6DA163BF932A15755C0A9659C8B63&n=Top/Reference/Times%20Topics/Subjects/I/International%20Relations&scp=5&sq=al%20tuwaitha&st=cse.

[37] In *The Great War for Civilisation*, Robert Fisk laments the US military's neglect in preventing the pillaging and destruction of all Iraqi embassies excepting those necessary to the country's oil infrastructure.

[38] RM Frost, *Nuclear terrorism after 9/11* (New York, 2005).

[39] F Nietzsche, *Thus Spoke Zarathustra*, trans RJ Hollingdale (Penguin Classics, 1961 (1883)) 82.

radical Islam.[40] This is what bin Laden meant when he said that, to some commentators, it seemed that he and former President Bush were in cahoots, with the shared goals of rousing the *umma* and draining America's resources. Michael Scheuer was one such commentator:

> U.S. forces and policies are completing the radicalization of the Islamic world, something Osama bin Laden has been trying to do with but incomplete success since the early 1990s. As a result, I think it is fair to conclude that the United States of America remains bin Laden's only indispensable ally.[41]

Robert Kagan buoyantly asserts that Europe is 'enjoying a free ride in terms of global security'.[42] Only if he means a ride on a rickety rollercoaster many of us want to get off is he correct. How many thinking Europeans feel safer for the presence of an unprincipled, nuclear hyperpower? How many sensible Londoners felt safer for the alliance with Bush?

It might be said that the partial displacement of religion in the United Kingdom and America left the seat of objective truth empty and it has been occupied by a distinctly fundamental belief in the rational merits of liberal democracy plus capitalism. Kagan argues that the 'central point of Francis Fukuyama's famous essay, "The End of History", was irrefutable: The centuries-long struggle among opposing conceptions of how mankind might govern itself had been definitively settled in favor of the Western liberal ideal'.[43] Of course, I do not dispute that liberal democracy, properly understood, has very attractive features (to capitalism, I come later). Moreover, these features could well reduce the incidence of terrorist violence in the world. But to argue that the Western liberal ideal is irrefutably, definitively the best possible way for mankind to govern itself smacks not of liberalism but of fundamentalism, for though liberalism is designed to allow all to live, within certain bounds, in the manner each sees fit, it is distinctly *illiberal* to argue that such liberalism is the only way to oversee human life on earth.

What, for example, if a community, after long consideration and rational debate, decides, quite reasonably, having road-tested the Western liberal ideal and found it morally wanting and insufficiently communal, that it might be best able to ensure peaceable flourishing and happiness by dedicating itself to a religious code, necessitating study and charity but obviating the need for formal suffrage and usury? Would such a society be backward? Would it be a miraculous historical anomaly? Hardly. On the other hand, it is arrogant, oppressive and, albeit in a paradoxical sense, *illiberal* to argue that the Western liberal ideal is a one-size-fits-all answer to human society. That this protest is unfathomable to the

[40] R Dreyfuss, *Devil's Game – How the United States helped unleash fundamentalist Islam* (Metropolitan Books, Henry Holt and Company, 2005) 16.

[41] M Scheuer, *Imperial Hubris* (Brassey's, 2004) xv.

[42] R Kagan, *Of paradise and power : America and Europe in the new world order*, 1st edn (Alfred A Knopf: Distributed by Random House, 2003) 54.

[43] *ibid*, 81.

pied pipers of the Western liberal ideal does not prove the primitivity, backwardness, or barbarity of the protest; instead it betrays the sanctimony, ignorance and parochialism of the pipers. It is easy for pro-democratic intervention to be tainted as condescension, and easier still in circumstances where the interveners claimed pro-democratic intentions only as an afterthought.[44]

Whether or not it was right or legal to launch the wars in Afghanistan and Iraq, the manner of their conduct might well have drastically reduced our security. Irrespective of the real motivations for war-making, attacks that are perceived to be driven by hatred and intolerance incite hatred and intolerance. Niccoló Machiavelli wrote that no matter how powerful one's armies, in order to enter a country one needs the goodwill of the inhabitants.[45] In wars ostensibly rescuing populations from the barbaric Taliban and the tyrannical Saddam that goodwill should have been easy to establish and preserve, but it was squandered by the manner and conduct of our operations. How are Iraqis to distinguish between one set of torturers and another? What effect did the total absence of post-conflict plans for democracy have on Iraqi faith in their new stewards?

In Iraq, on 26 April 2004, US helicopter gunships and tanks fired on a mosque in Fallujah, toppling its minaret. It was reported that insurgents were using the mosque to pin down marines with rocket-propelled grenades and small arms fire.[46] The point here is not to criticise the targeting of a religious building, perhaps justified in the circumstances, if it had been converted into an insurgent stronghold. But, immediate military advantage aside, the symbolic resonance of destroying holy buildings ought to be part of the calculus. Such destruction represents a public relations triumph for radical Islamists, not least because it is a violation of America's obligations under the 1954 Hague Convention on Cultural Property.

In war, these actions can be difficult to avoid – the difficulty of avoiding them should be part of the decision to resort to war in the first place. In the case of the minaret, calling in air support might have made sense, but if the war is really 'on terror' it most certainly did not. In a war, where troops are billeted all over a country, they inevitably disrupt, but more probably, injure and kill the local population.[47] Where terrorists, who blend into the local population with greater ease than soldiers, are the targets, the risk of injury to civilians and incurring their hatred increases exponentially.

[44] A similar point was well made by Rabinder Singh, in his lecture, at the London School of Economics, entitled 'Iraq and the Law', 14 November 2007.

[45] G Bull, *Niccoló Machiavelli, The Prince* (Penguin Classics, 2003) 9.

[46] J Burns, 'The Struggle for Iraq', *New York Times*, 27 April 2004, available at: query.nytimes.com/gst/fullpage.html?res=990CE0D9113AF934A15757C0A9629C8B63&scp=1&sq=fallujah%20US%20bomb%20mosque%202004&st=cse.

[47] N Machiavelli, *The Prince*, trans G Bull (Penguin Classics, 2003) 11.

Fallujah was the site of another public relations disaster for US forces, prolonging the bitter conflict.[48] On 28 April 2003, the 82nd Airborne Division took up a position in a school. According to local clergymen, the parents were incensed at the commandeering of the school. They marched on its gates to demonstrate. The American soldiers, fearing they were under siege, fired on the crowd and, according to the local clergymen, wounded 70 and killed 20. 82nd Airborne say they were fired upon first, and dispute the numbers. The fact of the matter is that such gross miscalculations, perhaps inevitable in a war, are public relations suicide in a war on terrorism. Moreover, the Allied forces exposed themselves to criticism for genocidal behaviour. In the minds of residents of Fallujah, America had come to destroy Islam, and hated Iraqis.

The treatment of Iraqi prisoners did nothing to dispel this impression. Three members of the same 82nd Airborne Division said that in their 2003 and 2004 tours, the beating of Iraqi prisoners for amusement was routine.[49] Measures which are, or appear to be driven by hatred and intolerance provoke hatred and intolerance in return. In a war on terrorists, intelligence as to their networks, infiltration of their cells and surveillance of their activities are all localised, precision instruments. The Allied campaign in Fallujah was something akin to picking teeth with a cutlass.

Furthermore, in legal terms, according to the International Military Tribunal's Nürnberg Trial, the International Law Commission, and the jurisprudence of the International Tribunal for the Former Yugoslavia, it is a violation of the customs of war to seize, destroy or wilfully damage religious or educational institutions – here mosques and schools.[50] When such acts are coupled with discriminatory intent, they qualify as persecution. Aside from the staggering inefficacy of these tactics, the US are in clear breach of the laws of war, and are perilously close to committing the crime against humanity of persecution. American democracy betrayed its virtue in Iraq. Working its will among the people it has found itself woefully inadequate and unprincipled. Is democracy to be delivered by war criminals?

The presidential pleiad had more bright ideas. In the story of Melibee and Dame Prudence in Chaucer's *The Canterbury Tales*, Seint Jerome's counsel is as

[48] For conflicting accounts, see M Gordon, 'Why Falluja remains a crossroads', *New York Times*, 9 April 2004, available at: www.nytimes.com/2004/04/09/international/middleeast/09FALL.html?ex=1217044800&en=67c0114a875b3f0f&ei=5070; and in Mark Juergensmeyer, 'Debunking the myths' in DS Hamilton, *Terrorism and international relations* (Calouste Gulbenkian Foundation; Center for Transatlantic Relations Paul H Nitze School of Advanced International Studies Johns Hopkins University, 2006) 54.

[49] E Schmitt, '3 in 82nd Airborne Say Beating Iraqi Prisoners Was Routine', *New York Times*, 24 September 2005, available at: www.nytimes.com/2005/09/24/politics/24abuse.html?scp=1&sq=fallujah%2082nd%20airborne&st=cse.

[50] *Prosecutor v Naletilic and Martinovic*, ICTY (2003) Case No IT-98–34-T, paras 205–7; and see generally H Abtahi, 'The Protection of Cultural Property in Times of Armed Conflict: The Practice of the International Criminal Tribunal for the Former Yugoslavia' (2001) 14 *Harvard Human Rights Journal* 1.

follows: 'Dooth somme goode dedes that the devel, which is oure enemy, ne fynde yow nat unocupied'.[51] The modern version of this advice is that the idle mind is the devil's workshop. With respect to military strategy, this has been taken to mean that it is far better to enlist rather than to disband the military in an enemy state. As Holmes points out, Lt Paul Bremer III et al's decision to strip Iraqi men of their livelihood was hardly likely to endear the Americans to the local population.[52] Furthermore, if tyranny was the real target, then the Iraqi soldiers could be expected to hate it as much as any other human being, and would have been obvious and valuable allies. If however, the Iraq war was more a matter of venting primitive revenge instincts against a badly defined racial group, the disbanding of the army made perfect sense. That the latter is not some fantastical theory was supported by former President Bush's speech on the fifth anniversary of Operation Iraqi Freedom. Instead of referring to the Iraqi troops as soldiers, as dictated by the reciprocal respect of warring nations, the President chose the term 'death squads'.[53] One can expect embattled troops to develop stylised perceptions of their enemies but it is disappointing to hear such polemics from civilian leadership.

Another problem with Iraq and Afghanistan is that both required swiftness of action like any military campaign, but then strength in numbers to stabilise the new order. Machiavelli counselled as follows:

> [N]el pigliare uno stato, debbe l'occupatore di esso discorrere tutte quelle offese che li é necessario fare; e tutte farle a un tratto, per non le avere a rinnovare ogni di, e potere, non le innovando, assicurare li uomini e guadagnarseli con benificarli. Chi fa altrimenti, o per timiditá o per mal consiglio, é sempre necessitato tenere el coltello in mano; né mai puó fondarsi sopra li sua sudditi non si potendo quelli per le fresche e continue iniurie assicurare di lui.[54]

> [W]hen he seizes a state the new ruler must determine all the injuries that he will need to inflict. He must inflict them once for all, and not have to renew them every day, and in that way he will be able to set men's minds at rest and win them over to him when he confers benefits. Whoever acts otherwise, either through timidity or misjudgement, is always forced to have the knife ready in his hand and he can never depend on his subjects because they, suffering fresh and continuous violence, can never feel secure with regard to him.[55]

There are two points to make here. First, that a sixteenth century strategist could have picked holes in the Allied strategy in Iraq casts doubt on the assertion that we are facing a new variety of enemy. The weapons might be different, but the

[51] G Chaucer, *The Canterbury Tales* (Various publishers, 14th Century), The Tale of Melibee, 1595.

[52] P Bremer, 'How I didn't dismantle Iraq's Army', *New York Times*, 6 September 2007, available at: www.nytimes.com/2007/09/06/opinion/06bremer.html.

[53] G Bush and G Brown, at 5th Anniversary of Operation Iraqi Freedom (2008).

[54] Niccoló Machiavelli, *Il Principe* (La Riflessione, 2006) 24.

[55] G Bull, *Niccoló Machiavelli, The Prince* (Penguin Classics, 2003) 32.

enemies are men, as they always have been. Second, the failure within the failure to put enough boots on the ground in Afghanistan and Iraq led to the sort of protracted, insufferable quotidian insecurity that stirs resentment and hatred for any invading force. The benefits which have been conferred are too little, too late. Again, legal and moral disputes aside, the American-led invasion of Iraq displayed an amateurish misunderstanding of military prudence.

Understandably struggling to hold down the flaps on their makeshift democratic tent, American soldiers became easy targets for insurrectionist attacks. William Scheuerman observed that

> US forces respond to suicide bombings and indiscriminate acts of insurgent violence by themselves killing and abusing civilians. This spiral, of course, has worked to fan the flames of burgeoning anti-Americanism – in other words, precisely what al-Qaeda needs in order to thrive.[56]

Five years after the invasion, with the war still raging, then President Bush said that, the 'speed, precision and brilliant execution of the campaign will be studied by military historians for years to come'.[57] Indeed.

The point I am trying to make here is that military tactics and ethics, rationality and morality, far from being in conflict, often go hand-in-hand. What seem to be ruthless measures taken to improve security often decrease security in the long run. A further demonstration is the 'flypaper effect'. For bin Laden's foot-soldiers, the US-led incursion of Afghanistan and Iraq was, apart from textbook government-baiting, the mountain come to Mohammed. The presence of troops in the Middle East obviated the need for radicalised fighters to travel to kill 'infidels'. Far from pressing terrorists to the wall, America reduced al-Qaeda's operational expenses. According to the flypaper theory, most terrorists would be drawn to the two Middle Eastern battlegrounds, protecting Americans at home. This was all very well for the meantime, assuming an unlimited supply of flypaper. Long ago then, the Iraq war created a recruitment centre, a boot camp, and a live theatre, which has served to enlist, ossify and radicalise future enemies of America and its allies. It is now common knowledge that Iraq had no links whatsoever to al-Qaeda. The same cannot be said after six years of this war. And what happens when the flypaper is removed?

As Richard Dreyfuss puts it, 'a problem that could have been dealt with surgically – using commandos and Special Forces, aided by tough-minded diplomacy, indictments and legal action, concerted international efforts, and judicious self-defense measures – was vastly inflated by the Bush administration'.[58] One basic effect of withdrawal from the Middle East might be

[56] WE Scheuerman, 'Carl Schmitt and the Road to Abu Ghraib' (2006) 13(1) *Constellations* 108.

[57] G Bush and G Brown, on 5th Anniversary of Operation Iraqi Freedom (2008).

[58] R Dreyfuss, *Devil's Game – How the United States helped unleash fundamentalist Islam* (Metropolitan Books, Henry Holt & Company, 2005) 13.

further terrorist attacks in Europe and America. Osama bin Laden claims he only wants 'infidels' to 'leave our fields', but he can hardly be described as having direct operational control over the vast, disparate and sprawling network that is al-Qaeda. Tony Blair passed this poisoned chalice to Gordon Brown. President Obama must drink from it too. The new enemies will not be disillusioned, inexperienced novices, like the half-wits who drove a 4x4 into Glasgow airport and set themselves on fire, or the inept Piccadilly bombers. They will be battle-hardened, hate-filled, ideologically rigid, operations-savvy guerrilla warriors. Absorbing the hate created by Afghanistan and Iraq, and, on withdrawal, withstanding the inevitable terrorist attacks might be even more difficult than it was to react in a proportionate manner to September 11.[59] Once again, it was imprudent to sweep aside considerations of legality and morality; measures taken to improve security have further imperiled us in the long-term.

The irrational nature of the response to terrorism has infected legal thought too. Take the following excerpt from the extraordinary Mr Yoo and his co-writer, Robert Delahunty, as an example:

> Although customary international law does not bind the President, the President may still use his constitutional warmaking authority to subject members of al Qaeda or the Taliban militia to the laws of war. While this result may seem at first glance to be counter-intuitive, it is a product of the President's Commander in Chief and Chief Executive powers to prosecute the war effectively.[60]

Almost identical statements by legal scholars can be found in support of Hitler's prerogative powers. In plain English, Yoo's legal doctrine means that America is considered above the laws of war it helped establish and by which it expects its enemies to abide. It is a double-standard. A double-standard may seem useful in certain circumstances, like lying, or cheating, but it is of limited utility to a legal system in a liberal democracy, or, for that matter, in an international society comprising independent and equal sovereign states. More will be said on this sort of 'lawyering', if that is not too gracious a term, shortly.

This mention of double-standards brings me back to the terrible practice of torture. Alan Dershowitz, who has been demonised by that queer breed of liberals who do not believe in debate, suggested a system of judicial warrants for torture.[61] His complaint about America's usage of torture was that it was hypocritical. Better, he says, in a liberal democracy to torture openly according to a procedure established by the regular legislative method and subject to judicial oversight, than to cart people off to secret prisons and torture them secretly in

[59] Perversely, the best hope for security from terrorist attack might be civil war in Afghanistan and Iraq. Sadly, neither country appears stable.

[60] J Yoo and R Delahunty, 'Memorandum for Alberto Gonzales and William J Haynes, 'Re: Authority for Use of Military Force to Combat Terrorist Activities Within the United States', 17 October 2001.

[61] A Dershowitz, 'Tortured Reasoning' in S Levinson (ed), *Torture: A collection* (Oxford University Press, 2004).

the absence of any form of accountability. His suggestion might seem wrong-headed, but it is far less pernicious and far more coherent than the carte blanche approach proposed by the extraordinary Mr Yoo. The problem with the judicial instantiation of torture is, well, *nulla poena sine lege*. Even if torture is conducted in the clinical, sterilised, institutionalised manner envisioned by the Harvard professor, it is still punishment without proof of crime. Whether meted out behind closed doors far from accountability à la Yoo, or surgically administered in glass-walled torture chambers per Dershowitz, torture is an instrument of tyranny entirely inimical to legality and, I argue, liberal democracy.

Having criticised the approach of society to liberty, security and rationality, it is time to envision how a liberal democracy might respond to terrorism in a manner that preserves defensible notions of those three ideals, upholds a version of legality not evocative of palm trees, and in so doing, enables us to manifest some sort of collective integrity.

Barring genetic intervention, or the ego's conquest of the id, the human propensity for violence is ineradicable. Potential terrorists live among us and within us. In 1951, when the United States faced a different enemy, George Kennan wrote:

> something may occur in our own minds and souls which will make us no longer like the persons by whose efforts this republic was founded and held together, but rather like representatives of that very power we are trying to combat: intolerant, secretive, suspicious, cruel, and terrified of internal dissension because we have lost our own belief in ourselves and in the power of our ideals.[62]

So long as we have dynamite, disgruntlement and disenfranchisement there will be terrorism. The way to beat terrorism then, is to rid the world of those three factors, or at least stop them coming together in a combustible combination. Dynamite and disgruntlement would seem to be ineffaceable so the answer must be enfranchisement. But there is many a logical mile between this premise and the conclusion that ballot boxes should be delivered in armoured vehicles to the Middle East. That intelligent politicians currently trying to expedite this delivery can, straight-faced, spout absurd predictions about how long it will take to win the fight against terrorism, is unsettling. Their ability to make such forecasts is more likely attributable to an expertise in 'doublethink' than it is to genuine belief.

Thanks to the recklessness of Bush and the fecklessness of Blair, terrorism is here to stay for the foreseeable future. Consequently, there is no need for rushed policies or hasty legislation. Western polities need a rational, collective, long-term plan. Clive Walker suggests the institution of an 'investigative standing committee' to keep anti-terrorist legislation under constant review. He considers this approach superior to 'current-time slice' investigations such as those conducted

[62] GF Kennan, 'Where Do You Stand on Communism?' *New York Times Magazine*, 27 May 1951.

by Shackleton and Jellicoe. The enduring nature of the committee would allow it to acquire expertise in legal methods for the combat of terrorism.[63] Such a committee might be a good idea, so long as it is populated by people with not only legal brains, but also experience in counter-insurgency and enough memory or enough learning of the 'troubles' in Northern Ireland, and the glaring governmental botches of that era and the current campaign.

Subject to that suggestion, one very practical thing we can do to reduce the effect of terrorism on our lives is to worry about it less. (For those who do not worry about it – as you were.) For a start, learning to live with life's precariousness is to increase one's sense of well-being. Moreover, in the West, the chance of dying in a terrorist attack is still very low. Rather than expending their energies suspiciously eyeing the local mosque, many Brits could redirect that energy towards drinking or smoking or driving less, with far greater immediate boons in their physical security than come from glowering at the local Muslim population. Communicating with Muslims might help too. Further, there is precious little we can do to defend ourselves against those who have no concern for their own lives, except to create a world in which people do not elect to blow themselves up in the first place.[64] Again, this is not idealism, but a matter of political empowerment. This is not bleeding heart socialism but cold logic, because, angry nihilists aside (and, fortunately, of that ilk there are very few), terrorism is resorted to for two reasons:

(i) I cannot beat this enemy without undermining its support by killing civilians.
(ii) I cannot achieve my aims through peaceful politics.

Terrorism is the weapon of the weak. To prevent terrorism in the first place (remembering the lessons of the Report on the Responsibility to Protect) political enfranchisement and social empowerment are the best weapons in the armoury of a liberal democracy, particularly a healthy one.[65] This does not mean that terrorists or terrorist masterminds come from politically disabled or socially emasculated communities. Far from it.[66] But they do, without fail, purport to act for, and rely on the support of, such communities for their popularity, and frequently enough, for their suicidal foot-soldiers. (Remember the lesson of the Basque language). To a large extent, security is enhanced by the protection of other people's liberties and diminished by encroachment thereupon. On the basis of a historical survey of the liberal democratic response to terrorism, Paul Wilkinson argues that there is 'overwhelming historical evidence that effective and preferably timely programmes of political and socio-economic reform are the best antidote against the rise of anti-democratic mass movements of the

[63] CD Walker, *The prevention of terrorism in British law* (Dover NH, 1986).
[64] N Machiavelli, *The Prince*, trans G Bull (Penguin Classics, 2003) 65.
[65] See ch 3 above, fn 80.
[66] M Sageman, *Understanding terror networks* (University of Pennsylvania Press, 2004).

extreme left or the extreme right'.[67] Nowadays, the pre-emption of anger must take place on a global scale; paradoxically the socio-economic empowerment of the Middle East is the best defence for the West. In sum, oppressing others is an effective way to endanger oneself, unless you annihilate them completely, per Machiavelli – which presumably is not in the contemplation of Western governments.

> The best fortress that exists is to avoid being hated by the people. If you have fortresses and yet the people hate you they will not save you; once the people have taken up arms they will never lack outside help.[68]

After September 11, the question, 'Why do they hate us?' was debated by Americans. There has been some mockery of this inquiry. In the mouths of some, the question was a positive exercise in self-reflection but for others, it was accompanied by wounded innocence. Several points can be made about, and in response to the question. First, the distinction between 'they' and 'we' is incoherent, and ultimately unhelpful. This question is side-stepped here to be confronted in the next chapter on amity and enmity. Second, America's prominence, opulence and success might evoke jealousy and even hatred. Third, if 'they' are Muslims and 'we' are Americans and co, then the overlap between Islamic values and our values is huge. There is more reason for amity than enmity. (More on this soon.) Fourth, Mohsin Hamid was correct to say that US interventions abroad, which are mere footnotes (if that) in American history, are the titles of chapters to other communities.[69] In respect of the chapter in the history of Afghanistan entitled 'Repelling the Soviets', Dreyfuss argues that 'there is no question that the U.S. support for the mujahideen … devastated Afghanistan itself, led to the collapse of its government, and gave rise to a landscape dominated by warlords both Islamist and otherwise'.[70] Furthermore, apart from its active interventions, few Americans are aware of the sheer passive presence of America abroad.

> If there were an honest count, the actual size of our military empire would probably top 1,000 different bases in other people's countries, but no one – possibly not even the Pentagon – knows the exact number for sure, although it has been distinctly on the rise in recent years.[71]

Notwithstanding the nobility of American intentions on some of its international adventures, foreign policy is a game of risk, and, to give only the simplest

[67] P Wilkinson, *Terrorism versus democracy : the liberal state response* (Routledge, 2001) 79.

[68] G Bull, *Niccoló Machiavelli, The Prince* (Penguin Classics, 2003) 70.

[69] M Hamid, 'Why do they hate us?' *Washington Post*, 22 July 2007, available at: www.washingtonpost.com/wp-dyn/content/article/2007/07/20/AR2007072001806.html.

[70] R Dreyfuss, *Devil's Game – How the United States helped unleash fundamentalist Islam* (Metropolitan Books, Henry Holt and Company, 2005) 288.

[71] C Johnson, 'The Arithmetic of America's Military Bases Abroad' (2004) HN Network available at: hnn.us/articles/3097.html.

example, helping one people, however altruistically, might cause irreparable damage to another, generating the hatred that manifests itself in violent extremism.

Discounting total lunatics, the chances of a human being concluding not only that it is a capital idea, but a personal duty to blow themselves up, or in some other way jeopardise the lives of innocent civilians, are vanishingly slim. Jealousy of opulence or freedom, discarding the pathologically obsessive, simply will not provide that impetus, and the human survival instinct and generally limited moral concern vouchsafes that no amount of indoctrination will compel even the least robust-minded of lemmings to explode themselves because of the moral degradation or plight of a distant society.

By contrast, two factors, which will provide more than ample motivation are the invasion of homelands real or imaginary, and the murdering, injuring or raping of kin, real or perceived. Negotiating with terrorists is not generally necessary, but listening to understand their grievances can be very helpful in the attempt to undermine their support and stem the flow of terrorist attacks. That said, it is a mistake, in a world where private actors can amass enormous wealth, to assume that terrorists need the support of the masses. Attentiveness to grievances does, however, remove the temptation to turn to terrorism. In this context, we can observe that the consistent message of al-Qaeda's figurehead has been 'we will not cease our raids until you leave our fields', and that 'which ever state does not encroach upon our security thereby ensures its own'.[72]

Truth be told, military bases abroad often do little to provide security at home and many state security measures at harbours and airports are, at best, akin to closing the garden gates to keep out ravens. Moreover, it is impossible to provide security for every possible target, particularly when terrorists are unscrupulous enough to attack soft targets like cafés, train stations and theatres. This is why terrorism can be so effective. It is high impact (depending on the malleability of the target government) and cheap. The London transport bombings on 7 July 2005 cost less than a good bottle of whisky.[73] Fact: terrorists can continue perpetrating their heinous crimes inexpensively for the foreseeable future.

In contrast, military deployments in foreign countries are vastly expensive. The operations in Afghanistan and Iraq drain our economies, damage our moral standing and increase the threat of terrorist revenge attacks. These problems pale into insignificance alongside those of our troops. The difficulties they face are reminiscent of those confronting the Russians fighting an almost contemporaneous counter-insurgency in Chechnya. Lt General Evgennii Abrashin complained that Russian 'forces are so busy just trying to ensure their own security' they never get around to fighting the 'resurgent guerrillas'.[74] Unlike the Russians

[72] B Lawrence (ed), *Messages to the World: The Statements of Osama bin Laden* (Verso, 2005).

[73] EJ Hobsbawm, *Globalisation, democracy and terrorism* (Little Brown, 2007) 141.

[74] M Kramer, 'The Perils of Counterinsurgency – Russia's War in Chechnya' (2004) 29 *International Security* 4, 9, 20.

(though I doubt it), we might have the upper hand, although whether it is worth having is up for discussion. Just as for the Russians, under-staffing, poor equipment, inhospitable conditions, god-awful food, and a suspicion that there is no end in sight to wars being fought for all the wrong reasons mean that morale is understandably dwindling. To make matters worse, the constant threat of sudden death or debilitating injury posed by land mines, improvised explosive devices and mortar attacks ensures that our troops are constantly on edge, operating under high levels of psychological stress.[75]

Detention is also very costly in financial terms. Arbitrary detention and torture have other non-pecuniary costs outlined above. Prudence does not militate for such tactics. Though there are those who speak of the usefulness of 'human intelligence', a CIA euphemism for information procured by torture, it is no substitute for good old-fashioned spy-work, such as surveillance and infiltration.[76] An executive using torture instead of surveillance, infiltration, phone-tapping and surprise searches is like a carpenter using a hammer to smash screws into wood. Information procured in these old-fashioned ways (with the possible exception of bugged calls) has the advantage of utility in future trials. Information procured by torture cannot be used in court (though there is some leniency towards evidence procured by foreign torture) and, as Guantánamo Bay evidences, actually functions as an obstacle to bringing people to justice.[77] Detainees against whom there is cogent evidence are not being tried for fear of them telling tales of their maltreatment. This creates a situation in which causing people to disappear or letting them languish in jail is preferable to criminal justice; hardly a policy becoming of a civilised liberal democracy.

Worse still for an administration which has opted for policies of systematic torture are detainees who turn out to be innocent. The case of Mr Khalid El-Masri, a German citizen, is a salutary example.[78] He alleged that, after being abducted whilst holidaying in Macedonia, whisked away to a detention unit and tortured for five months, it became clear to his CIA custodians that, due to the similarity of his name to that of their target, they had intercepted the wrong man. Instead of having the simple human decency to return him to his life, his job and his family in Germany (who, in any event had given him up for dead and moved away) his tormentors released him, of all places, on an Albanian mountainside.

El-Masri's innocence was not in any doubt, but even if he had been the most odious of international terrorists, responsible for orchestrating the deaths of

[75] 'Are British troops at breaking point in Iraq?' *The Independent*, 18 October 2005, available at www.independent.co.uk/news/world/middle-east/are-british-troops-at-breaking-point-in-iraq-511404.html.

[76] PB Heymann, *Terrorism, Freedom and Security* (MIT Press, 2003) 121.

[77] See for a note on the state of play in the UK, RS Brown, 'The House of Lords Ruling on Torture: A and Others v Secretary of State for the Home Department' (2006) 15 *Italian Yearbook of International Law* 153.

[78] *El-Masri v United States* (Fourth Circuit Opinion, 2 March 2007).

thousands of innocent, non-combatant Americans, the treatment he allegedly suffered at the hands of the CIA operatives would have been illegal under settled international law, including two of the most important instruments of world order, namely the Convention against Torture and the Geneva Conventions. Abduction and torture are the tools of global tyranny, not of any self-respecting liberal democracy.

Such actions also risk bringing the entire domestic justice system into disrepute. In October 2007, the US Supreme Court declined to entertain an appeal against a holding in the Fourth Circuit that the state secrets privilege prevented the courts from hearing El-Masri's claim.[79] One hopes that the invocation of the privilege is not simply the administration's desire to cover up its spectacular ineptitude and suppress the crimes against humanity it has committed in the name of freedom. The worst feature of this story (if it is possible to single one out) is that there is no need for an administration fighting terrorism to trample on civil liberties, resort to these medieval means, and create embarrassing situations for itself. As Phillip Heymann has argued,

> there is every reason to believe that our court system can handle a case of anyone arrested in the US for planning terrorism, at least if the arrest is delayed long enough for investigators to learn what they are seeking to learn about other participants and the nature of the plan; for by then, they will also have enough information to charge and convict for a crime of conspiracy.[80]

The holidaying El-Masri, on his way to Macedonia, can hardly have presented an imminent threat to American security. Far cheaper, much slicker, and infinitely more effective would have been simply to tag, track and tail him for a spell. Instead, America's agents squandered money, time, manpower and their international reputation.

In the British context, Walker has made a similar point:

> Proscription and exclusion probably make police work more difficult, the former by encouraging secrecy, the latter by removing suspects from known haunts and contacts … as the police recognise, there is little advantage in prosecuting petty offenders, there is a great deal more to be gained by keeping them under surveillance and following the leads they provide.[81]

These arguments are backed up by the social anthropology of terrorism. I would argue that the main practical lesson of Marc Sageman's study of terror networks is that effective intelligence is needed to unravel them.[82] Clumsy military and executive action only stoke the fires of religious fundamentalism, giving terror networks based on a radical interpretation of Islam a Medusa-like capacity. Terror networks grow out of close social ties, and mesh with almost brotherly

[79] *El-Masri v United States* 128 S Ct 373 (2007).

[80] PB Heymann, *Terrorism, Freedom and Security* (MIT Press, 2003) 171.

[81] CD Walker, *The prevention of terrorism in British law* (Dover NH, 1986) 179.

[82] M Sageman, *Understanding terror networks* (University of Pennsylvania Press, 2004).

alliances and militaristic loyalty. Thus, the capture and mishandling of one member, or of a member of the community for which the network purports to act, perpetuates the radicalisation of the node, generates free propaganda for terrorist recruitment drives, and invites revenge attacks.

More effective by far, is information gathering about, and surveillance and infiltration of groups who often move in packs, meet in set locations and live together in close quarters. Such tactics encroach on liberty less, have greater security dividends, and make more sense. Nevertheless, counter-terrorist operations must be conducted with great care. Irrespective of the intelligence assessment that, in the United Kingdom and the United States, the greatest terrorist threat is considered to come from Islamic radicals, this does not justify singling out the Islamic diaspora for surveillance and so forth.[83] Measures taken that harass may be interpreted as racially motivated and further alienate minority communities. Rather than racial profiling, behavioural analysis is far more likely to result in sensible policies and far less likely to inflame the interracial tensions that promote terrorism. Here, measures protecting liberty and security converge rather than diverging; moral policing turns out to be prudent policing. Naturally, none of this prevents police investigating a Muslim community where there is evidence of criminal activity.

At this point, it is worth reporting the alleged botching of the investigation into the plot to use liquid explosives to destroy transatlantic flights. According to the BBC, the Americans jumped the gun, moving on associates in Pakistan, forcing the British hand. NBC reported that a British senior official wanted to wait for evidence that would secure longer convictions. On 9 September 2008, after more than 50 hours of deliberations, the jury did not find any of the defendants guilty of conspiring to target aircraft, though three of the eight men on trial were found guilty of conspiracy to commit murder.[84] This might have been a case of premature incarceration by the Americans, but Frances Townsend, assistant to the President for Homeland Security denies any disagreement with the British authorities. If the men were indeed plotters, an early interference with liberty prevented a conviction, and a long-term gain in security.

A similar observation can be made about the suppression of free speech. Though this will be dealt with in greater detail later, we can note for now that responsible reporting of terrorist attacks and the motivations for those attacks will have two probable effects. First, it allows the common man to condemn the usage of indiscriminate killing for political gain. Second, it allows for the airing of the grievances that (genuinely or otherwise) motivated the attack. The mere airing of those political issues is a form of appeasement, but there is no harm in

[83] JM Schwartz, 'Misreading Islamist Terrorism' in J Margolis, T Rockmore and AT Marsoobian (eds), *The Philosophical Challenge of September 11* (Blackwell Publishing, 2005) 52.

[84] 'Three found guilty in August 2006 UK Liquid Explosives Plot', *Transport Security Administration*, 8 September 2008, available at: www.tsa.gov/press/happenings/terror_plot_hearing.shtm.

increasing visibility of territorial or political claims. Conversely, the suppression of free speech denies the common man the opportunity to judge for himself whether the means used are justified by the ends pursued, and any underreporting or misrepresentation of terrorist gripes merely serve further to exacerbate the underlying frustrations. States should not be afraid to put up for terrorists a platform on which to hang themselves. Again, it does not stand to reason that restricting a liberty has any benefits in terms of security; moral reporting is prudent reporting.

I would like to spend some time here exploring this relationship between what is rational and what is moral because, like the image of liberty being balanced against security, political expediency and morality are often portrayed as opponents. Dante Alighieri, in his diatribe against the moral turpitude in the Church, citizenry and State said that 'among the bitter berries, there is no place for the sweet fig to grow'.[85] This view, that one cannot govern without getting one's hands dirty (Sartre) or that one has to do bad to do good (Machiavelli), has pervaded and perverted the war on terrorism. Frankly, it has produced better literature than it has policy. Although many ancient philosophers like Panaetius adopted the opposite position, that nothing can be advantageous unless it is right and nothing right unless it is advantageous, they found it a hard stance to maintain without reference to spiritual boons for the virtuous man,[86] or fear of punishment in the afterlife: Locke, for example, argued that virtue 'has another relish and efficacy to persuade men, that if they live well here, they shall be happy hereafter'.[87] But it need not be the case that virtue is only justifiable by reference to soteriological, otherworldly gains.

Kagan's ultimately unrealistic romanticisation of the United States as the national embodiment of the mythical, moral outlaw, enforcing the law whilst flouting it with impunity, is a perfect characterisation of the Bush administration's 'dirty hands' mentality. Trying to distance himself from this view, Barak Obama, addressing a Berlin audience, said that, no state, however great, can go it alone. Cicero said that a splendid reputation and the goodwill of their allies are essential for governments, 'so how can unpopularity and infamy possibly be to their advantage?'[88] Indeed, there are prudent reasons for states to abide by the laws by which they expect others to abide, and to adopt a multilateral rather than unilateral stance. Alexander Hamilton enlarged on this:

[85] Dante Alighieri, *The Divine Comedy*, trans M Musa (Penguin Classics, 2003) Canto XV, 66.

[86] 'The perverted intelligences of men who are animated by such feelings are competent to understand the material rewards, but not the penalties. I do not mean the penalties established by law, for these they often escape. I mean the most terrible of all punishments: their own degradation'. M Grant, *Cicero: Selected Works* (Penguin Classics, 1974) 63.

[87] J Locke, *The Works of John Locke* (Thomas Tegg, 1823) 150.

[88] *Cicero: Selected Works*, trans M Grant (Penguin Classics, 1974) 193.

> An attention to the judgement of other nations is important to every government for two reasons: the one is, that, independently of the merits of any particular plan or measure, it is desirable, on various accounts, that it should appear to other nations as the offspring of a wise and honorable policy; the second is, that in doubtful cases, particularly where the national council may be warped by some strong passion or momentary interest, the presumed or known opinion of the impartial world may be the best guide that can be followed.[89]

So, Hamilton provides two entirely prudent reasons for cooperation rather than domination.

Further, open lines of communication, constant consultation, and collaborative enterprise, aside from sweetening diplomatic relations, allow a state to head off conflict before it occurs. Conversely, the sort of global tyranny that has characterised the American response to terrorism, featuring abduction, arbitrary detention of foreign nationals, rendition, missile attacks, targeted killings and torture, has hampered the fight against terrorism by polarising the world, offending allies by encroaching on their territory, maltreating their nationals, and making enemies of communities who get caught up in the poorly targeted, indiscriminate or disproportionate violence.[90] Such actions impede the project of international intelligence, policing and judicial cooperation that can cut across national and cultural boundaries.[91] A good example of collaborative international intelligence in action was the thwarting of the ricin plot by MI5 and the *Direction de la Surveillance du Territoire*.[92] The adoption of means frowned upon by potential partners in counter-terrorism efforts prevents such healthy alliances from forming. Even Machiavelli, the immoral politician's night nurse, advised against princely scrupulousness: 'it cannot be called prowess to kill fellow citizens, to betray friends, to be treacherous, pitiless, irreligious'.[93]

Torture and, for that matter, targeted killings seem to offer short-term gains in security, but have long-term detrimental effects. The ban on torture, a true commitment to liberty, far from being a disability, enables a liberal democracy to retain for itself moral stature, and the legitimacy that comes from a consistency of principle known as the rule of law. And as for targeted killings, how can a liberal democracy try and punish murderers and yet murder foreign citizens, without trial, in its own name? Contrariwise, where a democracy condescends to use torture and targeted killings, it becomes indistinguishable from the criminal

89 A Hamilton, 63 F Papers.

90 P Gilbert, *New Terror New Wars* (Edinburgh University Press, 2003) 92.

91 JM Schwartz, 'Misreading Islamist Terrorism' in J Margolis, T Rockmore and AT Marsoobian (eds), *The Philosophical Challenge of September 11* (Blackwell Publishing, 2005) 54.

92 BW Bamford, 'The United Kingdom's "War Against Terrorism"' (2004) 16:4 *Terrorism and Political Violence* 737, 745.

93 Niccoló Machiavelli, *The Prince*, trans G Bull (Penguin Classics, 2003) 29.

gangs it seeks to exterminate, sacrificing popular support and, for many, vindicating the radical nature of its enemies. In the judicial opinion of the Supreme Court of Israel on the torture of Palestinian detainees, Bharak J expressed these sentiments in the following terms.

> This is the destiny of a democracy: she does not see all means as acceptable, and the ways of her enemies are not always open before her. A democracy must sometimes fight with one arm tied behind her back. Even so, democracy has the upper hand. The rule of law and individual liberties constitute an important aspect of her security stance. At the end of the day, they strengthen her spirit, and this strength allows her to overcome her difficulties.[94]

Having argued that the protection of liberty is fundamental to, not inimical to the protection of security; having extolled her virtues, I would like to say something of her promiscuity. We are entitled, obliged even, to be a touch cynical about liberty. The light from her torch might illuminate but it can also blind. Liberty's proper role is not monarchic but that of a handmaid. Justice is the Queen of all virtues. The man who says that law is for the protection of freedom is worshipping an empty chair.

The extent to which liberty is of any service to men is debatable. All the choices we make are contaminated; every decision of our conscious minds is tainted; each reflection on reflection itself is infected by a prolonged state of affairs, called childhood, over which we had no control. That is to say, all of our free thoughts flow from circumstance governed by chance. We are never free of these beginnings. Our every contemplation, our every action, is to that extent predetermined, coloured and unfree. Moreover, even if we were capable of thoughts unconnected to the station of our departure, however rational we may feel from time to time, much of our conscious activity is instinctive; it is driven not by intelligence and reason, but by instinct and urge.[95] And because we are terrified by this notion of petrified fate, liberty is the most convenient, most emotive, most readily believed of the illusions available to a ruler. This inbuilt impotence, the notion that one's bootstraps are only so long, is anathema to the American way of thinking, of dreaming about self-empowerment through liberty.

Liberty, freedom to choose, can be as much a hindrance as it is a help, and restraints are as much a help as they are a hindrance. Think of the reluctant smile with which a revising undergraduate awakens to a rainy summer's day. Bad weather makes his confinement to the library seem more palatable because his liberty to waste away his youth relaxing on the Backs is restrained. Liberty is the enemy of our student; the rain is his friend. Good goalkeeping coaches will tell their charge to stand up as long as possible not to limit but to increase the options

94 *Public Committee Against Torture in Israel v State of Israel* (1999) HCJ 5100/94, at 37.

95 FW Nietzsche, *Beyond Good and Evil*, trans J Norman (Cambridge University Press, 2002) 86.

available to an oncoming striker, causing him to squander a wealth of choice in embarrassing indecision. The goalkeeper who dives too early makes the striker's choice easy for him by narrowing the range of available options. Liberty is the enemy of the striker, and the hasty goalkeeper is his friend.

In modern Western society, comparatively free of the demands of the Church and no longer in the shadow of the ideal being, where we are crowned and mitred lords over ourselves; we genuflect before mirrors.[96] Today's consumerist society is infused with the ideology of self-creation. The self is no longer something fit only for subordination to a set of ideals but something to which we should aspire, something to be 'found', 'improved' and 'expressed'. But the question of quite how or why the self is to be found, improved and expressed is the source of significant anxiety.[97] We are oppressed not by a lack of choice but by choice. Where am 'I' to be found? By reference to what standards should I improve myself? What should I express and how? These are not trivial questions, and they are burdensome for human beings, who, when confronted with unlimited choice, are hesitant, where they are not paralysed. The Lord's Prayer itself asks that someone else's will be done. This obsession with liberty does represent an important difference between the current secular and the historically more spiritually predisposed man of several generations past. It is worth remembering that liberty pertains to a 'can' rather than an 'ought'. The notion that liberty longs for a meaningful master was never better encapsulated than when Nietzsche asked: 'Are you such a man as *ought* to escape a yoke?'[98]

The disconcerting nature of abundant liberty, accentuated by consumerist society, is indexed to terrorism. Forms of fundamentalism that find their fringe expression in terrorism have at their core a rejection of choice and a repudiation of the value in plurality. Consequently, by subjecting the self to a rigid set of ideals, they combat the cognitive dissonance, the confusion, stemming from the liberty to choose between a bewildering number of versions of the I.[99] Fundamentalism is an aegis for agency and panoply for plurality. Its domination of all aspects of the being liberates the mind from the oppressive task of creating meaning by itself for itself. In this sense, in terrorism, terrorists paradoxically find all the things that are hard to peg down in modern Western society, viz security, dignity, belonging, purpose, identity, self-expression and, perhaps most importantly, liberty, the most meaningful liberty being discernible in enslavement to values.

96 See generally, C Taylor, *In a Secular Age* (Harvard University Press, 2007).

97 R Salecl, 'Worries in a Limitless World' in Peter Goodrich, Lior Barshack and A Schuetz (eds), *Law, Text, Terror* (Glasshouse, 2006).

98 FW Nietzsche, *Thus Spoke Zarathustra*, trans RJ Hollingdale (Penguin Classics, 1961 [1883]) 89.

99 The phrase 'cognitive dissonance' is used by Habermas in J Habermas and J Derrida, *Philosophy in a time of terror: dialogues with Jürgen Habermas and Jacques Derrida* (University of Chicago Press, 2003). The usage of the term here is not an endorsement of his approach to this topic.

Man is emancipated from liberty not only by fundamentalism, but also by law. Through law, we set boundaries on our freedom, precisely in order to make that freedom tolerable. Too much liberty in society results in anarchy in the same way that too much liberty in a man's mind results in cognitive chaos. We tie the bonds of law around ourselves so as not to sully or injure each other in the throes of indecision or orgies of misdeeds. It is a mistake to think of law only as a defender of liberty when its true calling is helpful suppression. Democracy is a particularly compelling reconciliation of liberty and compulsion.

One might argue that a democracy is a society made up of people who wish both to rule and obey and yet neither to rule nor obey – where the people pander to the rulers who pander to the people.[100] From this standpoint, it is easy to understand the fundamentalist distaste for democracy – though a liberal democracy purports to leave space for all faiths, it is inherently Godless, because man is the highest authority. But herein lies democracy's beautiful and pragmatic appeal. This appeal is intoxicating, 'of the people, by the people, for the people', but there is more than a trace of fundamentalism in the uncompromising espousal of democracy, especially when it is falsely equated with liberty or emancipation. Democracy is inherently purposeless. Absent ideas about what to do with our voices, it resembles an exquisitely crafted yacht in want of a crew, charter and captain.

It could be argued that libertarian fundamentalism comes to the fore in pro-democratic intervention – a degree of unmaskable narcissism taints the self-referential promotion of democracy abroad. It is bizarre then on two grounds to intervene in a society to liberate that society. First, liberty requires a master. Liberation for liberty's sake is arguably pointless. Second, it is not clear that liberal democracy contains any more liberty than an autocracy. Indeed, in a liberal democracy, the additional burdens obtain of ruling oneself, and ruling one's rulers. Third, surely it is a contradiction in terms to force a society to become a liberal democracy. As Ignatieff puts it, either 'these premises freely convince others or they are useless. They cannot be imposed, and we violate everything we stand for if we coerce those who do not believe what we do'.[101] Coercion in a democracy is premised on consent, however hypothetical that consent might be. The fabric of this theory will not stretch to cover a foreign society of non-voters. Philosophical chastenings of a meaningless liberty apart, from a more pragmatic slant, it does seem overly ambitious for Western powers so amateurishly to attempt to promote democracy in parts of the world where intelligent, stable autocratic governments are expert in sabotaging it.[102]

[100] FW Nietzsche, *Thus Spoke Zarathustra*, trans RJ Hollingdale (Penguin Classics, 1961 [1883]) 46.

[101] M Ignatieff, *The lesser evil: political ethics in an age of terror* (Edinburgh University Press, 2003) 169.

[102] 'Power Politics: Iran, Saudi Arabia and Leadership in the Muslim World', 16 January 2008, Center on Law and Security at NYU School of Law (Toby Craig Jones).

Having attempted to prescribe more sensible ways of thinking about liberty, security and rationality, I would like, now, to see how these themes relate to those of the foregoing chapters – language and image, war and crime. As has already been noted, the discourse of homeland security had the effect of relocating the American homeland in America.[103] In a sense, this was a consolidation of American identity, but it was an unhealthy one. As Kaplan puts it, talk of the homeland generates insecurity, as it is a place 'haunted by prior and future losses, invasions, abandonments'.[104] This relocation or redefinition of American identity led to a dislocation within America, a drawing of battle lines between true Americans and those to whom that designation was, normally for reasons of ethnicity or perceived difference, denied. Ideas of ethnicity and value can be absorbed into the identity of a community, to be guarded as it would guard its borders, and, as we have seen with liberty, to be projected. The aggressive projection of liberty – vigorous proselytising worship of an empty chair – has manifested itself in a totalising emptiness, an annihilation of all value, excepting the toxic values of shared ethnicity. Guantánamo Bay is the epitome of this annihilation.

It is revealing to consider language and imagery, rationality and security together. Our impressions of events outside our immediate experience are constructed by the media.[105] The wisdom that the printing press is the greatest weapon in a commander's armoury must now be amplified to account for television and the internet. A huge proportion of human experience is channelled through screens. Misdescriptions of events can lead to irrational actions. Afghanistan and Iraq were wrongly described as self-defence because both took place after September 11; worse yet, they were misportrayed as reprisals because the targets in Afghanistan and Iraq had little or nothing to do with the perpetrators of the suicide attacks. Irrational actions stemming from misdescriptions have jeopardised security by sowing seeds of mistrust and hatred. Much of the incoherence in American foreign policy is due to the clothing of blunt romantic urges, namely revenge, in the language of rationality, viz self-defence. But rationality is the best disinfectant for rhetorically contaminated politics. It is a shame that Americans did not stop and really investigate what it was they were being asked to endorse when Bush started catering to their tastes by peppering his speeches with expressions like 'dead or alive', 'let's roll' and 'smoking out of holes'.[106]

[103] A Kaplan, 'Homeland Insecurities: Transformations of Language and Space' in ML Dudziak (ed), *September 11 in History: A Watershed Moment?* (Duke University Press, 2003).

[104] *ibid*, 63.

[105] J Habermas and J Derrida, *Philosophy in a time of terror: dialogues with Jürgen Habermas and Jacques Derrida* (University of Chicago Press, 2003) 149 (Borradorri).

[106] M Byers, *War law: international law and armed conflict* (Atlantic Books, 2005) 152.

Before moving on to look more closely at the theme of ethnic hatred that has crept into the discussion, it is useful to contemplate how what has been said about liberty, security and rationality ties into the previous chapter's arguments about war and crime.

It is quite possible that a constituency formed in the United States and, to some lesser extent the United Kingdom, in support of the Afghanistan and Iraq wars, on the basis that they might create something approaching total security from terrorist attack. But such total security belongs to the realms of fantasy not rationality. As James Crawford has observed,

> just war theorists have traditionally objected to preventive wars against a hypothetical or alleged long-term threat because no nation can ever achieve total security. Any nation trying to do so will not only fail; it is likely to engage in massive unjust violence in its quest for imperial certitude.[107]

The inflated image of a global war on nihilist terrorists or, worse, evil itself, is unhelpful as it destroys fact-sensitive, rational reactions to events. The aforementioned misunderstandings of the dynamics of liberty and security, and the misdescriptions of events are compounded by mistaken identification of the enemy. By swallowing the common bilge that global terrorists do not have understandable private and public grievances, that they care only to instill fear, take life and cause destruction, and that they no longer have an essentially telluric character,[108] governments get intellectual indigestion, producing constipated policies. Osama bin Laden and Saddam Hussein might not have been very nice men in the past, but military attack was an appropriate method of dealing with neither. Moreover, to think both could be fought in the same way with the same tools was dim-witted in the extreme.

As Wilkinson put it (before we were knee-deep in the Middle Eastern quagmire) 'there is no universally applicable counter-terrorism policy for democracies. Every conflict involving terrorism has its own unique characteristics'.[109] Consequently, each requires a uniquely calibrated response. Wilkinson also said that the response ought to be measured because, once 'regimes and factions decide that their ends justify any means or that their opponents' actions justify them in unrestrained retaliation, they tend to become locked in a spiral of terror and counter-terror'.[110] The resistance in Afghanistan and Iraq is convinced that we are murderous maniacs knowing neither limit nor principle. Though this is unlikely to be a popular proposition, I would go so far as

[107] JM Schwartz, 'Misreading Islamist Terrorism' in J Margolis, T Rockmore and AT Marsoobian (eds), *The Philosophical Challenge of September 11* (2005), quoting James Crawford.

[108] See, for this wrong-headed view, M Rosenfeld, 'Habermas's Call for Cosmopolitan Constitutional Patriotism in an Age of Global Terror: A Pluralist Appraisal' (2007) 14(2) *Constellations* 159, 160.

[109] P Wilkinson, *Terrorism versus democracy : the liberal state response* (Portland OR, 2001) 229–30.

[110] *ibid*, 13.

arguing that we have forfeited our right to complain at, and are complicit in the horrendous treatment of captured British and American soldiers and contractors.

In the previous chapter, I gave several examples of actions that have been interpreted by Afghanis and Iraqis as hatred, or intolerance, or even as evidence of genocidal intent. The indisputable, ugly fact remains that the vast majority of those killed in the Afghanistan and Iraq wars, let alone the staggering numbers of refugees created by the conflicts, had absolutely nothing to do with September 11. Afghan and Iraqi refugees account for almost half of all refugees under UNHCR's responsibility worldwide, totalling 4.7 million people. Pakistan is host to the largest number of refugees worldwide (1.8 million).[111] It would be a safe bet to say that a great many of these people abhorred those terrorist atrocities for the same reasons we did. Sadly, a safer bet would be that many now retrospectively applaud the hijackers' vision and sacrifice.

As Holmes comments, it would have made sense to try, and to punish Khalid Sheikh Mohammed shortly after his capture, because it is this enlightened individualisation of culpability that not only helps people focus their outpourings of grief, but, in so doing it delivers them from the primitive temptations of feudal violence. Such violence has an incendiary potential. America has destabilised and endangered Muslim heartlands. It has sent the appalling message that Muslims might not be spared even if they renounce terrorist violence. Rather, they might 'become targets of America's lethal but poorly focused fury', their families might be bombed, their kin might be swept up, detained and tortured. The difficulties of fighting insurgents might well increase as more sophisticated weaponry becomes available to private actors. In such circumstances, where governments can no longer monopolise violence to the extent that fights are worth fighting, it would seem that the only way for them to retain power is to attain moral authority and win a reputation for reason.

And, it is prudence, not just morality that counsels focused, tailored, well-targeted responses. In any counter-insurgency, the military or police must show, with precision operations, that it does not pay to be an insurgent, but, on the contrary, it redounds to one's benefit to support the counter-insurgency, and to put down the tools of terror. The innocent must be separated from the guilty, lest indiscriminate violence drive the innocent to the guilty. It is to these grotesque failures properly to pinpoint the enemy that I now turn.

[111] UNHCR Global Trends Report, available at: www.unhcr.org/4a375c426.html.

5

Amity, Enmity and Identity

'You were seen. You were seen.
Coming from the Shankill
Where are you from?
Where is he from?
The Falls? When? What Street?'

Ciaran Carson, 'Question Time' in *Belfast Confetti*

OSAMA BIN LADEN reminds his followers never to 'forget this enmity between us and the infidels. For the enmity is based on creed'.[1] For those wondering about how consistent this is with his faith, it can usefully be compared with Islamic discourse in which enmity is one of the hall-marks of evil, injected into the hearts of men in order to stir up bloody conflict.[2] The term 'enmity' will be used here to indicate a hostile disposition, characterised by ill-will and hatred, and stemming, it will be inferred, from sanctimony and ignorance. In contrast, I will use the term 'amity' to denote friendliness, geniality, a welcoming disposition, and a public nature of inquisitive cultural aperture. These two terms are designed to help us consider the dynamics of identity that have featured in our response to the terrorist threat. 'Identity' is understood here as the shifting topography of the self, as the mind's map of the landscape of the 'I'. Identity's features and boundaries are unstable – they change in relation to both internal dynamics and, to a greater or lesser extent, the transmutations in the features and boundaries of the identities of others. Identity has an intimate tryst with amity and enmity. To paraphrase Samuel Huntington, human nature is such that, often we only know who we are when we know *against* whom we are. Having introduced the three titular concepts, we can now look back at the roles they played in the Anglo-American response to terror.

Notions of racial and religious difference have vitrioled modern British and American counter-terrorism policy, dulling our senses to the insidious and self-defeating effects of directly or indirectly discriminatory legal and political measures. In what follows, I shall attempt to describe these effects and then

[1] M Scheuer, *Imperial Hubris* (Brassey's, 2004) 15.

[2] KAA Fadl, '9/11 and the Muslim Transformation' in ML Dudziak (ed), *September 11 in History: A Watershed Moment?* (Duke University Press, 2003) 96.

suggest how they might, in the future, be remedied so that our legislative and executive acts are no longer warped by the primitive politics of credal irreconcilability.

The first awkward meetings of people of different cultures, brought by tired feet, buses, trains, ships and planes into towns and cities, carried along wires and bounced between satellites onto screens in homes, and the subsequent peaceable colonisation of chunks of Western lands and settlements by emigrants from the East has, inevitably – given man's predisposition to fear his fellows – led to an increase in xenophobia. Predictably, economic and personal insecurities have sought refuge in the comforting politics of collective ethnic and cultural exclusivity. Eric Hobsbawm observes that, in the United States, seven million families live in 'fortress compounds', half of those in communities 'where access is controlled by gates, entry-codes, key cards and security guards'.[3] In Europe, the threat of Islamic terrorism is high on political agendas, and yet, as Kofi Annan saw it in 2001, 'it is xenophobia and the political manipulation of fear of foreigners that pose the greatest threat to democracy, or at least to the quality of democracy'.[4]

It is common knowledge that, after September 11 in that hateful year, both the United Kingdom and the United States designed detention policies distinguishing between citizens and non-citizens. Such policies, though they might correspond to the more basic wants of a shell-shocked public, might be objected to on both moral and practical grounds. In moral terms, crude, discriminatory measures are destined to rupture human society along rival national and consequently ethnic lines. Cicero argued that discriminating against aliens subverts 'the whole foundation of common community – and its removal means the annihilation of all kindness, generosity, goodness, and justice'.[5] Aside from its moral repugnance, this 'removal' of amity between humans, the creation of distinctions in terms of race, is far from pragmatic if the goal is the reduction of enmity in an irrevocably interconnected world. Modern communities, be they familial, professional, cultural, religious, epistemic, cyberspatial or racial, are scattered all over the globe. It is counterproductive to attempt to buy security for an 'us' at the price of insecurity for an overlapping 'them'.

Furthermore, if attempts to draw clear lines of delineation between ethnic groups were futile in Hitler's *Reinigung*, in our contemporary society of increasingly hyphenated ethnicity they are artificial in the extreme. And, more than ever before in human history, igniting the tinderbox of racial enmity is like setting fire to one's own lawn. Still, racially motivated attacks in Europe on Muslims were

[3] EJ Hobsbawm, *Globalisation, democracy and terrorism* (Little Brown, 2007) 147.
[4] K Annan, 'Democracy: An International Issue' (2001) June-August *UN Chronicle*.
[5] *Cicero: Selected Works*, trans M Grant (Penguin Classics, 1974) 168.

eerily reminiscent of the twilight before the *Pogromnächte* that darkened the continent before, during, and in the aftermath of World War II.[6]

In the United Kingdom, official discrimination against foreign terror suspects eventually stuck in the judicial throat.[7] The detention law in question empowered an executive officer to imprison any person without either charge or trial if he reasonably believed their presence in the UK to be a risk to national security, and whom he reasonably suspected of being a terrorist.[8] Individuals who could not be deported (because of a risk of their being tortured in the recipient state) could be detained under immigration powers. The law was defended on the basis that the 'prison', like the courts of Jesus College, Cambridge, had only 'three walls'; that is, the detainees were free to leave the UK. However, given that the only reason they were not deported in the first place was the risk of torture, their somewhat bleak choice was between indefinite detention at Her Majesty's pleasure or the risk of torture at someone else's. It is important to note that this scheme provided only for the detention of foreign nationals, not British nationals representing an identical threat. Before passing the discriminatory law, the UK entered an Article 15 derogation to the European Convention of Human Rights on the basis that it was facing an emergency 'threatening the life of the nation', namely terrorism.

When the detainees challenged the compatibility of the detention scheme with the Convention, seven of nine judges in the House of Lords, in a decision that has come to be known, after the high-security prison in question, as the *Belmarsh* ruling, held that, though they would not overturn the executive's determination that the UK was facing a public emergency, they did not consider that a discriminatory detention regime met the standard set by the Convention for entering a derogation. That is to say it was not 'strictly required by the exigencies of the situation' – the condition in Article 15. Baroness Hale perhaps best encapsulated the kernel of the judgment: 'if it is not necessary to lock up the nationals it cannot be necessary to lock up the foreigners'.[9] She also admirably highlighted the pointlessness of indefinite detention in a three-walled prison given the international nature of terrorism and the fact that it is a bane on all states.

> What sense does it make to consider a person such a threat to the life of the nation that he must be locked up without trial, but allow him to leave, as has happened, for France where he was released almost immediately?[10]

[6] See 'New Incidents Heighten Tensions Among British Muslims', *New York Times*, 23 July 2005, available at: www.nytimes.com/2005/07/23/international/europe/23muslims.html?_r=1&scp=1&sq=racially%20motivated%20attack%20muslim&st=cse&oref=slogin; 'The New Berlin Wall', *New York Times*, 4 December 2005, available at: www.nytimes.com/2005/12/04/magazine/04berlin.html?scp=3&sq=racially%20motivated%20attack%20muslim&st=cse.

[7] *A v Secretary of State for the Home Department* [2004] UKHL 56.

[8] Anti-Terrorism, Crime and Security Act 2001, Part 4.

[9] *A v Secretary of State for the Home Department* [2004] UKHL 56, para 231.

[10] *ibid*, para 230.

In the face of such trenchant judicial criticism, the absurdity of the detention policy is patent. However, the question still remains how a bungling, racially discriminatory rule sneaked into the statute book. Several answers spring to mind. First, the legislation was enacted in a hurry when the images of September 11 were still burning on the back of everyone's eyelids. Second, the legislature no doubt had a genuine concern to avoid sending people off to be tortured matching their concern to defend the state. Third, the government (naïvely, as July 7 proved) probably did not contemplate that British nationals would pose a threat similar to that of transients or immigrants. Fourth, the UK leadership had precious little understanding of the threat it was facing, but felt the pressing need to be seen to be 'doing something' to neutralise that threat.

Another, slightly more sinister reason why a statute, arbitrarily discriminating on the grounds of race, crept into our law books, is that the prejudicial attitudes of mind pervading the imperial project, perfectly depicted in Kipling's poetry and Conrad's novels,[11] did not disintegrate with the British Empire. In the 1980s, Salman Rushdie asserted that Britain, the last colony of the Empire, was 'two entirely different worlds, and the one you inhabit is determined by the colour of your skin'.[12] Thirty years later, those two worlds continue to coexist. Men of Pakistani descent who consider themselves British and Londoners before they consider themselves Pakistani endured escalating alienation in the wake of September 11. Their scant consolation is breathing space on the underground and the bus. Sideways glances and brusque dealings increase frustration amongst British Muslims, who experienced feelings of stigmatisation and rejection, turning inwards for solace. If the irrationality of fighting terror in Iraq was not immediately apparent, it should have been after July 7 2005, when four home-grown British terrorists attacked their own capital city, killing 56 people, including themselves. British aggression against Muslims in Iraq was cited by two of the bombers in videotaped statements recorded prior to their deaths.[13] One of the bombers, Germaine Lindsay, who grew up in Huddersfield, converted to Islam five years before his suicide, and was known to have expressed extreme anti-Western, anti-white sentiment. It is not hard to imagine how these sentiments became radicalised in Huddersfield, which, at least in my experience of the town, during school and college, is poisoned by racial enmity and a bizarre, informal segregation, even (if not particularly) in its institutions of higher education.

The heavy-handedness of Allied operations in Afghanistan and Iraq, especially the usage of interrogational (and, sadly, recreational) torture, coupled with Pakistanis' new arbitrary status as terror suspects at home, exacerbated the

[11] J Conrad, *Heart of Darkness* (Penguin Classics, 2007 [1899]).

[12] S Rushdie, *Imaginary Homelands* (Granta Books, 1991) 134.

[13] 'Video of London Suicide Bomber Released', *The Times*, 6 July 2006, available at: www.timesonline.co.uk/tol/news/uk/article683824.ece.

minority's sense of persecution and discontentment.[14] Vulnerability and anchorlessness, prevalent amongst young Muslims who feel dislocated from their parents' histories and downtrodden by their own society, are easily capitalised upon by radical recruiters, who can instill not only a sense of brotherly belonging and worldwide community by reference to the notion of the resurgent *umma*, but also a feeling of higher meaning, dignity, self-respect, and purpose – in a word, Identity. It is fair to say that racists in British society and those who turn a blind eye to their bigotry are partly to blame for the deadly decoupling of British citizens from British society. July 7 was not mere individual but societal suicide. For the men who killed themselves, it was a second death. For Britain, it was self-flagellation.

In retrospect, it is plain that the terror generated by September 11 mixed with a very real American ability to lash out. Vulnerability was intolerable to America, who in what now looks like an orgy of violence, seemed to be engaged in an effort to prove to herself that military and economic superiority equated with genealogical ascendancy. This fierce self-assertion was accompanied by thinly veiled suspicion of the foreigner, described, somewhat tepidly by Jürgen Habermas as a 'slight mistrust'.[15] Martha Nussbaum was less generous:

> [T]he Americans who in July 2002 mistook a family of actors from Kerala in South India, speaking and writing Malyayalim, for Arab terrorists from some 'terrorist group' and had them arrested when their flight landed were displaying an appallingly high level of cultural and human illiteracy, no doubt reinforced by the divisive rhetoric of the 'war on terrorism' … This is a failure of our educational systems and we must do better.[16]

The brutal handling in America's infamous Cuban base of legally, if not morally innocent men, who were rounded up by militia, transported like animals, and are held incommunicado indefinitely, would be considered entirely unacceptable for even the very worst of convicted American criminals. The number of suicide attempts at Gitmo shows that many detainees would prefer the death sentence to the indefinitely enduring regime of torture to which they are subjected. The message this sends to the Islamic world is that Muslim lives are worth less than American lives. Worse still were the photos of naked inmates led around on dog collars and the revelation shortly before the seventh anniversary of 9/11, that Australian troops kept four suspected Taliban insurgents including a 70-year-old

[14] DS Hamilton, *Terrorism and international relations* (Calouste Gulbenkian Foundation; Center for Transatlantic Relations, Paul H Nitze School of Advanced International Studies, Johns Hopkins University, 2006) 29 (Farhad Khosrokhavar).

[15] J Habermas and J Derrida, *Philosophy in a time of terror: dialogues with Jürgen Habermas and Jacques Derrida* (University of Chicago Press, 2003) 26.

[16] MC Nussbaum, 'Compassion and Terror' in JP Sterba (ed), *Terrorism and International Justice* (Oxford University Press, 2003) 249.

man for a day in something akin to a chicken coop.[17] One does not have to look far for comments on public rooms on the internet endorsing this sub-human treatment, describing the suspects as 'vermin' and calling for 'mass deportation of refugees'. Such messages, which many Muslims feel are the sentiments to which the counter-terror allies are pandering, were loud enough to deafen moderate ears to any of the reconciliatory platitudes served up at annual White House Ramadan dinners.

That the system of torture 'survived its disclosure' is a damning indictment of American society.[18] Cicero thought a person was beyond the reach of argument if he saw nothing wrong in harming a fellow man. Whether or not America sees nothing wrong with herding up and torturing innocent men, ostensibly for her own protection, the belief that Americans are beyond argument, that they will defend themselves at all costs, only grants gravitas to the radical preaching and damning testimony of men like Al-Zawahiri and Khalid Sheikh Mohammed, according to whom the West only hearkens to the language of force.

Europe's tolerance for America's brash disregard for international law was a touch puzzling. Robert Kagan would cite European weakness or femininity as if weakness and femininity were unappealing or unintentional features of modern Europe. Kagan ignores that, after the bloodshed of the twentieth century, it is a matter of comfort (if not pride) for many Europeans that collectively, the continent is either slow or unable to take up arms. But more than just impotence informed European tolerance for America's Middle Eastern escapades. In many ways, US culture – violent movies, ubiquitous economically clad women, abundant 'bling', lewd lyrics, junk food in servings for the gluttonous, gas-guzzling cars, nihilistic college drinking, and an insatiable appetite for money and power – is the culture that we love to hate. It is quintessentially human to humour post-9/11 America because, behind the pomp and bluster, she seems to be the very personification of the fragility, cowardice, and vice of everyman. America, a child of colonialism, has succumbed to the temptations of brutality and licentiousness, and we love and tolerate her in the same way that we might disdain, yet tolerate (and to some extent revel in) a rebellious teenage daughter making mistakes we once made. The Bush administration's policy was redolent of adolescence.

Perhaps the most dangerous doctrine of modern times is the 'clash of civilisations', first coined by Bernard Lewis in 1990, made famous by Huntington in his book of that title, and as we have seen, harnessed by Bush and bin Laden

[17] 'Taleban suspects held in dog pen', *BBC Online*, 2 September 2008, available at: news.bbc.co.uk/2/hi/south_asia/7593434.stm; 'Taliban dog pen', *The Daily Telegraph*, 2 September 2008, available at: www.news.com.au/dailytelegraph/story/0,22049,24286455–5006009,00.html.

[18] Danner, 'Torture and Truth' in *Abu Ghraib – The Politics of Torture* (North Atlantic Books, 2004).

alike to convince their listeners of the inextinguishable animosity of their enemies. The 'theory', in Huntington's exposition, is as follows:

> The underlying problem for the West is not Islamic fundamentalism. It is Islam, a different civilization whose people are convinced of the superiority of their culture and are obsessed with the inferiority of their power. The problem for Islam is not the CIA or the U.S. Department of Defense. It is the West, a different civilization whose people are convinced of the universality of their culture and believe that their superior, if declining power imposes on them the obligation to extend that culture throughout the world.[19]

So, to recap, according to Huntington, Islam's problem is the West and the West's problem is Islam. Now this might make a nice jingle, but as a doctrine or a fundament for foreign policy, it leaves much to be desired. The theory must be considered in this argument because its influence on Anglo-American strategy is profound. It is argued here that the clash of civilisations exists only in the rhetoric of those with an interest vested in such a clash and in the gullets of those gullible enough to swallow it. Habermas contends that, the 'so-called "clash of civilisations" is often the veil masking the vital material interests of the West (accessible oilfields and a secured energy supply, for example)'.[20] Veil or otherwise, as should be clear from the above glance at divisive and discriminatory detention policies, Huntington's theory has terrible potential as a self-fulfilling prophecy.

Fortunately, like a great many simplistic theories, it is totally unsound – it has three main structural flaws. First, 'the West', in the way Huntington uses the appellation, is a puerile attempt to describe the multi-faceted and heterogeneous political, religious, and ethnic constellation west of the Bosphorous as if it were a unified social block of same-thinking people. Equally, one only has to visit a handful of diverse Muslim communities, for example, in Britain, India, and Turkey to appreciate that Islam is a discursive, multi-layered, ever-changing cultural tradition of immense scope and rich variety. To treat it as a simple, stable, social anvil is a gross oversimplification.

That said, it would be rash to chide the view that some parts of the Islamic world have struggled under the subjugating bane of colonialist meddlings and post-imperial capitalism. To that extent, some Muslims have justified feelings of resentment, but the Islamism of reactionary groups is an empty and impoverished movement, in which the only tenets are anti-tenets of American and capitalist culture.[21] It bears no resemblance to the rich, modern, religious life contemplated in the Qur'an.

[19] SP Huntington, *The clash of civilizations and the remaking of world order* (Simon & Schuster, 1996) 218.

[20] J Habermas and J Derrida, *Philosophy in a time of terror: dialogues with Jürgen Habermas and Jacques Derrida* (University of Chicago Press, 2003) 36.

[21] KAA Fadl, '9/11 and the Muslim Transformation' in ML Dudziak (ed), *September 11 in History: A Watershed Moment?* (Duke University Press, 2003) 80.

Paradoxically, the second structural flaw of the 'clash of civilisations' theory is that it generally underplays the homogeneity of all humans. In her study of the roots of religious violence in India, a wide-ranging antithesis to Huntington's doctrine, Nussbaum contends that, 'human beings are not so very different from one place to another'.[22] Indeed, it would seem, as Allott put it, that however 'exotic' other cultures may be, none are 'alien' to us: 'Always and everywhere, the struggle of human life and the responses of socializing humanity have a family resemblance'.[23] More particularly, Huntington's thesis disregards or discounts the frequently overlapping values even of its own caricatures of Western and Islamic society. As Khalid Abou al-Fadl has observed, Islamic tradition engenders respect for five core values, namely life, intellect, reputation, dignity and property. In Islamic doctrine, these are the proper due of not only Muslims but every individual.[24] Though the devil is in the detail, these precepts can hardly be described as foreign to a Western world; on the contrary, they are positively revered in the languages of science, liberalism, and human rights. I am unaware of any trait, urge, or instinct, wholesome or unwholesome, behind any human action or society, that cannot be traced in my own culture, and if I subject my own psyche to a scrutiny sufficiently honest and unforgiving, I know I can discern it there too, or at least I can find a place it might take root.

The third fissure in the theory of the clash between Islam and the West is that it ignores the ancient cross-fertilisation, ongoing intercoagulation, and frequently peaceful coexistence of human cultures. Carelessly applied gloss and thick statistical fudge are necessary to sustain the clash of civilisations doctrine. To Huntington, black Americans are non-Western peoples, and India, a modern democracy with 130 million Muslims, is a Hindu civilisation.[25] Apart from being offensive and irresponsible, such misdescriptions are intellectually indefensible. The overriding image of the clash of civilisations fantasy is of Islam eternally pitted against the West in mortal combat. Frankly, this image is not going to help us understand why West Yorkshire boys blow themselves up in London. Noting that terrorists live amongst us in Western cities, such as London and Hamburg, Jacques Derrida derides the notion that the threat emanates from foreign cultures: '"terrorists" are not, in this context, "others", absolute others whom we, as "Westerners", can no longer understand'.[26]

[22] MC Nussbaum, *The Clash Within: Democracy, Religious Violence, and India's Future* (The Belknap Press, 2007) 336.

[23] P Allott, *Eunomia: new order for a new world* (Oxford University Press, 1990) 69.

[24] KAA Fadl, '9/11 and the Muslim Transformation' in ML Dudziak (ed), *September 11 in History: A Watershed Moment?* (Duke University Press, 2003) 96.

[25] For criticism of these oddities, see S Holmes, *The Matador's Cape: America's Reckless Response to Terror* (Cambridge University Press, 2007) 150, and A Sen, 'Civilizational Imprisonments' in Joseph Margolis, Armen T Marsoobian and T Rockmore (eds), *The Philosophical Challenge of September 11* (Blackwell Publishing, 2005) 102.

[26] J Habermas and J Derrida, *Philosophy in a time of terror: dialogues with Jürgen Habermas and Jacques Derrida* (University of Chicago Press, 2003) 115.

A further shortcoming of the imagery of a civilisational clash is that it inadequately charts the transcultural currents along which terrorism flows, and is ill-equipped to explain the effects of political power in an interconnected world. In this world where information and money surge across borders, where planes cheaply carry people across thousands of miles, the clash we have to worry about, as Nussbaum contends, is not between Islam and the West, but it is within our shared societies, and, ultimately, within ourselves.

The new home-grown British terrorists of July 7 threaten to expose the societal double-standard according to which *revenge* is an appropriate response to a terrorist attack by someone thought of as 'foreign', whereas a *rehabilitative* response is apt where the terrorist is 'native'. Two prominent examples come to mind. First, although John Walker Lindh admitted joining al-Qaeda and fought alongside the Taliban, as a Californian, he was sentenced in a Virginia Courtroom, was able to strike a plea bargain, and it is anticipated he will serve his sentence in North California, nearer to Ma and Pa. Second, in the aftermath of the Oklahoma bombing – the most deadly terrorist bombing on US soil excepting September 11 – initial calls for violent reprisals died down when it was discovered that the perpetrators were not Middle Eastern terrorists but homegrown hotheads; US army veterans who hated their government's policies. The perpetrators were tried like normal criminals: as Noam Chomsky satirised, 'there was no call to obliterate Montana and Idaho' and 'there were efforts to understand the grievances that lie behind such crimes'.[27]

What lies behind the preferential treatment of Americans gone astray? Surely it is worse, treasonous, that they attacked their own country? The answer might lie in the inability to diagnose and remedy prejudice. Where we fail to understand another person, imagining the reasons for their emotions and actions, we betray our emotional retardation. Such deficient empathy can be traced back to a lack of understanding or even fear of the self; that is to say, the projection of malevolent or disgusting characteristics onto other racial or religious groups is often a product of a contempt for or an incapacity to sympathise with one's own proclivities and perversions. In order to distance ourselves from behaviour in other cultural groups, we convince ourselves of their inferiority – their inhumanity. Nussbaum concludes that '[s]hame, in the context of nationalism, typically involves a self-referential component: what is stigmatised in the other is what is feared and repudiated in the self'.[28] Feelings of disgust, contempt, and superiority informed the rhetoric of purification, decontamination and objectification preceding the Holocaust. A frustration at the insuperable limitations of our frail bodies can result in a collapse of sympathy. A well empty of compassion can be filled with aggression so that in extreme cases, this desire to expunge our

[27] N Chomsky, '9/11: Not since the war of 1812', available at: www.scribd.com/doc/93592/Noam-Chomsky-Not-Since-The-War-of-1812?ga_related_doc=1.

[28] MC Nussbaum, *The Clash Within: Democracy, Religious Violence, and India's Future* (The Belknap Press, 2007) 205.

vulnerabilities, this impossible effort to purge ourselves of human propensities, manifests itself in a seemingly achievable genocidal project. It is perhaps for this reason that the worst wars are fought by the closest relations and similar societies.

Understanding others is challenging, for it is ultimately impossible fully to plumb the endless abyss of another person. Therefore, the need for empathy, in the face of even apparent unreasonableness, is key to emotional maturity and to appropriate, amicable, worldly responses. When we consider that parochial reasonableness is the fundament of British and American criminal law, the blinkered nature of our approach, and the limitations of our empathy come into view. Of course, replacing prejudice with empathy does not mean condoning errant or unreasonable behaviour. On the contrary, a more searching scrutiny of our motivations and darker predilections facilitates more appropriate, and where necessary, harsher punishments.

If we return for a moment to the metaphor of identity as the shifting topography of the self, and apply it to society, we can reflect that when a map is charted, it not only records but generates boundaries. That which is outside the boundaries – the forbidden zone – is actually internal to our identity. In Allott's formulation, it is 'inside by being perceived from inside as outside'.[29] The importance of this realisation for legal philosophy is clear. Thought of cartographically, the law includes what it excludes. In other words, our settled decisions of what counts as unconstitutional are part of our constitution, a matter made clear when they vary over time (think of *Roe v Wade* on abortion). What we do not accept is as much a part of us as what we accept. Not only in its foundational documents or premises, but in its every statute and administrative decree, society defines its identity through law.

On the international plane, the structures of identity and law are thrown into relief:

> since the interstatal arena is not conceived of as a society … its social development is that of the international relations of diplomacy and war, as the internal public realms lead their separate lives and interact only intermittently and more or less fortuitously.[30]

Dogmatic adherence to the hackneyed structural postulate of international law – the property-derived doctrine of state sovereignty – does nothing to ameliorate this divisive state of affairs. A growing, albeit formless, international community, and beneath that, a global civic society is beginning to confront the deleterious effects of what might be called the orthodoxy of borders.

But where the goal is the peaceable administration of human affairs, are borders not inevitable? Is it not the case that politico-social circles will inevitably be drawn according to the living preferences of different groups? These questions introduce the themes of hospitality, tolerance and cosmopolitanism, which

[29] P Allott, *Eunomia: new order for a new world* (Oxford University Press, 1990) 81.
[30] *ibid*, 245.

have fascinated philosophers from the beginning of human history. They were addressed in the context of liberal democracy's struggle against terrorism by Habermas and Derrida.

In his famous essay, *Perpetual Peace*, Emmanuel Kant defined hospitality – which he saw as the basis for world citizenship – as the right of a stranger not to be treated with hostility when he arrives on another's territory.[31] Derrida points out that this is a rather impoverished understanding of hospitality, and that pure hospitality is not a limited licence or conditional invitation.[32] This observation reveals the ceiling of hospitality, it is the level of tolerance we will extend to an outsider, including whether we will permit their entering our territory at all – think of the multiplying border restrictions or the abuse of immigration laws to detain and deport non-Americans. Habermas notes that this threshold is set by the existing authority and it is this reality that tempers Derrida's enthusiasm for the concept of tolerance; it is the obverse of the intolerance of the ruling class; there is a certain condescension to the notion of tolerance.

Habermas attempts to neutralise this problem by arguing that, in a liberal democracy, given the equal rights of citizens, and their 'reciprocal respect' for one another, no one person can unilaterally impose their preferred boundaries of tolerance.[33] Clearly, the utility of tolerance as a concept quickly runs out and this is where discourse comes in, which is more helpful in setting boundaries because of its 'peculiar self-reference that makes it the vehicle for self-correcting learning processes'.[34] The foundational premise of liberal democracy is that of equal rights, but it is worth asking whether the habitual voting of a citizen, the secret expression of their own preferences, engenders empathy for others. The genius of liberal democracy is that it dilutes and exploits men's selfishness by reducing their preferences to one vote in a multitude. The flaw in this idea is that it officially excuses every citizen from reflection on public goods, requiring of them only that they state their own preferences.

This structural selfishness of a liberal democracy does nothing to help a non-citizen, who technically, has no voice, and is unlikely, as we have seen from America and Britain's silent acquiescence in torture, to rank amongst a habitually selfish citizen's priorities. Human rights are a device for remedying this deficiency, but it is arguable that they have done little more than give us a language in which to talk about different claims to entitlement. Behold the chink in liberal democracy's moral armour. It is institutionally intolerant. For this reason, Gandhi thought that Indian democracy, Indian *empathy* would be improved by each citizen's focus on the cultivation of themselves, the inner person.

[31] I Kant, *Zum ewigen Frieden. Ein philosophischer Entwurf* (1st edn, 1795).

[32] J Habermas and J Derrida, *Philosophy in a time of terror: dialogues with Jürgen Habermas and Jacques Derrida* (University of Chicago Press, 2003) 107.

[33] *ibid*, 18.

[34] *ibid*, 46.

Habermas, according to his unwavering belief in the mantra 'it's good to talk', thinks that if identity and culture animate constitutional structures nationally, then internationally, a commitment to constitutionalism will rescue us from this enmity. In his words, 'public, discursively structured processes of opinion-and-will-formation make a reasonable political understanding possible, even among strangers'.[35] In what follows, I shall try to inroad into the structural selfishness endemic to liberal democracy, for it is apparent that this institutional intolerance works against us in our attempt to understand how to foil terrorism.

Adam Smith wrote that, the 'most frivolous disaster which could befall himself would occasion a more real disturbance' to a man of humanity in Europe, than the deaths of an 'immense multitude' in a Chinese earthquake.[36] This will not do. We ought to treat the well-being of other societies with the same concern we reserve for our own, at least to the extent of caring how our societies interact in an interconnected world. Modernly, we enjoy the benefits of international news coverage and this window onto the world presents us with an unprecedented historical opportunity to open the umbrella of our concern to shield our furthest neighbours. This is not altruism. In a disenchanted world of international communication, impressionable, vulnerable and sexually frustrated young men, infinite private wealth, readily available, easily portable destructive weaponry, irremediably porous borders, and affordable international travel, it is at our peril that we protect the rights of those at home by trampling on the rights of or ignoring the plight of those abroad.

The real clash of civilisations is not a conflict that can be fought with ships on the Black or Mediterranean Seas, let alone with predator drones in the mountains of Pakistan. Rather, it is in our localities, in our streets, and homes. The roots of the present day antagonism between fringe Islamism and the united Allied front, lie not in failed integration, or abortive multiculturalism, or distopian cosmopolitanism, but in prejudice. When irrational, self-loathing enmity is replaced by rational, self-critical amity in human hearts and minds, terrorism will lose its appeal. It is far easier to dismiss a suicide bomber as fanatical than it is to understand what kind of desperation it is that drives a person to turn himself into a bomb.

People of a pluralist world, or citizens of a liberal democracy need education enabling them to 'reach out in the imagination, allowing another person's experience into oneself'.[37] Imagination, empathy and expression are critical to the advancement of society and are prerequisites to a society's long-term health where the same depends on the input of its citizens, as, of course, it does in the promise that democracy makes to itself. Rather than a clash of civilisations,

[35] J Habermas, 'The Postnational Constellation and the Future of Democracy' in Habermas (ed), *The Postnational Constellation* (Polity Press, 2001) 78.

[36] A Smith, 'Of the Sense of Duty' Part III in *The Theory of Moral Sentiments* (1853) 193.

[37] MC Nussbaum, *The Clash Within: Democracy, Religious Violence, and India's Future* (The Belknap Press, 2007) 296.

Nussbaum perceives 'a clash inside the person, between the forces of fear and reactive domination and the forces that lead to compassion and respect – a "clash" that must be mediated through effective education and a decent public culture'.[38] If we truly wish for the flourishing of our systems of liberal democracy, it is no mental quantum leap to realise that inter-cultural dialectic is in our best interests. Similarly, Habermas argues that conflicts begin where distorted communication results in reciprocal mistrust. In sum, only the empathetic interpretive ability of individuals can insulate society from flammable misunderstandings.[39]

Admittedly, it is easier to realise the importance of empathy than to design ways of inculcating it, such a project would be far beyond the scope of this argument and is certainly beyond my ability. This, however, can be said: in the England in which I grew up, history, religious education, art, theatre and foreign languages were not compulsory subjects beyond the age of 13. It was therefore perfectly possible for relatively sentient citizens of one of the most revered parliamentary democracies in world history to reach adulthood without any understanding of, and without reflecting on their own or other political cultures, and without developing skills of self-expression and empathy that one would imagine are the lifeblood of democracy and public life.

Nussbaum, in *The Clash Within*, records how Rabindranath Tagore's school, Shantiniketan, enacted ceremonies from each world religion, combining theatre, history and religion to develop skills of self-expression, understanding, and empathy. Indubitably, empathy must be taught and learned in our schools; it does not automatically inure with maturity.

Religion is fascinating; it moves people, societies and nations, is a source of epiphany, inspiring fables of human sacrifice for others, and conversely, is instrumentalised for evil-doing in the most dramatic conflicts of our times. It is anything but boring and yet this juicy, wholesome subject is often converted by poor schooling into the driest, most inedible of educational muesli. It is nothing short of reprehensible that Britain fails to illuminate or even reveal to its children the rich tapestry of cultures that make up its complex nationhood. Educational woes aside, it is clear that the communicative empathy of Europeans and Americans must extend beyond the liberal democratic ideal. How then, can we imagine a society of all humankind, when borders are inevitable? One answer to this might be to conceive of world society as a series of concentric circles of government, one outside of the other, where the length of the circumference is determined by the breadth of cooperation needed to create an agreeable, durable policy for the issue in hand. Global warming for example, would be an issue demanding the cooperation of all societies; the circle would therefore have

[38] *ibid*, 79.

[39] J Habermas and J Derrida, *Philosophy in a time of terror: dialogues with Jürgen Habermas and Jacques Derrida* (University of Chicago Press, 2003) 35.

the greatest circumference. The smallest circle would correspond to matters such as the listing of an historical building or the registration of a village green in a given town centre.

This vision is of a world of tolerant pluralism limited by a shared commitment to renounce the usage of certain means to push political agendas. It is a minimal notion of subsidiary world citizenry, where each citizen enjoys the right to political participation (which is only possible in conditions of basic security and need not entail formal democracy) and is obliged to eschew aggression in the espousal of their views. The crystallisation of political participation and basic security ought to reduce the incidence of resort to aggression. By aggression here, I mean to rely on the definition I suggested in chapter three: force used other than in the defence of others or self-defence, or excessive force employed in self-defence or the defence of others. In such a vision, international laws backed by international enforcement are far from being fantastical.

In line with Michel Rosenfeld, it is argued here that the fundamentalist positions of, say, Protestantism or Islamism, are not inherently inimical to fruitful exchange, or to pluralism, so long as aggression is not the chosen mode of persuasion.[40] Pluralism – equal respect for all versions of the good so far as is practical – is, like its progenitors, Liberty and Equality, essentially valueless; as such, it can antagonise those who would prefer a more stable version of the good, a more substantial base on which to build society. Here, it is helpful to shift one's focus to forbidden means; that is to say, propagate any version of the good, subject to limits on the acceptable modes of its propagation. I readily accept that this is based on a belief about what is pragmatic in an international society with a shifting power base. It is suggested that this version of procedural pluralism can help forge a common human political bond, based firmly upon a wholesale repudiation of aggression. Without consensus on a colourless definition of terrorism, such a common human jurisprudential bond is beyond our reach. To dispel confusion, it should be noted at this stage, though this will be elaborated in due course, that the version of social, procedural pluralism espoused here is not to be conflated with legal pluralism. Legal pluralism is impossible according to the understanding of law preferred here.

The discussion here can be rounded off by reflecting on Carl Schmitt's idea of the political. For the German philosopher, the political constituted the assertion of a collective identity at the expense of other collective identities. Habermas regards this as 'false and dangerous in view of its practical consequences'.[41] Schmitt's version of the political certainly seems peculiar, if not unnecessarily antagonistic. But he is not the only philosopher who contemplated violence as part of politics. Recall the afore-mentioned Clausewitzian construction of war –

[40] M Rosenfeld, 'Habermas's Call for Cosmopolitan Constitutional Patriotism in an Age of Global Terror: A Pluralist Appraisal' (2007) 14(2) *Constellations* 159.

[41] J Habermas and J Derrida, *Philosophy in a time of terror: dialogues with Jürgen Habermas and Jacques Derrida* (University of Chicago Press, 2003) 38.

for him, it was a mere continuation of politics by other means. I would like sharply to distinguish my understanding of the political from that of Schmitt and Clausewitz. As I understand it, violence is what happens when politics stop; the political is a discursive, syncretic phenomenon. It is prior, central, and subsequent to the formation of identity, and manifestly does not contemplate other than defensive violence in the pursuit of its ends. Is it not preferable to say that violence occurs where politics have failed?

Schmitt's philosophy has been criticised as an invitation to violence. However, his work repays careful reading. In several passages, he forecasted the problems we face today, and he offers up one insight of great service. Totalitarianism, terrorism and fundamentalism feed on the idea of an enemy, racial, credal or social. Contrariwise, as Schmitt noted, the concept of humanity excludes the notion of an enemy. We should be wary of powerful governments which purport unilaterally to prescribe a universal version of the good and who think that their version has many enemies. Echoing Schmitt, Ronald Dworkin argues that even if they are not in violation of international conventions, the Bush administration's security measures transgress the principle of shared humanity that underlies them all.[42] Humanity is a concept, the cultivation of which is a responsibility incumbent on every overlapping society of man. It is our shared identity, and our task is to make peace with the inevitable differences outside of that core commonality. Rejecting the usage of certain means, whatever the grandeur of their political or religious ends, is a suitable starting point. *Proice tela manu, sanguis meus!*[43]

Having endeavoured to elucidate some basic ideas revolving around amity, enmity and identity, and how a liberal democracy ought to approach these issues in its response to terrorism, I would like to draw together some of the strings of the argument so far, by reflecting on how the ideas in this chapter merge with those preceding it.

How do the themes of this chapter relate to the usage of language and image in the last decade? The natural human tendency to mask vulnerability with aggression is easily exploitable in the aftermath of terrorist attacks. After September 11, perhaps taken aback by the sheer size of the attack, 'ABC news anchor Peter Jennings invoked the image of Pearl Harbor and CBS labelled its coverage, "Attack on America"'.[44] From the first hour then, this *idée fixe*, this Nelsonian insistence on looking at the attacks through the lens of war determined America's response. If America had been attacked, of course, a trial would not do. America must, as tradition dictates, retaliate.

[42] R Dworkin, 'Terror and the Attack on Civil Liberties' in T Rockmore, J Margolis and AT Marsoobian (eds), *The Philosophical Challenge of September 11* (Blackwell Publishing, 2005) 86.

[43] Virgil, *The Aeneid of Virgil* (Macmillan, 1902) 135. Anchises cries to his progeny, Caesar, 'Cast from thy hand your arms, oh blood of mine'.

[44] TY Ismael and JS Ismael, 'September 11 and American policy in the Middle East' in J Strawson (ed), *Law after Ground Zero* (London, 2002) 161.

The sparks of enmity are fanned by incendiary descriptions such as former President Bush's invocation of the 'crusades' to explain the Middle East incursion. Given the common understanding of the crusades as religious slaughter, Bush's comment did little to smother rumours of a clash of civilisations. Another example was an injudicious Pope Benedict XVI's Regensburger speech, in which he referred to violent features of Islam, as if examples of divine violence and terrible plagues did not abound in the Bible.

Many commentators have complained, justifiably, that in American media coverage of the 'War on Terror', the 'lens provided projects an immensely homogenised Islamic Arab "world" devoid of the humane, enlightened and magnanimous societal achievements of Western – more specifically American – civilisation'.[45] Notwithstanding the skewed nature of this coverage, it has an indirect impact on non-whites. Arabs, Hindus and Muslims have suffered social ostracism. Islam itself, instead of meaning 'surrender' or 'submission' has become synonymous with the opposite; with insurgent uprising; beards and turbans are equated not with spirituality and observance but with the brutality of the Taliban.

Not only the words but also the actions of the Bush executive have had perilous symbolic resonance. As Byers explains, in the early years of World War II,

> German soldiers shaved off the beards of Orthodox Jews. In January 2002, US soldiers did the same to Islamic fundamentalists captured in Afghanistan, before flying them to a detention centre at the US naval base in Guantanamo Bay, Cuba … [This] probably violated the detainees' right to human dignity under the Third Geneva Convention, several international human rights treaties and customary international law. At best, it was patently insensitive and unnecessary.[46]

As part of the entertainment programme at Gitmo itself, the Qur'an was kicked around in front of detainees. The inflammatory message that such actions send to the Islamic world (which, of course, as we saw earlier, is irrevocably part of our world) cannot be doused down with diplomacy. Disrespecting, torturing and murdering prisoners of war, particularly in a war suspected to be a vile scramble for loot, is deeply imprudent. Americans captured by militants should not count on cordial hospitality. Further, having seen photographic evidence of Allied maltreatment and murder of detainees, militants are more likely to exhibit a steely resolve and resist capture right down to their last measures of devotion and resistance. Again, we have made our war more difficult for ourselves. In World War II, it became received wisdom that the net effect of killing prisoners of war was, as rumours and reports seeped out, to ossify the resistance of enemy soldiers. Not much has changed, except that now, in the age of the internet, this simple military prudence applies a fortiori because news of murder and maltreatment spreads like bush fire.

[45] *ibid*, 159.

[46] M Byers, *War law: international law and armed conflict* (Atlantic Books, 2005) 147.

We can make a similar observation about indiscriminate killing in general. Ferguson concludes that, contrary to the exorbitant predictions of war strategists, Allied firebombing in World War II did more to increase defiance than defeatism.[47] Likewise, the American policy of targeted killings: Is it not just wishful thinking that imprecise missile attacks on the extended families of Islamist militants will create a strategic advantage in the war on terror? Are they not more likely to enrage people who previously bore no grudge against America and to create sympathy for Afghanistan's insurgents in Muslim populations entirely unconnected with the conflict? After limited initial victories, America is literally regenerating al-Qaeda.

The discussion in this chapter also ought to influence our thinking about the paradigms of war and crime. Above, I proposed a form of procedural pluralism extending beyond a dogmatic and dangerous obstinacy about the boons for pluralism inherent in liberal democracy. The insistence that other societies accept our way of reconciling different views is neither democratic nor is it loyal to the core ideal of pluralism. The first philosophical pre-requisite for a more mature procedural pluralism is the worldwide renunciation of certain forbidden means in the pursuit of political interests. Retaliation, aggressive war, and the use of excessive or recklessly targeted force are no better than terrorism.

All too frequently, foreign policy, based on an assumption of the fundamental enmity of outsiders, is designed to promote the primitive and eventually self-defeating goal of advantaging our own societies at the strategic expense of others. As a result, one of the great struggles facing all communities is to redirect blood, sweat and treasure currently poured into the barricading of their defences, or the ability to project threat globally, into the well-being of their contemporaries. Echoing the conclusions of the International Commission on the Responsibility to Protect,[48] Heymann has argued that, America has 'little to lose and much to gain by showing concern for the well-being – the nutrition, health, education, governance and human rights – of Muslim populations around the world'.[49]

The mourning of the legal paradigms of crime and war lost on the battlefield of the war on terror is premature. In the way that the eyes combine two images into one superior view, the conflation of the foreign enemy and native criminal has the potential to sharpen rather than blur our moral vision. This merging of the man-made frames of crime and war, discernible in the mutual enrichment of human rights and humanitarian law, may help judges, politicians and laypeople alike descry and then focus on the moral and ætiological dynamics of cyclic violence, aggression and defence.

[47] N Ferguson, *The War of the World* (Allen Lane, 2006) 565.

[48] International Commission on Intervention and State Sovereignty, 'Responsibility to Protect' (2001)

[49] PB Heymann, *Terrorism, Freedom and Security* (MIT Press, 2003) 44.

Reference was made above to the crucial decision in *Belmarsh*, in which the UK House of Lords disapproved of a racist policy created to address the perceived problems of suspected terrorists. It is clear that neither discriminatory nor indefinite detention programmes are satisfactory solutions, and might even risk agitating radical elements in society as well as undermining support for the state. I would like to consider here how the United Kingdom and the United States might have designed more intelligent, more effective policies for dealing with suspected terrorists, using legal and moral principle as a guide. I will do this by looking first at the trajectory of one famous US detainee, on trial in Cuba at the time of writing, and then by briefly discussing how the British government could react to terror suspects, without discriminating in a manner incompatible with the promises it has made to itself.

In the first situation, the self-anointed 'executive director of 9/11', Khalid Sheikh Mohammed, was picked up, thanks to an informant's text message, in Rawalpindi, Pakistan on 1 March 2003. He was transported to Afghanistan and then to what the CIA regarded as the '51st state', Poland, to a so-called 'black site', where he was treated to the full range of interrogative techniques: 'the intensity of his treatment – various harsh techniques, including waterboarding, used about 100 times over a period of two weeks – prompted worries that officers might have crossed the boundary into illegal torture'.[50] Arraigned before a Military Tribunal at Guantánamo Bay on 5 June 2008, after five years in American custody, three years of which were in secret CIA prisons, Mohammed, after denouncing his lawyers as agents of the Bush crusade, told the military judge that he too was seeking the death sentence and ridiculed the court as the 'Inquisitionland' following the purgatory of systematic torture.[51]

This can hardly be described as a public relations triumph for the United States. Having squandered the opportunity to extradite, charge, indict and try their high-profile detainee in open court, America tarnished its reputation with countless human rights violations, transgressions of the Geneva Conventions and, now, is making a mockery of its own principles of fair trial, all in order to play into the hands of an egomaniac mass murderer. To make matters worse, the CIA will have a difficult time convincing anyone that torture was necessary or effective: the interrogator, Mr Deuce Martinez, who succeeded in giving Mohammed the opportunity he clearly wanted to glorify himself as the 'architect' of the most deadly terrorist attack of all time did not lay a finger on him. Instead, he used the tried and tested technique of creating rapport by reference to shared human experience. Mohammed even took to writing poetry to his new

[50] 'Inside a 9/11 Mastermind's Interrogation', *New York Times*, 22 June 2008, available at: www.nytimes.com/2008/06/22/washington/22ksm.html.

[51] '9/11 Suspects Arraigned at Guantánamo Hearing', *New York Times*, available at: www.nytimes.com/2008/06/05/washington/05cnd-gitmo.html?_r=1&scp=2&sq=mohammmed%20arraigned&st=cse&oref=slogin.

friend's wife. From the informer's text message to the interrogator's tactful tactics, empathy and intelligence proved to be the best weapons against terrorism.

Conversely, it was perhaps a combination of enmity and ignorance about the identity of their foes that led the CIA to tear up the rulebook.

> 'I asked, "What are we going to do with these guys when we get them?" recalled A.B. Krongard, the No. 3 official at the C.I.A. from March 2001 until 2004. 'I said, "We've never run a prison. We don't have the languages. We don't have the interrogators"'.[52]

There is another dimension to the Mohammed saga. American civil liberties organisations are almost certainly right that the detainee will not receive a fair trial in Cuba. But had he been tried in America, a fair trial might have been impossible due to the intensity of the natural desire to blame someone for the atrocious crimes of September 11.

Hence, it is worth considering whether a neutral, international court composed of judges from different jurisdictions would be more appropriate for the trial of such controversial figures; the International Criminal Court presents itself as a suitable instance for terrorist trials. This argument is bolstered by historically hypocritical state usage of the term 'terrorist', which, as we have seen, is all too frequently employed to smear perfectly legitimate militia or resistance forces with the tar and feathers of criminality. A court of independent, international character is more likely than national institutions to be unbiased in its assessment of those charged with terrorist crimes.

In this respect, it is worth touching on one of the more controversial (extra-)legal categories deployed by the Bush administration; that of 'unlawful combatant', which, in essence, has been used to deny detainees the protections due to both criminals and prisoners of war, opening up legal black holes and legitimising any form of treatment. This cynical attempt to duck accountability has tainted a perfectly useful category. Indeed, there is no inherent flaw in the claim that someone is an 'unlawful combatant'. To my mind, the term adds nothing to the phrase 'terrorist', or for that matter, 'war criminal' and reflects that a person is alleged to have used forbidden means.

Were there an international court with jurisdiction over terrorists, states contending that such persons had violated the laws of war, or had committed crimes against humanity, could turn them over, sparing themselves from the inevitable criticism that they themselves were violating the laws of war by mistreating civilians and avoiding exposure to the risk that the inertia of prolonged detention seduced officers into torturing. It would be sensible to have a maximum term unrelated to the continuance of hostilities for which states could hold people they consider unlawful combatants. After the expiry of such a term, states would be obliged to release the detainee, or turn him over to the jurisdiction of the international court. Thus, the staple American excuse – that

[52] 'Inside a 9/11 Mastermind's Interrogation', *New York Times*, 22 June 2008, available at: www.nytimes.com/2008/06/22/washington/22ksm.html.

the war on terror is ongoing and the detainees must therefore, like prisoners of war, remain in detention indefinitely, lest they rejoin the hostilities – would be circumvented. Space precludes a full elaboration of such a system but it is certainly worth considering as an alternative to the damaging, and counter-productive treatment that Mohammed has endured.

In the United Kingdom, nine men were arrested in December 2001 by the UK government. They were detained for over three years, without charge or trial, and, perhaps worst of all, without access to any of the 'intelligence' against them; in short, without being told why they had been stripped of their liberty. Their solicitors referred to them as having been 'entombed in concrete' by dint of the long periods (up to 22 hours a day) they spent in their cells. Civil liberties groups dubbed Belmarsh, the high-security unit where the men were held, 'Britain's Guantánamo'. Winston Churchill, who had some experience of a similar policy, brought in to tackle the Fifth Column in times of much greater peril to the nation, commented:

> The power of the Executive to cast a man into prison without formulating any charge known to the law, and particularly to deny him the judgement of his peers, is in the highest degree odious and is the foundation of all totalitarian government ...[53]

How could our modern government have tackled the threat allegedly posed by these men, without betraying its own time-honoured standards of hospitality and legality so basely? Five interrelated points can be made. First, in all the public statements made by British politicians, one is hard pressed to discern a single reason to believe anything other than that the existing criminal justice system could comfortably handle a case of someone plotting a terrorist attack.[54] Persons whom the police reasonably suspect can be arrested, charged, questioned, indicted and tried for preparatory and conspiratorial crimes. If they are found guilty, they will go to jail; if not, they will have been legitimately in custody long enough to interrupt all but the most flexible of terrorist enterprises.

The second and third points are closely related. Rather than helping, sweeping up terror suspects positively hinders the security and police officers in gathering the necessary evidence to support charge and conviction – it is counter-productive to take budding terrorists off the streets when there is not enough proof to sustain a conviction for at least three reasons: (a) stripped of their liberty without so much as an explanation, any individual is likely to develop a healthy fear of, if not, unquenchable rage against the government; (b) it is far better to watch the movements of suspects and take the time to amass enough proof of their evil designs to imprison them for life, legitimately; and (c) eventually foot-soldiers have to communicate with their commander. Absent strategy, impatiently collecting pawns does nothing to facilitate getting at the King.

[53] W Churchill, Comment (1 November 1943).

[54] PB Heymann, *Terrorism, Freedom and Security* (MIT Press, 2003).

The third point is that a prohibition on the usage of wiretap evidence (recordings of telephone conversations and such like) puts the government in an unnecessarily awkward position.[55] It might know and yet may not prove terrorist intent. Our objection to wiretapping should be that it is an invasion of our privacy, but as long as sufficient safeguards exist (such as a system of judicial warrants) to ensure that only genuine suspects are bugged, our concerns melt away. To prevent such evidence, once procured, from being used in court is needlessly to punish good police work. It is to throw the baby (conviction) out with the bathwater (intercept evidence). Fourth, old-fashioned surveillance is one of the most effective, least intrusive methods for unravelling terrorist networks, which exhibit many telltale characteristics easily spotted by diligent case officers. Where the goal is to seek out enmity without exacerbating it by victimising minority groups, surveillance is key.

Fifth and finally, the most effective method of beating terrorism is deep cover – infiltration. If the threat is from Islamist radical groups, Britain has a good-sized pool of intelligent, bi- or trilingual, young Muslim nationals who would like nothing more than to protect their fellow citizens and their country, by helping lock up those who would manipulate their religion for violent ends.

We can conclude this chapter with some closing observations on how the ideas on amity, enmity and identity interact with what was said before on liberty, security and rationality.

If it was not obvious before the 'war on terror', it should be now; the liberty of minorities is frequently threatened by democracies, where populist surges of fear result in an irrational scapegoating of innocent communities. Liberal democracy, where the 'liberal' part is inherently malleable, like in the United States and the United Kingdom, can very swiftly become terrifyingly illiberal. More will be said on these dynamics later, but for now, we can note in the polemical terms of Arundhati Roy, that in this war on terror, 'Enduring Freedom for some means Enduring Subjugation for others'.[56]

Similarly, Dworkin noted that Americans without any Muslim connections run no risk whatsoever of being 'locked up in a military jail'; the balance we strike then, is not between our security and our liberty, but between the security of the majority and the liberty of minorities. He argues that we should think about that 'as a matter of moral principle not of our own self-interest'.[57] These are fine sentiments, but we can also argue from self-interest: the security that is 'won' by sacrificing minority rights is often a sham; it is fool's gold.

[55] M Elliott, 'The "War on Terror" and the United Kingdom's Constitution' (2007) I *European Journal of Legal Studies* available at: www.ejls.eu/index.php?mode=present&displayissue=2007–04 6; see also PCR Committee, London, Stationery Office, 'Antiterrorism, Crime and Security Act 2001 Review: Report' (2003).

[56] A Roy, *Power politics*, 2nd edn (South End Press, 2001).

[57] R Dworkin, 'Terror and the Attack on Civil Liberties' in T Rockmore, J Margolis and AT Marsoobian (eds), *The Philosophical Challenge of September 11* (Blackwell Publishing, 2005) 86.

Though we may feel safer when the government locks up suspected miscreants, if there is no proof to charge them that is a very good general indication they have done nothing wrong. Holmes argues that governments who make such calculations are 'implicitly subordinating the cognitively demanding guilty/innocent distinction to a bright line that they have less trouble finding, namely the difference between them and us'.[58] Detention of innocent people is not only morally wrong (per Dworkin), and susceptible to racial abuse (per Holmes), but it is likely to exacerbate not eliminate threats. In this chapter it has been argued that the safeguarding of minority liberties, by, for example, using surveillance instead of draconian detention powers, redounds to the collective security of the majority. Protecting minorities, we insulate the majority from enmity.

Nussbaum's work is of great importance. She has illuminated the fact that a fear of foreigners is more probably informed by ignorance than knowledge. The unreal sense of insecurity this brings, and the irrational enmity it can generate, are counter-productive in both daily life and military command. A misleading individual perception of threat, triggered by a different complexion or a slightly flatter nose, can spread like a virulent virus throughout a nation because of, not in spite of, its democratic constitution. These reflections tie back into the odd inability of political leaders to admit, and by extension, for the public to accept, that it is nigh on impossible decisively to 'win' the war on terror, unless someone can uninvent dynamite.[59]

Only through education can we achieve a greater understanding of our own proclivities and the identity of others. Only through sharing our cultures can we cure democracy of its tendency to magnify our prejudices, catalysing a terrorist threat we have hitherto failed properly to appreciate. Andrew Norris insightfully warns that

> it is a fool's gamble to seek safety in injustice – just as it is a fool's gamble to assume that one's enemy is wholly irrational, and not motivated by an anger and frustration that one might share, and that one might help alleviate. This will no doubt be difficult. But it is not as hopeless a task as ridding the world of evil, nor is it as likely to undermine our own legal and moral order.[60]

Embracing heterogeneity and defending justice takes courage, courage absent in those who misguidedly seek reassurance in homogeneity. Enmity for others, often born of an unrealistic rejection of the fragility of human life, stems from insecurity of the self. Conversely, amity and security are intrinsically linked and can be mutually reinforcing. Armed with this understanding, in the next chapter, we can confront our more primitive urges, our fears, and our perversions.

[58] S Holmes, 'In Case of Emergency: Misunderstanding Tradeoffs in the War on Terror' (2009) 97 *California Law Review* 303.

[59] The expression, 'a different complexion or a slightly flatter nose' is borrowed from J Conrad, *Heart of Darkness* (Penguin Classics, 2007 [1899]) 7.

[60] A Norris, '"Us" and "Them"' in T Rockmore, J Margolis and AT Marsoobian (eds), *The Philosophical Challenge of September 11* (Blackwell Publishing, 2005) 39.

6

Sex, Terror and Perversion

There is just one thing I cannot grasp, and that is how the indulgent can ever set a limit on their desires?

Marcus Tullius Cicero

THE SUBJECT-MATTER of this chapter relates so closely to its predecessor that its inclusion here was irresistible, and, betraying the structure embraced so far, observations on how these notes relate to the foregoing will not feature at the end, but can be considered implicit in all of what follows. Sex, terror and perversion do not need any extensive preliminary explication, except perhaps to say that all three are closer sisters than one might initially imagine.

Some of the terrain covered here is loose and will require a certain robustness on the part of the reader. The first topic, sex, is, as it were, approached from several angles; the second, terror, focuses on its key feature – the fear it aims to produce. The discussion of perversion is particularly ugly in aspect, noting, as it must, the maltreatment meted out in ostensible protection of our security. By way of succour, the next chapter is far easier on the eye, dealing as it does with sublimity. Nevertheless, much of what immediately follows is not for the faint-hearted and should be prefaced with an apology. Sadly, no serious investigation of our often feral responses to terrorism can omit this material. To do so would be to study the scene of a murder without having the phlegm to look at the corpse.

No longer crucial to the survival of the human race, sex has officially left the realm of need, and passed into the realm of pleasure: as a matter of fact, scientific progress means that reproduction no longer necessitates the ungainly meeting of bodies, but more importantly than that, the ungainly meeting of bodies no longer entails the possibility of reproduction – procreation has become recreation. Sex is a matter of choice now more than ever before in the history of human society. Consequently, arguments about why, how and, most apropos, with whom we may recreate are at the heart of modern liberty.[1]

It is no surprise, therefore, that the most emphatic way to strip someone of their liberty, involves literally stripping them, then violating their sexual autonomy. A more convincing assertion of dominance than those methods made

[1] C Fried, *Modern liberty and the limits of government*, 1st edn (WW Norton & Co, 2007)

notorious by the Abu Ghraib photographs is hard to imagine. As Holmes points out, there was also no better way than sexual torture for the US troops to confirm the unfair stereotype that Americans are violent sexual perverts.[2] The best publicist for the version of Islamic jihad propagated by Osama bin Laden has been the US Military Police – words to the effect of 'God help us' accompanied the release of harrowing images of emaciated, bruised men forced to masturbate, or being led around like dogs.

There is a sinister inverse parallel between men's sentiments about women and torture, which I will try to elaborate. For the subconscious, women are a disagreeable reminder of male mortality. Nothing makes a man more vulnerable than the female, as nature dictates that women are what is wanting in men. Men seek security in the denial and oppression of their insecurity, that is, men seek domination over women in order to conquer the weakness that is their attraction to and innate need for women.

A man's delight at the female form and her disposition can oscillate to disgust with terrifying velocity. In a way, our attraction to women is the source of this disgust, a contradictory urge, which has no better portrayal than Willem de Kooning's painting, *Woman I*.[3] He perfectly depicts not only man's perception of the ferocity of femininity but also the deleterious effect that this perception has on women. The figure, a combination of fertility idols and modern glamour girls, leaps off the canvas, an aggressor, a threat, and yet somehow, she retains enough of her feminine wiles to evoke a sense of sympathy in the observer, who cannot help but feel, in the harsh light of her unbearable aspect, that Kooning's exaggeratedly jagged brushstrokes have done her beauty some injustice. The enduring power of the painting derives directly from Kooning's ingenious depiction of *Woman I* as a victim-aggressor. I want to underline that a male distaste for insecurity causes delight to swing to disgust or an intense fear of rejection, and by extension, of death. This volatile valence occurs at the seedy rendezvous of lust and bloodlust, love and hate, attraction and repulsion.

By virtue of their potential to further a race, women have always been the victims of man's emotional caprice. They become the focal point for our repulsion-attraction for another race. But men have not escaped either. As Ferguson reports, Himmler wanted Nazi doctors to find economic ways to sterilise Jews, Russians and Poles; Professor Claus Clauberg tried to destroy Jewish uteruses with irritant fluid; whilst Doctor Horst Schuman preferred firing x-rays at men and women to render them infertile. This concerted attempt to purge the Reich of its impurities was contradicted by the sexual desire felt, even

[2] S Holmes, *The Matador's Cape: America's Reckless Response to Terror* (Cambridge University Press, 2007) 272–5.

[3] Antonio Saura's, *Retrato imaginario de Brigitte Bardot* (1962), might well have been inspired by similar sentiments; it is at least a similarly brilliant depiction of the fear and loathing harboured by men with respect to powerful female sexuality.

in concentration camps, by the master race for those officially thought of as vermin. Of course, some even fell in love.[4]

Inversely, torture, something that should be the subject of universal disgust, can become addictive, even cathartic, in the visceral intoxication of cruelty. Torture of men by women of another culture is a triple humiliation: racial, sexual and physical. However, torture of men by men is a way of indulging and at the same time denying homosexual fantasy, by dominating and disrespecting another man. It is also a means of combatting one's own sense of physical vulnerability by exerting a tyrannical control over another man, who can always present a threat, but, more profoundly, by subordinating a symbolic embodiment of our own human frailty. Like Kooning's anti-idol, the men in US military custody are victim-aggressors. They were 'bad men' in the parlance and fantasy of the Bush administration, and yet they are innocent victims until proven otherwise.

Torture is often presented as the antithesis of legality, and though this is illuminating in terms of procedural protocol, it can unhelpfully cloud law's relation to force. Law would not be law if it did not involve dominion, a constraint on liberty; its relationship to violence then, is that of a sister-by-marriage (in law). Domination is integral to, not inimical to law just as it is integral to torture.

Perhaps the role played by sex in torture is obvious; less apparent is its impact on terrorism, and our response thereto. The collusion, in Joseph Conrad's *Under Western Eyes*, of terrorism and sexual assault is not mere literary playfulness, but a realisation of a close tryst between fear, sex, death and violence. It seems that, just as an inexorable attraction to women is also the source of an existential aversion, women are imagined by men to embody the potential for the furtherance but also the destruction of our societies. Wyndham Lewis thought that women's role was 'the manufacturing of children (even more important than cartridges and khaki suits)'.[5]

When, through the lens of the enmity discussed in the last chapter, we observe women's potential for furthering the human race, the phenomenon of birth-rate anxiety becomes easier to understand. Oddly, sex, enmity and terror are accomplices. The best demonstration of this is the inexplicable threat supposed to emanate literally from the wombs of a rival group, as if babies were frightening. Frequent features of genocidal campaigns are the usage of rape to destroy bloodlines and violence done to pregnant women's wombs in ad hoc vivisections.[6] In the Indian context, Nussbaum diagnoses the Hindu Right's fear that 'Muslims also (unlike the British) symbolise sexuality run rampant, sexuality out of control, a flood or tide of sex and birth that threatens to drown the

[4] N Ferguson, *The War of the World* (Allen Lane, 2006) 465.
[5] W Lewis, 'A Super Krupp – Or War's End', *Blast 2*, 16.
[6] N Ferguson, *The War of the World* (Allen Lane, 2006) 456.

nation'.[7] What else can explain that in the violent conflagrations in Gujarat, the radical right-wing extremists ripped foetuses from pregnant women's wombs, incinerating them in ready-made fires? As Nussbaum explains, 'the idea that Hindus, despite constituting 82 per cent of the population, are in the position of a persecuted minority, is ubiquitous in the Hindu right'.[8]

Holmes astutely observes the same demographic anxiety and birth-rate envy in Huntington's *Clash of Civilisations*.[9] Similar ideas of a nebulous, multiplying threat poison modern Britain, where the white majority stands in an even larger ratio to the Muslim minority than do the Hindus in India. This irrational, cowardly and, frankly, shameful fear fuels the argument for pre-emptive violence, for stamping out the foreign fire before it gets out of control. Frenzied stamping is a good metaphor for British foreign policy in the early part of this millennium.

Sex, however threatening it is when it results in babies, is almost omnipresent in modern advertising. Such is the allure of sexual pleasure, it can even be used to sell suicide.

> The martyr has a guarantee from God: He forgives him at the first drop of his blood and shows him his seat in Heaven. He decorates him with the jewels of faith, protects him from the torment of the grave, keeps him safe on the day of judgment, places a crown of dignity on his head with the finest rubies in the world, marries him to seventy-two of the pure virgins of paradise and intercedes on behalf of seventy of his relatives.[10]

The Hadith reinforces the argument that there is a morbid ancestral relation between sex – normally associated with the production of life – and death, sexual fulfilment and violence. It ought to go without saying that the hijack of this sort of text by those who ague impressionable youngsters – enlisting them to kill themselves and innocent civilians – is anathema to Islam. What is perhaps less readily admitted is that we all share responsibility when people are so alienated from proper influences, or are socially outcast to the extent that they become hungry enough to gobble up the absurdity that God will reward them for killing defenceless men and women, including their co-religionists.

Stories of suicide bombers who originate from Muslim diasporas in Western society tell of a loss of status,[11] an initial insatiable curiosity for Western women that sours with rejection into an acidic revulsion. Peripatetics will know of the sense of castration that accompanies first attempts to convey oneself in a foreign

[7] M C Nussbaum, *The Clash Within: Democracy, Religious Violence, and India's Future* (The Belknap Press, 2007) 204.

[8] *ibid*, 58.

[9] S Holmes, *The Matador's Cape: America's Reckless Response to Terror* (Cambridge University Press, 2007) 147.

[10] A al-Tirmihdi, *Hadith Collection* (Vol 4, Book 23, Ch 1, No 1, p 620, publication date unknown).

[11] S Holmes, *The Matador's Cape: America's Reckless Response to Terror* (Cambridge University Press, 2007) 29–30.

tongue across the already high gender and racial hurdles. Osama bin Laden tells virgin voyagers into Western society, with its depressingly omnipresent sexual imagery, to 'think for themselves' but also that the 'sitting around and giving lessons' is nought in comparison to pledging your 'soul and head' to God. Perpetual virgins and, depending on who you read, a permanent state of erectile arousal are the promised goodies for an alienated, sexually insecure, European Muslim youth who have guilty feelings about wanting what they often cannot get, and what they feel they would be disgusted by if they had.

And so it transpires that young, vulnerable Muslim men, frustrated by wholesale rejection by supposedly easy white women, embrace the ready-made tribal virtues and 'religious rectitude' of violently reactionary brotherhoods.[12] Violent disgust replaces virile desire as they are transported by frustration from the fringes of society into fringe societies. Love for men fills the chasm created by lust for women; but such an artificial substitute cannot sustain a human being. The prophets of suicide promise a cleansing, enduring eroticism of a hero's death, a martyr's destiny that ends a banal and futile life on earth with the glory of religious significance in the fight for transcendental truth, beauty and justice. Death, sex, transcendental truth and power emancipate oversexed, confused and impotent youths from their hitherto pathetic lives. Furthermore, the imaginary purifying fire of professedly religious violence extinguishes the sinful feelings of earthly temptations for the seemingly selectively promiscuous Western womenfolk.[13]

I alluded earlier to the classic tactic of radical anti-Western preaching: the denunciation of the turpid sexual profligacy of Western society. Suicide bombers are encouraged to deliver themselves from temptation, but also to rescue their victims from self-destructive wickedness. If we want to combat such ideologies, we must, at the very least, attempt to understand how our choices might seem to cultures in which there has not been a public disavowal of restraints on private sexual behaviour, and where the public are not subjected to the bombardment with sexual imagery to which we have become accustomed in the West. It is worth reflecting on the notion that when we sacrifice sexual morality on the altar of an all-embracing liberty, we might well appear disgusting to others, not because our societies are inherently repulsive, but because of the human tendency, discussed above, to project fears about one's own perverted proclivities onto other societies. I am not suggesting wholesale change, only self-awareness. Sexual disgust, then, far from being irrelevant to the terrorist threat, turns out to be of some importance. The case of Mohammed Bouyeri, murderer of the Dutch filmmaker Theo van Goth, lends credibility to the theory that initial excitement at the prospect of sexually liberated European society can quickly turn to disgust, reactionary piety and murderous hatred when intimate relations

[12] I Buruma, 'Extremism: the loser's revenge', *The Guardian*, Saturday 25 February 2006, at: www.guardian.co.uk/world/2006/feb/25/terrorism.comment.

[13] D Benjamin and S Simon, *The Age of Sacred Terror* (Random House, 2002) 165.

with Dutch girls fail to materialise in the convenient way they do in the imagination. Rejection is the prelude to revulsion.

Modern media converge in a veritable ocean of information; disparities between indigent and affluent are more apparent than ever before; private insecurities that afflict the wretched, can, where they affect a group, take on a public character; and global groups are more easily formed due to the networking opportunities made possible by mobile and online communication. So circumstanced, a group's collective insecurity is like tinder and can be ignited by clever manipulators into a desire for violent dominance. Very little is needed for a majority group to feel threatened by a minority. It would seem that a combination of swelling minority numbers (due to immigration or birth rate), intermarriage 'threatening the racial purity' of the majority, and economic instability can stoke an innate human tendency to establish pseudo-superiority through violence.[14] Both terrorists and politicians can instrumentalise these conditions to their own ends.

It is helpful to remember that we cannot really distinguish between politics and personality. Private bitterness is channelled into political activity. 'The way' writes Conrad, 'of even the most justifiable revolutions is prepared by personal impulses disguised into creeds'.[15] Personal outrage, or a desire for vengeance can grow into political aggression. As Holmes points out, in Al-Zawahiri's *Knights under the Prophet's Banner*, he 'speaks bitterly of his comrades and "brothers" who were "killed by acts of torture" or "killed under torture". He explicitly justified jihad as "retribution for … the souls of the tortured people throughout the land of Islam"'.[16] Nothing emerges so clearly from a critical reading of Al-Zawahiri's opus than that the shortcomings he singles out for criticism in the 'Western world' exactly mirror the deficiencies he fears in his own psyche and, by extension, the fate he wishes to avert for the 'Muslim world'. This is a (con)fusion of the personal and the politico-religious, the elision of the enemy within and without. Along the same lines, an entire group might project its self-loathing into symbolic acts of cleansing, rectifying, self-edifying violence against another group. Dominating others can cathartically counteract a sense of collective weakness or insecurity. It can give people a sense of expelling impure or weak elements in the self.

On the national plane, Nussbaum argues that, there

> can be little doubt that the aggressive hardness of current Israeli masculinity is a reaction, in many cases quite self-conscious, against the perceived softness and weakness of European Jewish manhood, which brought untold misery and humiliation upon the Jewish people.[17]

[14] N Ferguson, *The War of the World* (Allen Lane, 2006).

[15] J Conrad, 'The Secret Agent' in *The Portable Conrad* (Penguin Classics, 2007) 436.

[16] S Holmes, *The Matador's Cape: America's Reckless Response to Terror* (Cambridge University Press, 2007) 284.

[17] MC Nussbaum, *The Clash Within: Democracy, Religious Violence, and India's Future* (The Belknap Press, 2007) 197.

Israel has good reason to feel threatened but it is certainly worth investigating both the ætiology and the prudence of the somewhat uncompromising nature of her foreign policy, including torture and targeted killings. Were European Jews not castigated for their successes rather than their failures?

Now, the usage of torture with impunity is not only a wholesale rejection of supposedly established and immutable law, it is a rejection of the accountability traditionally considered inherent in the notion of liberal democratic government; conversely, it constitutes an expression of untrammelled political power, ie, tyranny. Perhaps intimidated by this false image of power, the European Court of Human Rights has adopted an imbalanced stance on torture. Though it is forthright, absolute and unconditional in its ban on the deportation of people to countries where they are at risk of torture or ill-treatment, it has been of no assistance whatsoever to those who have actually suffered torture and have been denied recourse to justice in their home state.[18] I have lamented this state of affairs at length elsewhere,[19] so for now, it suffices to note that this half-way house is an intolerably uncomfortable resting place for European countries professedly committed to the eradication of that most egregious misuse of state power.

More profoundly perhaps, in the new world of bewildering religious, philosophical and spiritual plurality, the state use of torture is also a claim to certainty about the 'dictates of conscience', a claim to mastery of the moral universe. This claim to ethical surety might spring from collective uncertainties, the great unsettling spiritual uncertainties about which Dostoevsky wrote *The Brothers Karamazov*. It might be that these existential tribulations plague a disenchanted America, which must, for the sake of its very identity, believe in the absolute rightness of its founding principles. On one interpretation, no doubt preferred by incredulous Americans who reject any notion of their Œdipean guilt, the Bush administration violated the time-honoured tenets of American nationhood, including respect for equality and liberty. On another interpretation, prevalent amongst Europeans with short memories, the war on terror has simply thrown the unprincipled nature of America's nationhood into relief, unless of course, racism, terror or tyranny can be called principles. The reality might be that it is unfair to attempt to pigeonhole the kaleidoscopic American mindset. This notwithstanding, it is hard to resist the conclusion that there was enough of a concentration of characters, who we can politely call 'short-term strategists' in the Bush administration (think of the Horner-Rumsfeld correspondence on the merits of madness) who thought that scrupulousness in defence of her interests, often located abroad, was America's greatest weapon. Inevitably, this is saddening for those who defend the notion that the USA is a federation of values as well as states.

[18] Compare *Saadi v Italy* (Application No 37201/06) 28 February 2008 with *Al-Adsani v United Kingdom* (Application No 35763/97) 21 November 2001, ECHR 2001-XI.

[19] RS Brown, 'Access to justice for torture victims' in F Francioni (ed), *Access to justice as a human right* (Oxford University Press, 2007).

Like sex, fear does not lend itself to rational analysis. We often marvel at the fearlessness of children, who hurl themselves off climbing frames or hurtle down ski-slopes. However, Nietzsche thought of fear as man's original and fundamental sensation. Do we school ourselves in fear, that is, learn to be afraid, and, if so, how serviceable is fear? We often speak of the irrational nature of fear, that it clouds our judgement, or causes us to freeze at the very moment when rapid movement would be advisable. This is not to deny that fear is real.

In America, the post-9/11 trauma was very real. Sleeplessness, depression and a fear of future terrorism plagued the population. In the United Kingdom, fear of world war was higher in 2004 than it was in 1954. It is clear that fear can have a large fictional element. As Francis Fukuyama put it, in 2006, 'many neo-conservatives continued to see the world as populated by dangerous and underappreciated threats'.[20] This comment is reminiscent of Ciaran Carson's observation that 'IRA men were practically invisible ... seeming to exist by rumour or osmosis in a narrative dimension largely inaccessible to the overwhelmingly non-combatant Catholic population'.[21]

When fear is driven by popular fiction or urban myth, or where it is irrational or exaggeratedly high, there is little hope for enlightened policy-making or accurate threat assessment. Fear prevents us from thinking straight, and it can suppress our conscience too. Irrational, immoral people will rubber-stamp irrational immoral politics. Rather than increasing security, fear can inform policies that decrease security by unnecessarily imperiling and provoking other societies. Furthermore, it can tempt a government to squander defence resources by concentrating on unlikely threats. Perhaps the best example of this is the doctrine attributed to Dick Cheney: 'If there's a 1% chance that Pakistani scientists are helping al-Qaeda build or develop a nuclear weapon, we have to treat it as a certainty in terms of our response'.[22] If threats that have a one per cent chance of materialising are treated as certainties, one is left wondering what resources are left over for threats having a two per cent, 10 per cent, or 20 per cent chance of materialising. Clearly, such a mindset is a recipe for an imbalanced defence policy. Pursuant to this 'logic', innocent communities have been confronted with aggression whilst America and Britain turned their backs on more realistic threats. What about the threat of escalating tension with Russia or Iran, or the germination of home-grown terrorist cells, or the combined threat of a weakening in defences at home necessitated by extended campaigns abroad and Chinese economic growth and remilitarisation? Where a society becomes

[20] F Fukuyama, *America at the Crossroads: Democracy, Power, and the Neoconservative Legacy* (Yale University Press, 2006) 62.

[21] C Carson, *The Star Factory* (Arcade Publishing, 1998) 117.

[22] R Suskind, 'The Untold Story of an Al Qaeda Plot to Attack the Subway', *Time*, 19 June 2006, available at: www.time.com/time/magazine/article/0,9171,1205478,00.html?cnn=yes.

mentally enslaved to an inaccurately depicted external enemy who poses an exorbitantly assessed threat, it risks squandering energy that could be better spent elsewhere.

The terror created, in Cheney's words, of a 'low-probability, high-impact' nuclear attack on America, bears a disconcerting resemblance to the conditions for detainees in American custody. Guantánamo Bay survivors describe how the pain caused by torture was nothing compared to the anticipation of future torture, and the potentially infinite detention. He who fears hell, then, careers towards it.

So, the subject-matter of terror contains a fictional element; the stuff of hearsay and rumour; it can be irrational, wildly skewing our responses; and it might well instill in us a desire to imperil others. But there is yet a darker face of fear – it can be a self-indulgent fantasy; indeed, that humans derive some pleasure out of fright is not a controversial assertion; such pleasure is unproblematic where it is confined to roller-coaster rides and horror films but we should be wary of our cinematic or literary fantasies colouring our readings of the real world. America, 'in its formative decades lived in a state of substantial insecurity';[23] it wrestled off monarchic rule, and expanded its frontiers. It was a violent conception and one that has been mythologised in popular fiction. I will say more on America as the personification of the virtuous outlaw who so frequently appears in its movie culture, in the chapter on the public man; but for now, we can concentrate on the characters created to mobilise armies.

George Orwell's *Nineteen Eighty Four*, first published shortly after World War II, is perhaps the most persistent and depressing modern example of art-imitating-life-imitating-art. His enigmatic 'Goldstein' is our bin Laden, perversely the greatest ally of our ruling class, the excuse that can be wheeled out for any policy, however draconian. In Oceania, the enemy represented 'absolute evil, and it followed that any past or future agreement with him was impossible'.[24] Bush made the almost identical assertion that America had been attacked 'by evil' and that '[w]e're not facing a set of grievances that can be soothed and addressed. We're facing a radical ideology with inalterable objectives'.[25]

As for the impossibility of past agreement, Americans had a few advantages over Orwell's Oceanians. First, some US citizens were able to remember former President Bush Senior's financial support of Saddam Hussein's regime and the CIA's backing of Jihadi resistance to Soviet incursion into Afghanistan. Second, unlike Oceania's residents, Americans are not actually prohibited or prevented from learning about the cultures with which they are told they are at war.

[23] R Kagan, *Of paradise and power : America and Europe in the new world order*, 1st edn (Alfred A Knopf: Distributed by Random House, 2003) 30.

[24] G Orwell, *Nineteen Eighty Four* (Penguin Books, 1954 (Secker & Warburg [1949])) 31.

[25] G Bush, 'President discusses War on Terror at National Endowment for Democracy', *White House Press Release*, 6 October 2005, available at: www.whitehouse.gov/news/releases/2005/10/20051006–3.html.

Whether they availed themselves of this opportunity is quite another matter. One would have thought that an informed population might have put up more of a protest when the bounty hunt for a terrorist in one country metamorphosed into the deposition of a dictator in another. In Britain, some of the population, though clearly not a large enough constituency to stop the offensive, was attentive enough to notice the government's rolling substitution of the justification for its twin wars; 'WMD' was not originally an acronym for 'We'll Make Democracy'. If it is bad military policy to fight protracted campaigns, it is imbecilic in the extreme to start wars without a clear idea of what is to be achieved. As we have seen, a moving-the-goalposts-as-we-go-along approach risks achieving nothing. Bin Laden is still at liberty. Saddam had no weapons of mass destruction and, at the time of writing, not even the most biased of commentators would describe Afghanistan or Iraq as stable democratic states.

If the British-American policy was actually just thinly veiled 'deterrence', or a Clintonian 'don't tread on us' message, involving the attempt to strike fear into the hearts of terrorists with terrible, and almost invariably reckless reprisals, it was – aside from being ethically indefensible and patently illegal – totally imprudent.[26] This sort of policy must be distinguished from a perfectly legitimate display of superior fighting ability – efficiently and effectively fending off an attacker – which works as a deterrent to future attack, and is morally hard to fault.

Measured self-defence is the equivalent of breaking the bully's nose to stop him strangling you for your lunch money. In contrast, invading a country that bears no relation to the dead men who attacked your cities, toppling its leader, dismantling its army and occupying it without even the faintest scintilla of a plan for settlement or stabilisation is a sure-fire investment in prolonged, internecine hatred. The United States and the United Kingdom have incurred infamy and enmity, two accolades that are greatly counterproductive for any society wishing to create an atmosphere of long-term security.

Whilst I was writing this chapter, Blair's successor, Prime Minister Gordon Brown, who many hoped might distance Britain from America, addressed troops in Camp Bastion, Afghanistan, on his way to watch the laudable British effort in the Chinese Olympics. Comparing the courage of the troops to that of our athletes, he reminded the soldiers what they were fighting for – 'freedom and justice' – before assuring them that 'you know what you are doing here prevents terrorism from coming to the streets of Britain'.[27] I am hard-pushed to accept that Brown believes this emetic rhetoric; that he thought continued alignment with reviled American troops, his shoulder-rubbing with their despised Commander-in-Chief, and fighting a bloody and intractable counter-insurgency

[26] For a similar view, see S Holmes, *The Matador's Cape: America's Reckless Response to Terror* (Cambridge University Press, 2007) 10.

[27] 'Olympians will salute you, Brown tells troops', *The Times*, 22 August 2008, available at: www.timesonline.co.uk/tol/news/politics/article4578623.ece.

in an inhospitable, mountainous land would make people in Canary Wharf any safer. Politically astute Londoners might well wonder whether the relatively simple act of divorcing the United Kingdom from its violent union with America would increase their security more than forcing a warped version of democracy down the throats of militant Muslims almost four thousand miles away.

It is not the establishment of democracy, which may or may not include a preference for periodical secret ballots, that will prevent terrorism, but the satisfaction of people's basic desires and the inculcation of the rule that killing innocents is a poor choice of means to bring about change. No mistake ought to be made about it, the real threat to world stability comes not from the dispersed, lightly-armed peons of pan-Islamist terrorism; it comes from the potential for hasty, misconceived and heavy-handed state overreactions, not to speak of the terrible and unpredictable chain reactions they might set in motion. This, if anything, is the lesson of the events that triggered World War I – Gavrilo's Gift.

But it is not only fear that has driven our reaction to terrorism off the road. We must also confront our relationship to violence, which would seem to bear more than a shade of the perverse. Again, perversion, as a topic, is hard to pin down so I shall content myself with making some observations, and asking some probing questions.

The first observation to make is that violent emotion and sexual emotion are experienced in similar ways, and both can be addictive. In his historical fiction, *The Middle Parts of Fortune*, recording the very human experience on the Somme and Ancre fronts, Frederic Manning describes the 'pleasure in killing', the 'ecstasy of battle' and that 'there was some strange intoxication of joy in it'. He is frank about the relation of this sort of ecstasy to sex:

> Afterwards all the insubordinate passions released by battle, and that assertion of the supremacy of one's own particular and individual will, though these may be momentarily quiescent from exhaustion, renew themselves and find no adequate object, unless in the physical ecstasy of love, which is less poignant.[28]

But what relevance do the blood-soaked battlefields of the Somme have to life today? Hobsbawm argues that 'the sight, sound and description of violence in its extreme forms are part of everyday life, and the social controls on its practice are consequently diminished'.[29] This is perhaps putting it a little high but exposure to fictional violence and human carnage in the news media must have an effect on our evaluation of its social role. Michael Sherry observes that

> war defined much of the American imagination … to the point that Americans routinely declared 'war' on all sorts of things that did not involve physical combat at all.

[28] F Manning, *The Middle Parts of Fortune: Somme and Ancre* (Filiquarian Publishing, 2007) 78.
[29] EJ Hobsbawm, *Globalisation, democracy and terrorism* (Little Brown, 2007) 127.

> Thus, militarization reshaped every realm of American life – politics and foreign policy, economics and technology, culture and social relations, making America a profoundly different nation.[30]

Sherry's point is that warfare's dominance of the American mindset led to the adoption of a martial lexicon, which then shaped behaviour in other fields. This is perhaps a longer and more careful route for arriving at Hobsbawm's seemingly abrupt conclusion that the social constraints on violence have slackened.

More generally, it is worth asking whether we are becoming addicted to the BBC and CNN reports of yet another suicide bombing in Baghdad, yet another storming of a Taliban stronghold, yet another war hero coming home in a casket. These victuals of violence, stories of martyrs, heroes and anti-heroes, seep into our brains like drip-fed death and depravation. Do they quench a bloodlust, helping us stomach the bland normality of our privileged existence? Can it be that Iraq was invaded not to topple a tyrant but to battle the tyranny of city banality? And is our fear of terrorism similar to the escapism offered by virtual reality games or Tom Clancy novels; is it a perverse diversion? What purpose, for instance, does the daily terrorism threat report serve? Are New Yorkers more vigilant as they enter the train on an orange threat day? Do Londoners queerly enjoy eyeballing rucksack-wearing men of a brown complexion over the top of the daily rag? Does a taste of fear make our otherwise nauseatingly dull journey to work more palatable?

These questions refer to a perversion that is hard to tie down. However, the war on terrorism was characterised, like all wars, by a very real perversion that would be unbelievable but for the equally incomprehensible photograph albums of the perpetrators. In March 2004, CBS released pictures taken by members of the US military of detainees at Abu Ghraib. Some of these images, such as the hooded detainee on a box wired up to electrodes, the naked human pyramid, and the forced group masturbation, are branded on the collective memory so they will forever haunt our recollection of the millennium's first decade.

One story helps bring out several layers of perversion that otherwise go unsifted. In October 2003, Manadel al-Jamadi was captured by an elite Seal commando force in a raid near Baghdad. Less than a month later, after having been transferred into CIA custody at Abu Ghraib detention centre, Manadel died. Though he was repeatedly beaten, his death reportedly resulted from being subjected to what is called 'Palestinian hanging' or 'strappado', a technique used frequently in medieval times and in sadistic sex games, in which the victim is hung from the roof by their arms, which are bonded or handcuffed, behind their back. This technique is preferred by torturers because, though it results in no obvious external injuries, it hurts a lot, by causing massive internal damage, including dislocation and paralysis, and, on occasion death.

[30] M Sherry, *In the Shadow of War* (Yale University Press, 1995).

The first layer of perversion is the torture itself, which, naturally, is a violation of the laws of war, of human rights and the most basic dictates of conscience; the treatment is made all the more perverse because Manadel was picked up in connection with a bombing at the offices of the International Red Cross, an organisation dedicated to preventing precisely such maltreatment.

The second layer of perversion is that officers Sabrina Harman and Charles Graner in charge of Manadel's by now bagged and iced corpse, thought it an opportune moment not for grief, or remorse, or a confession of guilt but to have their pictures taken grinning and gesturing a thumbs up. The stripping of victims and the taking of pictures are not new. In 1942, at the mass execution of Jews in Dubno, victims were stripped to 'degrade and humiliate', but also to satisfy personal 'prurience'.[31] There too, photographs were taken. The second layer of perversion, then, is voyeurism or the brazen documentation of the outrageous.

The third layer of perversion is the psychological damage that such activities can have on individuals and society. Harman, something of a diarist as well as a photographer, wrote the following disturbing and confused letter to an intimate friend on 20 October 2003. It perfectly captures how her morality and personality were perverted by what she saw, and how, in her view, society was perverted by what was hidden from view.

> One of the guys took my asp and started 'poking' at [a detainee's] dick. Again, I thought that's funny, then it hit me, that's a form of molestation … The only reason I want to be there is to get the pictures and prove the US is not what they think. But I don't know if I can take it mentally. What if that was me in their shoes. These people will be our future terrorist. [sic] Kelly, its awful and you know how fucked I am in the head. Both sides of me think its wrong.[32]

The fourth layer of perversion relates to American fear and self-efficacy. Torture of another is a way of asserting dominion but also of reducing the prestige of the victim in the torturer's eyes. A comedian in the US was castigated for making a favourable comparison of the bravery of the 9/11 hijackers to that of Allied high-altitude bombers. When a victim of torture shows fear, fear of death, this dispels the awe and reverence the torturer has for those who would give their lives to their ideals in martyrdom operations. It is to this mentality that the infamous Bybee memo speaks (see below). Torture must take the victim close to death in order to prove to the torturer that the victim is afraid to die. As an aside, following Falk, it can be argued that the relationship of high-altitude or predator drone pilots (drones are remote-controlled) to targets is asymmetrical like that of torturer to tortured, rather than the symmetrical relationship between regular war combatants.

[31] N Ferguson, *The War of the World* (Allen Lane, 2006) 450.

[32] P Gourevitch and E Morris, 'The woman behind the camera at Abu Ghraib', *New Yorker*, 24 March 2008, available at: www.newyorker.com/reporting/2008/03/24/080324fa_fact_gourevitch?printable=true.

The fifth and most disturbing layer of perversion is that the command to, 'make it hell for them so they talk', did not originate in a prison in Abu Ghraib but in the White House. The strategy of scapegoating and deniability adopted by the Bush administration contributes to a total lack of accountability on the part of those in command. As mentioned earlier, in international criminal law, the doctrine of *command responsibility* is used to establish the responsibility of a commander for the crimes of his subordinates. The United States had a leading role in establishing this rule of customary international law.

In Manila in 1946, in the trial of the Japanese Commander for the Philippines, Yamashita, a the United States Military Commission held that, where 'there is no effective attempt by a commander to discover and control the criminal acts, such a commander may be held responsible, even criminally liable, for the lawless acts of his troops'. Furthermore, the trial commission was content to hold that Yamashita knew, or must have known about the crimes of those in his charge, because the rapes, torture and executions were so 'extensive and widespread, both as to time and area, that they must either have been willfully permitted by the accused, or secretly ordered by the accused'.[33]

One example of official acquiescence or complicity in the foul means resorted to in the war on terror is Donald Rumsfeld's affirmative response to a request for his authorisation of the usage of 'mild, non-injurious, physical contact, such as grabbing, poking in the chest with the finger, and light pushing' in interrogations. Rumsfeld added, in handwriting, the following note to the bottom of the document: 'However, I stand for 8–10 hours a day. Why is standing limited to 4 hours? DR'.[34] Perhaps the subtle differences between his choice to stand at a desk in the White House and being handcuffed to a ceiling in a Guantánamo cell were lost on the civilian administrator. By dint of his alleged personal approval of interrogational torture, the US-based Center for Constitutional Rights argues that Rumsfeld was instrumental in abuses at Guantánamo Bay and Abu Ghraib. Amongst the others accused of gross dereliction of duty are Attorney General Alberto Gonzales and former CIA Director George Tenet.

Despite the well-documented involvement of civil servants at the highest level, the official line on the torture pictures was that they were not representative of America. But America is a country founded in inequality, where for 32 of the first 36 years of independence, the president was a slave owner;[35] where more black men are in prison than in college; where the conduct of war, prison

[33] '*In re Yamashita*, Decision of the United States Military Commission at Manila, 1945–46' in L Friedman (ed), *The Law of War: A Documentary History* (Random House, 1972) 1596, 1597.

[34] D Rumsfeld, 'Request for authorisation of counter-resistance techniques from William J Haynes II, General Counsel' (27 November 2002) available at: www.defenselink.mil/news/Jun2004/d20040622doc5.pdf.

[35] D Losurdo, 'Preemptive War, Americanism, and Anti-Americanism' in Tom Rockmore, Armen T Marsoobian and J Margolis (eds), *The Philosophical Challenge of September 11* (Blackwell Publishing, 2005) 167.

construction and the management of detention are booming private industries.[36] It is conveniently forgotten that the statutes of the Southern states prohibiting interracial sexual and marital relations were used as templates by the Nazis.

In a subsequent chapter, I will ask whether America, like Sophocles' Œdipus, ought feel guilt for horrible acts it committed but did not perceive. For now, in the context of this chapter and the last, we can ask whether it would be more plausible, and honest to admit that the confounded photographs are just records of venerated, structural violence in American society? Alternatively, are Sabrina's snaps the pictorial manifestation of the hitherto unspoken or privately whispered sentiments of a large xenophobic constituency? Holmes wonders whether the collapse of military morality came not from a need to procure information but from more sinister, emotional urges.

> Could the motives behind the decision to tear up the rulebook on interrogation have been more visceral than rational? Is not the dominance of expressive over tactically rational impulses in Administration interrogation policy strongly suggested by the techniques actually employed, for instance, forcing detainees, whose identities and backgrounds were barely known, to wear bras and to bark like dogs while dragged around on leashes?[37]

If we are to believe that visceral rather than rational motives drove interrogation practices, does this also explain why the US set the bar for torture so high? Pursuant to Jay Bybee's memorandum for the Bush administration, only physical pain 'equivalent in intensity to the pain accompanying serious physical injury, such as organ failure, impairment of bodily function, or even death' counted as torture.[38] This is a ribald aphorism. Indeed, a better view is that indefinite detention alone ought to qualify as torture if it is without access to lawyers or family, without charge and seemingly without any hope of a hearing, let alone a fair hearing, let alone restoration to freedom. Would drowning not be more pleasant by virtue of its brevity? Harold Koh, Dean of Yale Law School, quite rightly called Bybee's contribution to US jurisprudence, 'a stain upon our law and our national reputation'.

What is my liberty worth if it is bought at the price of another's? Are some people more equal than others? In 1998, a UNICEF Report found that UN sanctions had resulted in the deaths of an extra 90,000 Iraqi children every year since 1991. Presented with a similar interim statistic in May of 1996, on the television programme *60 Minutes*, the US Ambassador to the United Nations, Madeleine Albright said: 'We think the price is worth it'. Is this a faux pas, a lapse from virtue into venality, or a clue to a cold calculus where children's lives

[36] Matlin, 'Abu Ghraib: The Surround' in *Abu Ghraib – The politics of torture* (North Atlantic Books, 2004).

[37] S Holmes, 'In Case of Emergency: Misunderstanding Tradeoffs in the War on Terror' (2009) 97 *California Law Review* 303.

[38] *Memorandum for Alberto Gonzales, Counsel to the President* [1 August 2002] re standards of conduct for interrogation under 18 USC §§ 2340–2340A.

can be considered part of a price worth paying? When sanctions became warfare in the wake of September 11, when the number of deaths caused by American policy increased exponentially, the Bush administration refused, in violation of the Geneva Conventions, to count the number of Iraqi civilians killed during the occupation. Though these questions will be dealt with more extensively later, we might for now hoist up the following question: Has economy swallowed humanity? If America is dependent on oil, can a child's life be measured against the price of a barrel? Is Albright saying it can, albeit rather cheaply?

Earlier, I mentioned the structural selfishness of liberal democracy. In this connection, it perhaps suffices to observe that the inbuilt institutional intolerance of our society is an acquiescence in vice and a discouragement of virtue. How does this relate to Albright's calculus? The approach of liberal democracy and the excessive emphasis on capitalist freedom devalues other, more substantial values, such as social justice and the well-being of foreign children.

Only perversion can explain how America, the self-anointed 'last, best hope for freedom', embraced the favourite and most formidable instrument of tyranny – arbitrary in communicado imprisonment. Of fundamental importance to liberty is the petition of habeas corpus, forcing a custodian to deliver up their detainee. A beaten, tortured, emaciated, sleep-deprived and professedly innocent detainee produces a strong effect on the judicial conscience, particularly in the absence of evidence to validate their imprisonment. Only perversion can explain why the President of a country that violently shrugged off English monarchic rule, was allowed to suspend the writ of habeas corpus, giving him, to quote Taney CJ,

> more regal and absolute power over the liberty of the citizen, than the people of England have thought it safe to entrust to the crown; a power which the queen of England cannot exercise at this day, and which could not have been lawfully exercised by the sovereign even in the reign of Charles the First.[39]

Only perversion can explain arguments run by the government to the effect that allowing legally innocent detainees to talk to lawyers would present an unacceptable security risk; that state secrets prevented the hearing of the indisputably innocent El-Masri's claim against the CIA for wrongful detention, abduction and torture; that it would be too burdensome for the government to corroborate that detainees were in fact captured on the battlefield, and not arbitrarily herded up by Afghan bounty hunters.[40]

82nd Airborne Division, whom we met earlier, detained Iraqis at a base called FOB Mercury, 10 miles east of Fallujah. The detainees were referred to as Persons Under Control, or PUCs, pronounced in the same way as the ice hockey puck. And we need look no further than systematic perversion to explain the

[39] *Ex parte Merryman* 17 F Cas 144 (1861) Circuit Court, D Maryland (Taney CJ).

[40] R Dworkin, 'Terror and the Attack on Civil Liberties' in T Rockmore, J Margolis and AT Marsoobian (eds), *The Philosophical Challenge of September 11* (Blackwell Publishing, 2005) 88.

recreational activity of 'puc-fucking'. Here is an excerpt from the testimony of a Sergeant in the division affectionately known by the Fallujah residents, not as the defenders of freedom of justice, but the 'murderous maniacs'.

> On their day off people would show up all the time. Everyone in camp knew if you wanted to work out your frustration you show up at the PUC tent. In a way it was sport. The cooks were all US soldiers. One day a sergeant shows up and tells a PUC to grab a pole. He told him to bend over and broke the guy's leg with a mini Louisville Slugger …[41]

Human Rights Watch concluded that such abuses recounted by soldiers of 82nd, 'can be traced to the Bush administration's decision to disregard the Geneva Conventions in the armed conflict in Afghanistan'.[42] Though it might be difficult to blame Bush, it is too easy to blame the soldiers, many of whom are as much victims of the recent American administration's foreign policy as the Iraqi civilians they have killed. From what little I understand of history's most prolific abusers of human dignity, they have not, contrary to popular perception, acted alone; on the contrary, they have a system of support behind them, including of course the army and their close administrative cronies, but also leaders of society: lawyers, diplomats and university professors, for example.

Two props for the contemporary political perversity deserve a mention. The first, senior British diplomat, Robert Cooper, argued that the challenge to the postmodern world is to get used to the idea of double-standards.

> Among ourselves, we operate on the basis of laws and open cooperative security. But when dealing with more old-fashioned kinds of states outside the postmodern continent of Europe, we need to revert to the rougher methods of an earlier era – force, pre-emptive attack, deception, whatever is necessary to deal with those who still live in the nineteenth century world of every state for itself … Among ourselves, we keep the law but when we are operating in the jungle, we must also use the laws of the jungle.[43]

I do find Cooper's theory challenging. As he well knows, the jungle has no laws, and lawlessness is precisely what characterised the Blairite internationalism he helped to craft. What Cooper is in fact arguing for, is not a clever double-standard, but when it comes to foreign policy, no standard at all, total unscrupulousness. What arguments like this help to do, is return us to the nineteenth century, to arms races, conquest, and clashing cultures, and to tear down the fragile achievements of those who would, naïvely, according to such openly duplicitous diplomats, attempt to establish rules that apply, without exception, to all people of all societies. The Russians and the Iranians, the

[41] Human Rights Watch, 'Leadership Failure: Firsthand Accounts of Torture of Iraqi Detainees by the US Army's 82nd Airborne Division' (25 September 2005), available at www.hrw.org/reports/2005/us0905.

[42] *ibid*, available at www.hrw.org/reports/2005/us0905.

[43] R Cooper, 'The post-modern state' in M Leonard (ed), *Reordering the world: The long-term implications of September 11th* (Foreign Policy Centre, London, 2002).

Japanese and the Chinese, might well ask, what gives a diplomat from a tiny island off France the right to decide that its leader gets to play King of the jungle?

Naturally, arguments like Cooper's found favour in the American academy. Kagan, ironically of the Carnegie Endowment for International Peace, tells us that America 'must support arms control, but not always for itself. It must live by a double standard'.[44] This is not the American dream, but the American fantasy, which is a dream not of freedom but of the virtuous outlaw. Cooper and Kagan are, with respect, labouring under a great misapprehension. A good argument can be made that a noxious cocktail of arrogance and ignorance informs these opinions that promise to send us drunkenly careering towards mutual oblivion.

A nation cannot provide moral leadership if it is bare-facedly duplicitous. There is a reason our political leaders are not above the domestic law. A peaceable international order cannot be established on the precarious foundation of institutionalised criminality; of a primitive philosophy of smash and grab: one rule for us, the self-appointed civilisers, and another for them, the backward savages. Is this not all depressingly familiar?

The central argument here is that a few, morally and prudentially unsustainable means must be renounced, including what Cooper confusingly calls, 'pre-emptive attack', by which, he presumably means, 'attack'. What kind of diplomat endorses deception? Cooper's suggestion is bewildering not because of its novelty – indeed, it seems to be a rather old idea, dressed up in second-hand terminological robes – but because of its sheer absurdity. Is humanitarian law to be expounded by war criminals, restraint imposed by unrestrained power, lawfulness taught by brigands, principle protected by hypocrites, peace guaranteed by war, and chastity preached by whores? The challenge for the modern world is not to live by double-standards; on the contrary, it is to agree to one, very simple rule for all, and consistently to castigate those who violate that rule.

Cooper's mention of deception brings me to that issue. In his essay, he was referring to old-fashioned deception; that is, deceiving other governments. A different kind of deception has coloured the war on terror, deception of the public, and this involved a departure from one of the conditions of democracy, namely transparency. In the British context, the 45-minute claim comes immediately to mind. In the US, the Center for Public Integrity reported that former President Bush and seven of his administration's top officials made at least 935 false statements in the two years following 11 September 2001, about the threat posed by Saddam Hussein's Iraq.[45] The apex of that pyramid of lies was perhaps the epistemic atrocity turned self-fulfilling prophecy that, 'you can't distinguish between al-Qaeda and Saddam when you talk about the war on terror'.[46] The

[44] R Kagan, *Of paradise and power: America and Europe in the new world order*, 1st edn (Alfred A Knopf: Distributed by Random House, 2003) 99.

[45] Center for Public Integrity, 'Report on Falsehood in the Bush Administration', 2008.

[46] GW Bush, discussing terrorism with Columbia President (The Oval Office 2002).

Commander-in-Chief's inability (intentional or inadvertent, it matters not) to distinguish between a terrorist network operating in eighty countries and the leader of one country, goes a long way to explaining his negligent deployment of the American military. Systematic dishonesty not only jeopardises the public trust vested in government but it undermines the integrity that democracy itself needs to survive.

This early attitude of falsehood became so entrenched that public statements by Bush and his cabal now tend to the ridiculous. To take just one example, five years on from the invasion of Iraq, Bush made a speech. Instead of owning the decision to disband the military, in a manner reminiscent of the constant rewriting of history in Orwell's *Nineteen Eighty Four*, he flagrantly misrepresented the decision taken in his name to disband the military, commenting that 'former regime elements took off their uniforms'.[47] In the knowledge that his troops had maltreated and murdered prisoners of war and had used earth-movers and tank-mounted ploughs to bury Iraqis alive in their trenches, Bush said that enemy 'death squads' were unconcerned with the 'conventions of war or the dictates of conscience'. He spoke of the discovery of Saddam's 'torture chambers' without, of course, reference to those he had established. He made a spurious comparison between the founding of America and the war in Iraq. Depending on the generosity of the listener, this is amplified spin, shameless hypocrisy, or downright mendacity.[48]

One of the most effective techniques used by the Bush administration was to describe the September 11 attacks as an original act of pure evil, rather than an understandable and desperate, yet nonetheless morally condemnable, act of revenge. Given the grand scale and unthinkable cruelty of the attacks on the World Trade Center, the image of a pure, original evil had enormous resonance with the American people, and naturally, if you are fighting pure evil, if your enemy is absolute, then absolutely anything goes. This rhetoric, the fantastic 'ticking bomb' conundrum, and the popular depiction in the media of torture as a standard tactic for combatting terrorism were perhaps the most influential factors in building the constituency for torture.

But the seed of torture germinated and grew, because it had a fertile ground in the American psyche. The most chilling insight came in former President Bush's State of the Union address in January 2003:

> All told, more than 3000 suspected terrorists have been arrested in many countries. Many others have met a different fate. Let's put it this way – they are no longer a problem to the US and our friends and allies.

The Chief Medical Officer, Dr Charles S Hirsch says that 2751 people died in the September 11 attacks. A clearer admission that the administration sought feudal and yet mathematical revenge could not be imagined: Bush was not

[47] GW Bush and G Brown, at the 5th Anniversary of Operation Iraqi Freedom (2008).
[48] *ibid.*

talking the simple language of an eye-for-an-eye, he was talking the language of violence that far exceeds that of the initial attack; not breaking the bully's nose when he strangles you for your lunch money, but killing his entire family, and decapitating his dog for good measure.

And although, in the administration's rhetoric, everything in Afghanistan and Iraq is being done not *to* but *for* the native people, scant concern for civilian life has been shown. Byers reports one example of this attitude pervading the previously banned policy of resorting to political assassinations. 'The air strike to kill Omar was called off because a lawyer at US Central Command was concerned about the risk of disproportionate civilian casualties. [Rumsfeld] sought – unsuccessfully – to reduce the number of lawyers in uniform'.[49] The most perverse decision of all, the Iraq invasion, a pre-emptive war, ie a war of aggression, justified on the grounds of the link between terrorism and Saddam Hussein, has become a self-fulfilling prophecy. Tom Rockmore speculates that the link was only visible to those with private interests in the oil industry, listing Rice, Cheney and Bush.[50] But the connection between Iraq and terrorism has now crystallised. Indeed, Iraq can be considered the birthplace of the child of terrorism that will mature in the next decade. Bush and Blair were its parents, Brown and Obama are its new reluctant guardians.

Above, I made some tentative observations about how sex, terror and perversion have featured in our response to terrorism, so that, in what follows, I can suggest how we might reconceptualise the law's relation to these topics, in order to avoid the self-defeating and immoral urges that have led us astray in our 'war on terrorism'. Some of the issues, which I skirted around here, are confronted head on in the penultimate chapter that concerns itself with our civic responsibility.

Law proscribes certain activities. It choreographs human interaction, banning certain modes of expression. It even presumes to draw lines across and between our bodies, prohibiting particular forms of consensual human intercourse. Law is, in part, the embodiment of the separate spheres of our bodies, and, willed by our minds, our bodies, by creating convention, embody law as they interact. Archytas argued that the throws of sensual pleasure leave no room for cerebral activity and it is in this tradition that sexual expression has been vilified by pious moralists and the enemies of liberty. But the ancient Greek's biological argument only really denounces prolonged sensual gratification for the sake of thought.

Aside from that, it is worth thinking of the act of sexual union, barring bizarre surgery and conjoined twins, as the closest possible physical union of two individuals – hence its historically central role in the consummation of love and in the curtailment of liberty. The repression of love-making in Orwell's Oceania was designed to keep the population's energies focused on war-making, to keep

[49] M Byers, *War law: international law and armed conflict* (Atlantic Books, 2005) 121.

[50] T Rockmore, 'On the So-called War on Terrorism' in T Rockmore, J Margolis and AT Marsoobian (eds), *The Philosophical Challenge of September 11* (Blackwell Publishing, 2005).

hatred and lunatic credulity at fever pitch: 'All this marching up and down and cheering and waving flags is simply sex gone sour'.[51] This is a part-sardonic, part-serious reference to the sense of peaceful contentment felt by lovers, a satisfaction that leaves no room for feelings of enmity. Taking Archytas (sex ousts thought) and Orwell (sex ousts hate) together, one might speculatively conclude that a lack or an excess of sensual pleasures are bad for society.

For what it is worth (by way of example), it would seem that the disturbingly high level of domestic violence in Bangladesh correlates to the taboos preventing expression of the female sexuality in public.[52] In the Gulshan District of Dhaka, a boy and girl will skip to school together holding hands, in the blissful ignorance of youthful innocence, unaware that such affection, if displayed in their adulthood, will not only be the subject of social opprobrium but has a chance of being replaced by a violent attitude. This is not to side with the Muslim feminist filmmakers or the so-called enlightened Western liberals who argue that gender roles engrained in Islam are to blame. Far from it. How can a dream be culpable? Is it not more realistic to argue that humans are responsible for their flawed attempts to instantiate the ideal? It is not too daring a proposition that the repression of amicable physical expression might result in increased violence. But it is with great care that we should attempt to understand the complex role of sex in other societies, and with patient empathy that we should attempt to understand their perception of its role in our own. Only such sensitivity can facilitate détente between the warring fringes of diverse cultures.

The point I am trying to make, in an admittedly roundabout fashion, is that empathy is not exhausted by understanding another, but includes also understanding his understanding of you. That further step is often crucial to bridging what might be called 'the incorrigibility gap' between two cultures. We might bristle at the notion that in another culture – take for example the rural parts of the Sylhet region in Bangladesh, famous for its tea gardens and tropical rainforests – it is customary for women not to be seen whilst eating, such that there are booths in eateries separating female from male diners by plastic partitions. This might offend or even outrage our sense of equality. We might consider it backward. And yet British men might without a sense of moral inconsistency lament the gradual attrition of the prohibition of female admission to London's better clubs. The root of the rules might well be the same, though they purport to derive from different doctrines, but these could well be normative overlays for a similarly unsophisticated sentiment common to both cultures.

In the case of Western sexual licence, the disgust we evoke in apparently strict, puritanical, or intolerant cultures can more easily be understood by reflecting on the almost identical criticisms levelled at an ethically unhinged Western society by our own churches. Bin Laden knows this, so, in one of his public statements,

[51] G Orwell, *Nineteen Eighty Four* (Penguin Books, 1954 (Secker & Warburg [1949])) 109.

[52] See Nari Jibon available at: www.siu.edu/~narijibon/DADV.htm.

after noting that Muslims believe in Jesus, made an appeal to American public morality, asking them to reject immoral acts such as 'fornication, homosexuality, intoxicants and gambling' and government policies of 'subjugation, theft and occupation'.[53] Interpreting another starts with self-analysis. True diplomacy is a journey inward as much as it is a reaching outward. The materials for bridging the incorrigibility gap are inside us all.

One lesson that might be taken from the usage by the CIA of 'Palestinian hanging' is that there is little, if anything, in other cultures that cannot be traced in our own, and, notwithstanding the uniqueness of persons, there is seldom an act of another that cannot be understood by a similar impulse in the self. Vanity and a fear of losing ourselves in the darker side of ourselves inform our reluctance to make the admission: *Homo sum, humani nihil a me alienum puto*. Indeed, the notion that human behaviour can be understood is the very basis of our criminal law. In spite of his portrayal in Western media as an irreconcilably homicidal zealot, there is nothing otherworldly in bin Laden's basic message: 'If the US does not want to kill its own sons … it has to get out'.[54] We set standards based on what we have in common. Establishing, enshrining and courageously defending that commonality is the challenge of the post-modern world.

It is the responsibility of our governments to encourage the embrace of other cultures. An embrace goes beyond mere contact, to involve a transmission of meaning. It should not be difficult in liberal democracies to resurrect the attitude that great ideas are dialectically produced, that diversity enriches, that homogeneity stifles rather than protecting. The very idea of liberal democracy ought to combat the human propensities to seek well-being, security and self-affirmation in similarity. It is by acknowledging and exposing these tendencies that we can be delivered from our wall-building, window-bolting, door-locking, border-patrolling, similarity-seeking, *exclusionary* political impulses. These impulses, though occasionally prudent in limited private spheres, must carefully be curtailed in political and public life.

For instance, if a Muslim Englishman of Pakistani heritage, different only by virtue of the colour of his skin or the name of his God, goes to the same school, grows up in the same community, plays cricket in the same league, and rides the same tube train as a white notionally Christian Englishman, it would be odd if the latter patrolled the borders of his selfhood so jealously as to deprive that fellow classmate, countryman, cricketer and commuter of that vital need, felt so acutely by all men in these vertiginously anonymous times, for solidarity, togetherness, fraternity and belonging. The embrace of other cultures is not an act of altruism or charity. It is plain prudence, for solitude breeds indifference to life, impotence craves power, alienation spawns enmity, and victimisation provokes violence.

[53] B Lawrence (ed), *Messages to the World: The Statements of Osama bin Laden* (Verso, 2005) 'To the Americans', 6 October 2002.

[54] *ibid*, 'Interview with Peter Arnett in March 1997'.

One interesting question thrown up by man's ongoing metamorphosis from rural beast to urban animal is whether the densely concentrated life of the concrete jungle will defang him, or whether it will sharpen his survival instincts. Though the great cosmopolitan cities, New York and London, at times seem to presage a diminution of racial animosity and a greater intermingling of cultures, big city life is also known for its anonymity, and for its hardness.[55] If city life portends a greater fragmentation of identity and a correlative alienation of the one in the multitude, we should not be too quick to tout urban cosmopolitanism as an answer to intercultural blood feuds, particularly given the ethnically pure 'villages' which make up our modern cities. Whatever the answer, whilst Habermas is correct to observe that conditions of fear inhibit meaningful communication, much of our fear of others would seem to stem from ignorance, so communication is a prerequisite for reducing our unjustified fear of unknown cultures. Mere moral imagination and education will not rescue us from this ignorance, a little courage is also required to conceptualise other human beings as complementary not hazardous. Much violence stems from cowardice.

No space need be wasted on the argument that policies of systematic torture pervert our values. More perverse still is that it stands to reason that torture incentivises suicide terrorism. As mentioned earlier, a terrorist is far more likely to entertain a suicide mission in the knowledge that, if captured, she will be subjected to torture.[56] Here, the broader lesson is that the adoption of dishonourable tactics encourages your adversary to adopt dishonourable tactics, making the fight meaner and harder.

Many bombings that we would describe as pure evil or inexplicable cruelty are understood by radical Islamists as fairness or equity.[57] During the 1991 Gulf war, captured American pilots were brutalised and raped.[58] During the war on terror, Iraqis have been brutalised and raped by Americans. The Bush administration's decision to jettison the Geneva Conventions was reciprocated by Iraqi soldiers, who perfidiously dressed in civilian clothes and waved white flags to deceive their opponents.

In *First Principles of Government*, Thomas Paine counselled as follows: 'He that would make his own liberty secure must guard even his enemy from oppression; for if he violates this duty he establishes a precedent that will reach to himself'. The British citizens who finally escaped wrongful detention in Guantánamo can surely vouch for this maxim. Ironically, as *The Road to Guantánamo* reports, the lack of linguistic ability in the American forces put the British (and therefore English-speaking) prisoners, not in what you would expect would be a secure position, as allies, but in the unenviable position of being more amenable

55 EJ Hobsbawm, *Globalisation, democracy and terrorism* (Little Brown, 2007) 34.

56 S Holmes, *The Matador's Cape: America's Reckless Response to Terror* (Cambridge University Press, 2007) 48.

57 *ibid*, 284.

58 M Byers, *War law: international law and armed conflict* (Atlantic Books, 2005) 121.

interrogative subjects. So, respect engenders respect and brutality will be repaid in kind – 'blood will have blood'.[59] Paine's maxim can be contrasted with that of General Horner, cited earlier, to the effect that 'if we are to achieve noble purposes we must be prepared to act in the most ignoble manner'.[60] But, as these examples show, rather than helping their ill-defined mission in Iraq, the lawlessness of the war made the conflict harder to fight, not least because in an important sense we can end up fighting ourselves.

Law, brutality and perversion have a closer relationship than one might at first blush imagine, for law requires force. As human beings, we are naturally, to a greater or lesser extent, in awe of superior force, and by degrees we not only need, but also desire to submit ourselves, to parents, to spouses, to religion, to leaders and to values we cherish. This is *l'amour du censeur*. We love those who can show us a path out of the bewildering maze of our own agency and we revere those who are able to make themselves a slave to their own values, for that is the greatest freedom.

Law is subjection. In a liberal democracy, we subject ourselves to law, which then objectifies us. The objectification itself is a subjection. Our subjection of ourselves to law puts the law in possession of us, but it does so on our terms; it is a lease, in perpetuity, in our bodies drawn up by us in a constitutional deed. The minutiae of the agreement are left to be worked out, but in essence, we give the keys to our shared shackles to law and it binds us together on our terms. Secretly, we keep a spare set of keys. There is no constitution that cannot be torn up by those it binds, no shackles strong enough to hold determined rebels.

Law is domination. It is bondage. And we love law because we love submission, particularly to a master so benevolent as ourselves. The democratic ideal is particularly appealing to disenchanted minds because it involves a submission to ourselves; self-worship. Law itself is a perversion of the condition of our freedom. Some argue that man-made law is a perversion of pre-existing natural or god-given tenets. Nonetheless, law, of any provenance, rescues us from the unbearable condition of liberty, or worse, the call to command. Law is the instrument of society's institution of human life. Part of the appeal of liberal democracy is that the vote allows us to deny the proposition that we vicariously enjoy power exercised on our behalf. Instead, we can boast that we share power, that we hold it in common. But the privilege of this deniability can only consistently be claimed if we take responsibility for what our government does with the power vested in it, a topic I will enlarge on shortly.

We cannot hide behind law for long. Notwithstanding the resemblance between law and perversion, law – clean, clinical and incorruptible – is wrongly presupposed to be the antithesis of perversion. Our sovereigns should be blind to the irrelevant differences of religious disposition and race. But we might not want

[59] W Shakespeare, *Macbeth*, Macbeth's speech, in Act 3, Scene IV.

[60] HK Ullman and JP Wade, *Shock and Awe* (NDU Press Book, 1996) (Horner).

to forget that law is an institution of human thought and feeling, it is the incorporation of society, and society is the mere embodiment of what we think or feel it should be. For better or worse, then, law's choices, or more precisely, our choices incorporated in law, are, more frequently than we care to admit to ourselves, and more obviously than we care to mention, between Venus and Athena, between our unspeakable naked desires and our immaculately turned out discernment.

It is in the nature of this text that the further on we press, the knottier the issues become. Though I have tried to avoid repetition, and though the reader can no doubt make some of the unspoken apparent connections for themselves, it is also necessary to consider how the topics of each chapter interrelate with what has been said before.

The relation between the subject-matter of this chapter and the ideas of language and image is fascinating. Perhaps the first warning that should be made is that platitudes and political nomenclature can lull us into the acceptance of moral double-standards, making a mockery of the values that our societies are ostensibly designed to express. When British diplomats couch aggression in the benevolent-sounding terms of protective internationalism, they are complicit in modern repetition of the sins of our imperial forefathers. Uniformed torturers are no better than Taliban torturers. State aggression is no better, though it might be more deadly, than non-state terrorism.

Fear and language permeate terrorism and law. Both terrorism and law are coercive and discursive. Both employ fear and force, both create narratives to control human behaviour. It is hoped that acceptance of the similarities between terrorism and law will help us understand the proper place of force in law, and the particular stresses exerted upon law by terrorism.

As individuals, we ought to demand a discontinuation of government and media fear-mongering. Fear can be healthy, but irrational fear has no place in policy- or war-making. Proper threat assessment is fundamental to re-establishing conditions in which intercultural dialogue can germinate. It is a sad reflection of cultural ignorance in Britain that mosques – places of secure repose, beauty, quiet worship, light and reflection on truth – have been stigmatised as terrorist recruitment centres. This stigma is self-fulfilling. There is nothing more likely to create a siege mentality among already isolated Islamic communities and to foment inflammatory, reactionary preaching than this unwarranted stigma and its pernicious social consequences.

One of the more salient links between sex and imagery finds its embodiment in the female; that is, it seems to be the unfortunate burden of the female body to be treated as a convenient vehicle, symbolic and literal. The act of and prohibition of genocide responds to an understanding of women as 'carriers' of a race, to be destroyed, with rape and then fire. Queerly, a 'logic' similar to that which informed the Hindu burning of Muslim women in Gujarat riots and motivated the sewing of cats into the wombs of pregnant Polish women by

Ukranian Nationalists,[61] informed the suffrage art and rhetoric that attempted to 'reinhabit the empty body of female allegory, to reclaim its meanings on behalf of the female sex'.[62]

Sex, rather than a means of procreation, has its role reversed in genocide and is used as a weapon, to break blood-lines, blocking the terrifying tides of fertility of another ethnic group. Sex can be an engine of death. In Nussbaum's study of Gujarati genocide, she observes that the rape and murder by radical Hindu men of the Muslim women symbolised a consolidation of power and dominion. As women carry a race, a particular womanhood can come to symbolise a nation and its plight. Irish women who, in their amorous liaisons with British soldiers, were perceived to have broken the bonds of ethnic identity were tarred and feathered by catholic extremists. Seamus Heaney used this practice as a metaphor for Irish politics in his poem, *Act of Union*, where Northern Ireland was the enigmatic, libidinous female, and Britain represented rational masculinity. Control over the female, by death or sex, represented ownership of the nation, and by extension, self-mastery and security.

At the other end of the British Empire, Nussbaum detects the exact same pattern in Indian men, who, she suggests, brutally subjugated their women as a response to their lack of control of their colonised homeland, and to the feelings of their own fecklessness in the face of masculine British power. The path from violence to sex passes dominion. So it is no surprise then that law, that other site of dominion, has much to say of sexual violence.

In the famous English case of *R v Brown*,[63] the barely concealed disgust of the Law Lords at the homosexual sadomasochistic practices of the accused seemed to inform a decision which, of course, was wrapped up in the terms of public morality and paternalism. And one must have sympathy for the Law Lords – many people, those who do not experience voyeuristic delight, would feel a certain turning of the stomach at such an intimate insight into the sexual practices of others – and yet, the case is to be regarded with some reserve. Disgust at the private, consensual, sexual practices of others is not a good principle of law by which to decide a case or build a policy. Such policies tend to be an attempt to block out part of the self. In the last two chapters, I have tried to show how enmity and fear have grown out of a primitive disgust, into a desire for dominion and discriminatory policies. We ought to be vigilant to executive actions orchestrated not by reason but by revulsion.

In the darkest observation in his book on America's reckless response to terrorism, Holmes touches on what might be the bond between perversion and symbolism in the usage of torture by the Bush administration: 'That many of those who are physically abused are perfectly innocent makes torture a more

[61] N Ferguson, *The War of the World* (Allen Lane, 2006) 456.

[62] L Tickner, *The Spectacle of Women: Imagery of the Suffrage Campaign* (Chicago University Press, 1998) 209.

[63] *R v Brown* [1994] 2 All ER 75 (HL).

appropriate not less appropriate response to 9/11, for the 9/11 hijackers killed perfectly innocent people themselves'.[64] This would certainly be consonant with the interpretation preferred here of Bush's 2003 State of the Union Speech in which American revenge seemed to take on cold arithmetical quality. We have witnessed a descent on all sides into barbarism and torture of the most odious varieties, which leads us to two quick points on the nexus between perversion, war and crime.

In Fallujah, Iraq, in April 2004, four Blackwater USA contractors were mutilated and killed by resistance forces. Their charred bodies were dragged through the streets and strung up over the Euphrates. The reported reaction of the US forces which had arrived with the intention of renouncing the controversial methods of the 82nd Airborne Division, was to besiege the city, allowing only women and children out of the perimeter. The street warfare that then commenced, which involved over a thousand marines, attack helicopters, war planes and an AC-130 gunship, and was, in the army's own admission, 'messy',[65] cannot be explained in the language of criminal justice, or even of lawful war.[66] After only a few days of fighting, wire services had reported over 300 Iraqi civilian fatalities.[67] Perhaps such tougher tactics can be explained by Cooper or Kagan; perhaps the law governing such actions *is* the law of the jungle. Perhaps the actions of our men and women abroad cannot be judged by the principles we esteem at home. Perhaps, those of us who think this is wrong fail to pass the post-modern challenge of accepting double-standards. Perhaps we cannot envision Cooper and Kagan's island paradise of legality and reciprocal respect at home and utter lawlessness beyond its beaches. The world is a dangerous place, but it is made more so by the refusal of some to respect rules designed for all.

As the reader will recall, the High Level Panel on Challenges, Threats and Change thought that lawlessness would make for a poor solution. It concluded to the effect that all human societies naturally perceive threats, so unilateral preventive action – in the words of Cooper, 'pre-emptive attack' and, in the cryptic terminology of Bush, 'dealing with threats before they materialize'[68] – cannot be allowed because it would invite anarchy: 'Allowing one to so act is to

[64] S Holmes, *The Matador's Cape: America's Reckless Response to Terror* (Cambridge University Press, 2007) 276.

[65] E Schmitt, 'Marines Battle Guerrillas in Streets of Falluja', *New York Times*, 27 October 2008, available at: query.nytimes.com/gst/fullpage.html?res=9501E1DB1238F93AA35757C0A9629C8B63&sec=&spon=&&scp=5&sq=fallujah%20contractor%20mutilate&st=cse.

[66] M Byers, *War law: international law and armed conflict* (Atlantic Books, 2005) 126.

[67] D Barstow, 'Security firm says its workers were lured into Iraqi ambush', *New York Times*, 27 October 2008, available at: query.nytimes.com/gst/fullpage.html?res=9C0DE4DB1238F93AA35757C0A9629C8B63&scp=2&sq=fallujah%20contractor%20mutilate&st=cse.

[68] President Bush Discusses Global War on Terror, 29 September 2006, Wardman Park Marriott Hotel, Washington DC.

allow all'.[69] A better solution would seem to be to defend the principles we guard so jealously at home in our dealings abroad; to demand only of others that which we are prepared to deliver ourselves. To take away the liberty of a man accused of murder, we want 12 of his countrymen to be sure of his guilt, we would not even listen to hearsay against him; we would not ruin his life on a whim. Why then did we take the country to war on a third-hand whisper, ruining the lives of countless (because not counted) Iraqis and many British families alike?

True to say, our liberty is important to us but, unchecked, it is a motor of inequality. Gross inequalities make communication within a country strenuous, and they can make it almost impossible for us to empathise across cultures. Fried is right to argue that blatant inequality destroys what is common to humanity. Nonetheless, liberty is crucial to the improvement of law. Law threatens to destroy individuality and dominate individuals with its generality, its public reason, and its monopoly on force. To allow enough deviation to facilitate change and yet to restrict deviation to create cohesion is the task of law. This requires a measure of obedience and rebellion from its masters and subjects, that is to say, in a liberal democracy, from its subject-masters.

Much of the challenge of responding to terrorism is in channelling rebellion into discursive outpourings to prevent the outbreaks of non-legal violence. As in games with enduring appeal, in the legal game of liberal democracy, room for creativity, for rebellion, must be built into the rules, and scope for changing the rules to accommodate changing forms of creation and to avoid forms of deviation that threaten the endurance of the game itself, must be built into its super-structure, its constitution. The oft-cited tension between liberty and security ignores this complementary aspect of their relation – enabling participation, or more precisely, self-determination, restrains violence.

Pressing on, we can note that perversion can be an attempt to discover the law. Again, in the realm of speculation, much sexual perversion and, I would argue, violent perversion is an exploratory, diversionary quest for limits in a seemingly limitless world. It could be argued that Guantanámo Bay is a superpower's search for a law beyond itself to which it is desperate to submit. America is seeking subjection for herself in the subjugation of others. The piety of men who fly planes into buildings is awesome and formidable for a spiritually rudderless American society, in which the only, rather uninspiring value is to value the values of all. The judicial opinions on the Cuban camp, with their historical exegeses on the British Royal prerogative, and their melodramatic dissents about future threats, seem to reflect America's desperate search for the limits not only of the court's jurisdiction, but also of her own identity. America is destroying herself to (re)create herself.

[69] High Level Panel 'Report on Threats Challenges and Change (A59/565)' (2 December 2004).

Returning briefly to Iraq, the decision taken by Lt P Bremer III in May 2003 to disband the Iraqi military, which, to be fair, he tabled before military strategists, Bush and Rumsfeld, was a superb way (in stripping men of their livelihood) to incur the wrath of trained killers, to turn very influential public opinion against the liberators, and to swell the numbers of resistance fighters.[70] In the Fallujah street-fighting, American confidence in their new Iraqi Security Forces was rattled, because they feared that insurgents and terrorists had somehow infiltrated these corps. What a surprise it must have been that Iraqis found it easier to win hearts and minds than American troops, who had barely finished their own education, let alone attempted to learn the local language. General John P Abizaid, another of the unwitting architects of the Iraqi resistance, said: 'we attempt to do our best with regard to vetting people'.[71] One can only imagine the sophisticated set of questions put to Iraqi volunteers. Perhaps it starts with 'Do you believe in freedom?'.

Earlier, I alluded to the irrational and self-defeating nature of the fantastical and fictional elements of our fear. The fact remains that the likelihood of an American being shot by a family member is far greater than that of being the victim of any form of terrorism. With respect to the personal use of weapons, the 'US is quite exceptional, as it is in a rising rate of homicide over the past two centuries as against a declining one in Europe'.[72]

In America then, homicide is a far more pressing societal problem than Islamist suicide, though one would not think so, to judge by the media attention lavished on the latter. We feel indignation when one of our arbitrarily defined 'own' is killed by one of a crudely defined 'them' that we do not feel when we kill one another. It is almost as if we perceive a special prerogative for those who kill those with whom they are acquainted. Further, when the surface of the problem is scratched a little, it does not seem too outlandish a suggestion that the number of private arms in America reflects the insecurity endemic to the native psyche, and that, for Americans, defence and justice start at home. One image of America, now somewhat muddied, is of decency and friendliness to foreigners. Another, recently more prevalent, is of a warrior people on an indiscriminating warpath.

In *Il Principe*, Machiavelli advised leaders not to concern themselves with suicide missions: 'anyone who has no fear of death himself can succeed in inflicting it; on the other hand, there is less need for a prince to be afraid, since such assassinations are very rare'.[73] His advice goes beyond the world outside of

[70] P Bremer, 'How I didn't dismantle Iraq's Army', *New York Times*, 6 September 2007, available at: www.nytimes.com/2007/09/06/opinion/06bremer.html.

[71] D Barstow, 'Security firm says its workers were lured into Iraqi ambush', *New York Times*, 27 October 2008, available at: query.nytimes.com/gst/fullpage.html?res=9C0DE4DB1238F93AA35757C0A9629C8B63&scp=2&sq=fallujah%20contractor%20mutilate&st=cse.

[72] EJ Hobsbawm, *Globalisation, democracy and terrorism* (Little Brown, 2007) 144.

[73] N Machiavelli, *The Prince*, trans G Bull (Penguin Classics, 2003) 65.

il corridoio vasariano, the elevated passage commissioned by Grand Duke Cosimo to walk from his palace to his place of work, across the Arno, without descending into the rabblesome Florentine crowds. There *are* things we can do to protect ourselves against suicide terrorism, and there are certainly ways of reducing the incidence of such attacks, but the sort of subtle security measure and social fine-tuning that are worthwhile options for a liberal democracy cannot be performed with tank columns, helicopter gunships or predator drones. Accepting the fundamental defencelessness of our lives against those prepared to sacrifice their own is a step towards designing sensible policies against terrorism.

Why then, do politicians, particularly in America, choke on this admission of our fragile mortality? Holmes argues that, confessing to 'America's defencelessness … must be extremely difficult psychologically, especially for individuals emotionally invested in, not to say exhilarated by, America's global military supremacy'.[74] Reprisals, such as the Clinton missile attacks mentioned earlier, are easier to describe in terms of blind terror, emotional urge and cowardice, than in the language of prudent policy, rational threat management and courage. Irrational faith in the capacity of military power to terrify terrorists into submission and to mask an inherent national cowardice has perverted the Allied response to terrorist threat.

That perversion extends way beyond political leaders to philosophers. Take for example the following suggestion from one of the most famous theorists of rights of our times:

> The U.S. 'war' against terrorism can have no formal end: it may last at least a generation. Congress must therefore stipulate a maximum period – say, three years – for which anyone designated a prisoner of war in the campaign against terrorism may be held, though Congress would retain the power, so long as organized international terrorism remains a serious threat to extend the period, either in particular cases or in blanket extensions of a stipulated maximum period, on a showing of necessity and after suitable debate.[75]

Though he adds the obligatory inverted commas around the word 'war', Dworkin has been so affected by the rhetoric, by the terrifying nature of the threat and by the need, pressingly felt by civil libertarians, to scrabble for a numerical compromise, that he would institute a power of indefinite detention for as long as organised international terrorism remains a serious threat. If the executive determines the level of the threat, which it inevitably must, and also determines who is a prisoner of the war, which it inevitably must, then where do we find protection of the hallowed rights of the individual lauded in his books and essays? Is Dworkin's three-year detention without charge not a touch despotic? The British were up in arms about 90 days.

[74] HK Ullman and JP Wade, *Shock and Awe* (NDU Press Book, 1996) 311.

[75] R Dworkin, 'Terror and the Attack on Civil Liberties' in T Rockmore, J Margolis and AT Marsoobian (eds), *The Philosophical Challenge of September 11* (Blackwell Publishing, 2005) 93.

Whatever objections might be raised against such a power in terms of civil liberty, there are two more important sources of criticism. First, liberal democracy is constructed on the premise of a freedom that would be shattered by a power of long-term detention vested in the executive. Dworkin's suggestion might undermine individual rights, but, more depressingly, it would undermine the idea(l) of America. Second, such a power jeopardises the whole structure of government. Repression is an invitation to revolt. Rather than ameliorating the threat of terrorism, the abnegation of habeas corpus by unilateral classification of terrorists as prisoners of war, is likely to exacerbate rebellious sentiments.

A further exacerbation of rebellious sentiment can be expected as a result of the deafening message of injustice broadcast by the fact that the International Committee of the Red Cross has not been allowed access to CIA black sites or to the US airbase on British-owned Diego Garcia. Such clandestine, Kafka-esque government shatters the principle of transparency so important to the democratic ideal. Compared to these holes in humanity, Guantánamo Bay might be considered a summer camp. Foolish fear made of freedom a farce.[76]

The content of this chapter was of the darker, introspective variety and it might leave us wondering how we might combat the enemy within our societies and within us all. On first sight of the people hurling themselves from the World Trade Center inferno and, subsequently, of photographs of the worst atrocities of the British-American campaign, many people responded, first by invoking God and then with a literal turn or return to faith. The argument here shadows that turn, moving from gloomy examination of the very worst baseness of man, to a consideration of the lighter side of his perception, of another world, of loftiness and of the sublime.

[76] For a similar sentiment, see MC Nussbaum, *The Clash Within: Democracy, Religious Violence, and India's Future* (The Belknap Press, 2007) 92.

7

Temporality, Spirituality and Sublimity

If atheism were generally accepted, every form of religion would be destroyed, and cut off at its roots. There would be no more theological wars, no more soldiers of religion – such terrible soldiers! Nature, having been infected with sacred poison, would regain its rights and purity. Deaf to all other voices, tranquil mortals would follow only the spontaneous dictates of their own being, the only commands … which can lead us to happiness.[1]

Julian Offray de la Mettrie

THE PROMINENCE IN the debate about the war on terror of the grand-sounding titular themes is such that it would have been remiss to omit this material. In what follows, I try to formulate some considerations about the perceptions of time, religion, and the sublime that have led us to prefer myopic over more long-sighted counter-terror strategy and to shoehorn brutal policies into our laws.

First though, something must be said about those grand-sounding themes. I have preferred the term 'temporality', as it more aptly captures the notion of there being a difference between profane, or linear, as opposed to perfect, boundless or pooled time; that is, it encapsulates the distinction between the ticking clock and eternity. Here, I am interested in different ways of thinking about time. The word 'temporality' has the added benefit of prefiguring the discussion of spirituality and sublimity by alluding to a sempiternal realm coexisting with our conventional perception of the world. Incidentally, secularity and profane or linear time have a special link in that the etymological root of 'secular' is the Latin '*saeculum*', meaning a tract of time.

But there are many other ways of thinking about time. Time seems to warp for great sportsmen, who seem to have more time than other athletes as a result of their mastery. Great works of art have a timeless appeal, like Michelangelo's *Davide*, or Leonardo's *Adorazione*. Time stops or seems irrelevant in the face of spectacular natural surroundings. These are everyday variations in our perception of time, but science introduces plenty of ambiguity into our understanding of time too.

[1] Mettrie, *L'homme Machine*, quoted in AE McGrath, *Twilight of Atheism* (Rider, 2005) 33.

In the *Brief History of Time*, Hawking challenges the Big Bang Theory, arguing instead that there persisted a situation in which time and space were indistinguishable, in which the concepts of before and after were redundant, and in which the universe was not created, it just was. Philosophers through the ages have constantly referred to dual planes of time, the first in which we age and experience the changing days and seasons, and a second, which is boundless and unchanging, in which time, in truth, is meaningless. History, human records of times past, may be read like a book. But it would seem that half of us are blind, a good proportion don't like to read, some are dyslexic, others see but are mute, and all are biased. In this discussion, I wish to pick apart the concept of time a little in order to expose its core meaning for law, lawyering, and policy-making.

The next titular concept is spirituality. I have used this term to indicate something other than, but including religiosity. Max Weber told us our world was 'disenchanted'; Charles Taylor recently finessed that position by saying that modern people are 'buffered' in contradistinction to their 'porous' pre-modern ancestors. He explains that spirits, demons and cosmic forces do not impinge on our lives in the way they used to: buffered individuals are apparently unafraid of such phantasmic encroachments.[2] That said, even if religion is in decline, spirituality – a sense of there being forces at work that cannot be entered in the clinical register of science – is alive and well.

But the decoupling of religious authority from our daily to-ings and fro-ings – I speak only for the United Kingdom and United States – has set us adrift in a bewildering and featureless ocean empty of authoritative signals for our journey through life. Many people feel a debilitating disorientation in a loss of the deep identity and sense of togetherness produced through communal worship, or at least generated by a shared fear of hellfire.

The reason why our journey through life is dizzying is not its lack of destination, but its lack of a departure point. Like Hawking's universe that was never created, but just is, it is difficult to get a helpful foothold on the meaning of our existence without the a priori bases of religion. Modern mobility – spiritual, economic and geographic – means that, in the West, we now go off in search of ourselves. This journey without a destination and without a departure point can be religiously rudderless and, though it can be fun, it might be punctuated for many by longer or shorter periods of intense psychological vulnerability, whether they are aware of it or not.

This vulnerability can agitate us, especially when we reflect on how we destroyed our idols intentionally. Cai Guo-Qiang's *Age of not believing in God*, features wooden dolls and figurines punctured with countless arrows. It is an allegory, ambivalent to religion, for man's destruction of his own work, for the tearing up of spiritual fabric, but also for acupuncture – healing through piercing oneself – and, by extension, for salvation through destruction.

[2] C Taylor, *A Secular Age* (Harvard University Press, 2007) 38.

In popular discourse, religion has been destroyed and science is hailed as our salvation, but, and I think time will testify to this, science is a poor substitute for God, for the simple reason that where God gave people what might be called 'the Why?', science only seems to respond to 'the How?'. Special new technology might help a war veteran with multiple amputations clamber out of bed in the morning, but it might not help him find a reason to do so. Whereas religion is portrayed as medieval, mystical, whimsical and feminine, science is modern, practical, empirical and masculine. But the brave new men of the 'How? Society' must reach into other realms when confronted with 'the Why?'. Science and religion seem to be reluctant combatants.

In researching this theme, the most sophisticated consideration of terrorism I found was in the unlikeliest of sources, the Bible. In the Book of Exodus, against the background of Egyptian persecution of the Children of Israel, every issue of any importance in the modern debate on the 'war on terror' is not only introduced but treated in such a way as to engage the reader in its crucial complexities.

The first usage of the word 'terror' comes earlier in the Bible, but the Book of Exodus introduces the first instance of terrorism; the usage of fear to secure political results in the familiar sense. Perhaps most surprisingly, the terrorist is none other than God, but predictably enough, God acts through His human agent, Moses, who calls forth pests (frogs, lice and boils) but, when the Pharaoh refuses to comply, eventually sends more terrible (disease, locusts and darkness afflictions) against the Egyptian people culminating in the death of the first-born of Egyptian families.

Leaving aside the very apparent themes of transcendental justice and cosmic war, there is much more of interest in this text. Intriguingly, the issues of faith, human agency, and freedom are immediately brought to the fore. God seems to be conducting both sides of the affair. He moves Moses' hand, but he also hardens the Pharaoh's heart, paradoxically meaning that God perpetuates the bloody stalemate.

The themes of collective responsibility and the individuation of guilt (discussed in the next chapter) are also vividly discussed. Not only the Pharaoh, but all the Egyptians are punished for the persecution of the Children of Israel. God does a great deal of smiting, and if the punishment of the first-born is difficult to justify (how can infants be culpable?) the smiting of the cattle, who certainly had no hand in the Children of Israel's suffering, is without rhyme or reason. The indiscriminate nature of the heaven-sent plagues epitomises the core characteristic of terrorism.

The theme of deterrence, more a feature of the Allied response to terrorism than terrorism itself, is also colourfully portrayed in the Exodus. Eventually, of course, the Pharaoh apprehends the error of his oppressive ways and desists. But what is the meaning of his choice when God was in control of his resistance? On one view, God hardened the Egyptian ruler's heart long enough to escalate the conflict to a level at which God could manifest his infinite power, smash Egyptian idols, convince the Children of Israel that only fear of God was acceptable, and establish his omnipotence forever more on earth. His omnipotence is a matter we will have to address later, but for now we can note that it begs the classic question: If there is a God, and he is truly all-powerful, why does he tolerate (and in this case, perpetuate) such suffering?

Naturally, whatever one may think of these terror tactics from on high, in the popular idea, God is sublimity personified. But the human imagination is such that the idea of the ideal being or form is not limited to celestial spheres, indeed, it has also been a driver of art, politics and philosophy. Conceptions of the sublime take many forms, amongst them supreme power, beauty and grace: For many people, it is in their confrontations with nature, or the vastness of the sea, the earth or space that a proximity to or an appreciation of the sublime is experienced. Nietzsche, for example, pictured Zarathustra retreating into the wilderness, as if drawing strength and inspiration from nature for his meetings with the mundane men of the marketplace. Christ too spends 40 days and 40 nights in the desert.

Taylor described the effect of the wilderness on the human psyche cluttered with the quotidian in the following way:

> The sight of 'Excess', vast, strange, unencompassable, provoking fear, even horror, breaks through this self-absorption and awakens our sense of what is really important, whether this be the infinity of God, as with Burnet, our supersensible moral vocation, as with Kant; or, as with later thinkers, our capacity for heroic affirmation of meaning in the face of a world without telos – the truth of eternal recurrence.[3]

In the present context, Taylor's comment raises two questions: First, does his notion of 'excess' allow us to reinterpret the scenes of carnage from *Exodus* as God's necessary demonstrations of his absolute power? By hardening the Pharaoh's heart, perpetuating the Egyptian-Israeli standoff, does the Deity merely create conditions under which His supreme power can be proven beyond all doubt? And, here is the nub, did this tactic of unrestrained, disproportionate violence permeate the Horner-Bush-Rumsfeld strategy of showing that America will 'stop at nothing' to achieve its goals, and to evidence its unconquerability? The similarity is striking and disquieting.

Second, what is this 'really important' stuff that we forget in the humdrum of the everyday? For Taylor, it is, of course, the ideal, the aspiration to greatness. In Allott's words, the 'ideal is the goal we aim at but never reach; [it is] the idea that the human mind can order its activity and judge its activity in conformity with the permanent possibility of *self-perfecting*'.[4] Pierre-Joseph Proudhon put it in similar terms, claiming that we are born perfectible, but we shall never be

[3] *ibid*, 339.

[4] P Allott, 'Lecture', at Rome, The Pontifical Academy of the Social Sciences, XIII Plenary Session (2007).

perfect.[5] He meant that the total of what humans could achieve, and what they actually will achieve are different, that we will never realise our potential. Though this might sound depressingly like 'we are doomed to fall short of our aspirations', I would suggest that the ideal is even more elusive than that. Here, the suggestion is made, for a reason I will elaborate later, that we cannot even envisage the ideal, that it is not only beyond the reaches of our attainment, but also our imagination. It is not that we see the target yet miss; rather, we take aim in the dark. Kant's understanding of sublime experience tends to tally with this interpretation. He thought that the ideal was formless or boundless and, consequently, like Hawking's mind-boggling theory of the universe, it harangues the imagination because the mind cannot quite be wrapped around it.[6]

The basic objection to this understanding of the ideal as something nebulous is that we are surrounded by manifestations of the sublime: a masterpiece in the Louvre, a ceiling in the Vatican City, a perfectly balanced equation, a Wagnerian symphony, our dream mate. But philosophers have rejected these earthly counterfeits as approximations of the ideal. Edmund Burke distinguished between beauty – that which is well-formed and pleasing to the eye – and sublimity – that which has the power to compel and destroy us – and Plato too warned against alluring women, who were mere pretenders to sublime beauty. So, in this good company, we can feel confident in the assertion that the ideal is fundamentally inconceivable but, it will be argued, its intangible nature does not undermine its utility for understanding law and terror. On the contrary, the acceptance of the enigma of the sublime will help us a great deal. The conflation of ideas of physical beauty with sublime justice is not only lacking in sophistication, but it can have truly horrific results. Consider the following passage from one of the twentieth century's most amateurish of philosophers:

> In heedlessly ignoring the question of the preservation of the racial foundations of our nation, the old Reich disregarded the sole right which gives life in this world. Peoples who bastardise themselves, or let themselves be bastardised sin against the will of eternal Providence, and when their ruin is encompassed by a stronger enemy it is not an injustice done to them, but only the restoration of justice.[7]

This all seems a long way from law and terrorism, but the association between the sublime, rule and fear was explicated by Burke, in his *Philosophical Enquiry into the Origin of our Ideas of the Sublime and Beautiful.* He concluded, after reflecting on death, 'the king of terrors', that terror and power fed into one another. He could think of 'nothing sublime which is not some modification of power'. Later, he explains that the institutional power of 'kings and commanders' has a symbiotic relationship with terror. And Burke was not alone in realising the tryst between

[5] PJ Proudhon, *Philosophie du Progrés* (Originally published in 1853, (1946 edn)) 27–30, and PJ Proudhon, *De la Justice dans la Révolution e dans l'Eglise* (first published in 1858, (1930 edn)) 233.

[6] Kant, *Zum Ewigen Frieden: Ein philosophischer Entwurf* (first released 1795).

[7] A Hitler, *Mein Kampf* (Secker and Walberg, 1925) ch XI, 'Nation and Race'.

these odd bedfellows. For Kant, the violence of war had something of the sublime, and for Chaucer, sublime beauty came with the threat of merciless aggression.[8]

As for law, it also contains something of the sublime, perhaps in the beauty of its construction, in its abject disregard for individuality, in its aim of *sublimation* itself, or in the looming spectre of force at its rear. Presumably, law's sublimation is only sublime if it corresponds with justice. These ideas might be frustratingly formless at this stage, but I will try to give some shape to them in the remainder of this chapter. For now, it suffices to note that the seemingly inexplicable relation between law, force, beauty and the sublime is the lifeblood of this argument. These ideas will hopefully become more pronounced and take shape in the conclusion.

Perhaps in finishing the introductory part of this chapter, it is worth noting that the uncanny connection between outwardly irreconcilable concepts, such as time, beauty and justice, can better be described as a collapse. Throughout philosophy, poetry and religion, one finds that, at their very apex, these notions implode into one another and become indistinguishable. This finding explains why I have collected temporality, spirituality and sublimity in one chapter. Such an obscure comment perhaps requires some elaboration.

Writings throughout the ages have recorded moments in a lifetime when a person comes to a halt, time seems to cease, every other experience (past and future) is gathered up in one unity, and without reflecting, like a tuning fork, one has the uncanny sensation that one's being sounds in harmony with the natural order. Such moments are often connected with being in isolated landscapes, because, in its serene grandeur, nature is taken to mirror or merge with the infinite expanse of time, and the boundlessness of the ideal. Ramond's reverie on the banks of the Lac de Bienne is a superb example:

> Tout concourt à rendre les méditations plus profondes, à leur donner cette teinte sombre, ce caractère sublime qu'elles acquièrent quand l'âme, prenant cet essor qui la rend contemporaine de tous les siècles et coexistante avec tous les êtres, plane sur l'abîme du temps.[9]

If all the happenings of all time, all the ideas, actions and emotions of all people, great and small, were gathered into a single repository, and a perfect mind considered that collection of events, pondered on it with perfect objectivity, and concluded how to proceed henceforth, well, that observer could see justice done.[10] In the fourth book of the gay science, Nietzsche thought just such an

[8] Kant, *Zum Ewigen Frieden: Ein philosophischer Entwurf* (first released 1795). The first line of Chaucer's Merciless Beaute, goes: 'Your eyen two wol slee me sodenly, I may the beaute of hem not sustene, So woundeth hit through-out my herte kene'.

[9] D Mornet, *Le Romanticisme en France au XVIIIe Siécle* (Ayer Publishing, 1971) 72.

[10] 'In der Tat: dies ist Eine Farbe dieses neuen Gefühls: wer die Geschichte der Menschen insgesamt als eigenen Geschichte zu fühlen weiß, der empfindet in einer ungeheuren Verallgemeinerung allen jenen Gram des Kranken, der an die Gesundheit, des Greises, der an den

observer would experience 'humanity'. He stubbornly insisted on man's or at least a future man's ability to achieve this omniscience. Maintaining my stance as to the fundamental unthinkability of the sublime, I do not think I consign us to mediocrity if I nominate this sort of omniscience as a spiritual, not a human event; put briefly, I dispute that visions of justice can be arrived at by rational means alone.

The ultimate aspiration of humankind must be the kind of collapse portended by omniscience. It would render the distinction between law and justice otiose and untenable. The law we make presupposes its own annihilation at the moment of its eventual perfection through its alignment with the ideal form and substance given to us by the incogitable ideal of justice. This ultimate aspiration is impossible. And yet, it is only this unspoken, incomprehensible, unattainable goal that makes the human legal project tolerable. This intuition, this suspicion that we might well be able to improve the grim prevailing state of human affairs by reference to an immeasurable yardstick is not intellectual snobbery; it is an argument of policy and pragmatism. The ideal is a prop in our attempt to erect unstable meanings in this life against the edifice of the impossible. It might be why we make coffee instead of committing suicide.

On that happy abstract note, we can begin a consideration of the war on terror itself and how these concepts help us process the events of the last decade. Thinking about the war on terror in temporal terms is a salutary exercise. The first noteworthy aspect of the Allied response to September 11 and later, July 7 was an almost obstinate ignorance of history. For instance, it is worth asking how enthusiastic the British public would have been to send its sons and daughters to what Gordon Brown calls the 'crucial' war in Afghanistan had it reflected on the historic inhospitality of that country's snow-covered passes to British forces, who more than once before have retreated from those harsh terrains in inglorious defeat.[11] At the time of writing, Brigadier Mark Carleton-Smith opined that the war could not be won, and British Ambassador Sherard Cowper-Coles, who read

Jugendtraum denkt, des Liebenden, der der Geliebten beraubt wird, des Märtyrers, dem sein Ideal zu Grunde geht, des Helden am Abend der Schlacht, welche Nichts entschieden hat und doch ihm Wunden und den Verlust des Freundes brachte –; aber diese ungeheure Summe von Gram aller Art tragen, tragen können und nun doch noch der Held sein, der beim Anbruch eines zweiten Schlachttages die Morgenröte und sein Glück begrüsst, als der Mensch eines Horizontes von Jahrtausenden vor sich und hinter sich, als der Erbe aller Vornehmheit alles vergangenen Geistes und der verpflichtete Erbe, als der Adeligste aller alten Edlen und zugleich der Erstling eines neuen Adels, dessen Gleichen noch keine Zeit sah und träumte: dies Alles auf seine Seele nehmen, Ältestes, Neuestes, Verluste, Hoffnungen, Eroberungen, Siege der Menschheit: dies Alles endlich in Einer Seele haben und in Ein Gefühl zusammendrängen: – dies müsste doch ein Glück ergeben, das bisher der Mensch noch nicht kannte, – eines Gottes Glück voller Macht und Liebe, voller Tränen und voll Lachens, ein Glück, welches, wie die Sonne am Abend, fortwährend aus seinem unerschöpflichen Reichtume wegschenkt und in's Meer schüttet und, wie sie, sich erst dann am reichsten fühlt, wenn auch der ärmste Fischer noch mit goldenem Ruder rudert! Dieses göttliche Gefühl hieße dann – Menschlichkeit!'

[11] For a general history, see A Forbes, *The Afghan Wars* (Kessinger Publishing, 2004 [1892]).

Classics at Oxford, submitted that an 'acceptable dictator' was the best solution. Political historians will be forgiven for finding all this tediously familiar.[12]

Equally, England's expertise in the what-not-to-do of counter-terrorism appeared to play no part in the crafting of the response to Islamic radicalism. Of course, there are differences between Irish nationalists and Islamic radicals, but the similarities are instructive too, and certain responses are inappropriate to both. For all the talk about facing 'new threats' and 'new enemies', there was a disconcerting similarity about the newsreels. Though Blair practically held hands with Bush, he does not seem to have taken the opportunity to enlighten the latter as to England's valuable experience, or to recall it himself.

Many British people were or ought to have been haunted by a sense of déjà vu. All of Westminster's inflammatory botches in the Irish theatre; arbitrary detention, torture, heavy-handed occupation, and the occasional massacre were repeated and amplified by Washington in its offensive against radical Islamists. Castlereigh was revisited at Guantanámo Bay, wall-standing became water-boarding, Diplock Courts were revamped as Military Commissions, and the screams of Bloody Sunday resounded on Blackwater Sunday. It was as if our support of the Allied efforts required an Orwellian series of victories over our own memories. Truly, those who forget the past consign themselves to its repetition. It was like being governed by goldfish.

This governmental aversion to historical reflection has a telling parallel with the fundamentalist adherence to original texts to the exclusion of the undulations of history. This attitude was brilliantly parodied by Rushdie in *The Satanic Verses*:

> History is the blood-wine that must no longer be drunk. History the intoxicant, the creation and possession of the Devil, of the great Shaitan, the greatest of the lies, progress, science, rights – against which the Imam has set his face. History is a deviation from the Path, knowledge is a delusion because the sum of knowledge was complete on the day Allah finished his revelation to Mahound.[13]

We touched upon the human ambivalence to boundless time above, but do we also have a schizophrenic approach to profane time, to human history, and progress? If we dig a little deeper we find that this might be the case. As Taylor observes, 'Good Friday 1998 is closer in a way to the original day of the Crucifixion than mid-summer's day 1997 … Higher times gather and re-order secular time. They introduce "warps" and seeming inconsistencies in profane time-ordering'.[14]

At the time of writing, the seventh anniversary of September 11 was marked by communal mourning, which had the effect Taylor describes; it was a

[12] 'Defeat is not yet inevitable', *Independent*, 8 October 2008, 24 and 26; 'We can't defeat Taleban', *Times*, 6 October 2008, available at: www.timesonline.co.uk/tol/news/world/asia/article4887927.ece.

[13] S Rushdie, *The Satanic Verses* (Vintage, 1988) 210.

[14] C Taylor, *A Secular Age* (Harvard University Press, 2007) 55.

remembrance, recalling a past event into the present. It brought September 11 2001 closer to the present day than would have been possible without setting aside, for a moment, our purely linear understanding of time. Put simply, it took us back. This phenomenon can be observed in philosophy too. In Platonic teaching, for instance, the eternal, timeless realm was also a plane of metaphysical propositions, that is, immutably true or sublime ideas. Man's role on earth, therefore, is one of transposition, the imperfect mimicry of cosmic order.

In contrast, Saint Augustine argued for a gathering of past into present consciousness in order to project a future. This investigation of historic time might serviceably be interpreted as the collapse of the present under the weight of the learning of the past and the hopes of the future. For Augustine's God, time was static and simultaneous, a snapshot in which the divine eye was all-seeing and thus omniscient in the way I described above. Understood in this admittedly particular fashion, Augustine's position in our discussion is at the gateway between the secular and sempiternal realms, where history meets philosophical spirituality, where time meets the sublime.

If one reflects on modern history, the ongoing decline of monarchy, and with it the decomposition of the King's immortal body, might be thought contemporaneous with the profanation or flattening of our understanding of time. Irrespective of one's stance on the institution of Kings, it is worth asking whether we squeezed out some valuable, if indefinable, material by ironing out the spiritual kinks in the time continuum.

But we seem to be reluctant to press out all these kinks. We are apprehensive of both limits and limitlessness, we crave a date of creation and yet wish for an eternal afterlife; we suffer from temporal strands of claustrophobia and agoraphobia. James Usher's estimate that everything was created at 6pm on 22 October 4004 BC neatly limits the mind-boggling infinite or static past proposed by some scientists. And science has been schizophrenic too. At first it wanted to destroy but now seems to support the notion of gathered or boundless time. At the time of writing, beams were being sent around the Large Hadron Collider to, if you will, recreate the conditions of creation, to give us insight into how the universe began by finding what scientists have dubbed the 'God particle', the secret piece in the jigsaw of everything.

But this will bring us no closer to meaning or motivation. We turn to religion or to higher Platonic planes to avoid the cramped juridical categorisations of earthbound law. We crave both the prosaic and the perfect, daytime and dreams, a concrete plan for the year, but a transcendent reason to crawl out of the warmth of our beds every morning. We walk on the earth gazing in wonder at the night sky. We delight in looking out to the vastness of the sea but panic and swim for shore when we can no longer feel sand under our searching feet, or worse, brush against some foreign life-form in the deep.

Stronger spirits are capable of both greater reduction (think St Francis of Assisi) and expansion (think Julius Caesar). One only has to glance at the point where Byron enjoyed swimming, where the sea surges against the rocks at Porto

Venere, to appreciate his quest for the extraordinary. It is no accident that a romantic tirelessly hounding the sublime happened upon a spot of such barely believable beauty. There, photography (man's attempt to stop, capture, or warp time) almost seems profane. It is as if we are fixated with the sublime but know that we cannot accommodate it in our quotidian agenda.

In short, the message of this section is that a little vertigo is stirring, but that too much will have us hurling ourselves into oblivion. We need law to plan our tactics on earth, but justice to set our strategy for law, rules to guide our activities and ideals to guide our rules. It is symptomatic of humankind's moral rudderlessness that many people prefer to locate the origin of the prohibition on killing in a story about a man receiving instructions from a deity on a mountain, than in the basic injunctions of morality. We do not want our rules of public law inscribed on tablets of stone, but many insist our Ten Commandments simply must be.

At this stage, we can tap into an important seam in man's understanding of time. Though the Ten Commandments are said to be inscribed in stone, the event, Moses' receipt of God's utterances is understood by many to have occurred not in profane history but, as Taylor puts it, 'in some higher time, or on some unspecified higher plane of being, that of, say, Gods or heroes'.[15] But earlier we noted the dangers of 'homogenised' time, legendary events, and an obstinate disregard for history. It can result in bungling policies on earth.

It might be that September 11 now exists in both realms, the profane and the mythical. It was real, but from the offset had a sense of surreality about it. It was an impossible occurrence. The literal inferno of the Twin Towers has reintroduced a very real fear of hellfire into the modern American psyche. Paraphrasing Edmund Gosse, we could say that the smashing of America's secular symbols jolted us out of an opium-dream of comfort, and shattered the self-indulgent poltroonery of Western life. Terror launched a surprise attack on peace; poverty ambushed luxury; and spirituality hijacked secularity. The terrorist atrocities furnished modern Americans with a departure point. It was tangible myth writ large.

September 11 became that a priori foothold we were scrabbling for. It is erroneously considered an original, momentous, inexplicable event and a manifestation of pure evil.[16] It was, for many, an event of biblical proportions, not least due to the deeply symbolic interpretations and the apparent unfathomability of the motives for such a crime against humanity. What possible reason could anyone have for killing all those innocents? The apparent unanswerability of that question placed the attacks outside rational, profane history, and a cosmic battle, described in the Manichean terms of good and evil, began. Both sides made

[15] *ibid*, 271.

[16] A Nuzzo, 'Reasons for Conflict: Political Implications of a Definition of Terrorism' in T Rockmore, AT Marsoobian and J Margolis (eds), *The Philosophical Challenge of September 11* (2005).

identical claims as to the perfect beastliness of the opponent in order to justify the unjustifiable measures they adopted in combat.

Though the motivations for September 11 have been explained in territorial and political terms; though they are easily traced back to human motivations, this sort of down-to-earth, Hegelian analysis was rejected, and the myth that those behind the hijacking had radical, inalterable, cosmic objectives was embraced. The attacks on the Pentagon and the World Trade Center blew holes not only in buildings but, to borrow Taylor's term, in the 'buffered self'. As a result, spirits are back – and we have received them with a mixture of fear and fawning.

We need look no further than *Exodus* to know that fear is integral to religion, but ought we be afraid of religion itself? The Mettrie quote used to introduce this chapter is typical of those who believe that religion is noxious, and that we should barricade our minds against spirituality. Indeed, bin Laden, who by all accounts, is not a very nice person, claims that the conflict between the Allied forces and Islamic insurgents is 'fundamentally religious in nature'.[17] Richard Dawkins captured the feelings of many when he said that, whereas religion could be considered nonsense prior to Autumn 2001, it must now be considered dangerous nonsense. In America, the Nebraska State Senator, Ernie Chambers, even tried (unsuccessfully) to sue God for the 'widespread death, destruction and terrorisation of millions upon millions of the Earth's inhabitants'.[18]

Louis Pojman even argues that the Islamic religion is the problem:

> Religion is surpassing nationalism as the foremost threat to world peace and stability. Although the majority of Muslims may eschew the terrorist's tactics, there is something in Islamic culture that predisposes it to violence, the idea of jihad, the holy war against the infidel.[19]

Is this not utter rubbish? The 9/11 hijackers did not fly Islam into buildings; the Qur'an did not explode in cafés and embassies. Planes and bombs were used. And these are the gifts to humankind of *science*, not religion. Whatever is said of religion, science not religion gave us the power to annihilate human life on earth. We ought to be at least as afraid of launch bases as we are churches, as preoccupied by bombs as we are religious books. That said, it is silly to confuse means with motives; science does not cause terrorist bombings, people do. Equally, those who argue that science gave us the 'How?' but religion gave us the 'Why?' of mass murder are absolving the belligerent human readers of religion of the blame they thoroughly deserve. But in reality, the only thing in Islamic culture that predisposes it to violence is common to all cultures, and that is

[17] B Lawrence (ed), *Messages to the World: The Statements of Osama bin Laden* (Verso, 2005), 3 November 2001, Letter to al-Jazeera's Kabul Bureau.

[18] 'Legal case against God dismissed', *BBC News Online*, 16 October 2008, at: news.bbc.co.uk/2/hi/americas/7673591.stm.

[19] LP Pojman, 'The Moral Response to Terrorism and Cosmopolitanism' in JP Sterba (ed), *Terrorism and International Justice* (2003) 139.

human nature. Would not an objective assessment of British or American history reveal a similar predisposition to violence?

Taylor understands that part of what we find disturbing about members of our own societies, like Shehzad Tanweer, who turn to terrorism is that their acts undermine our notion of security, not only physical, but also ethnic or cultural. How can someone like Shehzad, who works in a fish-and-chip shop, plays cricket, attends Leeds Metropolitan University, who was in countless ways an archetypal Englishman, blow himself up, wreaking havoc on a London tube train? Are we again porous? Did spirits slip through our borders into the minds of our youth? What does being English mean if such things can happen? Such angst-provoking questions leave us looking for quick, off-the-shelf answers, and religious fanaticism is one. In the minds of people like Pojman and de la Mettrie mosques do not have the repute of places of communal worship knitting together the social fabric, but seem to take on the aspect of centres of indoctrination for tearing it asunder.

Granted, in the mouths of clever manipulators, religion can stir revolutionary sentiment, but an axe in the hand of a forester is different altogether from an axe in the hand of a murderer. The axe does not chop down trees or lop off heads on its own. To say that religion is the source of terrorism is about as cogent as saying that bombs are the source of terrorism. No specific usage for planes or bombs is contemplated in any religion of which I know. But does religion drive Islamic terrorism? Stripped of religious window-dressing and superfluous scriptural decoration, bin Laden's own sentiments appear entirely secular. His most frequently recurring messages are of self-determination, self-defence and fairness. He keeps abreast of America's aims and responds with political, moral and territorial rhetoric. Here is an example:

> This is a defensive *jihad* to protect our land and people. That's why I have said that if we don't have security, neither will the Americans. It's a very simple equation that any American child could understand: live and let others live.

There must be some doubt as to the veracity of bin Laden's claim that this is a religious conflict. Perhaps he is not a man who really thinks that a crusader war is in progress but someone who knows, as Hitler did, that you cannot galvanise a people into action with half-hearted statements.[20] Perhaps bin Laden is just a ruthlessly rational man with an axe to grind.

Recalling the introductory discussion of the sublime, here are some questions: If belief in the ideal, in a heavenly afterlife, with or without perpetual virgins according to individual preference, motivates people to improve their earthly conduct and ameliorate the hardships of others in this life, is not God validated without proof of his existence? Is the quintessential purpose of the mythological not precisely this, to facilitate our flourishing not after but before death, here on

[20] W Laqueur, *No End to War: Terrorism in the 21st Century* (Continuum International, 2003) 25.

earth? Inspiration and escape are basic to human well-being. And is it not pedantic and antisocial to argue that socially useful earthly action undertaken based on the promise of heaven is devoid of moral value, even if that might be true as a matter of intellectual accuracy? Good behaviour in the present, irrespective of its motivation by reference to the afterlife, retains its social value. To say it is otherwise smacks of secular snobbery.

What if we were to flourish, to achieve justice on earth (an impossibility)? Would that not obviate heaven? Would a celestial sphere become otiose to human requirements; would God not expire contented on a cloudy bed? In that impossible event, has the myth/threat/promise of his existence not served its purpose? And if so, why criticise it so vehemently? If that aspirational ideal is an illusion but it can, like an axe, do a considerable amount of good, is it quite as bad as Pojman would have it? And is it not entirely irrelevant whether on the one hand, eternity, or the metaphysical plane, or its various alleged inhabitants, or simply the ideal form, are considered to exist beyond the reaches of living human realisation or whether, on the other hand, they are imaginary constructs of the human mind, considered (perhaps involving the mind in a subtle self-contradiction) to be outside the bounds of human imagination or visible only in flashes, glimpses, or epiphanies?

Despite the religious fervour that drives the Allied response to terrorism, religion has had a very bad press in British and American intellectual circles. The upshot of the puerile 'is religion good or bad?' debate is that spirituality is considered by many antithetical to politics. Here, then, we can analyse how this attitude sits with the basic tenets of liberal democracy and address the less facile inquiry as to what role religion ought to have in law and policy-making. The argument to which I am about to offer a rejoinder is that faith is inimical to, or should be excluded from, liberal democratic politics. The form that this argument has taken in the war on terror is that of a comparison of 'backward' Islamic societies choked by a religious stranglehold on state institutions – where religion is a public matter, with 'progressive', enlightened liberal democratic societies liberated by a pluralistic disposition to religion – where religion is a private, not a public matter. Public argument about Truth is suppressed so that people can peacefully live their lives according to their private truths.[21]

Though this deserves a little attention in subsequent chapters, for now I would like to question the extent, at least so far as America is concerned, to which the dichotomy between reason and religion is false. In other words, is the exclusion of faith from politics in America only ostensible? Tareq and Jacqueline Ismael have argued that the religious orientations of Western political leaders and their frequent invocations of religion are not stressed in the English-speaking media. Religious symbolism and imagery is not seen as bearing on decisions emanating

[21] R Phillips, 'The War against Pluralism' in JP Sterba (ed), *Terrorism and International Justice* (2003) 104.

from Washington or London.[22] Anecdotally, anyone who watched the American presidential campaign could not have failed to see that reference to God is absolutely standard in peroration. More telling still, in the 1983 case *Marsh v Chambers*, the US Supreme Court found that legislative prayer is 'deeply embedded in [the] history and tradition of this country'.[23]

These were, of course, the Ronald Reagan years. Dreyfuss, author of the *Devil's Game*, drew an analogy between the Christian Right and Islamic fundamentalism. He point out how support for the Christian and Islamic Right 'converged neatly during the Reagan administration, which eagerly sought alliances with both. So influenced were some Americans by the Cold War that militant Christian right activists and fervent Zionist partisans of Israel cheerily supported Islamic fanatics in Afghanistan'.[24] Having publicly dubbed the USSR an 'evil empire' and portrayed the arms race as a simple struggle between 'right and wrong', he argued, in words that would not be out of place on a radio sermon, that there 'is sin and evil in the world, and we are enjoined by Scripture and the Lord Jesus to oppose it with all our might'. How would Erasmus, who was reviled by the prudential nature of much private prayer, feel about the dubious public use of religious rhetoric today?

Are such considerations anachronistic? Would such sentiments be laughed out of today's political speech? Well, no. Even before September 11, polls showed that 70 per cent of Americans believed in the Devil. And the then President Bush, possessed of Reagan-like insights into moral and religious rectitude, proclaimed that America 'is chosen by God and commissioned by history to be a model to the world of justice'. Adolf Hitler made almost identical assertions. He considered the Germans the 'people of God', and claimed that he felt himself called upon to do 'the work of the Lord' and desired to obey his will.[25]

The argument here is not that Americans are religious fanatics, but the more modest contention that we should be slow to accept the proposition that religion and politics are separate in the United States. And this leads us to another question, considered below, as to whether or not religion and politics can be separated, whatever the formal rules about the generation of law might say. Is it not fair to say that the aim of politics, like religion, is justice; and the product of politics and religion is law? At least for true believers, injunctions stemming from their religion take precedence over the enjoinders of whatever state they might happen to be in; that is, conflicts between man-made law and God's edicts are resolved by believers in favour of the latter.

[22] See generally, TY Ismael and JS Ismael, 'September 11 and American policy in the Middle East' in J Strawson (ed), *Law after Ground Zero* (London, 2002).

[23] *Marsh v Chambers* (1983) 463 US 783.

[24] R Dreyfuss, *Devil's Game – How the United States helped unleash fundamentalist Islam* (Metropolitan Books, Henry Holt & Company, 2005) 12.

[25] D Losurdo, 'Preemptive War, Americanism, and Anti-Americanism' in T Rockmore, AT Marsoobian and J Margolis (eds), *The Philosophical Challenge of September 11* (2005) 171.

In light of the more than passing resemblance between the statements of the infamous German and American leaders, we can reconsider Dawkins' pithy claim that religion is dangerous, and can consider a speculative suggestion (which anyway cannot be proved): The collusion of religious sentiment (worship of God) and nationhood (worship of land and self) in modern America – the widespread American belief that their nation is the last, best hope for freedom for mankind, that it is the source of infinite justice on earth – is the reason why Americans acquiesce in torture, encroachment onto other lands, extra-territorial targeted killings and aggressive war. For, where your country is the sole hope for boundless goodness and a cosmopolitan heaven on earth, where there is no other chance for man to be delivered from evil without your grace, what trivial earthly wrongs can possibly matter? The answer is 'None'.

Whatever America does, in the mind of some Americans, it is justified by America's *mission*. This is the most parlous group delusion that has ever afflicted human societies. History has seen it before, and I stress that it is not an exclusively American sentiment. It has swelled the chests and heads of Germans and Greeks, Russians and Romans, the British and Belgians, and many other races which found themselves momentarily on top of the man-pile, or ahead by a nose in the arms race. It is just America's turn, and she, like all the others, has disgraced herself with hubris. Pascal was not quite right to say that men never do evil so completely and cheerfully as when they do it from religious conviction. They are most cheerful when they do it out of love of a God who bears a distinct likeness to themselves, their kin and countrymen. Should we not worry about this 'God Delusion'?

Shifting the emphasis from spirituality onto sublimity, those at the head of such missions express their fundamentalist certitudes with unwavering confidence in their understanding of history, the wishes of their preferred deity, and just desserts. Both Bush and bin Laden have shared their insights into infinite justice. Judith Shklar is vociferous in her execration of those who indulge in such posturing: 'no form of arrogance is more obnoxious than the claim that some of us are God's agents, his deputies on earth charged with punishing God's enemies'.[26] That said, the fact of the matter is that the greatest threat is presented not by terrorists but by the massive military apparatus of the state. Dante was perturbed by the elision of religious and national fervour. The following excerpt expresses the apprehension we ought to feel when an elected representative, who is openly religious, no longer fears God's fury, but thinks they are doing God's work.

> Soleva Roma, che 'l buon mondo feo,
> due soli aver, che l'una e l'altra strada
> facean vedere, e del mondo e di Deo.

[26] JN Shklar, *Ordinary Vices* (Harvard University Press, 1984) 29.

L'un l'altro ha spento; ed è giunta la spada
col pasturale, e l'un con l'altro insieme
per viva forza mal convien che vada;

però che, giunti, l'un l'altro non teme.

On Rome, that brought the world to know the good,
Once shone two suns that lighted up two ways:
The road of this world and the road of God.

The one sun has put out the other's light;
The sword is now one with the crook – and fused
Together thus, must bring about misrule,

Since joined, now neither fears the other one . . .[27]

The point I want to make here, with Dante's help, refers back to my earlier assertion that as human beings, we are chronically incapable of grasping the sublime. Whatever sublimity is, it is fundamentally inconceivable – it is beyond us. We should therefore regard officials' claims that they know what is just, good or right with a healthy scepticism, if not disdain. However, that the sublime is unthinkable does not undermine its utility. René Descartes thought that the innate sense we have of the perfect helps us understand our own infinite imperfections, and imperfectability. The usefulness of the ideal, then, is its function as a spur in our sides, and as a reminder that whatever we think is right, we might well be wrong, epistemelogically and/or ontologically. This conviction of the presumptuousness of human claims to divine or sublime justice was, to my mind, the greatest driving force behind the *Divina Commedia*. It is perhaps best encapsulated in the following stanzas:

Però ne la giustizia sempiterna
la vista che riceve il vostro mondo,
com' occhio per lo mare, entro s'interna;
che, ben che da la proda veggia il fondo,
in pelago nol vede; e nondimeno
èli, ma cela lui l'esser profondo.

And so the vision granted to your world
Can no more fathom Justice Everlasting
Than eyes can see down to the ocean floor:
While you can see the bottom near the shore,
You cannot out at sea; but nonetheless
It is still there, concealed by depths to deep.[28]

Where does this leave us? The attempt to prove that there is objective justice is a waste of time, and beside the point. The basis for my assertion that objective,

[27] Dante, *The Divine Comedy*, trans M Musa (Penguin Classics, 2003), *Purgatorio*, Canto XVI, 106.

[28] Dante, *The Divine Comedy*, trans M Musa (Penguin Classics, 2003), *Paradiso* Canto XIX, 58.

sublime justice is 'out there' is not scientific, but a mixture of faith and pragmatism. As flawed people, we ought not claim that we are able to deliver justice. By what shibboleth shall we distinguish true manifestations of justice from imposters to her transcendent throne? Justice is but a whisper, a notion, a glimpse of a dream chased away by consciousness. It can never be entrapped in our laws, committed to a page, or delivered in a speech. In injustice, we feel its disapproving gaze. It moves endlessly in front of us, forever out of reach, but always close enough to encourage us onwards. Rather than asserting where or what it is, we should content ourselves with the more modest mission, proper to our limited capacities, of discovering where and what it is not.

In this light, we might see radical ideologies propounding absolute claims to right and wrong, truth and untruth, good and evil, as mere political flares. They burn hot and bright, briefly illuminating the ideological landscape, but also blinding those who look too directly into their flames. Inevitably, they burn out, and spiral, spent, to the ground, leaving us in a darkness all the denser for the brief, hollow promise of light.

In what follows, an attempt will be made to distil out of the above observations some implications for the law pertaining to terrorism.

First, something of history and the common law: In the final ecstatic image of Nietzsche's *Zarathustra*, time seems to implode: 'My world has just become perfect', cries the protagonist, 'midnight is also noonday'.[29] Similarly, in the culmination of Dante's experience of paradise, the poet is acutely aware of time, love, light and space collapsing into one. These are not just the deranged ramblings of philosopher-poets; rather, they have a deep resonance for the administration of human affairs. As I said above, an analysis of historical mistakes did not feed into the British Government's counter-terrorism plan.

Historical records, particularly those where facts are subjected to rigorous testing, such as in the common law and some public inquiries, are an ingenious man-made means for collapsing time. They help us bring the accumulated wisdom of the past to bear on the trials of the present. They collapse time, and, in so doing, help us more accurately to approximate justice in our legislative, judicial and executive measures. As philosophy seeks truth in the pitting of contrasting opinions against each other, history is borne of the friction between rival cultures. History, and for lawyers, the common law, is *social reason*. The common law, far from just incrementally responding to societal change, collapses time to further justice. As for history, it might well always be tainted by the inadvertent subjectivity of the historian, but we are better off with it, than without it. The state, with its vast resources, has no excuse for failing to consider alternative histories, thereby coming even closer to an accurate narrative of what happened in the past.

[29] F Nietzsche, *Thus Spoke Zarathustra*, trans RJ Hollingdale (Penguin Classics, 1961 (1883)) 331–3.

But, on both sides of the Atlantic, social reason was lacking – the war on terror was characterised by hasty legislative measures and an almost belligerent disregard for the realities of the situation as compared with historical threats. How can we guard against these errors? Mill thought one answer would be to institute a standing panel of expert legislative draftsmen, for, in his view, legislation was a 'work of skilled labor and special study and experience'.[30] Holmes puts a useful gloss on this suggestion:

> Truths do not simply accumulate like stones heaped upon a pile; some are destroyed by the advance of knowledge. Under rapidly changing conditions, bureaucrats and specialists can be crippled by what they 'already know'. Hard-won insights tend to become objects of veneration and irrational loyalty – as we are constantly being reminded by all those generals anachronistically fighting the last war.[31]

So we must be able to draw on historical awareness, to collapse time, without becoming slaves, in a changing world, to stultified past masters. In the context of terrorism, this discussion takes on a different complexion, for it is coloured by the dynamics of emergency.

When faced with emergencies, governments introduce extraordinary legislation or declare a state of martial law. The danger here, put as plainly as possible, is that the curtailments on liberty normally deemed necessary by legislators eager to reassure a panicky public tend to be oppressive, inflaming anti-establishment sentiment. The oppression therefore exacerbates rather than extinguishes the reasons for the conflict, or worse, it introduces new reasons for discontentment, turning moderates into radicals. Fiona Aoláin notes a further disturbing trend:

> There is also a strong correlation between the length of an emergency and its impact on an ever-growing number of citizens. The general experience is that while emergency powers may start out as (and be approved for) use against targeted groups of citizens and others, the longer the emergency persists the wider the application of the powers conferred against a wider net of citizens and non-citizens alike.[32]

Formulated differently, the encroachments on liberty, anti-government protest or diffidence, and increasing deference shown to the executive, form a vicious circle from which it is difficult to escape, and a state of emergency becomes normality. A standing panel of experts comprising lawyers, historians, sociologists, experts in conflict and politicians of different parties would be able to act as a bulwark against misguided measures, preventing governments slipping into the vortex of permanent emergency, and steering the flow of governmental enthusiasm

[30] JS Mill, *Considerations on Representative Government* (Kessinger Publishing, 2004) 103.

[31] S Holmes, *Passions and constraints: on the theory of liberal democracy* (University of Chicago Press, 1995) 191.

[32] FN Aoláin, 'The Individual Right of Access to Justice in Times of Crisis' in F Francioni (ed), *Access to Justice as a Human Right* (2007) 69.

towards measures likely to increase security in the short-term without jeopardising it in the medium-term. Permanent expertise can prevent permanent emergency.

The importance of preventative and permanent measures against terrorism is particularly acute in the current climate. Though we are promised a timely end to the war on terror, anyone with half a brain will realise that this will never come. Unless measures are taken to reverse the pattern of executive interference with liberties, we can expect a disintegration of cosy normality into a permanent state of emergency. One only need glance at Pakistani or Bangladeshi politics to know that this is not a very pleasant state of affairs. Again, this is not the plea of a civil libertarian. It is in the interests of government to refrain from slipping into the vortex of permanent emergency, where increasing oppression increases opposition, increasing oppression. As Hannah Arendt insightfully noted, violent governmental oppression 'appears where power is in jeopardy, but left to its own course it ends in power's disappearance'.[33]

Alongside permanent panels for conflict prevention and cure, governments would benefit greatly from a united front against international terrorism, in the form of an agreed upon international criminal jurisdiction. That terrorism is an international phenomenon is confirmed by the provenance of al-Qaeda's foot-soldiers, many of whom have joined the Taliban. Pakistanis, Afghanis, Bangladeshis, Indians, Iraqis, Uzbeks, Iranians, Germans and Brits fight shoulder-to-shoulder against British-American forces in the Pakistani hill territories.[34] The International Criminal Court would, but for various notable refusals to take part, be a perfect venue for the trial of terrorists.[35] It would also, perhaps more importantly, signal a renunciation of certain violent means, such as the indiscriminate killing of non-combatants, torture or political assassinations, which we can all agree ought to be universally forbidden.

Parallel to permanent jurisdiction, any pretence of justice must not contemplate immunity for certain actors. This important corollary to international criminal jurisdiction finds expression in Resolution 2005/35 of the UN Office of the High Commissioner for Human Rights, which mandates that states provide 'those who claim to be victims of human rights or humanitarian law violations with equal and effective access to justice, as described below, irrespective of who may ultimately be the bearer of responsibility for the violation'.[36] The aforementioned 'Hague Invasion Act' is the embodiment of international lawlessness and is hostile to any notion of international legality. Powerful states should be

[33] H Arendt, *On Violence* (Harvest/HBJ, 1969) 52.

[34] 'Taleban reveal arms suppliers', *BBC Online*, 18 September 2008, available at: news.bbc.co.uk/2/hi/south_asia/7622335.stm.

[35] FN Aoláin, 'The Individual Right of Access to Justice in Times of Crisis' in F Francioni (ed), *Access to Justice as a Human Right* (2007) 82.

[36] N Ronzitti, 'Access to Justice and Compensation for Violations of the Law of War' in F Francioni (ed), *Access to Justice as a Human Right* (Oxford University Press, 2007) 98.

first, not last, to sign up to the ICC, for they need its protection the least. That America actively opposes the ICC project – a minimal equality among peoples – is an embarrassment to its leaders and a tacit admission of vulnerability.

Many people argue that justice is a process that unravels over time; that the law's protection of rights is necessarily less vigilant in emergencies; that executives should be immune for measures taken in the heat of the moment; that counter-terrorism cannot be second-guessed from an armchair. But is it not wrong to think of justice as a process? There might be less time to ask questions in emergencies, but that does not, contrary to popular myth, entail that ex post accountability is unjust. To abrogate from principles of executive accountability as well as the protection of basic liberties, on the basis of a state of emergency is to throw the baby out with the bathwater. Perhaps law is a process; perhaps law, particularly the law of nations, is our fitful and interminable procession towards justice. I have kept this all rather abstract here, but I want to elaborate on this notion of ex post accountability in the chapter on civic responsibility, with what I consider to be a very important tale from America, which illuminates, better than any other I have heard, a healthier understanding of the relationship between necessity and legality than the hawkish mantra that necessity trumps legality.

Having made some suggestions about how thinking about time can help us use law intelligently, the discussion can now turn to spirituality, and how it might rally to our aid in combatting terrorists.

The first point of view to which I would like to offer a rejoinder is that there is some sort of violence inherent in Islam. Though the terrifying plagues in *Exodus* sent by God himself should be enough of a riposte to any Christian making this argument, the prejudicial view of Islam has taken an unrelenting hold of British and American opinion. For a start, a very good way to provoke anyone to violence is to assert that their credo is inherently violent. It is therefore unhelpful in the extreme to maintain that Islam is violent, unless we want Islam to be violent.

However, there is another very down-to-earth way of responding to the accusation that Islam contains the seed of conflict. The first important premise to note is that, for believers of all religions, whether we like it or not, we are a constituent part of the divine – we generate (the) divinity, and (the) divinity constitutes itself through us and our stories about divinity. Gandhi, for instance, considered the different religions of his multi-credal state to be diverse converging paths towards the truth. To employ today's parlance, his was a humanist or moralist understanding of religion. Nevertheless, many staunch believers reject this image of different converging paths. For them, their path is the only true route to peace, enlightenment and paradise.

It is contended here that this obstinacy (which is a feature of atheist bigotry too) lies behind the assertion that any one particular religion has violent tendencies. The frank way of refuting this obstinacy is to say, well, on any view, it is highly improbable that the various Gods will present themselves and fight to the death, or that a sign will be sent by *the* God(s) to the unequivocal and undeniable effect that he/she is the only one, (assuming his/her perfect knowledge of the demography of the universe). Hence, believers will have to content themselves with divergences in belief and embrace one another on the alternative bases for tolerance in each religious code, and on the basis of a shared spirituality.

The argument that any one religion is superior to another is almost farcical because it is an assertion admitting of no earthly proof. As a result, by denigrating another's religion, one degrades one's own. By deriding belief in another God, one makes a mockery of one's own credo. This is not to say, for the sake of argument, that no one religion has it right. It is not inconsistent to argue that moral or religious truth exists, truly to believe in one's own God, whilst arguing that no one on earth, or no one likely to present themselves, can possibly have the final say on it. The disposition endorsed here is not so much syncretism as settled henotheism.

Further, that perfect truth or justice are unascertainable and unattainable does not make it inherently pointless talking about them, or striving towards them. Those without the courage to accept the absolute impossibility of perceiving or achieving truth and justice, or who shudder at the prospect of never creating or finding meaning for their lives, take refuge in the comfortable certitude of the sort of fundamentalism that fosters violent propagation of beliefs. But this is cowardice not courage.

Arguments that assail religion as dangerous, and hail science as the source of any worthwhile truth, are equally absurd. Scientists, who have given us guns, bombs, missiles, and other less efficient means with which to kill ourselves, who argue that religion is dangerous nonsense, are inhabitants of a crumbling Potemkin village. But the critics of religion call victims of religious conflicts as their witnesses:

> [W]hen religion enters the picture, as in Fallujah, it transforms the struggle. It expands timelines into eternal goals and expands the rewards of the strugglers into cosmic rewards; it transforms a realistic struggle into a cosmic one and changes the character of the battle.[37]

But these witnesses are not necessarily credible. Arguments like de la Mettrie's – 'well, look at all the religious soldiers' – ignore the very earthly, human reasons for these wars, which include, inter alia, self-defence, revenge, bigotry, jealousy, xenophobia and intolerance. As we observed earlier, bin Laden's goals are territorial and his justifications are drawn from (twisted) moral reasoning, even if both are steeped in religious rhetoric. Religion might provide the register but not the reason.

[37] DS Hamilton, *Terrorism and international relations* (Calouste Gulbenkian Foundation; Center for Transatlantic Relations, Paul H Nitze School of Advanced International Studies, Johns Hopkins University, 2006) 60.

Furthermore, as conflicts intensify, it becomes harder to find rational reasons to continue fighting. 'Religification' of the war rhetoric or the 'cosmification' of conflicts is therefore a natural development of continued bloodletting, where positions become entrenched and stylised, where further violence and death can only be justified by fanatical, transcendental truths, which hide the real pathologies of violence, and mask the fact that it is addictive and self-perpetuating. As Arendt observed, violence becomes an end in itself. This has far less to do with God's power than it does man's weakness. War suspends our capacity for empathy. Take the following example. An American interrogator described a German parachutist, captured in the Battle of the Ardennes and, at 18, barely a man, as a 'totally dehumanized Nazi', 'a carefully formed killing machine' but then went on, apparently without any sense of the irony, to say: 'I could have killed him in cold blood, without any doubt or second-thought, as I would a cockroach'.[38] This is not to say that the interrogator was inhuman, but that there is nothing special in any race preserving them from inhumanity.

Consequently, instead of pointing the finger at Islam, it would be far more sensible to denounce the un-Islamic nature of terrorist violence. Terrorism might be many things, but it is hardly pious. Indeed, in the Islamic tradition, again contrary to modern wisdom, just as in the Christian and Jewish traditions, suicide is a sin, for one's life is not one's own to take. The critics of religion cannot rely on the credibility of the suicide bombers either. Holmes makes the point that, seeking

> death to avoid the tribulations of life is a sign of cowardice, not courage. The incentives in such a case for deceptive signalling are so great, in fact, that no public pronouncements by a suicide terrorist can provide decisive evidence about his private motivations.[39]

Holmes might be right, but I would argue that a retention of spirituality, an empathy for things religious, or at least a rejection of the snotty deprecation of all God-belief, is crucial to understanding our world. We are superstitious, we do resort to prayer in adversity, and many of us, secretly, stupidly, think we are right about most things because we have special access to the truth. A strictly scientific disposition is unhelpful in sociological analysis, and might well be counter-productive in conflict scenarios, where emotions are running high. Again, science is super at answering the How? questions, but it is inept when it comes to answering the motivational Wherefore?. Taylor describes the demerits of the scientific disposition succinctly.

> The prestige of the disengaged model can easily override this everyday experience. Reality is summoned, as it were, to conform to what this stance can pick up. A powerful homogenizing a priori is at work here (perhaps a little too reminiscent of Kant),

[38] Quoted in N Ferguson, *The War of the World* (Allen Lane, 2006) 548.

[39] S Holmes, *The Matador's Cape: America's Reckless Response to Terror* (Cambridge University Press, 2007) 20.

> perverse in its effect. I say 'perverse', because we ought to hold that method and stance be adapted to the nature of the reality concerned, whereas here, albeit unwittingly, reality is being arraigned before the bar of Method; what doesn't shape up is condemned to a shadow-zone of the unreal.[40]

For many British and American commentators, it is in this 'shadow-zone of the unreal' that suicide bombing takes place. The Israeli-Palestinian conflagration is a good example. It is far easier to denounce mothers who acquiesce in their offspring being conscripted as suicide bombers as monstrous than to understand their desperate intergenerational motivations, or to empathise with their unenviable position as the victim of the victims, or to comprehend the pride they feel for their courageous children. Those who want to paint the enemy in the colours of fanaticism do not want to hear arguments about the strategic logic of suicide terrorism and its usage by secular organisations, as this might mess up their portrayals of religion as dangerous nonsense. But, as Robert Pape has made clear, suicide bombing is cheap and effective, and its recruiters are anything but fanatical.[41]

It is worth pausing to query whether those who denounce religion as violent have spent any time actually reading the original texts of the more popular world religions. Notwithstanding their dramatic content and some fairly unpleasant excerpts, it is readily apparent that the thrust of the scriptures is towards peace between various creeds, not war; towards, to borrow from the Cambridge Platonists, the 'theiosis' and consequent pacification of man through agape or meditation or Islam and so forth.

Indeed, it might well be that the factors informing this aversion to religion, behind the mock piety of those protagonists of the profane who claim that religion produces war, are the *rigidity* of religious precepts condemning violence and the connected notion of self-abnegation in the common good – tenets which do not sit well with modern liberal democracies, their institutional intolerance, and their secular, self-interested national economic goals. To claim that conflict has 'religious' roots, apart from involving a stubborn ignorance of glaring earthly indices, is a tactic of those incapable of peaceable neighbourliness, of those who have no interest in reaching reconciliation, or of those who seek a scapegoat to deflect attention from their own agenda. It is a comical feature of modern human affairs that claims of divine right can often be traced back to prosaic human wrongs. The bottom line of this argumentation is that religion is not dangerous: like medicine, its effect depends on both the administrator and the patient. Certainly, the exclusive truth claims in religion can be dangerous weapons in the hands of a certain type of administrator, but is not the confidence in objective truth claims rooted in the character of such a person? Would not a

[40] C Taylor, *A Secular Age* (Harvard University Press, 2007) 286.

[41] RA Pape, 'The Strategic Logic of Suicide Terrorism' (2003) 97(3) *American Political Science Review* 344.

differently disposed individual find other things in religion, invitations to self-doubt and respect for others being amongst them? The point here is that the eradication of religion postulated by de la Mettrie would do nought to erase the human character traits that make belief systems dangerous. Blaming religion or science is an abdication of responsibility.

Thus far, I have tried to defend religion's virtue, but it would be remiss not to extol it a little too. When it comes to conflict-avoidance and reconciliation, one of the most favourable features of popular faiths is the reminder of the need for self-doubt, the iteration that we are imperfect, errant, calamity-prone, fallible, and that whatever we might think good or right on the basis of our scriptural readings, might not parry with divine justice or the whole, sublime truth. This religious prescription for permanent uncertainty is distasteful to the professedly pious who admit of no doubt, and to those who have, for psychological or putatively pragmatic reasons, chosen a philosophical diet of scientific certitudes or moralistic sureties. Further, it would seem that those who are sure of their convictions and their role are more inclined to use violence to defend or impose them than those who carry with them a dutiful, self-deprecating, self-doubt. A proneness to violent conflict then, has more to do with false certainty than it does true piety.

In sum, to denounce another's religion or faith is to discredit one's own. To lambaste all religion or faith, and to scoff at scripture, apart from usually involving the antagonist in an attempt to disprove that which cares not for and admits of no proof, is to jettison some of the most valuable provisions available to man – it is to throw overboard the priceless stock of human mythology and to abandon a cargo of agape of inestimable worth. This is not to deny that the fantasy land of religion becomes dangerous when it eclipses the world in which we live to the exclusion of the light shed on human affairs by history, philosophy and the sciences.

Having attempted to rescue religion from its current besiegement, we can perhaps begin to consider how it ought to feature in the modern state, and in particular, whether a constitution can be calibrated to ameliorate the sort of discontentment that results in terrorism.

Many modern scholars believe that immediacy of faith in the lives of believers erodes or precludes democratic sentiment and habit: it prevents them from separating politics from religion.[42] But, it is unclear why we would want believers to keep their faith to themselves, or to draw a mental distinction. Are not religion and liberal democratic politics striving for the same things – *l'observation de la justice et la pratique de la bienfaisance*?[43] The stuff of religion and politics is not fissile. Taking Islam as an example, Fadl makes a crucial point:

[42] L Weinberg and A Pedahzur, 'Introduction' in L Weinberg and A Pedahzur (eds), *Religious Fundamentalism and Political Extremism* (Frank Cass, 2004).

[43] C Taylor, *A Secular Age* (Harvard University Press, 2007), quoting L'Abbé de Saint-Pierre 222.

> [M]any classical jurists argued that, regardless of the political affiliation to a particular territory, the real or true abode of Islam is wherever justice exists (*dar al-'adl*), or wherever Muslims may freely and openly practice their religion. Therefore, it is possible for a territory with a Muslim minority that is ruled by non-Muslims to be considered part of the abode of true Islam.[44]

But some scholars think that religious belief and a political disposition are incompatible. Benjamin Beit-Hallahmi is as good an example as any. He tells us that 'we must realise that religious people have a hard time being true citizens in a democracy'.[45] Why must we? Because, he tells us, 'the idea of tolerance is alien to the spirit of historical religions'.[46] In Beit-Hallahmi's view, religious views and religious people stifle liberal democracy. Beit-Hallahmi seems to enjoy something of a burlesque. Intolerance, for instance, is inimical to both Islamic and Christian doctrine; both are heavily suffused with humanistic sentiment.[47]

Beit-Hallahmi's burlesque does not tally with my understanding of British or American polities. Liberal democracy is a system not for the suppression of, but for the *sharing* of different beliefs, green, blue, red, gnostic, agnostic and so forth. The key to it, therefore, is that each person's beliefs are accorded equal respect. And religion has no quarrel with diverse faiths or points of view. On the contrary, it, and spirituality more generally, can be regarded as a path to self-reflection, self-knowledge and contemplation of society and ethics. The major religions counsel the abnegation of the self and tolerance of others that are necessary to assure equal respect for diverse points of view, and yet encourage self-assertion and expression. Tolerance and self-expression are the building blocks of liberal democratic polities.

Religion and liberal democracy are not in inevitable conflict. On the contrary, liberal democratic procedures and religious conviction stand in a potentially complementary relationship. One temptation of faith is to deny our own agency, in the face of divine omnipotence; neglecting our role in the generation of a better world, of the ideal state, by attributing the creation of all things good to an external other. Democracy reinforces the consistent religious emphasis on human agency. There is a parallel temptation of secular modernity in mass society, to submit to a somewhat contradictory feeling of dangerous rudderlessness and entrenched helplessness. Religion can through faith furnish disorientated members of a modern democracy with both direction and stability.

Furthermore, faith – not the blind fire and brimstone type, but the thoughtful, discursive variety of religious observance I endorse here – reinforces mindfulness

[44] KAA Fadl, '9/11 and the Muslim Transformation' in ML Dudziak (ed), *September 11 in History: A Watershed Moment?* (Duke University Press, 2003) 101.

[45] B Beit-Hallahmi, 'The Return of Martyrdom' in A Pedahzur and L Weinberg (eds), *Religious Fundamentalism and Political Extremism* (Frank Cass, 2004) 32.

[46] *ibid*, 31.

[47] For a different view on the role of religion in al-Qaeda, see L Wright, *The Looming Tower* (Knopf, 2006).

of our fallibility (helping us tolerate other beliefs). It is a strong force pushing us toward self-betterment and public service (combatting the apathy fatal to liberal democracy). It contains readily serviceable, off-the-shelf moral maxims, imparting an obligation for subordination of the self (working as an important counterweight to the structural selfishness of secret voting).

Beit-Hallahmi is not alone in the view that religious people struggle to be democratic: The judges of the Strasbourg Court of Human Rights also showed a liking for this religious burlesque. In 2003, in a display of judicial innovation, the Grand Chamber concurred with the inferior Chamber, which, imaginatively, had concurred with the Turkish Constitutional Court, in considering that democracy was the antithesis of *sharia* because '*sharia*, which faithfully reflects the dogmas and divine rules laid down by religion, is stable and invariable. Principles such as pluralism in the political sphere or the constant evolution of public freedoms have no place in it'.[48]

This judgment seems to be based on the staggeringly implausible assumption that there can be no discussion about 'what Islamic law ought to be' amongst an estimated 1.2 billion Muslims; 22 per cent of the world's population. Though, as in any social structure, those wielding power are few, it is false to presume that ordinary people do not discuss the law and its shortcomings. Patently, the notion that ancient religious precepts can ever survive introduction into modern life is hard to defend, even with the strongest will in the world. But religion, all religion, is a discursive phenomenon, and as such, is perfectly compatible with democracy, a political system anchored in discussion. Conversely, fundamentalism, according to which life must be lived in a manner loyal to unchanging rules, is of course, incompatible with democracy. But *sharia* is not, and has never been, a system synonymous with fundamentalism, though unbending bigotry has a habit of masquerading as Islamic jurisprudence. An example of the coincidence of *sharia* with fervent zealotry was provided by the Taliban regime's activities early in the second millennium, including the premeditated destruction of the great sixth century rock sculptures known as the Buddhas of Bamiyan, the institution of the death penalty on 8 January 2001 for converts to Judaism and Christianity, and their generous hosting of Osama bin Laden.[49]

In its consideration of the compatibility of Islamic law with democracy, the Grand Chamber was particularly troubled by 'the way [*sharia*] intervenes in all spheres of private and public life in accordance with religious precepts'.[50] But the convictions held by any person, religious or otherwise, presumably pervade all

[48] *Refah Partisi (The Welfare Party) and others v Turkey* (Application Nos 41340/98, 41342/98, 41343/98, and 41344/98) (2003) 37 EHRR 1 (Grand Chamber), para 123.

[49] For a backdrop to this excessive intolerance and its status in international law, see F Francioni and F Lenzerini, 'The destruction of the Buddhas of Bamiyan and international law' 14(4) *European Journal of International Law* (2003) 619.

[50] *Refah Partisi (The Welfare Party) and others v Turkey* (Application Nos 41340/98, 41342/98, 41343/98, and 41344/98) (2003) 37 EHRR 1, para 123.

spheres of private and public life, or at least they should. Further, a person who is convinced of the way they ought to lead their private life, and sure of their public values is not destined to be alienated from democracy. On the contrary, such a person is of great utility to a democracy, being capable of the confident espousal of ideas crucial to debate. How favourably such a person would compare to the limp opposition politicians of today's Britain whose views change with public opinion polls, whose values are formed not in the heart and mind but in contradistinction to the unpopular policies of the government, and whose convictions are indexed only to their perception of the quickest route to power. On the other hand, a person incapable of tolerating (and empathising with) the views of others is a poor candidate for life in a liberal democratic state. With respect, the Grand Chamber was (rightly) concerned about fundamentalist bigotry and yet (wrongly) conflated that with *sharia*. As a result, there is more than a hint of siege-mentality about its conclusion.

It is salutary to note that there are logical miles between the *belief* that one's system of values is true and just, and the professed *knowledge* that they are so. This is the difference between faith and bigotry. Unlike faith and liberal democracy, bigotry and liberal democracy *are* in conflict. But, to conflate religion with bigotry is to confuse a characteristic with a credo, and obstinacy with belief. The distinction I am trying to make is parallel to my argument about the sublime; scilicet there is no harm in believing in a realm of eternal values but it is harmful to believe they can be imported wholesale into our human social structures. Such bigotry is as much a characteristic of staunch atheists as it is the faithful. As a matter of fact, if we were all better Christians or Muslims or otherwise and practised the public virtues in those faiths, we would have less need for democracy. It is only our selfishness and inability objectively to evaluate competing claims that necessitates a crude division of social power.

Naturally, procedural restraints on modalities of espousal of religion are desirable. As Habermas argues, 'complex life circumstances in modern pluralistic societies are normatively compatible only with a *strict* universalism in which the same respect is demanded for everybody – be they Catholic, Protestant, Muslim, Jewish, Hindu, or Buddhist, believers or nonbelievers'.[51] The name of the true path or deity should not be up for debate in parliaments, not only because such intractables are not resolvable in discussion, or evincible with proof, but because, at least modernly, the question is unhelpful, and for a society dealing with inequality, hunger and homelessness, the largely common principles flowing from religions are of greater present concern than their ultimate eternal source. Perhaps now, where few states can lay a realistic claim to even a general oneness

[51] J Habermas and J Derrida, *Philosophy in a time of terror: dialogues with Jürgen Habermas and Jacques Derrida* (University of Chicago Press, 2003) 32; see also J Habermas and J Ratzinger, *Ragione e fede in dialogo* (Marsilio, 2005).

of belief of their citizens – in other words, where unbelief and other beliefs are features of the mindscape of the masses – the wall between 'church' and state should be Chinese.

Religious authority perhaps should not be seen, but it most certainly should be heard. The absolute position, that religious sentiment should play no part in politics, is unsustainable. Belief – that is, the attempted, yet dedicated subjection of oneself to religion – real belief, is not a private diversion; it is an all-immersing lifestyle; it is a pocket yardstick used to measure, whether ex post or ex ante, each and every decision. Both religion and politics are systems for the elaboration of the good, whatever form that might take. Attempting to separate them is an exercise in futility. Believers cannot suppress their beliefs for the duration of a debate or leave their faith at the door of the polling station. For believers, though there may be a separation between earthly and celestial planes, there can be no separation between religious and secular domains or religious and public values. But this *reductio ad absurdum* is a far cry from the conclusion that private religious convictions are inhospitable to democratic constitutions. By way of example, if the Church has views on contraception, derived from a particular view of chastity and family life, that strike us as baseless, backward and socially harmful, it is well within the competence of members of the community opposed to these views to refute them on public health grounds.

Even where a state can claim oneness of belief amongst its citizenry, the need for discursive procedures in the public sphere does not necessarily diminish. Religions are *discursive* phenomena. We are constitutive of the ideal and constitute the ideal. The power to narrate what it means to be religious, to believe, and what religion means, belongs to each believer in equal measure. Where citizens disagree as to the ultimate being, as is the case in most states, it is not clear why democracy should not serve religion – in that it allows those who believe in the ultimate truth of their doctrine to dispute it with others convinced otherwise. Why is religion supposed to be inimical to democracy? Does it not provide a source of largely selfless principle, diluting the institutional intolerance permitted and promoted by secret ballots?

Espousal of one's convictions, religious or otherwise, is not anathema to but *integral* to liberal democracy. On the contrary, violent espousal is inimical to liberal democratic politics, but violence does not come from an overabundance of religious sentiment. Rather, it stems from a lack of perspective as to the validity of one's own views vis-à-vis those of others. Oppression of expressions of religious sentiment must be kept within narrow procedural bounds in a democracy. As Holmes puts it, 'the strategy of avoidance can exacerbate pent-up social tensions, eventually engendering terrorism or a revolutionary explosion by denying legitimate expression to deeply felt beliefs'.[52] Naturally, this cuts both

[52] S Holmes, *Passions and constraints: on the theory of liberal democracy* (University of Chicago Press, 1995) 233.

ways. If religious views are aired in public, they may also be criticised in public, but this criticism would be more meaningful if it were based on a realistic understanding of religion, and its potential part in the democratic play. It could even be argued that Beit-Hallahmi's intolerance of religion is more damaging to democracy than religion itself.

Prefiguring somewhat the penultimate chapter, it is contended here that a partial reclamation of the public sphere by spiritual authority would help us produce better laws, and avoid bitter wars. As Nussbaum explains, in late 1940s India, Prime Minister Jawaharlal Nehru's aim was to 'forge a policy whose key features were secularism (meaning not separation of church and state, since four major religions were given substantial roles in law-making, but equal respect among the religions)'.[53] In America and the United Kingdom, the co-opting of religious advisors and the canvassing of religious views would not threaten the legislative process; rather, it would enrich our decision-making. The moral bulwarks of religion are an important brake on the sort of populism that sucks a government into the vortex of permanent emergency, where increasing securitisation and anti-government violence become ends in themselves.

Religion and politics, prudence and morality can be blended in the constitution of a modern polity, with fruitful results, not least, by responding better and earlier to the 'pinching shoe'; that is, by responding to the claims of sections of society who are suffering uncomfortable restraints on their liberties. There is no necessary conflict between religion and liberal democracy. Rather, they can complement one another, particularly where the citizenry espouse a plurality of religions. There is nothing aslant about the proposition that religious plurality might enrich a society and, paradoxically, reinforce the power of the state. As Holmes explains, religious liberality 'strengthens the state, makes possible an armistice among rival sects, and promotes the supremacy of the crown'.[54]

The central point is that, irrespective of who is accorded the highest authority, politics, adjudication and religion are all discursive phenomena; all decisions are made according to the most persuasive reasons. The differences between a democratic and a religious polity can be more formal than substantive.[55] Pierre Legendre might have been right: 'We are prisoners of the fragmentation of the disciplines connected to the art of discourse. We are haunted by the representation of a rationality that starts from the secularisation of Latin Christianity'. It is the position here that we are constitutive of divinity, in Legendre's terms, we are animated building stones, *vivus lapis*. We instantiate the ideal.

[53] MC Nussbaum, *The Clash Within: Democracy, Religious Violence, and India's Future* (The Belknap Press, 2007) 115.

[54] S Holmes, *Passions and constraints: on the theory of liberal democracy* (University of Chicago Press, 1995) 125.

[55] On this, see M Diamantides, 'Towards a Western-Islamic Conception of Legalism' in Peter Goodrich, Lior Barshack and A Schuetz (eds), *Law, Text, Terror* (Glasshouse, 2006).

It will have been clear from the discussion of sublimity earlier in this chapter that the intention here is to underline the importance of the ideal for law-making and for counter-terrorism policy, whilst undermining the attitude of mind that arrogates to itself certainty about what the ideal solution might be.

There is a world of difference between, on the one hand, referring to the sublime inspiration for whatever plan you seek to promote, or appealing to your particular understanding of right or the good, and on the other, assuming inerrancy, and claiming that one's actions are undertaken pursuant to God's will or to a plan that is in itself sublime; there is a difference between quixotic motives and afflatitious presumptions. The former are laudable, the latter ludicrous. It is of the imperative that our actions are informed by our interpretation of some eternal, sublime goal – justice for example, but it is equally fundamental that we frankly admit our incurable fallibility and the chance that our brilliant plans might achieve less than lustrous results in reality. This frankness has the effect of moderating our zeal without dampening our enthusiasm, of tempering ambition with humility, and of diluting piety with humanity.

Though I will say more on this later, the arrogant civilian disregard for the possibility of error caused the British Army to stampede blinkered into Iraq. Similarly, this confusion about the role of the ideal oxygenates America's religious assurance that her modern moral order is correct: 'for Bush himself, 9/11 was all the proof he needed that "infinite justice", not mere human and partial justice, was on the American side'.[56]

The aesthetic formidability, the awesome destructive potential, of America's sophisticated war machines reinforces the conviction that God acquiesced in her possessing such power, and that she is doing His glorious work. America was drunk on the desire for revenge, intoxicated with religious fervour, and giddily keen to use her lethal gadgetry. History shows that the security of our societies is jeopardised by three sources of violence: crime, zealous nationalism and religious zealotry. Is it off the mark to say that Bush's America threatened to engulf global politics in a sea of zealous, religious, criminal nationalism?

The prerequisites for climbing out of the current Stygian quagmire are pungent, accurate criticism of the status quo, plus utopic thought, and hopeful action. Without a vision of the ideal form, and unless we strive to attain that ideal form, we resign ourselves to sloth, apathetic mediocrity. That the attainment of the ideal form is impossible is of no import; our inbuilt sense of what is not ideal means that sublimity is a disorderly ordering principle by which we can legislate for, regulate and adjudge the real. That the ideal form shifts rainbow-wise further away, with our every attempt at approach, is a reminder and nothing more of the eternal duty to progress. And it is right that it should shift, for every time we try

[56] S Holmes, *The Matador's Cape: America's Reckless Response to Terror* (Cambridge University Press, 2007) 210.

to achieve justice in law, we create new imbalances, offsetting the original equilibrium of injustice. I would like to deepen this line of thought.

It might be said that we need some form of imaginary model – be it justice or love, or God, or beauty – upon which we project our aspirations, in order to overcome our base instincts for those we know to be higher; to readjust our relationship to reality by artificially extending our potential. As Taylor puts it, the 'membrane of self-absorption has to be broken from the outside, even if what it liberates is internal to our more authentic selves'.[57] In the human experience, 'God establishes the new relationship with us by loving us, in a way we cannot unaided love each other'.[58] But – and this is what Taylor is alluding to in the first of these comments – for some people, imagining God's impossible love, or God's unattainable justice, helps them feel they can come closer to emulating it in their own lives. That is the function of the ideal – it stretches us.

Taylor's take is of course that of a believer, but religion is not a prerequisite of spiritual depth. A greater appreciation of the relationship between temporality, spirituality and sublimity comes for some from the simple acknowledgment that we are part of nature and not somehow outside of it. The fear of death, for example, which relates back to our irrational fears, can be averted (for some) by reflecting that they only die in a biological sense, explicitly defined by humans. Being worm-food is a death of sorts but it also involves one's conversion into different energy forms, back into the greater cycle of life itself, a cycle of life far more profound than the simple, insignificant effluxion of a single human lifespan.[59]

Pursuant to the format adopted thus far, I will now join some of the dots of the themes here and those of the foregoing chapters. Clearly, symbolism and semantics are integral to religion, time, and our impressions of the sublime.

We have already noted the powerful rhetorical resonance of religion (eg, bin Laden's invocations) and, conversely, the religious symbolism of excessive force (think of the plagues of Egypt or the quasi-mythical significance of September 11). In the secular realm, the idea of sublime order and beauty pervades our consciousness: Taylor recalls Mandeville's *Fable of the Bees*, where the attractive counter-intuition that private vice was conducive to public benefit was made notorious. This is relevant to our story, and, anticipating the next chapter, we can observe that the theories of Adam Smith and Jeremy Bentham – according to which, given the proper procedural conditions, self-interest can redound to the common benefit – are aesthetically hypnotic, and have duped many with their simplistic promise that unabashed self-interest is in the public good.

[57] C Taylor, *A Secular Age* (Harvard University Press, 2007) 338.

[58] *ibid*, 282.

[59] This sort of oneness-of-it-all approach found expression in Stoic philosophy. In modern times, it was brilliantly portrayed in the film, *Thin Red Line*, directed by Terence Malick, adapted from the novel of the same name by James Jones.

Next, there is a crucial link between the language in which conflict is described, and the unfolding of history. The rhetorical meta-conflict, that is, the conflict about what the conflict is (crime, civil disorder, civil war, international armed conflict) can affect the outcome, because it can affect the register of law applied and therefore, by extension, the level of discretion allowed to the law-giver/war-maker. Northern Ireland, for example, as far as UK law was concerned, was, since its founding, in the unhappily oxymoronic state of permanent emergency, and the Irish and British suffered as a result.[60]

In his 2008 seminar series at Columbia, on civil liberties, Stephen Shapiro made the point that, whilst violence or a state of emergency continues, judicial deference is shown to the state; when it is finished, however, curative decisions are made, deference ends, decisions are analysed, and decision-makers chastised. His point is not that judges are wise after the event, but that there is a restorative aspect to ex post legal proceedings. I want to make two further observations. One, judgments are very helpful historical records (when their political context is kept in mind). For instance, in a war with China, would the US repeat costly mistakes made with the Japanese by interning everyone in Chinatown, including Chinese Americans? Two, whoever wins the meta-conflict, the battle about what the conflict is, secures a victory in a battle that will actually affect the outcome of the war, because the rhetorical jousting, by swaying public opinion this way and that, determines the leeway a state enjoys in its response.

Hence, and I want to stress this, so long as we accept that global terror is a war, so long as we accept that interstate war-making is an appropriate response to private bomb-making, we change the parameters of that conflict, and of permissible responses by our governments, but also, crucially, by terrorists. So long as the war or emergency is ongoing, our inspection of laws will be ad hoc, and our judicial review will be lax. It is the Pandora's box of politics. So long as we unsuspectingly imbibe the rhetoric of terror, we will unquestioningly approve of the security measures. The *Hamdi* and *Belmarsh* litigation[61] may be seen as turning points in the meta-conflict about the war on terror, for the simple reason that they represented a waning of judicial patience with post-9/11 executive fiat.

Peace processes are important in themselves for expediting an end to conflict, but they are also crucial to policing the actions taken during the conflict: by recognising two separate entitled entities, peace negotiations open a window on the 'war/disorder' to the world, which normally remains closed for the duration of crimes or civil disorder. As is typical, a poet has summed up these points better than I ever could. In 'Question Time', in his *Belfast Confetti* collection, Carson announced: 'No, I don't trust maps, for they avoid the moment: ramps,

[60] The best discussion of these dynamics is by C Campbell, '"Wars on Terror" and vicarious hegemons: The UK, International Law and the Northern Ireland Conflict' (2005) 54 *International & Comparative Law Quarterly* 321.

[61] *Hamdi v Rumsfeld* 542 US 507 (2004); *A v Secretary of State for the Home Department* [2004] UKHL 56.

barricades, diversions, Peace Lines'. His point is that, particularly in a contradictory permanent state of emergency, maps, oddly enough, exist in the past and the future, but never in the present. A similar point can be made about law, it describes the past and prescribes the future, but is somewhat estranged to the present.

I asserted above that September 11 was portrayed by the British-American war lobby as an original, absolute event, to give moral clarity to their plans in the Middle East. Here, the further point can be made that the usage of the epithet '9/11' or rather, the omission of the year, has the effect of 'collapsing' or 'gathering' time, eternalising the event, and perpetuating its rhetorical force. Some people's lives were redefined entirely by the attacks on the Pentagon and New York's financial district. In the same way that clocks are rumoured to stop at the time of a murder, some individuals seem, since then, to have been in stasis. Harry Roland, the 'Ground Zero man', a self-appointed tour guide, visits the Trade Center site every day to demystify for tourists the mythical misapprehension that only two towers fell that day – 'Don't say two, 'coz it ain't true' – and to draw their attention to the uncounted homeless who died in the inferno.[62]

Perhaps the above consideration of the profane, human, rational reasons for terrorism allows us to rebut de la Mettrie's simplistic assertion that an end to religion would bring about an end to war. Is it not more realistic, and more attentive to the human thirst for story-telling and taste for the metaphysical to agree with Voltaire – *si Dieu n'existait pas il faudrait l'inventer*? Or, alternatively, in the unlikely event that the Large Hadron Collider somehow proves there is no God, would we not simply adulate people, ideas or objects as we revered deities? In this respect, it is interesting to note that, in his attempt to liberate man from God-worship, in *Thus Spoke Zarathustra*, Nietzsche seemed not only enslaved to religious symbolism but, in the end, shackled man to an idea of a new breed of man, with greater powers and self-possession – a god then. Whether or not his symbolism was intentional, it hardly gave us a ringing rejection of religion. Instead, it rather tends to confirm the utility of man-made myth. Of course, in a sense, this was precisely Nietzsche's point.

Arguments like de la Mettrie's also seem to ignore that the ideals and idols of the day, secular or sacred, will inevitably clash and conflict. This is not a cause for concern. Clashes and conflicts are required for growth. However, the proper modalities of those battles are, in human society, one of the most important themes of our times. How can we fight monsters when they rear their menacing heads? Dreyfuss, and countless other scholars, argue for nation- and religion-building in the Middle East, largely in the conviction that this will prevent little monsters growing into big monsters.

[62] D Barry, 'Preaching the gospel of Sept 11 to visitors', *New York Times*, 21 March 2003, available at: query.nytimes.com/gst/fullpage.html?res=9A00EFDE1E31F932A15750C0A9659C8B63. I had the pleasure of meeting Mr Roland myself, in March 2008, six years on from the tragedy.

But the British-American bunglers have made themselves unsuitable candidates for securing or aiding any constitutional or religious reforms. Any proactive proselytism on our part will now be seen by all Islamists and by many Muslims as imperialism and politico-religious supremacism. And so we find that the close alliance of America (and, by extension, Britain) with Christianity was not necessarily prudent, however rousing it might have sounded in speeches. Instead of harnessing the plurality of cultures and religions amongst British and American citizenry to steer ourselves quietly into a sovereign position above the cultural and religious skirmishes blighting world politics, we have aligned ourselves with one side of an eternal cosmic war that started in academic fantasy.

Moreover, by responding with such cumbersome ferocity to al-Qaeda, we have invested that movement with legitimacy (if only as a counter-imperialist force), increased the numbers of its supporters, and ensured its longevity for years to come. Far from preventing little monsters from growing into big monsters, we have achieved the opposite. As John Milton had it, 'obstructing violence meets for the most part with an event utterly opposite to the end which it drives at: instead of suppressing sects and schisms, it raises them and invests them with a reputation'.[63]

The post-Bush United States must now see that the peoples of far flung nations might not feel the need for American sermonising about statecraft as much as Americans feel the need to sermonise about statecraft; that America is not universally regarded as a prototype of perfect society. The alteration of foreign societies must originate with those peoples, if they so will it. Furthermore, if the aim is counter-terrorism, the so-called civilisation of Afghanistan and Iraq will achieve nothing if it is not accompanied by the taming of British and American political cultures, rightly regarded by many other societies as unruly and iniquitous.

States cannot effectively combat terrorism if they reserve to themselves the right to employ means which, by showing disdain for human life or liberty, reciprocate the terrorist calculus. To do so is not only to create enemies but to force the hand of one's enemies. Hence, the argument here was that we should focus on means which have a chance of being universally considered worthy of prohibition. Peace is not served by ensuring that war is as terrible as can be, but by gradually whittling away at the acceptable modes of warfare until we develop a collective conviction that egregious forms of executive fiat, be they torture, targeted killings, arbitrary detention, or indiscriminate killing of civilians, are considered incompatible with our self-understanding. This might sound sensible, but it did not parry with the early reticence of the United Nations towards

[63] J Milton, *Areopagitica* (1644), DM Wolfe (ed), *Complete Prose Works of John Milton* (Yale University Press, 1959) 542.

humanitarian law, that is, the law of war. Why, it was thought, should the UN concern itself with legislating for something it has prohibited?[64]

A final point may be made here about the relationship of time to law and justice, war and crime. When we think of damages, or reparation, we tend to think of moving a wrongdoer to compensate the victim of their wrong, or to restore the victim to the position they were in before they suffered a wrong. Our focus is on the individuals. And when we think of punishment, we tend to regard it as retribution for a wrong, but also as a display of institutional revenge or solidarity with the victim. Our focus is on individuals. But the forgotten potential of reparation is that it can repair the social fabric. Punishment too can be reparative; it can be salvific and cathartic, where it is just.

Take, for example, a police officer who, in desperation to save a kidnapped child trapped in a room with a dwindling oxygen supply, pokes the suspected perpetrator in the ribs, and stamps on his naked toes, to ascertain the suffocating child's whereabouts. We are caught between the proposition that the maltreatment of the suspect is wrong and the conviction that allowing the child to asphyxiate would be unforgivable. Law, over time, can reconcile this seemingly intractable conundrum. Punishing our police officer expresses the social conviction that what he did was illegal, even anti-legal, and that it was morally unacceptable; further, it allows him to rebalance his out-of-kilter conscience; but, more importantly, it restores, it *repairs* the social fabric, by correcting malversation in the administration of legality. This reparation is completed by the compensation of the victim of the policeman's maltreatment. However distasteful it might seem to pay out to the kidnapper of a child, the reparation symbolises the state's remorse about one of its officers resorting to a criminal act to rescue the victim of a criminal act. It says: 'We regret he had to do that'. This is not to say that the policeman was wrong to act in this way. Rather, it is to say it was right for him so to act but it would be wrong for him to go unpunished.

Turning to the earlier discussion of liberty, the suspect in the example above is used as a means to an end by the police officer – he is coerced to supply information on the dying child's whereabouts. We can measure these actions against the yardstick of the influential Kantian maxim: '*Handle so, dass du die Menschheit sowohl in deiner Person, als in der Person eines jeden anderen jederzeit zugleich als Zweck, niemals bloß als Mittel brauchst*'. Permitting myself a rough translation, this means that one ought always conduct oneself so as to treat one's own humanity – but also that of every other person – not merely as a means, but, at the same time, as an end. Torturing a suspected criminal for information, subordinating their dignity to the aim (however worthy) of finding the imperiled infant, is to transgress this principle. However, as I hope I have shown, after the event, the law can step in, to articulate our absolute rejection of the police officer's actions,

[64] N Ronzitti, 'Access to Justice and Compensation for Violations of the Law of War' in F Francioni (ed), *Access to Justice as a Human Right* (Oxford University Press, 2007) 97.

by punishing him, compensating the suspect, restoring our sense of legality and repairing (albeit imperfectly) the flouting of the suspect's dignity.

This brings me to a discussion of the role of liberty and ideals in the human constitution, and in that of society. We might all be able to agree that the greatest freedom comes from an active subordination of one's whim to wisdom, from passing up short-term pleasures in favour of the real, enduring long-term satisfactions. This is often represented in literature as triumphing over one's emotions: '*Bound heart, free spirit.* – If someone binds up his heart and takes it captive, he can give his spirit considerable freedom'.[65] We reserve our admiration for people who overcome their baser instincts in pursuit of more virtuous goals, not for desultory individuals who succumb to fleeting desires. Frivolity, indecision and petulance, unless pursued with life-long conviction, are seldom regarded as characteristics of human greatness.

This idea of subordinating one's passing fancies to venerable norms is typical of religious and spiritual teaching. It is also inherent in the idea of a 'constitutional' democracy, one whose democratic nature is delimited (and preserved) by principles prior even to democracy, such as equality and human agency. But this is a site of tension in constitutional theory. A constitution can always be torn up by the new leaders of society. There is a deep-set democratic resilience to time-honoured tradition, an aversion, if you will, to permitting 'certain dead gentlemen' to tyrannise us. Democracy's very strength, we are told by those who are sceptical about constitutional restraints, is in its flexibility. In the war on terror, for instance, we might be told that a democracy must be free of pesky constitutional fetters so that it can respond to new wars, new threats, and defeat new foes. But what if a free-wheeling, flexible democracy contorts itself to such an extent that it violates these prior principles of equality and human agency? What if it the majority in a democracy arrogates to itself powers that transgress the trust on which it holds those powers?

The notion of constitutional forbearance has a fascinating relationship to security, which can be illuminated with Montesquieu's help. He said that, in 'proportion as the power of the monarch becomes boundless and immense, his security diminishes'.[66] In light of this wisdom, we might conclude that when equality and liberty are violated in the name of the numerical power of democracy, the majority, in trying to protect its liberty, might, perversely, jeopardise it. At this stage, we can recall the notion of 'excess', of using excessive force to command obedience, to 'shock and awe', in the parlance of the US military. What we have learned from Montesquieu seems to gainsay the efficacy of these military tactics. There are ways of containing conflict and, similarly, ways to exacerbate, cosmify or religify it. One of the latter is targeted killings. As Heymann notes, such tactics, where they are accurate, might 'incapacitate,

[65] FW Nietzsche, *Beyond Good and Evil*, trans J Norman (Cambridge University Press, 2002) 61.

[66] C de Secondat Montesquieu, *The Spirit of Laws*, trans T Nugent (Hafner, 1949) vol I, 114.

disrupt, and deter, but they also create martyrs and thus stimulate imitation'.[67] Where they are inaccurate, they create converts to the terrorist cause. According to the BBC, in Tikrit in September 2008, marines besieged a building, believing it to contain the leader of a bombing network. The occupants failed to surrender so, after waiting one hour and issuing 'multiple warnings', the marines called in an air strike, obliterating the building. Iraqi officials say that none of the occupants had any connection to the insurgency. Though the United States admitted killing three civilians along with the suspected insurgents, their spokesman Colonel Jerry O'Hara, who obviously has a very singular understanding of causality, attributed blame to terrorists, 'who repeatedly risk the lives of innocent women and children to further their evil work'.[68]

Bringing temporality into this discussion of security and ideals, support for unsavoury characters might seem a rational short-term measure, but wherever hands become bloodied, conflicts have a tendency of becoming transcendental. Enthusiastic American support for hardened Islamists during the Reagan years was, as Dreyfuss says, a 'catastrophic miscalculation'. He argues that it 'devastated Afghanistan itself, led to the collapse of its government, and gave rise to a landscape dominated by warlords both Islamists and otherwise'.[69] To look at modern Russia, it can hardly be said that a decisive victory was won in terms of security.

Rational observation yields the result that security is a dangerous ideal that often gets the better of governments. As Jean Bodin admitted, 'Neither laws nor magistrates can restrain "bands of men" whose "rage will oft times most furiously break out"'.[70] On this understanding, absolute security is not an ideal but an illusion – it is a false idol. Attempts to create security frequently generate insecurity. Conversely, accepting a degree of perpetual insecurity, embracing mortality, welcoming the happy accident of life and greeting the imminence of death, often has boons both in terms of liberty and security. This is not to argue that states should give up all security measures but rather that we can link back our spiritual capacities to the dynamics of security and liberty, amity and enmity; that there might be a certain exhilaration awaiting us, not in daring military exploits, but in the brave commitment to trust, cultural aperture and empathy.

In academic literature and the critical press, rationality and religion, spirituality and reason are often pitted against one another as stylised foes. Again, Pojman provides us with a good example of this sort of thinking:

[67] PB Heymann, *Terrorism, Freedom and Security* (MIT Press, 2003) 48.

[68] 'US air raid kills Iraq civilians', *BBC News Online*, 19 September 2008, available at: news.bbc.co.uk/2/hi/middle_east/7625167.stm.

[69] R Dreyfuss, *Devil's Game – How the United States helped unleash fundamentalist Islam* (Metropolitan Books, Henry Holt & Company, 2005), eg at 288.

[70] Quoted in S Holmes, *Passions and constraints: on the theory of liberal democracy* (University of Chicago Press, 1995) 122.

> Invoking the authority of God and offering the rewards of eternal bliss, can be an incentive to extreme acts of virtue and vice … It is hard to reason with religious fundamentalists, for they generally hold their faith or religious assumptions to trump what we in the West call *reason*. Reason, for them, always functions as a strategy within the 'bounds of religion alone'.[71]

It is difficult to respond to this sort of comment in academic terms, but such opinions are so ingrained in the popular psyche that they distort our perception of God's role in the mind of a believer. Pojman's comments are intended as an indictment of tribal, insulated, Eastern, religious cultures, but are riddled with error. First, arguing that reason is a Western concept or capacity is an historical aberration. Amartya Sen gives two helpful reminders of Eastern rationality: In the sixteenth century, whilst Akbar, an Indian Emperor, was counselling freedom of religion, 'the Inquisitions were active in Europe and Giordano Bruno was being burned in the Campo dei Fiori in Rome'. Further, the 'decimal system, which evolved in India in the early centuries of the first millennium, arrived in Europe at the end of that millennium, transmitted by the Arabs'.[72] The second problem with Pojman's premise is that, the Iraq invasion being the prime example, as we have seen, it is far easier to describe and understand 'Western' reactions to terrorism in emotional or religious terms than by ratiocination. Third, Pojman's underlying point is that faith is dangerous, but a loss of faith can be depicted as just as dangerous as belief if we use a stylised character similar to Pojman's believers.

Ostensibly secular in form yet fervently religious in substance, America has proven how dangerous religion can be, but can we conclude with de la Mettrie that an entirely faithless, and therefore materialist, society would be any better? (We certainly cannot impose the like if we are committed to liberal democracy.) Predictably, Pojman recommends our cautious and critical commitment to world trade. Capitalism, if it can be called a social model, is atheist and might, undiluted, be as destructive as communism in that it has no pretence to social justice, but this is the stuff of the following chapter. Going back to Pojman's quote, would capitalist reason not be more likely to redound to the net benefit of humankind if it functioned within the bounds of social values prevalent in religious codes, if it were tempered with charity (as it often is in the case of individuals)? At the time of the American-Taliban alliance against the Soviet invasion of Afghanistan, conventional American wisdom was that communist materialism must be resisted by Christo-Islamic allies, united by faith. Former friends are now mortal foes, in large part because of ideology. Freud might say it is their similarity that informs their mutual hatred.

[71] LP Pojman, 'The Moral Response to Terrorism and Cosmopolitanism' in JP Sterba (ed), *Terrorism and International Justice* (2003) 139.

[72] A Sen, 'Civilizational Imprisonments' in Joseph Margolis, Armen T Marsoobian and T Rockmore (eds), *The Philosophical Challenge of September 11* (2005) 103.

In the foregoing discussion of rationality, an attempt was made to explode, or at least damage the notion that morality and prudence are separable. At the very least, we must admit that religion and rationality have a more subtle relationship than the crude opposition depicted by Pojman. For Derrida, this imaginary line of demarcation between reason and faith functions in the same way as the border between two countries, separating but intertwining their fates. This too is perhaps an oversimplification. Locke argued that morality was the most 'enriching purchase' but that it was only on the basis of boons in the afterlife that morality could trump prudence and capture the minds of men.[73] We might consider whether this appeal to rewards in the hereafter is necessary. Here, I prefer Cicero to Locke, who, rather than relying on posthumous dividends, bases his assertion that prudence and morality are one and the same on the integrity of the soul – one cannot, unless sick, live happily with a bemuddied conscience. Tillotson made a very similar point, which might appeal to those who do subscribe to a complete philosophy, such as Islam or Christianity, by arguing that religion and happiness, duty and interest are the same thing, considered from different perspectives. The basic point to grasp, and I concede that it is true perhaps only in an aspirational sense, is that we cannot live well in *male fides*. One cannot live the good life in bad faith.

Dante's depiction of the limitations of reason is compelling. Virgil, the poet, guides the bewildered and beleaguered protagonist through the circles of hell and purgatory, but, being a faithless philosopher, is unable to ascend into heaven, where the symbol of eternal love, Beatrice takes over. The symbolism is made even more powerful because Virgil is loyally portrayed, whilst Beatrice responds only in part to a real human being, but is largely an aspirational, fictional, or ideal character; Virgil is an ever-present companion, whereas Beatrice is someone altogether more mysterious. For Dante then, religion fills the gap between the real, the rationally achievable, and the Utopian ideal. It spans the abyss between the subconsciously conceivable and the consciously attainable. It needs to be stressed here that the utility of the ideal for law-making is separable from the sort of religious sentiment that informed Dante's masterpiece, but not from faith in the possibility of human betterment – in a word, hope.

One field of human affairs where human betterment is urgently required is race relations. In particular, our reading of academic texts must be attentive to the agenda, express or implied, of the author. Much space has been dedicated here to inviting the reader to look behind the 'clash of civilisations' theory at the preconceptions or policy goals that shape its neat contours, for these hidden motives have literally written the playbook in the match between Islamist terrorists and the Anglo-American alliance. For instance, Dreyfuss is very critical of Bernard Lewis' brand of historical scholarship:

[73] C Taylor, *A Secular Age* (Harvard University Press, 2007) 223.

> Although Lewis maintained a veneer of academic objectivity, and though many scholars acknowledged Lewis's credentials as a primary-source historian on the history of the Ottoman Empire, Lewis abandoned all pretense of academic detachment in the 1990s. In 1998, he officially joined the neocon camp, signing a letter demanding regime change in Iraq from the ad hoc Committee for Peace and Security in the Gulf, co-signed by Perle, Marin Peretz of *The New Republic*, and future Bush administration officials, including Paul Wolfowitz, David Wurmser, and Dov Zakheim. He continued to work closely with neoconservative think tanks, and in the period after September 11, 2001, Lewis was ubiquitous, propagating his view that Islam was unalterably opposed to the West.[74]

The theory of civilisational clash took hold not because of flawless scholarship, or because it was amenable to certain policy goals, but because the notion of a latent threat lurking in the East appealed to the popular psyche. Notwithstanding their differences, both Nietzsche and Nussbaum recognised that it is a sense of ethnic or racial or cultural insecurity that moves policies of exclusion and persecution. In particular, Nietzsche's comments on this theme were prescient:

> 'Don't let in any more Jews! And lock the doors to the east in particular (even to Austria)!' – so commands the instinct of a people whose type is still weak and indeterminate enough to blur easily and be easily obliterated by a stronger race.[75]

But it suffices to observe children's attitudes to one another to realise that absent exploitation, violence, or rival claims to territory, mere racial difference does not determine hostility.[76] It is crucial, therefore, not only to denounce violence borne of insecurity, but also to combat pseudo-histories, spurious rumours of economic exploitation, and speculative territorial claims. A government must consult alternative histories.

With respect to economics and territory, spirituality is a helpful tonic for diluting absolute claims to proprietary right. In most forms, spirituality is less about the reconciliation of the claims of the individual against those of the group, which preoccupy theories of social justice and rights, than it is about the blending of the self with the whole. This blend or bond or unity, usually perceived by people at epiphanic moments in their lives, might usefully be interpreted as the perfect state to guide our imperfect earthly attempts to achieve communal harmony. The afore-mentioned ability of the sublimity of nature to evoke in us feelings of our true purpose also has stirred emotions of unity or fraternity with the cosmos, the earth, fellow man, and even beasts. The solution

[74] R Dreyfuss, *Devil's Game – How the United States helped unleash fundamentalist Islam* (Metropolitan Books, Henry Holt & Company, 2005) 333–4.

[75] FW Nietzsche, *Beyond Good and Evil*, trans J Norman (Cambridge University Press, 2002) 142.

[76] S Holmes, *The Matador's Cape: America's Reckless Response to Terror* (Cambridge University Press, 2007) 140.

of the one in all, man in nature, earth in heaven, is not possible without some sort of spiritual synchrony; not a oneness of belief, but an appreciation of the value of the spiritual realm, per se.

This utility of deference to spirituality for its own sake is an important rejoinder to absolutist or fundamentalist arguments, such as the Wahhabi creed, which regarded moral philosophy or extra-textual thought as self-love or devil worship. This sort of belligerent textual fidelity has the paradoxical effect of undermining the credibility of one's own religion, for it groundlessly presupposes that other forms of spirituality are insubstantial and without foundation. Moreover, as Nussbaum suggests, it might be that 'variety, polymorphousness, and change are features of all real religions'.[77] Furthermore, though fundamentalists would be loath to admit it, and though it was perhaps flippant of Mill to say so, there is more than a grain of truth in the contention that the 'same causes which make him a Churchman in London, would have made him a Buddhist or a Confucian in Pekin'.[78] Faith can transcend earthly boundaries too. Take the following, symbolic, excerpt from a French aviator's report of armies in the Western Front of World War I.

> I could make out two similar gatherings among the Boche and ourselves, in these parallel lines that seem to touch one another: a crowd, a hub of movement and, around it, what looked like black grains of sand scattered on grey ones … Then I understood. It was Sunday and these were two services being held in front of my eyes: the altars, the priests and the congregations … These two gatherings were similar – so exactly similar that it seemed ridiculous …[79]

There is no space for enmity in visions of the sublime.

This is a useful juncture to consider again belligerent *un*belief and condescending atheism. Taylor, in *A Secular Age*, notes that 'the interesting issue is whether there could be any unbelief without any sense of some religious view which is being negated'.[80] If we think about it in this way, even atheism includes belief. (This is similar to Derrida's point about identity.) In short, by denying the possibility of a god, atheists generate the subject of their denial. This might be a pedantic point, but for us to deny the existence of something, it must exist somewhere, if only in the mind. Nothing that exists in the human mind can be foreign to us, and as such, deserves empathy at the least.

But religion is frequently rejected as rule-fetishism, and though irrational, institutionalised worship of idols can certainly become cumbersome, it is argued here that it is hard to attack religion without causing collateral damage to the notion of the ideal and the valuable human capacity for transcending the self, shattering the mundane and escaping the inexorable current of progress into the

[77] MC Nussbaum, *The Clash Within: Democracy, Religious Violence, and India's Future* (The Belknap Press, 2007) 227.

[78] JS Mill, *On Liberty* (Broadview Press, 1869) 15.

[79] N Ferguson, *The War of the World* (Allen Lane, 2006) 123.

[80] C Taylor, *A Secular Age* (Harvard University Press, 2007) 269.

calm ocean of the pointlessness of it all. Though some might reject the study of European Union Law as rule-fetishism or institution-worship, this does not undermine the utility of creating laws for Europe.

Turning to consider the difficult relationship of the sublime with human beauty, there would seem to be three consecutive obstacles in life's steeplechase. The first is the temptation to project that which is base in the self onto other races, the next is to err by worshipping anything human or human-made as if it were ideal, the last is excessive aversion to the human.

Francis Bacon wrote that the spirit of fornication was an ugly little 'Æthiope' and thereby arbitrarily linked what was considered base in his society with another ethnic group. The effect of this sort of 'thought' process on foreign policy is obvious. It tempts us into accession to the untenable proposition that by attacking another culture, we can destroy that which is objectionable in our own. Of course, aside from injuring our reputation with other societies, this sort of behaviour compounds what is repulsive in our own culture by denial. In short, prejudice has a deleterious effect on foreign policy.

The next trap is worship of the profane. Here, we can recall Plato's warning about the baseness of physical yearnings for pulchritudinous women, who were distortions, or perversions of the soul's longing for true beauty. Similarly, it is folly to take military supremacy as evidence of divine endorsement. Earthly might should not be confused with cosmic Right. In essence, this is a warning about aesthetic arrest. In the Romantic period, barren-looking moral precepts were rejected by those who saw artistic expression of beauty as the highest form of human flourishing. It would seem that, in thinking about law and policy, we ignore the allure of the aesthetic at our peril. Reason alone does not generate our laws.

This notwithstanding, philosophers wrestling their passions and resisting earthly inducements tend snobbishly to reject what is human, the beauty in the flaw. Of course, the suggestion that we have no higher purpose, and might as well submit to our carnal drives is distinctly offensive to the transcendentally disposed, and of precious little social utility. The third obstacle then, is the tendency to take this repugnance too far, so that it becomes unnatural, inhuman and repressive. The attitude towards sex of (ascetic) thinkers like Socrates, Nietzsche, Descartes, Kant and Gandhi can be fruitfully compared with those who embrace this essential aspect of humanity, like Tagore, Orwell, Russell and Nussbaum; those who arrange things into higher and lower pleasures, like Aurelius, Cicero or Mill; and finally, with the incurably romantic disposition of a Byron or a Wilde.

Presumably, the correct calibration of what might be termed a healthy embrace of humanity varies from individual to individual but it also might be said that the rigid sobriety of some sections of society compensates for the excessive lascivity of others. Understandably, during the long period of composition of *Les Miserables*, Victor Hugo swung from extolling the merits of the monastery to lamenting the cons of the convent. In fact, as he seems to conclude, playboys and priests might well benefit from more frequent colloquia: One can imagine lively debates as to who is more fulfilled or whose notion of beauty or the ideal is more refined. (James Joyce jokes in *Ulysses*, that apparently it was a nun who invented barbed wire.) These three traps can be avoided by acknowledging that law must always respond to human need without accommodating human greed or pandering to our vanities. Law should be the engine of our betterment.

I spent some time above on terror and religion, religion's use of terror as a motivator, and terror's use of religion as leverage. Here, however, I want to address a discrete point. Many believers are reluctant to confront the problem of why their own all-powerful and unfailingly benevolent god tolerates such evil and suffering in the world[81] so they seek other scapegoats for their grievances. Other societies with unfamiliar idols make excellent candidates. With respect to modern terrorism, it can certainly be argued that the core of al-Qaeda has nothing to do with Islam, and much to do with hatred for outside influences; hatred for the bewildering freedom presented by the lack of a priori belief – it is an anti-ideology. (Remember the disorientating journey without a departure point.) Fear of 'the demonic depth of human freedom' drives people to fundamentalist belief, to submission to a simple code.[82]

This is not a new phenomenon: in the Indian context, Christopher Jaffrelot argued that 'it was easier to mobilise Hindus *against* the Babri Masjid [a mosque in Ayodhya built, Hindus assert, on the site of a temple to Rama] than *for* anything else'.[83] How can we combat our propensity to locate blame outside ourselves and our own societies? How can we learn to be for instead of against? One answer can be located within religion. In both Christian and Islamic theology God, unlike humans, can take an objective stance on things, he can perceive perfect justice.[84] Though law can, through general regulations, cure human subjectivity and caprice, it cannot cure our incurable subjectivity of outlook. This notion forms part of the idea, central to religion, of that all-too-human fallibility which fundamentalism seems to forget. It is not the suggestion here that we model law on the perception of some omniscient being. Quite the contrary, it is suggested that we do the best we can to make laws and manage conflicts given our incurably subjective and limited outlook, without pretending that our results instantiate justice. The idea of the ideal functions as a helpful reminder of our subjectivity and limitations.

Before concluding this chapter, I would like to highlight the relationship between the sort of perverse political speech we noted earlier and time. When

[81] P Ricoeur, *Evil: A Challenge to Philosophy and Theology*, trans J Bowden (Continuum, 2007).

[82] *ibid*, 53.

[83] Quoted in MC Nussbaum, *The Clash Within: Democracy, Religious Violence, and India's Future* (The Belknap Press, 2007) 178.

[84] KAA Fadl, '9/11 and the Muslim Transformation' in ML Dudziak (ed), *September 11 in History: A Watershed Moment?* (Duke University Press, 2003) 96.

governments or other structures of social power co-opt the controllers of media and the academy, and pervert the presentation of reality and history, the struggle against misinterpretation and public misfeasance is not just a struggle for reliable information but also, as Milan Kundera once put it, the struggle of memory against forgetting. Hobsbawm rightly considered this to be the historian's valuable contribution to society. They help us to 'stand back, so far as possible, from the contemporary record and see it in a broader context and in a longer perspective'.[85]

This chapter considered the relationship of time, spirituality and the sublime to the war on terrorism and to law. The next chapter is far more materialistic, though it is not a complete departure from these themes, as it addresses two attempts to institute sublime ordering of human affairs, through economy and hegemony.

[85] EJ Hobsbawm, *Globalisation, democracy and terrorism* (Little Brown, 2007) 2.

8

Economy and Hegemony

All great things occur away from glory and the marketplace: the inventors of new values have always lived away from glory and the marketplace.

Nietzsche[1]

PART OF THE challenge of writing about terrorism is that, short of Shaw-like innovations, it necessitates the usage of terms with contested meanings. This chapter is no exception, so here, to begin the discussion, something should be said about what is intended by the terms economy and hegemony.

Hobsbawm stridently asserts that the 'era of empires has gone, but so far nothing has effectively replaced it. The number of independent states has quadrupled since 1913'.[2] He paints a picture of a world divided into small geopolitical spheres with varying internal features. Nevertheless, it would not seem to be the case that collapse, cession and decolonisation ended an epoch of imperium. Domination is, needs must, a wily changeling.

Nor is it adequate to say that America simply acceded to the throne previously occupied by European powers. Throughout her short history, America has never been an empire of the old school. As Desmond King points out, the United States has no territorial claim on any other country, largely because such a claim would be received with revulsion amongst US voters on account of their innate empathy for subjugated societies, and the sympathies of large ethnic minorities in the United States.

What can be said of the post-colonial international system? Perhaps the first point to make is that the infrastructure of world institutions, and the relationships between states, are the progeny of post-colonialism. Colonial powers did not simply decamp, up and leave, but did so on terms – conditions favourable to the exertion of a continuing influence.[3] With respect to Britain, a quondam hegemon, it is often wondered how so few people, on such a tiny island, can exert such great influence on world affairs. The answer perhaps is twofold. Few though

[1] F Nietzsche, *Thus Spoke Zarathustra*, trans RJ Hollingdale (Penguin Classics, 1961 (1883)) 79.

[2] EJ Hobsbawm, *Globalisation, democracy and terrorism* (Little Brown, 2007) 75.

[3] J Tully, 'On Law, Democracy and Imperialism' in S Tierney and E Christodoulidis (eds), *Political Theory and Public Law* (Ashgate, 2007).

they might be, the Brits are old hands at domination, and they play at the international negotiating table with the loaded dice of an international system they helped to design. Occupation is not a prerequisite of oppression.

Returning to American influence, Hobsbawm foregrounds the role of trade in the explanation of US dominance:

> The US hegemony of the second half of the last century rested not on bombs but on the enormous wealth of the US and the central role its giant economy played in the world, especially in the decades after 1945. Politically, it rested on a general consensus in the rich north that their societies were preferable to those under communist regimes ... Culturally, it rested on the attractions of the affluent consumer society enjoyed and propagated by the US, which had pioneered it, and Hollywood's world conquest. Ideologically, the US undoubtedly benefited as the champion and exemplar of 'freedom' against 'tyranny', except in those regions where it was only too obviously allied with the enemies of freedom.[4]

This lucid account perhaps underplays that the Americans have stretched out a 'safety net' of military bases abroad. So dizzying is the number of these sites, there is now a lively debate in a corner of the American academy as to the exact total. It can, however, confidently be asserted that there are now more than three times as many American bases abroad as there are countries on the globe. The express aim was to create a potential for force projection anywhere, at any time, or, more polemically, effectively to threaten everyone, everywhere, always. Although its capacity to proliferate these bases was in part dependent on economic predominance and ideological appeal, stripped of its frills, if America is or was an empire, in large part it was an empire of threat.

However, history does seem to tell us that, although superior force can certainly help found an empire, it will not, alone, sustain one.[5] The retention of imperial power requires a mobile, savvy elite schooled in anthropology, languages, international relations, theology, economy, government and war-making. The Bush administration's display in the Iraqi theatre of its sheer ignorance in these disciplines allowed it to deny any imperial designs.

In fairness to America, much of the castigation aimed at its 'new imperialism' is misplaced. US influence seemed to have less to do with an American desire to subjugate and more to do with the seemingly inexorable psychological arrest achieved by the idea of liberal capitalism. The feeling of being stuck on a runaway economic train has led people to lampoon those in First Class.

At the time of writing, we were told by Bush that Wall Street had been getting drunk, and by his critics that he was the one serving the drinks; piggy bankers were enraged with bankers; Main street was incensed with Wall street and the US embassy to the United Kingdom announced a move from Mayfair to Nine Elms. Depression has set in. Money, it seems, is central to our wellbeing.

[4] EJ Hobsbawm, *Globalisation, democracy and terrorism* (Little Brown, 2007) 45.

[5] *ibid*, 44.

Nietzsche, infuriated by the lure of the marketplace, wrote: 'Tell me: how did gold come to have the highest value?'[6] It is a rhetorical question but, given the entrenchment of monetary value in our society, it is arguably one worth having a stab at answering.

One great advantage of money over all other systems of exchange, over all other false-starting attempts to create social interaction across seemingly insurmountable cultural barriers, is its simplicity. It answers the primal grunt of desire. It talks where socialist ideologies stammer; cash is hard, where political ideals are infuriatingly soft. It can be held in the hand and exchanged for infinite varieties of pleasure. In short, it can be grasped. Orwell mused over the human aptitude for financial reckoning: 'Where the Lottery was concerned, even people who could barely read and write seemed capable of intricate calculations and staggering feats of memory'.[7]

That is why, when other inducements fail to bring people together, money sometimes succeeds. Thus, commerce has often been presented as a nostrum for international strife, and to the extent that it begins a process of transcending cultural and linguistic barriers, it is socially useful. Kant was convinced of the pacifying properties of trade, but did not present it as a driver of integration. For him, constitutionalisation and cosmopolitification would 'lead to the gradual replacement of military competition among states by economic competition, which is spread by "cosmopolitan right" and "mutual self-interest", so that "the spirit of commerce sooner or later takes hold of every people'.[8] Granted, trade has pacifying and integrative effects, but the potency of economic structures to subsume political ideology ought not to be underestimated. This is the other side of the coin: when economic volatility causes these market structures to collapse, a politicisation of ethnicity grows out of the ruins. Indeed, the current economic cataclysm does not bode well for friendly relations. I want to explore why capitalism and liberal democracy have a strained relationship. What are the dynamics of politico-fiscal freedom?

The liberalisation of society entails at least some privatisation of value judgements. Prima facie, democracy involves the public espousal of competing versions of the good. In fact, secret ballots can incentivise *private* interest, that is, self-interest, over public morality. People who cannot check how their fellows will vote have less incentive to consider the preferences of others before they cast their lot. Democracy might be said to result in an approximation of justice because, even if we all vote selfishly, each vote has equal weight, and no one can thereby subjugate another to his will. However, what I have called the structural selfishness of liberal democracy is hard to deny. This institutional intolerance

[6] FW Nietzsche, *Thus Spoke Zarathustra*, trans RJ Hollingdale (Penguin Classics, 1961 [1883]) 12.

[7] G Orwell, *Nineteen Eighty Four* (Penguin Books, 1954 (Secker & Warburg [1949]) 72.

[8] I Kant, *Zum ewigen Frieden. Ein philosophischer Entwurf* (1st edn, 1795).

validates and is reinforced by the sort of self-regard intrinsic to capitalist ideology, that, by looking after ourselves, we are somehow raising the standards of all.

According to this simple plan, wealth is applauded and revered for its own sake. This reverence relegates the political to the financial, by conflating self-service with public service. These structures have led Allott to argue that 'Democracy-capitalism has an intrinsic tendency to degenerate into the management of forms of *evil* – greed, corruption, immorality, crime, injustice'.[9] Whether or not one agrees with this strong formulation, at the very least, it can be argued that the minimal form of the state required to accommodate the conventions of capitalism *licenses* avarice, selfism and a disregard for ethics. Liberal democracy does not convert virtue to vice, but, without more, it certainly provides a fertile environment for that metamorphosis.

In a sense, the accumulation of wealth is deeply anti-social. Like the championing of liberty for liberty's sake, dedicating one's life to a pursuit of profits, without any other goal, is an empty activity, tantamount to stacking paper. Taking a step back, it is a sad indictment of Western culture that many people believe a country's success can be measured in terms of the average wealth of its citizens. Of course, it can if we are prepared to leave the abject conditions of other communities out of the calculus. Otherwise, we must admit to a collective failure.

In the same way that violence can become the end in a process where it was originally the means, and the original ends (defence of freedom, peace and happiness) can become the means for a continuation of violence, profit can become the end in a process in which it was originally envisaged as the means (pursuit of freedom, peace and happiness). In this way, a system can take on the aspect of a dog chasing its own tail or a horse in pursuit of a cart. Original reasons for action are subsumed in, subservient to, and explicable only in the logic of economics. This phenomenon might be described as the commodification of social life, and it has sickening consequences.

It can result, namely, in a devalorisation of values other than economic value, leading to a devaluation, in our collective psyche, of the intrinsic worth of what is human, and by extension, what is social. In its extreme form, this devalorisation has the consequence that anything that cannot be given a price-tag is valueless. Further, according to some theorists, there can be a devalorisation of 'use value', since what counts is 'exchange value' or, in other words, 'market value'. In plain English, in a society of customers, things, once procured, are no longer enjoyed. The effect of human subordination to economics is that simple pleasure (of eating, drinking and playing) is replaced by an all-consuming avarice for acquisition or exchange. To give a simple example, the quality of a wine is judged not by reference to its taste, but by the cost of a bottle. The powerful

[9] P Allott, 'Lecture', at Rome, The Pontifical Academy of the Social Sciences, XIII Plenary Session (2007).

pathologies of money precipitate the total destruction of the primary value of things and its replacement with market value.

The irony here is piquant. The result of the combination of two systems based on an adulation for private freedom, liberal democracy and capitalism can be that the 'private life and the private mind become *residual phenomena*'.[10] Though freedom is allegedly promoted by free-wheeling liberty, it is actually abnegated by the manner in which we have chosen to enshrine our liberty. What is more, in the attempt to achieve happiness through consumerism, the public sphere, civic values and political participation have been neglected. The over-exuberance of the self has not only alienated the self *from itself*, but it has alienated man from his society. Mass consumerism stifles public reason.[11] Where power in society is a function of money, the temptation is to make financial rather than social (or spiritual) investments. Coinage replaces suffrage and the delusion that freedom is capital disorientates the social body.

Perhaps the most subtle and therefore deadliest subversion involved in capitalism is not the oppression of the poor by the rich, nor the conversion of vice into virtue, but the subordination of the rich to profit. In the same way that rickshaw wallahs' legs are kept spinning by the *need* to make money, the wealthy are kept locked into the pursuit of profit by the *greed* for more money, a greed which can eclipse human value. Is this the proper light in which to observe Albright's reference to the deaths of Iraqi children resulting from UN sanctions as a 'price' worth paying? Does her calculus testify to the apotheosis of money over mores? The relevance of all this for law is patent: law describes and prescribes for society. Inevitably, it reflects, and crystallises these pathologies.

The self-defeating potentiality of these attempts to promote freedom is, once perceived, terrifying. In my view, it should not be ignored in a study of terrorism, particularly given its propensity to generate fear and loathing. Herbert Marcuse, thought to be an influence on the Baader-Meinhof group (later the *Rote Armee Fraktion*), thought that capitalist industrialisation produced a 'terroristic coordination of society', which, in turn, could provoke terrorism.[12] Against this backdrop, it is a useful mental exercise to recall that economic depression exists only in the mind, not in the sense that people do not suffer effects of it, on oil prices or mortgages, for example, but in the narrower sense that the tokens of trade and league tables of value of the world economy are nothing more than the outgrowth of human attempts to give order to reality.

It is perhaps worth distinguishing between our reaction to the results of, and corollaries to, these human attempts to order reality, such as the plight of refugees (a consequence of statal ordering), or poverty (a consequence of

[10] *ibid.*

[11] J Habermas and J Derrida, *Philosophy in a time of terror: dialogues with Jürgen Habermas and Jacques Derrida* (University of Chicago Press, 2003) 58.

[12] A Houen, *Terrorism and modern literature, from Joseph Conrad to Ciaran Carson* (Oxford University Press, 2002) 219.

economic ordering), and our reaction to a distant natural disaster, such as the devastating tsunami of 2004. The former, the plight of refugees and poverty are more obviously traceable to our input into the ordering of the world. The latter, though we have an undeniable and devastating effect on the environment, cannot so easily be attributed to human invention. And yet, our reaction to the natural disaster was a heart-warming outpouring of grief, funds and aid. Our reaction to the plight of refugees and poverty is, more often than not, one of total indifference. Is the difference that we are more disposed to alleviate suffering we had no hand in creating? Does our unwillingness to contemplate our collective guilt impair our charity?

It might be a happy outcome of international broadcasting that the scope of things we care about begins to extend to the effect of our lifestyles on the rest of the globe. Where terrorism is concerned, we ought to realise that international broadcasting cuts both ways. Presumably, a pauper does not feel poor until confronted with riches, until he sees the 'offensive prosperity' of others, to borrow Derrida's phrase. Human wants are susceptible to infinite extension. Thus, satisfaction will always, in part, be relative to one's position, though it might be tempered by a philosophical disposition. To this extent, it is worth reflecting on how our prosperous indifference resonates in poorer countries. Furthermore, when British-American modernisation, economic and cultural, spills over into other societies, a natural antagonism and repulsion takes root. As Habermas put it, the 'West in its entirety serves as a scapegoat for the Arab world's own, very real experiences of loss, suffered by populations torn out of their cultural traditions during processes of accelerated modernization'.[13]

To compound this anger, the darkest ironies of the recent history of capitalism, and the blackest sites in the war on terror are inextricably intertwined. It is easier to explain Afghanistan and Iraq by reference to economic than it is political motivations. War and commerce are brothers in arms and have been at least since the massive assembly lines of World War II. Evidence for this proposition is not hard to find. For a time, during the war, Boeing Seattle made 16 bombers a day and employed 40,000 people.[14] The military-industrial alliance is going strong. On 18 July 2008, for instance, the *Guantánamo Bay Gazette* reported the opening of the 'Blackwater' Close Quarters Shooting Range. The range was built by Bremcor, as part of a contract awarded for construction at the Naval Station.[15] Notwithstanding the shamelessness of this nexus between war and commerce, it is masked, to an extent, by theories of new internationalism or neo-imperialism, and it is to a consideration of these theories that I now turn.

Despite the utility of the rules we have developed for governing ourselves in the domestic forum, these rules have been cast aside by the British-American

[13] J Habermas and J Derrida, *Philosophy in a time of terror: dialogues with Jürgen Habermas and Jacques Derrida* (University of Chicago Press, 2003) 32.

[14] N Ferguson, *The War of the World* (Allen Lane, 2006) 528.

[15] 'New Blackwater Range', *Guantánamo Bay Gazette*, 18 July 2008.

alliance in the international arena. The example of pre-emptive self-defence has already been given. This would be intolerable in domestic law and, unsurprisingly, is intolerable in international society. Our foreign policy is our most important export so it should not be found faulty. Arguments that the Afghanistan or Iraq invasions were necessary to the survival of the United States and the United Kingdom have been given short shrift by other states and by clear-thinking commentators alike:

> [A]n individual accused of intentional homicide cannot successfully invoke a right to self-defense by claiming that he was only defending himself when he killed someone because the victim, in the future, might possibly have sold a gun to someone else who, in turn, might at some unspecified time have murdered the accused. Rather than pleading 'necessity' after acting on such reasoning, a preemptive self-defender would be better off pleading insanity.[16]

And yet, the argument that all states should abide by the same rules is treated with disdain in some quarters of the American academy. In a seminar of the Security Working Group at the European University Institute, Ivo Daalder, the current US Permanent Representative on the NATO Council, on being asked how America was to escape his own classification of a rogue state, being a state with nuclear capability and a record of human rights violations, his response was first to shrug, and when pressed for some sort of answer, Daalder simply commented that he believed that 'some states are more equal than others'. As far as I understand it, this attitude stems from the belief that economic power plus superior military capability plus formal democracy imbue a state with greater legitimacy than those without those characteristics, irrespective of whether or not that state systematically tortures, or has a history of the offensive usage of nuclear weaponry. In May 2009, the US Senate confirmed President Barack Obama's nomination of Ivo Daalder as US Ambassador to NATO.

Whilst many Europeans find this sort of attitude morally indefensible and theoretically baseless, many Americans find objections thereto antiquated, unrealistic or naïve. One booklet that might help us understand these communicational difficulties is Robert Kagan's, *Of Paradise and Power*. It is an extended essay that has achieved considerable popularity and, on that basis alone, is worth testing.

Kagan says, at the beginning of his booklet, pondering the divergent European and American approaches to force and multilateralism, that, despite 'what many Europeans and some Americans believe, these differences in strategic culture do not spring naturally from the national characters of Americans and Europeans'.[17] The first point to make is that Kagan comes dangerously close to

[16] S Holmes, *The Matador's Cape: America's Reckless Response to Terror* (Cambridge University Press, 2007) 318.

[17] R Kagan, *Of paradise and power : America and Europe in the new world order*, 1st edn (Alfred A Knopf: Distributed by Random House, 2003) 8.

talking about Europe as if it were a country. Part of the point, of course, of the European project, is the preservation of many different national and sub-national parts in the attempt to enrich the whole.

However, it is perhaps possible to tackle Kagan's argument on its own terms: he says that the 'ambition to play a grand role on the world stage is deeply rooted in the American character'[18] and it is not worth denying that the will-to-imperium, or the desire to 'civilize the uncivilized' is as much a part of some European psyches (French, Belgian, German, Italian, English, to name but a few) as it is the American mindset. Nevertheless, there are important differences. One, which will be discussed in more detail in the next chapter, is that where it might be said that Europeans revere a virtuous ruler, Americans reserve the highest esteem for a virtuous outlaw.

Few would disagree with Kagan's assertion that when 'Americans sought legitimacy for their actions abroad, they sought it not from supranational institutions but from their own principles'.[19] Of course, we must all legislate for, judge and, if necessary, condemn our own actions, but where we are operating well outside the sphere of our own society, failure to canvass the opinions of others, including those of the members of the society for whom we purport to act, is a noxious mixture of arrogance and ignorance. This ignorant self-assurance characterised the cabinet management of the Iraq invasion in the United Kingdom and the defiantly blinkered presidentialism in the US.

Kagan implies that the European response to the terrorist threat was one of denial. Europeans squeezed their eyes shut, ignoring the severity of the problem, because they were impotent to deal with it: 'When you don't have a hammer, you don't want anything to look like a nail. The perspectives and psychologies of power and weakness explain much, though certainly not all, of what divides the US and Europe today'.[20] A perfectly reasonable riposte to this argument is, as Holmes put it, that the United States, having a rather heavy hammer, tends to see foreign policy problems as tempting nails; that is, it opted for the military not because it was apt to combat terrorism, but because it was available. And it did so, as I will shortly argue, because it lacked other, more appropriate tools. Kagan seems to discount the possibility that Europeans might not have chosen to respond to terrorism with massive military deployment because that was not only a dangerous, but a potentially counter-productive course of action. Europeans have enough experience of terrorism to know how helpful and how dangerous the military can be.

Kagan is not convinced that Europe's relative experience causes it to react differently to threats. Instead he argues that because 'they are relatively weak, Europeans have a deep interest in devaluing and eventually eradicating the brutal laws of an anarchic Hobbesian world where power is the ultimate

[18] *ibid*, 86.
[19] *ibid*, 88.
[20] *ibid*, 28.

determinant of national security and success'.[21] This is a revealing claim. Consider this: if a professional arm-wrestler, in a group of men of assorted trades – let us imagine it comprises a chef, a cleric and a lawyer – asserted that the other men had an incentive to deny the merits of arm-wrestling because that would reveal their inferiority to him, the cleric, lawyer and chef might think that, by making that statement, the professional arm-wrestler betrayed the narrowness of his mindset, by revealing that he arbitrarily equated physical strength with superiority. 'What precisely', the lawyer might say, 'would the arm-wrestler gain, by defeating the cleric in his chosen contest of strength, and what would the cleric lose?' The cleric might gain a laugh, the arm-wrestler, though he might reassure himself that he was indeed stronger, might lose face in the eyes of the other men in the group, who regard him as a knucklehead.

The point here is that, just as it is in the arm-wrestler's interests to continue to rank men in terms of the strength of one of their limbs, it is in the interests of an American academic to construct his mental league table of world states by reference to the respective power of their militaries, instead, for instance by reference to the quality of their cuisine, sermons or their legal systems. Although presented in academic language and form, Kagan's argument has all the sophistication of an arm-wrestle. The point that seems to elude the Senior Associate at the Carnegie Endowment for International Peace is that no contest, except where the rules of the contest expressly stipulate its resolution by violence, has ever been resolved by violence. And, unless we believe that by killing someone, we 'win', or assert our superiority over them, the simple fact of human mortality is not enough to constitute such a stipulation in the made-up rules of human society.

Kagan might respond by saying, well the reality of international politics is that military power constitutes success. But this is a circular statement and it is empirically questionable. If success can be defined by reference to an ability to vanquish foes in a physical contest, then America is for now, according to its own yardstick, arguably successful. But we are constitutive of the ideal. We choose our ideals, and international relations do *not*, contrary to the primal grunts from some quarters of the academy, have to be this way.

It is empirically questionable, because America's chosen foe was terrorism, a foe it has proven itself singularly incapable of vanquishing. Holmes recognises that, when it comes to fighting terrorism, America is *not* a superpower. Using Kagan's own hammer analogy, America does not have the tools or the know-how for countering terrorism. Given its international nature, aspirant counter-terrorists must have international friendships and alliances. America preferred, in the early years of the war on terrorism, in its confident naïvety, to 'go it alone'. However, effective intelligence, including linguistic competence, is crucial to tracking terrorists, cracking their communications and infiltrating their cells. The

[21] *ibid*, 34.

linguistic competence of America's counter-terrorism officers is in dire need of improvement.[22] Furthermore, though it professes to lead the war on terrorism, America's experience in this field pales in comparison to that of the United Kingdom, or Spain, or Germany.

Indeed, though the threat of nuclear terrorism might loom on the horizon, American attempts at containment have been disastrously ineffective. The al-Tuwaitha debacle has already been mentioned. The suppression of nuclear terrorism cannot be dealt with militarily; it must be handled with multilateral intelligence to track down unscrupulous scientists and weapon development projects, international political accords to prevent proliferation and accelerate dismantling, and security operations to secure nuclear depositories.

Kagan's contention that 'the US can go it alone' is empirically dubitable for the further reason that history has taught us how great military power can tempt a state into ill-thought-out projections of force.[23] Overextended states topple, and countries attempting to sustain multiple, protracted military campaigns drain their economic resources, subordinating themselves to their creditors. Kagan is certainly not deaf to history. He states that 'modern European strategic culture represents a conscious rejection of the European past, a rejection of the evils of European *Machtpolitik*'.[24] This, at least, is correct. Europeans have refrained from mutual mass murder for over 60 years, and that, given the maelstrom of killing during the first half of the twentieth century, is a momentous achievement. What is tragic is that America, led by academics like Kagan, by embracing *Machtpolitik*, seems to think that European history contains no lessons for the United States, and that the US is somehow *sui generis* in world history. It is true that America's military might is unprecedented. But every self-proclaimed great nation was a little mightier than the last, until it was either destroyed by the next great nation, slowly eroded by waves of invaders, halted by a coalition of nations, or overextended itself.

It stretches credulity, even in the short history of mankind, that America thinks there is anything special about its historical trajectory, and yet the conviction is pervasive that the American 'lot is to be the one essential country' or the 'last best hope of earth'.[25] This is better rejected as a quasi-religious delusion. We have seen many a great nation collapse, brought to its knees by economic pressure, the tolls of waging wars, and a paralysis of political support. It has been done before and there is nothing American about it.

Kagan admits that Americans cannot conceive of an international order that is not defended by American power, and genuinely seems to believe that America

[22] See the Iraq Study Group Report at n 44 below; and 'Language skills an urgent need in changing threat landscape', 22 February, 2007, available at: www.federaltimes.com/index.php?S=2562275.

[23] *ibid*, 39

[24] *ibid*, 53

[25] W Berns, *Making Patriots* (Chicago University Press, 2001) preface, x.

is trustee of global stability, a view absolutely at odds with the perception of America in the rest of the world. Despite the fact that ill-advised support for US foreign policy brought death to London and Madrid, Kagan tells us that 'Europe may be enjoying a free ride in terms of global security'.[26] This would be amusing if only it were written in jest.

Thus far, I have attempted to consider economy and hegemony separately, if only for the sake of clarity, but now it is worth saying a few things about the relation between them. Modern American hegemony was never a territorial empire, though it now has the character of an empire of threat. However, it is fair to say that America did build up an ideological economic imperium, which, at the time of writing, is under serious strain. Theoretically, a purported nationalist hegemony based on a capitalist model is structurally unsound. As we have seen, the market has uncorseted itself from the constraints of state regulation, baring the inherent flaw in neo-conservative orthodoxy: the capitalist dogma is such that no one state can forever monopolise the markets, the best arms or the best scientists. The problem with the American economic game, much like football for the English (*quære* the much earlier Chinese game 'cuju'), is that there is nothing to guarantee that Americans will be best at playing it. The clearest demonstration of this is that America is now threatened by weapons it designed, manufactured and distributed. Unfettered private wealth and the advances (if that is the correct term) in the science of destruction mean that terrorists can now wage highly destructive wars. Laqueur makes the consequences of unregulated markets clear.

> Very small groups of people now have access to weapons of unprecedented destructiveness and, to repeat it once again, the smaller the group, the greater the likelihood that it will be motivated by wholly irrational motives. Second, there is the possibility that these small groups will look for powerful sponsors and that, on the other hand, governments eager to cause mischief may want to make use of such groups for their own purposes.[27]

Under the auspices of former President Bush, exponential increases in US military spending, the sort argued for by Kagan's father, Donald, were made possible by heavy borrowing from China.[28] America is now in enormous debt, which will eventually affect its ability to project threat. Market ideology derailed

[26] R Kagan, *Of paradise and power: America and Europe in the new world order*, 1st edn (Alfred A Knopf: Distributed by Random House, 2003) 54.

[27] W Laqueur, *No End to War: Terrorism in the 21st Century* (Continuum International, 2003) 221.

[28] 'US Ideology Takes a Knock', *BBC Newsnight*, 30 September 2008, available at: news.bbc.co.uk/2/hi/programmes/newsnight/7645438.stm.

national hegemony.[29] It should now be apparent that 'the ideal of market sovereignty is not a complement to liberal democracy, but an alternative to it'.[30]

These dynamics of economic and hegemonic power have serious consequences for law and the stability of the international order, particularly in light of what we can describe as the structural precariousness of the politico-economic model promulgated by the Bush administration. How can we learn from these experiences?

If there is anything to be drawn from the above, it is that liberal democracy and largely unregulated capitalism do not fit neatly together in a political jigsaw puzzle. Though both are ostensibly designed to maximise freedom, together they can destroy the value of freedom, or rather they can lay bare the pointlessness of freedom for its own sake. If we enshrine management forms of an empty value, we are condemned to existentialism at best and nihilism at worst. The cure to these pathologies lies in the realisation that liberal democracy is more than the mere periodical casting of votes; it is discourse, reason and solidarity too.

People like to point fingers at Wall Street or at Bush or the WTO, but there was no single perpetrator of the current ideological ordering of world affairs. Rather, it is a corollary of the subtle and incremental replacement of value with currency, and debate with purchase – our generation of this insipid ideological empire was passive; most of us are guilty of acquiescence, or a lack of foresight, not design. What should be abundantly clear is that, without 'the political taming of an unbounded capitalism, the devastating stratification of world society will remain intractable'.[31] Governments must regulate the markets in order that the markets do not regulate the governments. In other words, parliaments must be the marketplace of values.

Similarly, it is unhelpful to say that capitalism, globalisation or Americanisation caused 9/11. These abstractions are meaningless. But, all actions have their context: foremost in the minds of all those who enjoy the benefits of capitalism must be the international effects of the policies mobilised to sustain its pathologies. To give the indigent and downtrodden a sense of unity and common purpose by offering them a simple reactionary ideology is to fan the flames of insurrection and terror. It is to build an army out of disparate elements by giving them the common enemy of gaudy greed.[32] And, of course, bin Laden never misses an opportunity to create an elision in the common psyche between war

[29] M Rosenfeld, 'Habermas's Call for Cosmopolitan Constitutional Patriotism in an Age of Global Terror: A Pluralist Appraisal' (2007) 14(2) *Constellations* 159, 163.

[30] EJ Hobsbawm, *Globalisation, democracy and terrorism* (Little Brown, 2007) 103.

[31] J Habermas and J Derrida, *Philosophy in a time of terror: dialogues with Jürgen Habermas and Jacques Derrida* (University of Chicago Press, 2003) (Habermas, at 36).

[32] 'The idea of a coalition between the extreme left and the extreme right, between nationalism and socialism (or, to be precise, anticapitalism) goes back to the Soviet Union in the 1920s, appearing in the early 1930s on the margins of the Nazi movement (Otto Strasser), and then taken up in the 1980s by the French rights and on a more primitive ideological level by American neo-Nazis such as the Aryan Nations Congress and WAR, calling for support of the

and commerce, criminality and capitalism: American troops, he says, 'merely fight for capitalists, takers of usury, and arms and oil merchants, including the criminal gang in the White House'.[33]

It is crucial to the defensibility of our foreign policy, to the popularity of the British and the Americans, and therefore to their security, that liberal democracy is decoupled from illiberal interventions ostensibly designed to secure human rights or install democracy, but which, in actual fact, are aimed at consolidating economic interests. The elision, referred to above, of national military strategy with private economic goals – the unison of war and commerce – is counter-productive for Britain and America, however much individuals might stand to gain.

From 1995 to 2000, Dick Cheney was Chief Executive Officer of Halliburton, a company that, inter alia, provides reconstructive and security services to war zones. Immediately thereafter, he assumed office as Vice President in the Bush administration, and, unsurprisingly, was an energetic protagonist of regime change in Iraq. Subsequently, Halliburton has been awarded contracts in Iraq worth billions of dollars. That a man who has a private interest in the perpetuation of armed conflict is permitted not only to influence but to guide the most powerful military in the world is perverse in the extreme. The *New York Times* reported that 'Mr. Cheney still holds hundreds of thousands of stock options that have ballooned by millions of dollars as Halliburton profited handsomely from the war in Iraq'.[34] Charles Wilson was wrong to think that what was good for the country was good for General Motors and vice versa.

Leaving aside the lucrative deals for security contractors, the influence of economics on politics and the devalorisation of human value can be seen not only in the decisions to go to war, but also in the conduct of war itself. Commenting on the American use, in the Iraq conflict, of weaponry incorporating depleted uranium, Byers speculates that financial expediency tempered humanitarian concern in American military decision-making.[35] The European Parliament has long tried to introduce a moratorium on the use of such controversial weapons, but Britain and France have doggedly rejected its resolutions.

Instead of pandering to the United States like this, other societies should take the edge off American hubris by condemning its excesses and staunchly opposing the arguments of those, like Kagan, who endorse double-standards. As George Leaman puts it, 'we must insist that the United States abide by its professed

white working class against monopoly capitalism and the corporations': W Laqueur, *No End to War: Terrorism in the 21st Century* (Continuum International, 2003) 220.

[33] B Lawrence (ed), *Messages to the World: The Statements of Osama bin Laden* (Verso, 2005), 'To the people of Iraq: February 11 2003'.

[34] 'Dick Cheney Rules', *New York Times*, 3 June 2007 available at: www.nytimes.com/2007/06/03/opinion/03sun2.html?scp=1&sq=cheney%20rules&st=cse.

[35] M Byers, *War law: international law and armed conflict* (Atlantic Books, 2005) 124.

commitments to justice and the rule of law, and that it accept the same standard of behaviour that it demands of other countries'.[36] This is not an argument that need be won on moral terms. Rather, it is in American interests not to succumb to neo-imperial hubris. One of the motivations for the 9/11 attacks was American hypocrisy – its 'casual disregard of the standards to which it holds other nations accountable'.[37]

Westminster must bear significant blame here, for in 2003, Britain had the political independence, economic stability and moral clout to halt, or at least stall the Iraq war, which served to compound the resentment that motivated the 9/11 hijackers. Whatever subtle distinctions former Prime Minister Tony Blair tried to draw between American and British policy, he reduced his country to a US administrative outpost; and a rendition refuelling station. Britain is still paying the price, in British lives, for these mistakes. As we saw in the earlier discussion, ill-conceived measures purportedly taken to make us safer have significantly diminished our security.

But, again, to blame America and her European disciples is too easy. Before I make this point, it is perhaps worth remembering that although Americans might want their country to play a 'grand role', they do not have imperial aspirations. As we noted earlier, the anti-colonial, anti-imperial furnace in which the United States was forged means that the sensibilities of not only large American minority populations but also the white majority, are offended by the notion of territorial expansion, beyond, of course, the limited expansion foreseen by the founders – in a sense, in the initial statal accords, the embryonic America always had imperial ambitions.[38]

The American attempt to ensure it can project military power abroad is different to the travelling armies and foreign outpost settlements of an empire. This is about national interest, about coercing the rest of the world to accept economic integration on American terms. Nevertheless, whilst we can reject the notion of American Empire in the sense of extensive political dominion over satellite territories, we must acknowledge the American desire (irrespective of whether we consider it benevolent or malevolent) to consolidate its cultural, military and economic hegemony.[39]

James Tully argues that today's informal imperialism runs counter to the wishes of the majority of the population of the post-colonial world,[40] and this brings me back to the point about it being too simple to blame the US-UK axis.

[36] G Leaman, 'Iraq, American Empire, and the War on Terrorism' in T Rockmore, J Margolis and AT Marsoobian (eds), *The Philosophical Challenge of September 11* (Blackwell Publishing, 2005) 14.

[37] A Norris, '"Us" and "Them"' in T Rockmore, J Margolis and AT Marsoobian (eds), *ibid*, 20.

[38] I am grateful to George Fletcher for this point.

[39] C Johnson, *Nemesis: The Last Days of the American Republic* (Holt, 2008).

[40] J Tully, 'On Law, Democracy and Imperialism' in S Tierney and E Christodoulidis (eds), *Political Theory and Public Law* (Ashgate, 2007) 39.

For leaders, or a powerful ruling class in an emergent economy or 'baby state', in the short-term, it might with good cause seem far easier, safer and lucrative to submit to a British-American economic and military game plan, than it is to reject such rules on principle. This submission, an unspoken deed of servitude, is the original sin of some post-colonial states. In an attempt to ensure their survival, they have shrugged off slavery to embrace servitude.

In response to this state of affairs, Neil Walker argues that the variegated nature of informal imperial structures, that is, the blend of cooperative multilateralism, economic coercion and military duress, offers 'transformative possibilities'. It is certainly arguable that the current market chaos is evidence that such a transformation is underway. However, for any transformation to be worthwhile, the international community must comprehend that the problem is not so much America, as our susceptibility to buckle before thinly veiled threats. Returning to the question pitched in the introduction to this discussion: there is a more than a passing resemblance between a Mafia protection racket and the current world ordering. Racketeers cannot be beaten without concerted effort and a good deal of courage.

Courage is fundamental because, in the last seven years, we have seen the preparedness of the British-American alliance to turn its vision of the world into reality, forcibly importing democracy and securing economic footholds to secure future prosperity. Indeed, the American National Security Strategy of 2002 explicitly linked foreign policy to 'building the infrastructure of democracy [and] the development of democratic institutions'. This is revolution for the world.

The pro-democratic interventionism described by Ferguson,[41] according to which the United States increasingly involves itself in imposing liberal democratic institutions by governing other territories for fixed periods, is susceptible to manipulation by those with pernicious, or self-interested agendas. Further, though such a policy might sound nice in theory, it can be catastrophic in reality, as Afghanistan and Iraq have proven. There is nothing immediately wrong with democratic proselytism but persuasion is the proper tool of democracy; pre-emptive war is just aggression by another name.

It is pertinent here to query the assertion that non-democratic countries do not choose their leaders. This fallacy supports the Western presumption that non-democratic regimes without voting must be 'delivered from evil'. On the contrary, it is unclear how a people can choose democracy without previously having *chosen* monarchic, religious or autocratic rule. And there is nothing logical about the proposition that monarchic, religious or autocratic rule is necessarily malevolent. Indeed, as Ferguson himself has recognised, as a matter of historical fact, 'in some cases dictators may actually have been better for minorities than

[41] N Ferguson, 'The Empire that Dares not Speak its Name', *The Sunday Times*, 13 April 2003.

elected governments willing to give full vent to majority prejudice'.[42] Furthermore, the idea that man must awaken from a slavish, unenlightened mentality in order to enjoy democracy ignores the slavish, mindless nature of much of life in Britain and America. Formal voting tells us nothing of the quality or freedom of thought of the voters.

Defending democracy, that is, protecting it from invasion – 'fighting on the beaches' – is, of course, valorous. Promoting it by force of arms abroad is arrogant, illegitimate adventuring. If we believe in democracy, is it not better to let people choose both a system and their own leaders, at the time and in the manner they deem fit? Accepting this, moreover, does not in any way inhibit states from intervening in foreign jurisdictions on humanitarian grounds. We might do well to accept that importing democracy by force is to do a disservice to the idea, and, just as much as it promises to empower a society, it can impede the ability of peoples to determine their future for themselves.

Pro-democratic intervention has given America and the United Kingdom a bad press, particularly as it was long since clear that the interests of the newly emancipated citizens were not foremost in the minds of the interveners. Pro-democratic interveners should perhaps temper their zeal, in the knowledge that the mere existence of nominally 'free' societies puts enormous pressure on one-party administrations, dictatorships and religious regimes.

At this point, we can reflect on how the topics discussed here, economy and hegemony relate to the foregoing. The first interesting link is that of language to power. Prima facie, the predominance of English is a reflection of the power of the United Kingdom and the United States. However, that predominance does not necessarily perpetuate their might. On the contrary, as English skills become more prosaic in other parts of the world, the accessibility and transparency of the British and American societies and institutions increase. In contrast, other cultures remain impenetrable to linguistically lazy Brits and Americans.[43] Our influence is dependent on our linguistic and cultural capabilities.

As Holmes observes, 'our efforts in Iraq, military and civilian are handicapped by Americans' lack of language and cultural understanding. Our embassy of 1,000 has 33 Arabic speakers, just six of whom are at the level of fluency'.[44] And fluency is a notoriously flexible concept. The lower the ability of the typical official, the lower the bar is set for fluency. The sort of fluency helpful in counter-terrorist operations is the capacity to pass for a native speaker, including the ability proficiently to hold a conversation whilst eavesdropping on the one being held on the next table. But America need not have handicapped itself in this way. In New York alone, English is spoken as a first language in only half of all homes. The sheer number of minority populations in America gives it vast

[42] N Ferguson, *The War of the World* (Allen Lane, 2006) 227.

[43] S Holmes, *The Matador's Cape: America's Reckless Response to Terror* (Cambridge University Press, 2007) 255.

[44] *The Iraq Study Group Report* (Vintage, 2006).

linguistic and cultural resources. It can be argued that Westminster too has done a better job of alienating Muslim minorities than it has harnessing their natural faculties.

So language can damage power, but it can also disguise it. Earlier, I discussed how every description is also a prescription. A word, by virtue of being an abstraction, contains, at the same time, more and less than the object it describes. Each word, as it reveals, conceals too. Hence, a language can hide features of its subject or, more pertinently here, it can describe an unjust global order or an objectionable policy in seemingly acceptable terms. Furthermore, when it comes to actual conflicts, the precision with which we identify our enemies can, by surgically isolating guilty parties, or clumsily enraging innocent bystanders, have a tangible effect on the outcome of the conflict. The 'war on terror' has become bigger and meaner because of inaccurate descriptions.

In his discussion of terrorism in literature, Houen notes the link between economies of production and war, where instruments of death are regarded as life-givers. He cites Filippo Marinetti, the Italian futurist of the early twentieth century, who reported that in 'Japan they carry on the strangest of trades: the sale of coal made from human bones … Glory to the indomitable ashes of man, that come to life in cannons!'[45] Today, the centrality of commercial value to American ideology results in not poetic or figurative but explicit official linking of war and economy.

> The 2001 Quadrennial Defense Review speaks of using military force to defend our 'enduring national interest', of 'contributing to economic well being' through the 'vitality and productivity of the global economy' and 'access to key markets and strategic resources' (Department of Defense 2001). Thus, according to official Defense Department doctrine, the United States has a right to go to war to preserve the global neoliberal economic order.[46]

Such a strategy is to international relations what armed robbery is to banking. Anyone capable of distinguishing between this sort of 'defense doctrine' and the principles of forcible theft will render themselves incapable of distinguishing between a state and the armed band. The basic point here is that we, as a society, decide what is of value and what we wish to protect. If we decide that our economic power and, more precisely, our economic advantage over others is a legitimate military aim, we have all the morality of a mugger, and reduce democracy to delegated dacoity.

This is not to say that the British and Americans are indistinguishable from highwaymen, but at some point, the collective Nelsonian blindness to the policies and pathologies that support our politics must become culpable. Where political

[45] A Houen, *Terrorism and modern literature, from Joseph Conrad to Ciaran Carson* (Oxford University Press, 2002) 97, quoting from 'The Birth of a Futurist Aesthetic' in *Let's Murder the Moonshine* (trans 1991, Sun and Moon).

[46] JM Schwartz, 'Misreading Islamist Terrorism' in J Margolis, T Rockmore and AT Marsoobian (eds), *The Philosophical Challenge of September 11* (Blackwell Publishing, 2005) 62.

leaders become spineless yes-sayers to merchants, who might not trouble themselves with the effects of their dogma, politics and morality become subservient to the strictures of the markets. Untrammelled pursuit of private interest, which according to capitalist theory, is in the public interest, turns out to be diametrically opposed to global social welfare, including that of the rich.

It is perhaps no coincidence that we have seen a re-emergence of dangerous piracy off the coast of Africa, threatening peaceful sea-faring traders. Piracy, like aggressive war and torture, is one of the activities considered entirely antithetical to an international legal order. It is, in my view, important to realise that the disregard for international law shown by Britain and America does nothing to encourage others to respect the fragile norms of the international legal order. Furthermore, if militant Islamic organisations achieve control of the ports in Somalia, piracy and terrorism will become bedfellows. Oddly enough, such an unholy alliance might come to espouse a similar doctrine to that of the US Defense Department, justifying forcible seizure of other's property by reference to economic advantage. There is a further problem presented by piracy. Somali sea-robbers have already managed to capture a Ukrainian merchant vessel loaded with 33 tanks – enough to win a small war (or start a bigger one).[47] Not only the rightful owners will make tender for such destructive cargo and there is little to deter pirates (already internationally despised villains) from selling to the highest bidder.

Perhaps the most troubling connection between economy and hegemony is the privatisation of war, that is, the support and prosecution of war efforts by businesses. War is highly profitable for firms specialising in military hardware and security services. Where persons with a commercial interest in warfare are in charge of the national security policy of states, the prosecution of war for ethically indefensible motives and ethically indefensible conduct of warfare are the inevitable results. According to Hobbes, the state was created to protect us from each other, from being robbed, injured or killed by our neighbours. It would be a shame if states simply became instruments for robbery, injury and murder on a grander scale. Schmitt prophesied that a war waged to protect or expand economic power must, with the aid of propaganda, turn into a crusade and into the last war of humanity. It is hoped that this is not our lot.

Ominously, the Bush administration, during its expansive and expensive war years, avoided tax increases by borrowing heavily from foreign creditors. This has the effect of shielding the public from higher taxes in the short term, purchasing their indulgence for war policies, whilst exposing them to debt in the long term. America has, at least economically, enslaved itself. It will now have to satisfy its creditors before its conscience. Government cannot be run like a business unless one is content to subordinate the entire human experience to chasing profits.

[47] 'The Somali pirates: tanks, but no tanks' *Time Magazine*, 9 October 2008, available at: www.time.com/time/world/article/0,8599,1848772,00.html.

Equally, government cannot be run by businessmen, because not all ends are dividends. Governors owe a fiduciary duty to citizens and this should not be allowed to come into conflict with private interests, particularly where those private interests are advantaged by the perpetuation of warfare.

But war is not the only bane on human existence. Global inequality sustained by the loaded dice of the post-colonial world leaders is a source of immense frustration in many countries. Indeed, it is no great perversion of language to say that there is a great deal of 'structural violence' in the current world ordering. A good example, alighted upon earlier, was the effect of UN sanctions on child mortality in Iraq. However, repugnant as the consequences of these punitive measures might be, they can have no bearing on our assessment of the legitimacy of terrorism.

Jean Baudrillard contends as follows: '*C'est le système lui-même qui a créé les conditions objectives de cette rétorsion brutale. En ramassant pour lui toutes les cartes, il force l'Autre à changer les règles du jeu*'.[48] But though these dynamics may help us to understand the roots of outrage, to argue that they justify terrorism (as opposed to resistance) is to agree with bin Laden. Different foes must be fought with different weapons and conceptual clarity is a step towards reducing the incidence of violence – if we can agree on limits to legitimate violence, we strengthen our protests where its usage exceeds these parameters. Where we adopt double-standards, pursuant to Kagan's arguments, or consider ourselves above a law that applies to others, pursuant to Yoo's lawyering, we lose the platform from which to denounce the errant behaviour of others.

George W Bush was a disciple of such doctrines. By unsigning the statute of the International Criminal Court, persuading 90 other countries to promise not to surrender US citizens to its jurisdiction, and authorising himself to deploy the military to liberate Americans in Hague custody,[49] he made a Herculean attempt to tear down the edifice of international justice and establish, in its place, a monument to American lawlessness. It would be mistaken to presume that he was a rogue President, and did this single-handedly. Though the American judiciary could see the contradiction in Guantánamo Bay's role in a war fought for freedom, at times, they have gone out of their way to ensure that America's black operations remain shrouded in darkness. The afore-mentioned *El-Masri* litigation was an example of this, where the Supreme Court upheld the Court of Appeal's judgment that the government could invoke the state secrets privilege not merely to exclude certain information from a hearing, but to exclude the entire hearing of a German citizen's claim that he had been abducted and tortured by the CIA.

America's place above the law is often justified by reference to its role as guardian of the international order. Kagan argues that 'Europe's postmodern

[48] Baudrillard, 'L'esprit du terrorisme', *Le Monde*, 1 November 2001, available at: www.egs.edu/faculty/baudrillard/baudrillard-the-spirit-of-terrorism-french.html.

[49] M Byers, *War law: international law and armed conflict* (Atlantic Books, 2005) 145.

paradise cannot long survive unless the US does use its power in the dangerous Hobbesian world that still flourishes outside Europe'.[50] He means to say that our liberty is guaranteed by American security. This is presumably an appealing image for Americans searching for a justification for their country's actions in the last eight years, but it is a fiction. Kagan is deceiving himself. Of course, we need power to protect our freedoms, but the concept of power is not exhausted, as Kagan would have us believe, by military force. The whole point of this text is to argue that collectively, humankind *can* choose to renounce certain means. Power can also derive from the force of a proposition, or an ideal which can in turn be instantiated, policed and defended. The ideals of legality and civility cannot consistently be defended with means more typical of lawless brutality, like torture and aggression.

The war on terror, a war for freedom, must be seen in the context of the transformation of much of the world. The terms on which European colonialism came to an end favoured members of indigenous communities with the ability to emulate the leadership style of imperial leaders, and, under the economic duress of receding hegemons, to redesign their countries along the lines of Western legal, fiscal and corporate institutions. The demise of formal dominion was not necessarily accompanied by a joyous re-growth of liberty. The new structure of a global order, built out of innocuous acronyms – the UN, G2, G8, G20, IMF, WB, GATT and WTO to mention but a few – has massive influence on developing nations, which have sacrificed much of their native culture in order to ensure their enduring nationhood, in a world where their existence as a viable state is defined by their past masters.[51] In this way, the project of democratisation can make of liberty a mockery.

However, charged with oppression, capitalism pleads innocence. Money is but a freedom token. It can buy food, water and land, and, moreover, can be used to pay people to keep others off it. Capitalism claims to protect liberty, empower the entrepreneur and reward industry. But we have seen it ravage the developing world. Furthermore, even in the so-called developed world, the joys of disposable income and the limitless possibilities of consumerism have resulted in new forms of malaise. People of plenty are consumed by various addictions, to food, alcohol, drugs, shopping, profiteering and so forth: 'limitless consumption paradoxically provokes the moment when the subject starts "consuming himself"'.[52] The more we own, the more we can become owned by ownership – the less we possess, the less we expose ourselves to possession. In the 1999 film *Fight Club*, the protagonist is locked in a battle between the existential allure of mindless

[50] R Kagan, *Of paradise and power: America and Europe in the new world order*, 1st edn (Alfred A Knopf: Distributed by Random House, 2003) 75.

[51] J Tully, 'On Law, Democracy and Imperialism' in S Tierney and E Christodoulidis (eds), *Political Theory and Public Law* (Ashgate, 2007) 15.

[52] R Salecl, 'Worries in a Limitless World' in Peter Goodrich, Lior Barshack and A Schuetz (eds), *Law, Text, Terror* (Glasshouse, 2006) 138.

violence and the terrifying ennui of mindless consumption, between the nihilism of destruction and the nihilism of consumerism. The film reflects on how our attempts to create meaning can empty us of meaning, how man can subordinate himself to the manufactured. Furthermore, it is a helpful reminder of the reality that property and prosperity alone are no more a cure for fundamentalism than poverty and adversity are its cause.[53]

The empty, nihilistic pathologies of consumerism can afflict a nation, just as they can affect a person. As Elaine Tyler May reported, 'Topps, the bubble gum company that invented baseball trading cards in the 1950s, quickly produced and marketed "Enduring Freedom" card packets immediately after 9/11'.[54] There is perhaps no better parody of what I referred to earlier as the devalorisation of value. Patriotism here was expressed through consumerism. But, as we have seen, consumerism is an empty ideology. It does not, contrary to popular belief, express liberty. It enshrines only valuability (we can give things a price) and buy-ability (and then exchange them for money). Built over a chasm, it has the look of a trap.

However liberating capitalism might seem at first blush, it is healthy to be mindful that if something is my property, owned absolutely, it cannot at the same time be yours. Consequently, as often as capitalism liberates, includes and empowers, it constrains, excludes and disempowers. One man's property is always, in a sense, another's loss. Free trade, absent constraints, sets no limit on the freedom of the one to acquire property. Nor does it limit the acceptable subjugation of the other. Though a modern state will temper this possibility with guarantees of social justice, with welfare and basic provision, these fetters do not bind us in our actions across borders, and do not foreclose the possibility of the exploitation of other peoples. It is to the connection between the themes of hegemony and economy, amity and enmity that I now turn.

It seems that a false equation is made between weapons capacity and security. (I have already noted the futility of attempting to defend liberal democratic society from suicide bombings.) Indeed, it was common ground between the presidential candidates, John McCain and Barak Obama that American defence-spending was absolutely perverse. There are ways other than investment in the development of a military to ensure a society's safety. Investment in righting the wrongs of disparities in standards of living would do much more to improve the security of the American people, by ameliorating the sorry disaffection that plagues the developing world, and by improving America's woefully tarnished image. In a collection on terrorism, James Sterba homed in on this point.

> [The US] contribution to alleviate world hunger is (in proportion to its size) one of the smallest among the industrized [sic] nations of the world – roughly 11 percent, which

[53] JG Jansen, *The Dual Nature of Islamic Fundamentalism* (Cornell University Press, 1997) 5.

[54] ET May, 'Echoes of the Cold War' in ML Dudziak (ed), *September 11 in History: A Watershed Moment?* (Duke University Press, 2003) 47.

> President Bush proposes to increase to 13 percent; Britain's contribution is about three times as much, and Sweden, the Netherlands and Norway proportionately give about eight times as much.[55]

The sharing of America's prosperity – investment in 'soft security' – would have done more to protect America's long-term wellbeing than the enormous spending on 'hard security' – military improvement. Charity can spread trust and amity. The establishment of international military capability can sow fear and enmity. These dynamics are not those of greed so much as gluttony, the biblical sin of taking into oneself in glorification of oneself, and bringing about one's own destruction. Avarice, gluttony and brutality (understood as a cold disregard for human life) go together in modern America, like ominous, hooded malcontents lurking on the street corners of civility. It is not, however, all doom and gloom – the deleterious trends of untrammelled trade have been noted by people in the right places.

> [T]he president of the World Bank has come to the conclusion that for most of the world's population the word 'globalisation' suggests 'fear and insecurity' rather than 'opportunity and inclusion'. Even Alan Greenspan and US Treasury Secretary Larry Summers agree that 'antipathy to globalisation runs so deep' that 'a retreat from market oriented policies and a return to protectionism' are real possibilities.[56]

Nevertheless, these shades of American society bring me to the connection between the dynamics of domination and trade and the topics of chapter six: sex, fear and perversion. Taking the latter first, American land, on and off-shore, yields approximately three per cent of the world's oil and yet America consumes around 25 per cent. The energy dependency of the United States, and its effect on the economy, dominated the 2008 presidential debates. It is increasingly hard to deny that an insatiable thirst for oil drove the Iraq war. In fact, Daalder, a pro-interventionist, frankly admits that, without oil, no invasion would have taken place. This stands in ugly contrast with initial official claims of humanitarian motives and of necessary self-defence from an imminent nuclear threat. As George Leaman has observed, the perverse effect of political untruths is that democracy itself comes under the strain of 'the lying, fraud, and violence necessary to sustain this project'.[57] Virgil asked, '*Quid non mortalia pectora cogis, Auri sacra fames!*' (To what do you not drive human hearts, cursed craving for gold!)[58] Perhaps we are bearing witness.

This distortion of American democracy was compounded by the huge political influence of those who profit from war and literally need oil to drive

[55] JP Sterba, 'Terrorism and International Justice' in JP Sterba (ed), *Terrorism and International Justice* (Oxford University Press, 2003) 221.

[56] EJ Hobsbawm, *Globalisation, democracy and terrorism* (Little Brown, 2007) 110.

[57] G Leaman, 'Iraq, American Empire, and the War on Terrorism' in T Rockmore, J Margolis and AT Marsoobian (eds), *The Philosophical Challenge of September 11* (Blackwell Publishing, 2005) 17.

[58] Publius Vergilius Maro, *Aeneid*, Bk 2, line 521.

their business. The privatisation of war is part of a deeper pathology resulting from the influence of strong market ideology on weak democratic principle. (Remember Allott's warning that democracy-capitalism can catalyse the conversion of virtue to vice.) In America, for instance, there has been an enormous transfer of public services to private corporations. Hobsbawm observes that 'characteristic activities of national or local government as post offices, prisons, schools, water supplies, and even welfare services have been handed to or transformed into business enterprise'.[59] Private prisons in the States now make a profit from detention, so that they are incentivised to deprive people of their liberty for longer. Private companies make a profit from war-making, so that the perpetuation of conflict is in their interests. These developments are portentous, for the two quintessential functions of the state are criminal justice and the prosecution of war. The use of detention and force for private interest is the essence of tyranny – there are some affairs of a liberal democratic state that simply should not be conducted for profit by privateers (in both relevant senses of the word).

This observation is a key to unlock a further clarification. Terror has played a role in American adventuring abroad. As we saw above, Kagan says that Americans seek justification for their foreign policy in their 'own principles'. This might be the case for a hawkish neo-conservative political class, with vested interests in the perpetuation of warfare. But would it not be more accurate to say that the American *people* have been duped by political and media fear-mongering, suppressing their rational processing of foreign policy options, and silencing their collective conscience not only in respect of the huge death toll in Iraq and Afghanistan, but also tyrannical policies like targeted killings, indefinite detention and interrogative torture? It is not 'principle' but fear, or more precisely, the engineering of fear through threat reports, political statements and the press, that really drives American policy. This is the unpardonable exploitation of the seemingly incomprehensible and the willing credulity of a folk primed for self-destruction and scared into a stupor. And this must be right, for what principle can inform two wars of aggression?

Perhaps it is no principle at all. There is a nexus between sex and the hegemonic and economic aspects of our approach to law in the war on terrorism. When compared with 300 years ago, British and American societies now have what could be described as a more liberal or open disposition to sex. In days gone by, sex was considered taboo; now sexual signalling is ubiquitous in television, film, literature and advertising, and love, be it paternal, fraternal, platonic, sexual, matrimonial or spiritual, seems to have replaced sex as the taboo topic. It provokes a squeamish reaction amongst today's sexually savvy youth; emotional commitment is often scoffed at, whereas liberal sensual indulgence is lauded; love can be considered a handicap or a weakness in the more important

[59] EJ Hobsbawm, *Globalisation, democracy and terrorism* (Little Brown, 2007) 103.

project of procuring the money or experience that will bring about happiness. It might be that the incessant bombardment of the public with sexual imagery drowns out the pleas of empathy in human relations.

Shifting sexual preference and identity are key features of exaggerated consumerist and fashionable trends. Salecl tells us that the 'metrosexual rather than being a sexual identity is more a set of consumer identifications. So under late capitalism, shifts in identity and indeed in identifications are celebrated as the new vogue and turned into profit'.[60] Implants, enlargements, rejuvenations, reductions, suctions and, the *pièce de résistance* of consumerism, the designer baby, are endemic to a lack of appreciation for the inner values of human existence. The inane, pleasure-seeking solipsism of modern American life facilitated a distracted acquiescence in the destruction of American values.

Hence, a further point to make is that fickle, value-light Western ideology is easy game for fundamentalist organisations, which link capitalism to moral degradation and sybaritic depravity. The propaganda of Hizbul Tahrir, an Islamic political sect, blames capitalism for sex crimes committed in the United Kingdom.[61] Books in East End libraries in London advocate attacking scantily clad women. Such opinions and the organisations that espouse them are often regarded as backward; however, in another sense, they are very modern. Hizbul Tahrir, for example, is less than 60 years old. It is necessary to realise the dynamics of capitalism, so that phenomena that are, in part, produced by capitalism are not written off as aberrations or anachronisms. In fact, radical religiosity is a side-effect of the pressures of global ordering on capitalist terms. Fundamentalism and terrorist networks can provide support and solace for the wretched; those who have not benefited from, but who were further disenfranchised by, the globalisation of trade. It is therefore incoherent and naïve to argue that democratisation and the promotion of capitalist market ideology will somehow cure the world of terrorism. Instead, free trade and the global inequality it facilitates promise to agitate radicalism. To ignore these dynamics is to fail both to grasp the effects of a legal order premised on the ideology of democracy and capitalism, and to understand how effectively we can protect ourselves by protecting others. We ignore Somalia's desperate plight and tolerate its pirates at our peril.

Properly to understand the effect of economic ordering on spirituality, we must grasp the relationship of religion to hegemony too. This relationship has, historically, been contested by scholars on the battlefield of 'just war' theory. Augustine thought that a war would be just when undertaken for the common good by a nation-state that represents God in establishing order and justice on Earth. This is perhaps a harmless contention when confined to the cloister. In

[60] R Salecl, 'Worries in a Limitless World' in Peter Goodrich, Lior Barshack and A Schuetz (eds), *Law, Text, Terror* (Glasshouse, 2006) 142.

[61] W Laqueur, *No End to War: Terrorism in the 21st Century* (Continuum International, 2003) 66.

determining the justness of a war, according to Augustine, we have to ask whether it is undertaken altruistically, and whether the nation-state represents God. Answering the first question is perhaps possible. We can, for instance, step back from the deposition of Saddam and observe that the motives of the Allies were not entirely selfless. Answering the second question is simple. Given the notion of the ideal propounded here, pursuant to which no man or human organisation can ever achieve (or even perceive) ideal form, it is impossible to point at any one nation and claim that it represents God. Where, however, a nation comes collectively to believe it is fulfilling God's will, as with the German nation of the twentieth century and the American nation of today, it might tend to adopt policies that cannot be justified by reference to the more grounded dictates of basic morality.

To expect our countries, leaders and armies to interpret and translate celestial commands into successful, humanitarian, just military campaigns is wishful thinking. It is far better to accept our human fallibility and guard ourselves against ill thought-out invasions with a doctrine of just war based on self-defence and defence of others, which is neutral, religiously and politically (in that the justification of force is premised neither upon a deity nor an ideology). Such a doctrine would seem to boast a greater immunity to rhetorical infections and inflammations. A principle for human and state interaction, designed to be preventive of warfare, ought to apply equally to all and ought not to be of ideological or religious patronage.

Drained by their own wars, and forced to their knees by economic forces they unleashed, the United States and the United Kingdom ought to have recourse to the significant intellectual resources, and historical and social reason at their disposal in order to forge for themselves a durable plan and an identity for the future. A public debate is needed, and in that debate, politicians, the press and the common man must participate in candour to reinvigorate these flagging societies. The civic responsibilities of these social leaders are investigated in the next chapter.

Before beginning that chapter, it is worth noting the significance of the discussion of the dynamics of economy and hegemony for law. This can be enunciated simply. The law describes and prescribes for our economic and hegemonic designs and pathologies. Rather than protecting liberty and guaranteeing security, the law can become a vehicle for our instincts of oppression and domination. Though arbitrary detention, torture, targeted killings and aggressive war might be inimical to a civilised, sophisticated legal order, there is nothing to stop such policies becoming law in a society that values financial advantage and military superiority above the various interests of loosely defined others.

9

Parliaments, The Press and The Public Man

I'm the commander – see? I don't need to explain – I do not need to explain why I say things. That's the interesting thing about being the President. Maybe somebody needs to explain to me why they say something, but I don't feel like I owe anybody an explanation.

President George W Bush[1]

AT BASE, THIS chapter is about blame. Whose fault is it that so many civilians have died in American missile attacks in Pakistan?[2] Why did the Bush Administration not openly own the tactic of automated assassinations in the border regions? Who is to blame for the degeneration of the ideal of American freedom and the American intelligence service such that the latter defends the former with a grotesque violation of freedom, 'extraordinary rendition'? And how is it that the United Kingdom became entangled in a protracted war against a dictator and his people, who had nothing whatsoever to do with the terrorist attack used as a pretext for that war? Why, instead of realising that the settled, civic Muslim population in the UK was the best first line of defence against Islamist extremists, did the government adopt measures destined to aggravate the very rage which had motivated the attacks of 11 September? Why did we forget the lessons of the past and jeopardise our safety in the future? And, what does this mean for our laws? How did these things come about in our supposedly advanced cultures, and how, more importantly, can they be avoided by refining our understanding of laws and morality?

To investigate these themes, I will discuss organs of government: political leaders, parliaments, the judiciary, and the interplay between them. Thereafter, I consider the other two bastions of reason, the press and the public man. I distinguish, of course between the United States and the United Kingdom, where necessary, but the similar reflex of the two systems has been, to my mind, more revealing than their differences. Before I begin, a note on the differences – some commentators will use the recent violations of civil liberty in the UK to argue for a constitutional bill of rights. Those who think that this will provide a more secure foundation for our cherished freedoms should refer to recent American history, which, if anything, has proven the infinite elasticity of

[1] B Woodward, *Bush at War* (Simon and Schuster, 2002) 145–6

[2] 'Airstrike kills eight militants in Pakistan', *New York Times*, 24 October 2008, available at: www.nytimes.com/2008/10/24/world/asia/24pstan.html?_r=1&scp=3&sq=pakistan&st=cse &oref=slogin.

constitutionally enshrined norms (like habeas corpus), given pressure from presidents and people. Everyone knows that violations of rights involve taking something from someone. But it is too frequently forgotten that *the granting* of rights also involves taking something from someone. Irrespective of dusty constitutional guarantees and solemn promises of performance, sometimes, in the end, we have to take what is ours.

In what follows, I draw liberally on the work of Stephen Holmes, whose exposition of the occasionally paradoxical dynamics of power in a state with a system of checks and balances is instructive. There are two intertwining threads running through what follows. Perhaps the most important contribution of his work is the lucid exposition of the idea that restrictions on power can, oddly enough, enhance power and allow it to endure longer than untrammelled power. This is one thread. The other, which has already been elaborated throughout, is that of moral action being prudential, of what is right neatly dovetailing with what is advantageous.

In an attempt to secure advantage or the upper hand in the war on terror, Bush et al made a greedy grab for power. Recent American politics have been presidential to the extent that it is not clear if the leaders believe in the merits or utility of their constitutional democracy. Indeed, it is easier to make change and progress without having to canvass varied points of view, or pay attention to facts. But this is bad for democracy. And, democracy is more than pure voting, since it is discourse and the sharing and reciprocal refinement of opinions beyond that. Hence, the suppression or ignorance of minority opinion, though that might satisfy the whim and will of a majority, is deeply anti-democratic. Stifling of discussion and discourse suffocates democracy. This process begins the conversion of a democracy into a totalitarian state. But this is a subtle change; tyranny has more salient features.

The detainees at Guantánamo Bay enjoyed neither the significant safeguards of the American criminal justice system, nor the rights enshrined in the constitution, nor the protection of the Geneva Conventions. Surely a lawyer could not countenance the establishment of a space outside of all legal registers, an accountability- and oversight-free zone? On the contrary, some lawyers were more than happy to construct such a space. Amongst them were Jay Bybee and Alberto Gonzales, respectively Assistant Attorney General in the US Justice Department and Attorney General, and, of course, the extraordinary Mr Yoo, whom we met earlier. Yoo argued that, due to his status as Commander-in-Chief, though the laws of war do not bind the President, he could still subject al-Qaeda or the Taliban to the laws of war. Furthermore, Yoo told us, since the US was 'at war', Congress and the courts could no longer 'purport to second-guess or interfere with or even learn about the president's national-security decisions, however momentous'.[3]

[3] S Holmes, *The Matador's Cape: America's Reckless Response to Terror* (Cambridge University Press, 2007) 287.

According to this brand of constitutional theory, it was within Bush's prerogative power deliberately to 'deceive congress, the courts, and the public in the name of national security'.[4] This was news to many constitutional lawyers and judges alike, who thought that transparency and oversight were integral to democracy. Indeed, though Yoo insisted that his theory was entirely consonant with American constitutional jurisprudence, it seemed to contrast somewhat with venerable precedent. To take two prominent examples, in *Youngstown Sheet and Tube Co v Sawyer*, Jackson J held that the Founders did not provide for 'powers *ex necessitate* to meet an emergency' because, being streetwise, seasoned politicians, they were painfully aware of how such an expansive prerogative could 'afford a ready pretext for usurpation'.[5] Similarly, in *Brown v United States*, Story J readily accepted that the President has certain wartime discretion, but this did not mean that he could lawfully 'exercise powers or authorize proceedings which the civilized world repudiates and disclaims'.[6]

It would be presumptuous to contradict American lawyers of learning and position like Yoo, Bybee and Gonzales, but the outside observer is to be forgiven for a degree of confusion as to what America really stands for. Does she stand for constitutionalism, a separation of powers and democracy, per Madison, Story, and Jackson, or is she a presidential autocracy, internationally a law-only-unto-herself, per Yoo, Bush, and Kagan? And, more importantly perhaps, what view best serves America? William Scheuerman has made his position clear:

> [O]nce the cancer of normlessness is allowed into the legal system, it is only a matter of time before it infects healthy legal organs as well. By insisting that accused terrorists are subject to pure presidential prerogative, the Bush Administration opened the door to the terrible crimes of Abu Ghraib.[7]

Certainly, the usage of indefinite detention, torture and targeted killings would seem to support Scheuerman's contention that lawlessness will metastasise in the body politic. Now, Yoo might dispute the causal relationship between his constitutional theorising and the well-documented atrocities of Abu Ghraib (remember the fate of Manadel al-Jamadi). The US Senate has recently come to a contrasting verdict, denouncing Rumsfeld and other Bush administration officials for 'unconscionable' attempts to 'pass the buck to low-ranking soldiers whilst avoiding any responsibility for abuses'.[8] Hardly anyone will disagree that torture was regrettable and deeply immoral, but was anything to be gained by this expansion of presidential prerogative? Did it allow for effective threat management? Was it prudent? Holmes does not think so.

[4] *ibid*, 288.

[5] *Youngstown Sheet & Tube v Sawyer* (1952) 103 F Supp 569, affirmed.

[6] *Brown v United States of America* 12 US 110 (1814).

[7] WE Scheuerman, 'Carl Schmitt and the Road to Abu Ghraib' (2006) 13(1) *Constellations* 108.

[8] 'Abu Ghraib blame for US officials', *BBC News Online*, 12 December 2008, available at: news.bbc.co.uk/2/hi/middle_east/7780355.stm.

> By dismantling checks and balances, along the lines idealized and celebrated by Yoo, the Administration has certainly gained flexibility in the 'war on terror'. It has gained the flexibility, in particular, to shoot first and aim afterward. It has acted on disinformation, crackpot theories, theological certainties, and utopian expectations that could perhaps have been corrected or mitigated if traditional decision-making protocols had been respected and key policymakers had not 'spoken power to truth', silencing dissident voices and sequestering themselves in an echo chamber.[9]

It is hard to see out of a bunker; secrecy and cabinet cliquery are not conducive to informed, intelligent decision-making. Conversely, a president who seeks counsel from a wise, diverse and learned senate ensures that the fate of the country is not indexed to his own necessarily limited grasp of theory and fact. Broader still, an administration that avoids the temptation to erect a presidential palisade can, instead, construct its policies out of the solid stuff of informed public critique. *Head on*, by the artist Cai Guo-Qiang, thematises and parodies violent movements. In his piece, first displayed in Berlin, and at the time of writing in the Guggenheim, a pack of wolves, ignorantly careering towards the faintly visible Perspex wall in front of them represent the blind following the blind. His target is ideological collectivism and the tendency of fallible, insulated groups to follow paths of self-destruction, because of their imperviousness to reason and limited foresight.

The quote opening this chapter betrays an impoverished understanding of democracy, in which the concept is limited to special moments of express consent separated by long terms without oversight or criticism. Suzanne Spaulding has said of the Bush administration that

> a lot of their behaviour reflects, sadly, a fundamental lack of faith in our system of government; a fundamental lack of faith in democracy and in checks and balances; and a lack of understanding of the ways in which those are not a vulnerability, or a luxury for a time of peace.[10]

In the same debate, which took place at the Center for Law and Security at New York University, John Dean said that what really got his attention was the Executive Order, drafted by Gonzales and issued by Bush, which 'for all practical purposes repealed the 1978 law on preserving presidential records. The law, in essence, makes presidential records available to the American people, who really own them'.[11] In short, the shutters went up, and the quality of decision-making went down. As journalists will testify, the White House became a Dickensian Circumlocution Office.

Aside from the deleterious effects on the quality of governmental deliberation, secrecy has certain pathologies. The concealment of consultation can result in

[9] S Holmes, *The Matador's Cape: America's Reckless Response to Terror* (Cambridge University Press, 2007) 300–301.

[10] Presidential Powers, 26 April 2006, Center for Law and Security at NYU School of Law.

[11] *ibid.*

the masking of motive, allowing reasons which would not pass muster in public to inform policy choices. Holmes gives the example of the World War II relocation and internment of (US) West Coast Japanese for the ostensible reason that they posed a threat but really 'because government officials did not possess sufficient linguistic or cultural knowledge to discriminate accurately between innocent and guilty members of the group'.[12]

The more controversial the measure, the more tempting it can be for an executive to prevent parliamentary or judicial oversight. The most controversial tactic of all, pre-emptive self-defence, compounds the pathologies of secrecy and stonewalling, for it will always be resorted to on the basis of classified intelligence and in the absence of international authorisation. Budding pre-emptive self-defenders request our pre-evidentiary commitment. Where motives for war are classified or unchecked, the executive has the facility to fabricate the facts for itself, cheating the people into unreflecting hatred and panicky acquiescence to ill-advised and unwarranted aggression.

I have written elsewhere that a modern example of conniving judicial complicity in this sort of executive secrecy was the *El Masri* litigation, where national security was invoked successfully by the administration to prevent a hearing into the alleged abduction and torture of a German citizen.[13] It is hoped that the motive behind this masquerade is a tremendously important national security secret and not simply the desire to deflect attention from the incredible ineptitude that caused CIA officers to detain and maltreat a man for several months because his name sounded similar to that of a suspected terrorist. As Dworkin has it, 'the Bush administration claims that wartime security demands this secrecy and immunity from judicial and other supervision. That is an argument made by every police state'.[14]

I would be glad to report that we were spared such rhetoric in the United Kingdom. However, with respect to the contested Labour government attempt to create new detention powers, Tony Blair announced that he wanted to give the police the powers *they said they needed* to defend the security of the nation and its citizens. Prima facie, this is a reasonable-sounding contention. Of course, the police should have the powers they need to protect us. But it is only in a police-state that *policemen* are left to decide what level of policing is required. In a democracy, the citizens decide for them.

The judiciary has a delicate role in all this. Whilst not wanting to impede executive attempts to defend the nation, a domestic judge is aware of his

[12] S Holmes, *The Matador's Cape: America's Reckless Response to Terror* (Cambridge University Press, 2007) 225.

[13] *El Masri v United States* (Fourth Circuit Opinion, 2 March 2007). RS Brown, 'Access to Justice for Victims of Torture' in F Francioni, M Gestri, N Ronzitti and T Scovazzi, *Accesso alla giustizia dell'individuo nel diritto internazionale e comunitario* (Giuffre, 2009).

[14] R Dworkin, 'Terror and the Attack on Civil Liberties' in T Rockmore, J Margolis and AT Marsoobian (eds), *The Philosophical Challenge of September 11* (Blackwell Publishing, 2005) 87.

traditional role as a defender of the citizen's rights. International judges can be expected to take a deferential approach to the determinations of national authorities on how to handle internal unrest, due to their 'direct and continuous contact with the pressing needs of the moment'.[15] But to what extent is the assessment of national authorities, including the judiciary, clouded by the fog of war?

Judges are not isolated from the public. They read the papers, have political views, share the fears and desires of their countryfolk, and are aware of the precariousness of their position in a national emergency. They almost always consider themselves institutionally incapable of adjudicating on the risk to the nation, and defer to executive attempts to abrogate the constitution: the 'Constitution is not a suicide pact' (Arthur Goldberg J). But this metaphor is questionable. As Fletcher pithily puts it, 'there is many a logical mile between guaranteeing trials as prescribed by the Bill of Rights and imminent self-destruction of the nation'.[16] Indeed, it can readily be argued that the creation of 'lawless zones' goes far further down the path of destroying the American nation because the very concept of a nation presupposes moral, legal, and jurisdictional contiguity – in short, rights against the government. A nation, apart from being bordered land, is a bundle of principles.

In the United Kingdom, in the afore-mentioned *Belmarsh* case, Lord Hoffman's dissent, in which he repudiated the veracity of the government's claim that the life of the nation was threatened by terrorism, was very much a departure from judicial etiquette.[17] That said, it was a welcome departure. Perhaps Hoffman simply could not handle the slippery lies which had greased the path to Iraq. His dissent can be interpreted as a deeply political statement, a 'no' to scaremongering, but equally, one could simply say that, as a judge, he did not consider that it had been proven, on the balance of probabilities, that the United Kingdom faced an existential threat. How could it?

Some civil rights lawyers expect the courts to act like Hoffman, and 'defend' the constitution, but sometimes they ask too much. Judges are to apply the law, and if the law or policy, resulting from the democratic process, provides for 'water-boarding' or rendition flights for instance, it is perhaps not for a judge to take a stand against the people. Moreover, the strength of judges is always borrowed. Their shoulders are only as broad as contemporary consensus. Often, they will defend the constitution, or a reading of the constitution, only to the extent that they perceive public desire for their officials to be bound by its terms.

[15] *Ireland v United Kingdom* [1978] 2 EHRR 5, para 207.

[16] GP Fletcher, *Romantics at war: glory and guilt in the age of terrorism* (Princeton University Press, 2002) 102.

[17] *A v Secretary of State for the Home Department* [2004] UKHL 56, para 95; on judicial etiquette, see generally, D Pannick's enduringly progressive critique, *Judges* (Oxford University Press, 1987).

This is problematic in the United Kingdom given the extreme malleability of the constitution, and in the United States because the public has so much reverence for the virtuous outlaw.

The *Belmarsh* case was, of course, an example of judges standing up to the government, but the latter responded to the judicial determination that the detention scheme in question was incompatible with the United Kingdom's human rights obligations, 'by proposing unprecedented powers with potentially drastic interference with convention rights'. As Janet Hiebert has argued, this reaction 'underscores the need for continuing, robust *parliamentary* guardianship of fundamental rights'.[18] As Laqueur reports, in the summer of 2001, gangs of Pakistanis were torching shops and attacking the police in riots lasting days.[19] But instead of stalling new terror legislation that created a detention power discriminating between natives and foreigners, Parliament rushed it through. It would not be unfair to say that the war on terror has been characterised by congressional acquiescence and parliamentary obsequity.[20]

In the United States, Michael Vatis, a partner at the New York law firm Steptoe & Johnson, berated 'Congress's utter failure even to hold meaningful hearings into what's gone on – not only at Guantanamo and in Afghanistan and Iraq, but at secret detention sites around the world'.[21] Returning to El Masri's ordeal, the crucial point is that we cannot know whether the judges' decision was necessary. What we do know is that CIA agents should not be romping around Europe, abducting and torturing people. As I understand it, such transgressions are a matter for Congress. Now, back when Congress was not aware of these matters due to excessive White House secrecy, it had an excuse. Once the nightmare stories of torture and extraordinary rendition exploded into the public realm, why was the President responsible for these policies not removed from office? Is it that adultery in the Oval office shocks the conscience of the American people but extra-judicial torture and assassination do not?

A never-ending war on terror is particularly troubling because, as we know from experience, 'long term derogations from human rights obligations have a corrosive effect on the culture of respect for human rights'.[22] Where rampant presidentialism is received by parliamentary fawnery and hosted by judicial sycophancy, only the form of separated powers remains. In substance, this is autocracy. But our picture is incomplete. Today, to speak of three branches of government is anachronistic. Our gaze must be turned on that vital guardian of public freedom, the press.

[18] J Hiebert, 'Parliamentary Review of Terrorism Measures' (2005) 68(4) *Modern Law Review* 676, 679.

[19] W Laqueur, *No End to War: Terrorism in the 21st Century* (Continuum International, 2003) 62.

[20] Presidential Powers, 26 April 2006, Center for Law and Security at NYU School of Law.

[21] *ibid.*

[22] Joint Committee on Human Rights: Review of Counter-Terrorism Powers (Eighteenth Report of Session 2003–04 (HL 158/HC 713).

Leaders can be tempted to curtail the freedom of speech in wartime. The standard reason for this was perfectly captured by Attorney General John Ashcroft's comment before the Senate Judiciary Committee that 'those who criticize the post-9/11 curtailment of civil liberties "aid terrorists ... erode our national unity and diminish our resolve"'.[23] This is an interesting point for a high-ranking advocate to make in a democracy. Embattled leaders can fall into the trap of treating criticism of military policy as treason, and confusing dissent with insurrection. Those who question the wisdom of war risk being singled out as unpatriotic, even if their sentiments are informed by the entirely patriotic wish that their country avoids squandering its resources in endless wars. The American Council of Trustees and Alumni put the thumbscrews on 'liberals' by releasing 'a report that included a list of names of academics who had made public statements that questioned aspects of the war on terrorism'.[24] This was hardly a ringing endorsement of their purported commitment to academic excellence and freedom of expression in higher education.

Naturally, terrorism relies on media coverage for impact. Power grows as much out of the report of a gun, as it does its barrel. As Laqueur observed, 'Yussef el Qaradawi, the TV sheikh of the Al Jezira network, famous in the whole Arab world ... declared suicide terrorism the highest form of *Jihad* and therefore very commendable'.[25] Admittedly, the effect of such pronouncements can be devastating. In the early days of the war on terrorism, the White House was quick to request that ABC, CBS, CNN, Fox and NBC censor al-Qaeda material. The networks agreed to suppress al-Jazeera's footage, which created a deathly silence that should have been filled by an answer to the question: 'Why do they hate us?' Downing Street followed suit: Alistair Campbell pressurised the BBC, ITN and Sky to omit bin Laden footage. Did this censorship redound to the benefit of the British-American alliance? Hugh Miles argued that al-Qaeda made light work of these restrictions with its expertise in the usage of modern communications.

Though television appearances can validate causes, the suppression of material allows the public to draw the inference that the government is afraid of the message being sent. Further, censorship increases the sense of political disenfranchisement of terrorist sympathisers; as well as providing free propaganda for terrorists who tend to argue that the state regime is oppressive. Bin Laden's response was predictable and not entirely without credibility. He argued that American values

[23] ET May, 'Echoes of the Cold War' in ML Dudziak (ed), *September 11 in History: A Watershed Moment?* (Duke University Press, 2003) 49.

[24] *ibid*, 49.

[25] W Laqueur, *No End to War: Terrorism in the 21st Century* (Continuum International, 2003) 82.

> were revealed as a total mockery, as was made clear when the US government interfered and banned the media outlets from airing our words (which don't exceed a few minutes), because they felt that the truth started to appear to the American people.[26]

Another problem of suppressing factual reporting relates to what I said above about secrecy. If the public are ignorant as to what is going on, they are incapable of usefully engaging in debates about how to react. Thus, the government denies itself a crucial source of critique and innovation. The right to freedom of expression and the correlative right to receive information are regarded by embattled leaders as dangerous, but interfering with free speech is just as damaging to a democracy's natural defences. Curtailments on speech risk alienating the citizenry, which can provide valuable information on fifth column type activities, but can also actively contribute to national security doctrine. The first line of defence in a democracy is willingly formed by the people who enjoy its benefits.

A society threatened by terrorism should pull together, but there is a difference between pulling together and uncritical capitulation to the demands of an overweening executive. A pusillanimous media can hardly perform its role as a fact-finding watchdog, an irrepressible guardian of the public interest. Ironically, the worst suppression of free expression has been committed by the media itself. By churning out sensationalist 'infotainment' designed to maximise circulation, the media, that bastion of truth, has made intelligent thought nigh on impossible for vast swathes of the population.

The most effective instrument of tyranny is not torture, but an unscrupulous press. The Sun newspaper's headline that Brits were '45-minutes from doom' probably did more to pave the way for the Iraq invasion than any other factor. There was something noxious to the brain issuing from the ink of that headline. Brandeis thought, not without justification, that an inert people was the greatest enemy of freedom. Long ago, Plato counselled that the price of apathy towards public affairs is to be ruled by evil men. It is for this reason that blaming GW Bush, though he is of course blameworthy, is the intellectual equivalent of shooting fish in a barrel. Leaders aside, there was a 'thoroughly guilty stratum of intellectuals' including press editors.[27] More interesting and difficult still, is the question of the guilt, accountability and responsibility of that public institution of the lowest discernment and the greatest power, the masses.

We were told repeatedly about the threat of nuclear terrorism, of rogue states providing terrorists with nuclear arsenals or funding. Iraq, as weapons inspectors established, had neither nuclear programmes nor resources. Russia, on the other hand, had a problem of containment and control. Why then, did the United

[26] B Lawrence (ed), *Messages to the World: The Statements of Osama bin Laden* (Verso, 2005) in his interview with Taysir Alluni, on 21 October 2001.

[27] The phrase is Thomas Mann's from a letter to Joseph Pulitzer in the summer of 1945.

States not concentrate on helping Russia to locate and lock up its highly enriched uranium, a course of action far more likely to prevent nuclear terrorism than the antagonisation of the entire Islamic world? When the adversarial procedures in a democratic society – in the inner circle, or the Cabinet, in Congress, the press, and the courts – are functioning as intended, when the public man is kept alert not inert, this sort of erroneous mission is not embarked upon. When asked about what he thought of overwhelming public opinion wanting withdrawal from Iraq, half a decade on from the incursion, Cheney said: 'So?'. When asked if he cared what the American people think, the first word of his response was: 'No'. It is too easy to criticise Cheney's contempt for the American public. That contempt was in part earned.

This brings me to the difficult question of collective responsibility. The very suggestion that a group can be culpable for the actions of an individual will have some lawyers up in arms. However, to deny that perceptions of collective guilt (of the father, the kin or the creed) impel our judgements and actions is to ignore the role that it plays in the human psyche, in our motives, and in our shared mythologies. Further, to refuse to acknowledge the collective nature of responsibility for the actions of those who act on our behalf in a democracy is to abdicate from the throne on which the citizen set himself when he rejected the rule of Kings. It is suggested here that, irrespective of legal consequences, a collective can be *guilty* of failing to bring their representatives into line when they are out-of-line with what the collective wants.

However, we naturally feel that officials whose role it is to govern, and who are close to the locus of decision-making are more culpable than the citizen going about his private affairs. It could be argued then, that a person's culpability increases with their proximity to maladministration and stands in a proportionate relationship to their level of influence. Colin Powell for instance, who backed Barack Obama's successful campaign, was, five years ago, considered by some to be the only man who could have stopped the Iraq war. This is, of course, utter rot, but it suffices to illustrate that we attribute more responsibility to those with greater sway. Our individual responsibility is not an exact fractal of collective guilt. Rather, those wielding more power bear a greater burden for the actions of the whole.

Fletcher observes that the 'polycentric collective as a subject is basically foreign to the legal way of thinking'.[28] But what is modern society if not a polycentric collective? Is it that our conceptual tools are too blunt to trace the contours of collectives? Or is our moral imagination insufficient to evaluate our own complicity in the plethoric atrocities of the modern world? If we think for a moment about September 11, the attackers were not soldiers of a state, and the people they killed, though they were killed on American soil, were from at least

[28] GP Fletcher, *Romantics at war: glory and guilt in the age of terrorism* (Princeton University Press, 2002) 40.

70 different countries.[29] A slight gloss must be applied to this description. The attackers purported to act for a nascent nation of Islam, but also for existing real states, who suffered US oppression. Further, the attack was aimed at America and her symbols.

Now, for the police, a suicide bombing is a relatively tidy crime. The criminal enacts their own death sentence. But for the American government, it was a problem. First, the attack demonstrated our irremediable vulnerability, which is always bad for the incumbent power. Second, the public, whom governments are so keen to please, if truth be told, craved revenge (called 'justice') and, absent perpetrators, only a collective action could slake that craving. That craving (along with other factors) pulled America into Afghanistan, but became satiated somewhere in Iraq.

For members of the public in the United Kingdom and the United States, it is worth considering whether the current enemies of the state are also private enemies: am I for example, at war with the Taliban? This is a helpful exercise because our silent approval of the state's categorisation of a group as enemies will make of us an enemy to the target group: members of the Taliban might well consider themselves at war with me and my 'kind', whatever that means.

People respond to faint feelings of guilt in different ways. Haranguing a prominent scapegoat, like Bush or Powell – and it is not contended that they are innocent – allows us to deflect blame or wash our hands of responsibility. But there are other ways of addressing a besmirched conscience. Nussbaum records that, in response to the massacre in Gujahrat, students from Dehli's Jawaharlal Nehru University considered it important to visit the site, and to offer physical aid, 'as a type of penance for a collective Hindu guilt … thought of in terms of the Hindu concept of *praysaschit*, or atonement'.[30] Here, we can draw an interesting contrast: whereas, after September 11, the collective blaming of Afghanis and Iraqis seems unhealthy (not to say, incoherent), being a product of American desire for revenge, the collective guilt feelings of Hindus seem altogether healthy, being a product of sympathetic reflection.

We can of course interpret events in different ways in order to calibrate our response. An expansionist might call September 11 an attack on democracy, civilisation or world order. A reductionist might describe it as a domestic crime, committed by individuals. Similarly, the Iraq war might be characterised by an expansionist as an attempt to rid the world of Islam. The reductionist might

[29] D Archibugi and IM Young, 'Envisioning a Global Rule of Law' in JP Sterba (ed), *Terrorism and International Justice* (Oxford University Press, 2003). In this article, this reasoning is used to argue that terrorism should be conceptualised as a crime, and that this requires the strengthening of the institutions of international law.

[30] MC Nussbaum, 'Compassion and Terror' in JP Sterba (ed), *Terrorism and International Justice* (Oxford University Press, 2003) 32.

prefer to call it a British-American attempt to secure economic interests in the Middle East.[31] The correct interpretation tends to be a *via media*.

Fletcher categorises the reductionist take as typical of enlightenment philosophy, and the expansionist attitude is, for him, classic romantic thinking. These are helpful categories. Though Americans are 'children of the enlightenment', their policies are distinctly romantic. Part of the incoherence in foreign policy statements of the Bush administration was borne of a pathological inability to own up to the romantic urges informing their actions, coupled with a shameful habit of dressing those perfectly human, albeit disgraceful, emotional urges in the comforting swaddles of enlightened rationality. There is something more cynical there too. Ruthlessly self-interested actors in the upper echelons of American society, who, it seems, care little for America, dressed up policies destined to enrich their private enterprises in language designed to appeal to a population bent on revenge and incapable of understanding the very rational reasons why America might be despised.

To assert notions of shared responsibility is to say that we are all, in part, responsible for a world in which some people prefer to turn themselves into bombs rather than to continue living; it is not the same as excusing suicide bombing. Of course, the needless killing of innocents, commuters, workers, tourists and revellers is deplorable. Firing missiles at mosques, weddings, villages and schools is morally abhorrent too. Only an absurd romantic expansionist could consider a businessman at the World Trade Center responsible for the deaths of Iraqi children such that, according to divine justice, he should pay with his life. It is not, however, absurd to accuse that same trader of moral somnambulism, of an apathetical disregard, or reprehensible lack of interest in the policies sustaining his standard of living. Ferguson has illustrated this point by reference to US Cold War proxies:

> The truth about the Cold War then, is that in most of the southern hemisphere, the United States did almost as little for freedom as the Soviet Union did for liberation. American policy involved not only the defence of West European democracies like Italy, France and West Germany, which there is no doubt the Soviets tried their level best to subvert; it also meant the maintenance of dictatorships in countries like Guatemala where Communism – sometimes real, sometimes imagined – was fought by means of mass slaughter of civilians.[32]

The futility of the expansion of presidential prerogative is now clear. Bush had the lowest approval rating of any outgoing president in US history. Power reserved is power preserved. It is in the interests of the governors to secure the rights of the governed. Just as a brutish golf swing, unrestricted by the strictures of technique, is unlikely to transfer its raw force into a powerful and accurate

[31] *ibid*, 22.

[32] N Ferguson, *The War of the World* (Allen Lane, 2006) 617.

shot, capricious government, where power exceeds pre-set constitutional parameters, is likely to be weak and ineffective. The various trammellings of presidential powers are too frequently seen as pesky limits rather than facilitative constraints.

This argument need not appeal to ethics. It can be made in purely prudential terms: Bodin wrote that there is

> nothing that giveth greater credit and authority unto the laws and commandments of a prince, a people, or state, or in any manner of commonweal, than to cause them to pass by the advice of a grave and wise Senate or Council.[33]

A president who calls wise men to his counsel is not only likely to stay popular for longer, but he will increase his reputation for diplomacy, deal-making and wisdom. He also insulates himself from stupid errors, and spreads responsibility for mistakes. Ferguson gives the example of World War II Britain:

> [I]f Churchill had enjoyed the same untrammelled power as Hitler, he might well have lost the war, so erratic were his strategic judgments. It was the limitation of Churchill's power that was Britain's greatest strength – the fact that the other members of the British Chiefs of Staff Committee, notably [Alan] Brooke, were able not merely to disagree with 'the old man' but frequently to dissuade him. Britain waged war by committee. No individual's will was supreme. The armed services were forced to hammer out their differences and subscribe to a coherent strategy.[34]

Even where things do go wrong, as they are bound to in the administration of something so complex as a country, a government should not be afraid of admitting its peccadilloes, and compensating victims. Instead of lending their shoulders to blockade the doors to the courts, the Supreme Court should have granted El Masri, the alleged victim of CIA abduction and torture, a hearing and, depending on the merits, compensation. A government, in this case the Bush administration, is more palatable and attractive where it allows itself freely to be criticised, and is willing to be reproved and remorseful. A humble governor, one capable of self-correction, would not need to be replaced with such urgency. Towards the end of his presidency, Bush was regarded expressly by Democrats, and impliedly by Republicans, who seemed to keep him as far from their campaign as politically possible, as an unfortunate burden. Rather than it fortifying their position, it would seem that the avaricious accumulation of power is the least intelligent thing a leader in a democracy can do. Rude proclamations of power can awaken the sleeping lion of the people.

Similarly, executive secrecy and cabinet cliquery straightjacket our decision-making abilities. Views must be tested against those of intelligent opponents, not to the satisfaction of closely allied partners and invertebrate or like-minded

[33] S Holmes, *Passions and constraints: on the theory of liberal democracy* (University of Chicago Press, 1995) 116–17.

[34] N Ferguson, *The War of the World* (Allen Lane, 2006) 524.

yes-sayers. Arguments to the effect that the people do not know what it takes to protect a country, or that they do not want to know what is being done to protect a country, are hackneyed, unacceptable and invidious to democracy. A liberal democracy need not be ashamed of its methods.

Nor does liberal democracy necessarily mean that the wise few are made subjects of a foolish multitude. The public is remarkably shrewd in two respects, evaluating their own happiness, and judging character. Anent the public's natural gifts, there are several restrictions on those who participate in public debate. First, only those with an interest in influence do so. Second, only those who have a view do so. Third, only those who care do so. Fourth, only those who consider themselves competent do so, irrespective of their actual competence. Fifth, due to the ferocious, unforgiving nature of public debate, only those who are considered competent endure (except where incompetence is considered endearing).

Transparency is wrongly presupposed to be a burden on government. This is not so. Holmes points out that, whilst 'publicity is a disinfectant, a way of flushing out corruption and exposing abuses of power', it 'also exerts a more positive influence: it is a stimulant as well as a depressant'.[35] Consequently, intelligent leaders sure of the truth of their opinions and integrity of their motives will have no qualms about making them public, running them by the council of contradiction. Furthermore, when I know my decision will be tested in public, I am more likely to ensure that I have defensible reasons for its adoption. Public scrutiny therefore improves the decision-making process. Moreover, a thoughtful leader welcomes criticism, for deluded criticism will eventually strengthen his considered position as he easily elaborates its merits vis-à-vis that of the misguided critic. Poor argument will deliquesce against the flame of truth. Good argument can enrich understanding and refine policy. Only a churlish leader would deny himself that benefit. Congressional or parliamentary hearings and judicial review ought not to be regarded as necessary evils of the democratic process. On the contrary, democracy is served by these mechanisms, which check excess, test motive and improve decision-making.

The Pakistani Ambassador to the United States, Maleeha Lodhi, told the BBC that the United States has 'destabilized Pakistan', ignoring the enormous political and human costs on the front line of the war on terrorism. (There is truth in this comment even if Pakistan was not exactly stable prior to the war on terror.) For this reason alone, terrorism is here to stay. If something is constant, it is not an emergency. It is normality. It would not be an overstatement to say we live in an age of terror, and thanks to our bungled efforts to fight terrorism, history's page will not turn any time soon, so we have time to talk about what to do, calmly. Preventative measures can be debated and decided in parliamentary deliberations. There is no

[35] S Holmes, *Passions and constraints: on the theory of liberal democracy* (University of Chicago Press, 1995) 180.

place, except in responding to imminent emergencies, for presidential or prime ministerial invocations of prerogative or war powers. Spineless parliaments and cowardly congresses, which bend to prime ministerial or presidential fiat, are failing to perform their constitutionally allotted, procedurally fundamental role.

Of course, as Schmitt lectured, laws cannot predict emergencies. Naturally, the executive should have the freedom to react swiftly to crises without consulting judges or parliaments. But laws can allot roles and delineate procedures for the proper use of these powers. And if crises are constant, if our war (should you wish to call it that) is ongoing, then let us, together, debate the best way to fight it and deliberate the modes for countering the plague which is upon us, instead of burying our heads in sands of apathy and indifference.

Yes, as Abraham Lincoln, that heroic despot, told America, sometimes a limb must be amputated to save the body, but there is rarely so much haste that the threat posed by that limb is not double- and triple-checked by independent analysts. What makes Britain great is that the Prime Minister has the benefit not only of the collected ken of a Cabinet, but also a simulated public in Parliament. But, though we elect representatives to give voice to our views, we also put them in place because we think they are best equipped to decide. We want parliamentarians not to do what *we* would do, but to do what they think is best. At no time is phlegmatic parliamentary scrutiny more important than when the public is rendered insentient by fear.[36]

A formal separation of powers is all very well, but decisions must be made by people. Irrespective of one's constitutionally allotted role, the final arbiter in every instance must be the self. Each of us must be legislator, executor and judge. Especially, at the heady level of constitutional altercations between the various branches of government, the only valid appeals are to fact, reason and compassion. Where one wing of power has slackened, that slack must be picked up. Otherwise, presidential malversation is ingratiated by congressional nonfeasance, which is flattered by judicial abdication. Law is argument. It is in the making. When we argue about law, we exert the social power necessary to generate and sustain its meaning.

In February 2002, having tampered with the freedom of the press at home, causing a deglasnostification of American public life and a remarkable stupefaction of the common man, Bush told the Chinese that 'diversity is not disorder. Debate is not strife. And dissent is not revolution. A free society trusts its citizens to seek greatness in themselves and their country'. This is the theory underlying the preservation of free speech in a democracy. Indeed, free speech can suppress violence. Adversarial debate between opposed interest groups helps strike compromises and the availability of cathartic recourse to political expression reduces

36 For discussion of the respective roles of parliament and the judiciary, see S Tierney, 'Determining the State of Exception: What Role for Parliament and the Courts?' (2005) 68(4) *Modern Law Review* 668 and J Hiebert, 'Parliamentary Review of Terrorism Measures' (2005) 68(4) *Modern Law Review* 676.

the appeal of the resort to force. Further, reason and discourse are in a symbiotic relationship. Our reasoning is proved by the argumentative testing of ideas. Our discourse is facilitated by reasonable argument.

Contrariwise, the suppression of the speech of those who back their rhetoric with violence can be counter-productive. Indeed, the larger the constituency for an alleged terrorist cause, the less the stifling of free speech is the answer, as it implies that what is being said is persuasive, and the denial of access to political expression legitimates the resort to force. Locke knew that the conferral of free expression, however paradoxical it may sound, actually bolsters the government's powers, whereas, as he saw it, there is 'only one thing which gathers people for sedition, and that is oppression'.[37]

What is often forgotten in the hasty censorship of terrorist speech is that civilised people are outraged by terrorism. No one in their right mind endorses the indiscriminate killing of innocents as a means of political propaganda. As a result, benevolent and careful liberal democracies need not fear that terrorism will win powerful constituencies. Once aired, the noxious views of terrorist organisations will dissipate and become harmless. Furthermore, it stands to reason that factual reporting of the motivations for terrorists' attacks will increase the public's indignation at their illicit activities. Liberal democracy, on the other hand, has enormous moral authority because, properly understood, it denies itself certain means and methods in the political process. Where it loses the courage of its convictions and begins to adopt counter-terror tactics that involve strikingly similar calculus to the terrorists, the public finds it equally unconscionable to support either side.

Press freedom is so cherished that a government, securing it for journalists has a willing ally. A zealous, investigative press is not a hindrance to rulers; rather, it might even make valuable political commentary, and detect and expose dangerous fringe groups. The suppression of press speech suffocates public imagination and, as a consequence, stultifies the government. In this way, the 'outlawing of dissent, whatever the excuse, undercuts public reason as well as private rights'.[38] As President Abraham Lincoln believed, 'given the truth', the people 'can be depended on to meet any national crisis. The great point is to bring them the real facts'.

Here, I would like to make a short parenthetic observation. I have argued that for citizens to seek greatness in themselves and the nation, as Bush lectured the Chinese, the public man must be stimulated, his mind must be enriched, and his opinion must be sought on issues affecting the nation. In this way, his abilities can be gently harnessed for the commonweal. However, the mere existence of torture as a policy will strip a citizen of his willingness to contribute to public debate because of a heightened fear of arbitrary castigation and punishment. Torture is

[37] J Locke, *Two treatises of government* (Cambridge University Press, 1988) II at § 57.

[38] S Holmes, *The Matador's Cape: America's Reckless Response to Terror* (Cambridge University Press, 2007) 219.

inimical to democracy in this very fundamental way. And yet – and this is key – though such brutality is the antithesis of a civilised democratic understanding of legality, there is nothing to stop torture becoming law, except, of course, the mettle of the public man.

It is wrong to underestimate the influence of the press. The press is the portal through which we receive practically all our information. If it were a mere lens, there would be little cause for concern. A lens, however, it is not; it is an actor with a political agenda (self-sustaining like most) and financial projects. Its influence is so large that it deserves the circumspection usually reserved for governments. Media coverage prioritises or ranks the beneficent projects of Britain and America and designates our enemies.

With that influence comes the responsibility to send an exoteric message designed accurately to report and criticise, but not to inflame conflicts or unnecessarily to exacerbate public fright. In his tome, *The Great War for Civilisation*, Robert Fisk laments so-called 'generic' reporting which flagrantly violates all these precepts. Some American news-reporting uncritically echoed dubious political descriptions, and by using a series of images, linked prayer and communal worship of Islam to suicide bombing, when there is no necessary nexus between these phenomena.

A caveat is required here. It is wrong to presume that we read what the press print; on the contrary, they print what we read. It is in this light that we must regard the failure of the American media to grasp the threat posed by terrorism. As Laqueur points out, in the 1990s, 'there were far fewer foreign correspondents than forty or fifty years earlier'. Similarly, in 'the 1960s up to 40 percent of the news time on television was dedicated to foreign news. Thirty years later this percentage had shrunk to 10 percent or less'.[39] This is as much a shortcoming of the American people as it is of the American media. Kagan tells us that Americans want to play a 'grand role on the world stage'. In that case, one would expect them to have a far greater degree of cultural ken. Viewers of the last presidential campaign would be forgiven for their despair at the Republican running mate's quip that her ability, on a clear day, to see Russia from Alaska was some sort of substitute for foreign policy experience.

The media's retinue to the public is not straightforward. Coverage of terrorism can have unwanted effects. Consider the following: what relationship does the recent reporting of the Taliban killing a Christian aid worker have to our treatment of Taliban detainees? What effect does our viewing of al-Qaeda operatives cutting off heads with rusty blades have on our assessment of the acceptability of torture? Our approach to legality is mediated by the press. So, though grievances must be explained and tactics reported, care must be taken by the media, collectively, not to over- or under-report atrocities and the reasons for their occurrence.

[39] W Laqueur, *No End to War: Terrorism in the 21st Century* (Continuum International, 2003) 129.

Moreover, there is a difference between interviewing resistance fighters such as the Taliban, who, if truth be told, despite their hostility to foreigners and Christianity and their other obvious shortcomings, have a realistic claim to self-defence, and interviewing, for instance the hijacker of an aircraft, whilst hostages sit trembling on the plane. In the current situation, the former is vital journalism, and we ought to reserve our highest accolades for journalists who venture into Taliban-controlled zones, risking their lives, to bring us reports of Afghan sentiment. Interviewing the hijacker, however, is a different matter. It must be remembered, as I said earlier, that for terrorists, coverage is leverage and, absurd though it may be, the mere appearance of a person on television invests them with status and legitimacy. There is 'significant evidence of a contagion effect wrought by coverage' and 'sane people may see the terrorist model as a plausible outlet for their sense of rational grievance'.[40]

The media is a conflation of power and its representation. And, though this means that the traditional media must self-censor, the internet cannot be controlled or regulated. Hence, the public, through government, must self-censor too. Our lust, our *blood*lust, is self-perpetuating. In other words, the more we want to watch terrorism, the more we will see terrorism occur. Only education can steer us out of this circular rut. And, taking Nussbaum and Habermas together, it must be geared towards the development of empathy and communicative trust.[41] Education is fabulously difficult, but it is through education of its citizens that society invests in its future. When correctly orchestrated, formative studies put on by the government invest in individuals who then invest in society. As former President Bush implied, the empowerment of the individual empowers society. For a liberal democracy, the aims could be fivefold: to enrich society by enriching the minds of individuals; to instill a belief that violence is not the continuation of but the end of politics; to demonstrate that reason and discourse are integral to both peace and progress; to impart a capacity for empathy; and, finally, to convey, per Lincoln, that 'though a man's attributes may be far superior to those of his fellows, no man is so superior that he may govern them without their consent'.

I have come to think that, partly as a by-product of consumerism, we distinguish overzealously between our cherished private spheres and an optional public life. We forget that we are society, we are *vivus lapis*, and by virtue of our interactions with others, we are public; our minds are part of the collective consciousness – even the choice of reclusion is an expression of a version of the good. A hermit is a profoundly political animal. As trust between people is precluded by dishonesty, the relation between governed and government is

[40] B Nacos, *Mass-Mediated Terrorism* (Rowan and Littlefield, 2007) 24, quoting from the results of a study by Conrad Winn and Gabriel Weimann.

[41] J Habermas and J Derrida, *Philosophy in a time of terror: dialogues with Jürgen Habermas and Jacques Derrida* (University of Chicago Press, 2003) 36.

inhibited by mendacity, and comity between nations is hindered by deceit. Society, be it intimate, national or international, is weakened by untruths.

Moreover, distinctions between society, intimate, national and international, are fragile fictions. Even war, regarded by some as the ultimate political event, is intimate. It is more human than it is political. Civilian casualties always outnumber military deaths, and though war often spirals out of control into an attempt at complete annihilation, it is almost invariably accompanied by that most intimate act between aggressor and victim: rape. Closing our eyes or turning our heads is a political choice. It is inhuman to close our eyes to two wars being fought in our names and the objectionable manner of their conduct.

As members of society (domestic and international), we have a primary responsibility to denounce indiscriminate killing and other manifestations of brutality, whoever the perpetrator and whatever his cause.[42] In this way, convention will harden into rule, and violent protest will soften into civil dissent. In our daily interactions, we do not reserve for ourselves a right to attack others, except in defence of ourselves or others. It has never satisfactorily been explained why Britain and America implicitly consider themselves above this simple norm ensuring the civil ordering of human affairs. Perhaps the principles flowing from the normatively barren concept of sovereignty continue to push states and their citizens off course in their assessments of international morality.[43]

We bear a secondary responsibility to monitor our own egos, predilections and predispositions, for the foreign adventuring of the government is always an outgrowth of our domestic ideas. Even a complete disregard for foreign affairs carries a certain culpability because a leader, like a sommelier, will sell you what they think you will buy. Thus, public nonfeasance is a prerequisite for political misfeasance. As Jaspers put it, in his book on German guilt, *Die Schuldfrage*, '*es ist jedes Menschen Mitverantwortung wie er regiert wird*'. Again, permitting myself a rough translation: 'the manner in which he is governed is the shared responsibility of everyman'.

In order to combine what I called the primary and secondary responsibilities of the public man, the following formulation is perhaps useful: What others do in our name *is* who we are, and who we are will control what others purport to do in our name. I am, whether I like it or not, at war with the Taliban in Afghanistan and yet, quite what positional advantages on those ice-topped, craggy, inhospitable peaks do to improve the security of people in Peckham is beyond me.

Perhaps we have been sucked into the vortex of permanent emergency, portrayed earlier. Ignatieff has expressed a similar sentiment:

42 For a similar view, see A Cassese, *Terrorism, politics, and law: the Achille Lauro affair* (Princeton University Press, 1989).

43 P Allott, *Eunomia: new order for a new world* (Oxford University Press, 1990) 275.

> Coercive means cease to serve determinate political ends and become ends in themselves. Terrorists and counterterrorists alike end up trapped in a downward spiral of mutually reinforcing brutality. This is the most serious ethical trap lying in wait in the long war on terror that stretches before us.[44]

We ought to be mindful that the goal of security becomes pointless if we destroy that which we originally set out to protect, if the measures we take augment the evil against which they were employed. The key point is that liberal democracy is not an empty fortress. It is filled with precious principles that ought not be exchanged for short-term tactical advantage. Where these principles ('freedom' for the allies, and 'justice' for the terrorists) become the *means* of justifying the sole end of inflicting losses on the enemy, something has gone perilously wrong.

I want to deepen this discussion of responsibility or guilt. Guilt is too frequently considered a categorical concept. Instead, it is scalar in the following sense: White police officers who beat up an innocent black man are guilty. Those who stand by and watch without intervening might be described as guilty too. Even if their only misfeasance was nonfeasance, if their only crime was omission, they are still responsible for a gross dereliction of duty. Colleagues who work in the same department can be described as responsible for creating or tolerating an atmosphere of racial antipathy, which made such an assault conceivable. The Chief of Police is guilty of failing to instill respect for all ethnicities in his officers.

The police force, as a whole, is accountable, and though society may be shocked that racist persecution taints their law enforcement, it is also responsible, for the policemen are part of society. Police attitudes cannot be considered independently of the attitudes of their peers. A child may not be responsible but the wife of a policeman who titters at his racist jokes instead of reproaching his ignorance might well be thought blameworthy, in a moral, though not a legal sense.

Those most proximate to the abuse of power (the cowardly onlookers) and those with the greatest power to prevent such abuse (the Chief of Police) are most culpable, whereas those farthest from the abuse (the wife) and those with no power to understand or influence attitudes (the child) are least blameworthy or blameless. All are responsible. That said, none of this detracts from the guilt of the actual perpetrators. To refute their agency is to unravel the whole criminal law and with it, the possibility of social ordering.

If the manner in which he is governed is the shared responsibility of everyman, we should reject oppressive government that needlessly and foolishly curtails our freedoms, but with equal fervour, commitment and indignation we should reject oppressive government that tries to defend our freedoms by curtailing those of others, however distant they might be. If we do not, we are tacitly claiming racial superiority, we are morally complicit in their crimes, and

[44] M Ignatieff, *The lesser evil: political ethics in an age of terror* (Edinburgh University Press, 2003) 115.

though the law may have no claim on our persons, our conscience should have a claim on our peace of mind. How does this relate to the war on terror?

That Bush won an absolute majority of the popular vote after the invasion of Iraq is a damning moral indictment of the American nation, though it by no means discredits the individuals and organisations which opposed him. America is paying the price in blood and treasure for its poor judgement. Sadly, it will be the incumbent not the outgoing President who must repair the damage done to the nation. Moreover, the very existence of Guantánamo Bay is a heinous collective wrong committed by the American people, notwithstanding the valiant efforts of many to restore some notion of legality and moral consistency to the justice system. In the early years of the war on terror, the stench from the fœtid Cuban brig was walled in by barriers of high public indifference. As prosecutions began to fall apart, as the floor fell away from underneath the administrators at the Cuban camp, as prosecutors like Lt Colonel Darrel Vandeveld resigned because of 'systemic problems' with the military tribunals, one of the main reasons informing the Bush administration's decision to keep Gitmo open was that they had no idea what the legal consequences of closure would or should be.

On one view, it challenges our theories when things start coming back out of legal black holes. On the view of law propounded here, the American people simply do not know what to do with the fact that they, as a collective, acquiesced in the indefinite, incommunicado detention, and intentional degradation and maltreatment of innocent men. For a time, torture was the law, and that is very difficult to face up to, not least because everyone in America is responsible, albeit not legally culpable.

A unified Europe could have prevented the Iraq invasion. But it was not united in its resistance. The United Kingdom, rather than challenging America, sacrificed its loyalty to the aspirations of international law on the altar of solidarity with America, rendering itself a handmaiden. This happened despite notable but ultimately ineffective public protests, including that of Professor James Crawford, Whewell Professor of International Law of Cambridge University:

> On the information available, none of the exceptions that permit the use of force applied. There was no UN Security Council authorisation, and no imminent humanitarian catastrophe, and no imminent threat of the use of force by Iraq. I think it was unlawful in the beginning, and they haven't found anything since to make one change one's mind.[45]

[45] For Crawford's opinion and that of other UK experts, see, 'War On Iraq Was Illegal, Say Top Lawyers', available at: www.globalpolicy.org/component/content/article/167/35770.html.

Nevertheless, despite its failure to block the US invasion of Iraq, Europe retains the majesty and moral authority to interpose itself between the opposing fundamentalisms of British-American (inter-)nationalism and radical Islamism. That, it must do.

For the last time in this argument, I would like to reflect on how what has been discussed here relates to the foregoing themes. The public simply must keep a vigilant watch out for the misdescription of events. When we are told we are under attack, we really ought to assess that claim. Often we are threatened more by the media event than by the actual event. The famous 45-minute claim was preposterous for two reasons. First, as weapons inspectors were on their way to demonstrating, the late President Hussein had no nuclear capability. This sort of inquiry was beyond the public, but it was well within the power of the people to insist that the inspections were finished before an attack was launched. Second, a state's mere possession of a nuclear arsenal is hardly a reason to launch an attack. In fact, it is a very good reason not to attack. The same logic will have been apparent to Saddam, who, unless suicidal, would never have contemplated firing on the United Kingdom, even if he had the capacity, which he did not.

Furthermore, we might want to be more careful about our own use of language. I have already noted the widespread abuse of the term 'jihad', which is not used in the Qur'an to refer to warfare.[46] This formerly delightful term, full of ethical meaning and wholesome resonance has been abducted by fundamentalists and disfigured by the Western media. Absurdly, though terrorism, the slaughtering of non-combatants, would be inimical to the notion of jihad, terrorists are now limned as jihadists. It is a most inappropriate trope for al-Qaeda's troops.

Similarly, the statement that the United Kingdom is threatened by terrorism is unhelpful. Apart from failing to specify the nature of the threat, or whence it emanates, the usage of an '-ism' tends to magnify the danger, linking it to ambiguous 'movements', like Islamism or anti-capitalism. It is fair to say that al-Qaeda in its current form is a British-American innovation. Houen has useful guidance:

> One way to separate terror from its 'ism' is to try [to] map the multiplicity of factors involved in it. Only by thus drawing critique into the crises can we help to prevent violence and discourse from forming further explosive compounds.[47]

This attempt to control phenomena by using precise language helps people distinguish what, if anything, they are fighting for and against, and by extension, whether the question is one of crime or war, or both. Fletcher has a passage on this that deserves to be quoted in full.

[46] KAA Fadl, '9/11 and the Muslim Transformation' in ML Dudziak (ed), *September 11 in History: A Watershed Moment?* (Duke University Press, 2003) 101.

[47] A Houen, *Terrorism and modern literature, from Joseph Conrad to Ciaran Carson* (Oxford University Press, 2002) 278.

> In some respects, the concurrence of war and crime should appeal to romantics. With their zeal for individual self-expression, romantics should be attracted by the criminal's independence and authenticity. Committing a crime promises the recognition of the person as actor, as author of his or her own deed. But war has a similar appeal. The romantic begins with an overflowing self, then craves unity with others in a communal movement, but the self still craves recognition. The crime redeems the suppressed individuality of the conformist soldier.[48]

Terrorism then, like war crime, is the ultimate blend of self-expression, self-transcendence, self-abnegation and self-glorification. This explains why some people hate to love characters like Blair, rogue leader, and love to hate characters like bin Laden, lead rogue.

With respect to the responsibilities I have outlined above, governments should never be permitted to feel so comfortable in their own political latitude, and officials should never be permitted to feel so secure in their impunity, that they deign to send their troops into an aggressive war, to commit the original crime against humanity.[49] Further, it is only by insisting on the fair treatment of others that we can prevent the state of emergency becoming the prevalent governmental paradigm for the twenty-first century, precipitating what the Swedish political scientist and jurist, Herbert Tingsten, in 1934 called a 'liquidation of democracy'. Right now, this is crucial, for America considers itself to be in an ongoing, global war, where ordinary rules of respect for nations and their people have been ousted to make room for a cowardly new martial disorder.

At base, the only bulwark preventing the disintegration of democracy is the citizen. Democracy is only as strong as the constitution not of the state, but of the individual. Consequently, our fealty to our rulers should depend on their fidelity to our principles. Otherwise formulated, constitutional laws are but words; constitutional power is in our hands. Constitutions are spectral shackles imagined by the human mind. We are bound only by the fantasy of collective constraints. Constitutions are as changeable as the day-to-day balance of power between our passions and our reason. Most days don't challenge our substance. But those days come, and on some days, there is danger, real or imagined. Constitutional rules are futile attempts to bind our future selves. Nevertheless, the only effective fetter is recollection of why the rules were adopted in the first place. In a flash storm with zero visibility, a helicopter pilot is drilled to trust his instruments and never his instincts, which can be perilously disoriented. This allows him to reach his destination safely instead of mistaking up for down, with tragic results.

[48] GP Fletcher, *Romantics at war: glory and guilt in the age of terrorism* (Princeton University Press, 2002) 94.

[49] This is not intended to be a legal classification, merely to draw attention to the dynamics of international legal classifications.

Returning to the theme of guilt, Fletcher has argued that a 'sensitive approach to collective guilt challenges the degree to which individuals act in ways that are totally independent of the collectives and the nations in which their personalities are rooted'.[50] Allott goes further:

> The government of a statally organized society can, through all the forms of social power available to it, take control of the reality-forming processes of society, especially law and education, but also morality and history and art (including public entertainment). The government of a statally organized society may be in a position to determine the total social process and hence society's becoming.[51]

Earlier, in the chapter on liberty, I argued that we can never truly escape our origins, because all our decisions relate back to an original situation, called infancy, over which we had no control. Nevertheless, the whole criminal justice system is premised on the proposition that humans are agents, to some extent, of their own destiny. A man of a public disposition ought to at least attempt to evaluate the quality of his freedom, by reference to what policies sustain his freedoms and to the nature of his desires (are they innate, eg the desire for a mate, or are they generated by his surroundings, eg the desire for a particular laptop).

In this chapter, we have seen an interesting link between security and avaricious accumulation of executive power. This nexus was perfectly captured by Montesquieu's afore-mentioned warning that 'in proportion as the power of the monarch becomes boundless and immense, his security diminishes'.[52] We can apply this thesis to our nations too. Leaving aside the huge economic drain of warfare, by adopting policies of 'shock and awe', by indulging in a form of global tyranny run by sinister grab teams, who abduct, render and torture civilians, America has secured only increased insecurity for many years to come. Machiavelli argued for the extermination of enemies but when he did so, he envisaged well-defined adversaries, and swiftly prosecuted executions, not badly drawn foes, poorly targeted violence and protracted warfare. Paradoxically enough, we ought to keep our leaders and our armies in check not to diminish but to preserve their power. Holmes' advice for America epitomises this notion that power restrained is power preserved.

> What would really take 'strong nerves' … is the candid admission by our political leadership that the US must abandon its infantile hopes for 'victory' and must concentrate instead on managing and reducing, in collaboration with capable allies, largely self-created vulnerabilities that can never be completely removed because they

[50] GP Fletcher, *Romantics at war: glory and guilt in the age of terrorism* (Princeton University Press, 2002) 39.

[51] P Allott, *Eunomia: new order for a new world* (Oxford University Press, 1990) 204.

[52] C de Secondat Montesquieu, *The Spirit of the Laws*, trans T Nugent (Hafner, 1949) vol 1, 114.

> are simultaneously the sources of liberal civilization's identity, prosperity, and creative resilience in the face of ominously evolving threats.[53]

The acceptance of our irremediable human vulnerability to ruthless terrorists emancipates a population from slavery to the fear of an ineradicable threat. Responsibility for rational thinking about security, and in particular the accurate assessment of threats, rests primarily with government but also with the press, the judiciary and the academy.[54] A certain exaggeration can be expected of political leaders, though exactitude must be demanded of government. One of the most important functions of the academy and the free press is assiduously to expose 'doublethink'.

Orwell defined doublethink as the capacity to be aware of the falsity of a proposition whilst simultaneously convincing oneself and glibly asserting to others that it is true. In the aftermath of 9/11, Richard Clarke reported that he 'realised with almost a sharp physical pain that Rumsfeld and Wolfowitz were going to try to take advantage of this national tragedy to promote their agenda about Iraq', that although the nation had been attacked by terrorists, they conceptualised the problem as 'dictators'.[55] Not enough was done by the free press to test the unsubstantiated supposition that Osama bin Laden and Saddam Hussein were in cahoots, that terrorism and tyranny were part of the same problem and that, as that perspicacious strategist, Bush, had it, Iraq was the 'central front on the war on terror' against the 'Islamist fascists'.

The baseless cant that Iraq had weapons of mass destruction and links to al-Qaeda was publicly repeated by Bush and key officials on over 500 occasions.[56] In the land whose biggest export is entertainment, a violent, perverse fiction was allowed to refute the simple truth. Why is the modern mind so accommodating of fantasy and inhospitable to fact? Is it the case that the innately civic and social character of the average American, their *politikon*, was polluted by film, fantasy and 'infotainment'?[57]

And when Americans realised the full extent of the horrific means adopted to defend their liberty, was it then that they embraced the facile Manichean terms in which the conflict was couched? In a comment of 1988, which has equal currency today, Rushdie observed:

> When the activities of a nation's representatives begin to diverge so dramatically from its self-image as the guardian of freedom and decency, then the country has to find

[53] S Holmes, *The Matador's Cape: America's Reckless Response to Terror* (Cambridge University Press, 2007) 332.

[54] F Gerges, 'The Ultimate Terrorist: Myth or Reality', *Beruit Daily Star*, 12 March 2001.

[55] RA Clarke, *Against All Enemies: Inside America's War on Terror* (Free Press, 2004) 30.

[56] Center for Public Integrity, 'Report on Falsehood in the Bush Administration' (January 2008).

[57] MT Cicero, J Annas and R Woolf, *On moral ends* (Cambridge University Press, 2001) 140.

> ways of turning away from the truth into cosy simplicities (God, patriotism), in order not to see itself too plainly; in order not to see that its picture of itself is in many ways a false one.[58]

In this way, the Bush administration duped America into self-betrayal.

In the introduction to his history of twentieth century violence, Ferguson asks: why are men willing to 'identify one another as aliens when they are biologically so very similar?'[59] Fletcher, for his part, suggests that we 'live in the world but we need a home. And the Romantic spirit dwells in these yearnings for partiality and solidarity'.[60] Two elements of this are worth enlarging upon. First, yes, there is great joy in limited solidarity, particularly given the dizzying disarray of neoteric social, spiritual and cyberspatial phenomena. But such solidarity is but one step from insularity. Armed with this observation, if we go back to our discussion of identity, we can perhaps see that enmity, paradoxically, can grow out of excessively exclusionary forms of amity. Second, though there is nothing wrong with solidarity with our kith and kin, this ought not to oust the notion of humanity, which, as Schmitt observes, admits of no enemy. In a sense, our moral reflections must stretch further than our local communities, so that the bounds of amity are drawn around humankind. Fletcher is strategically sympathetic to the romantic mindset, but we should court romantics with caution, for rather than being conflict averse they seek clash and resistance as forms of growth. This is unproblematic where clash and resistance take place on an intellectual plane, but it is an adulteration of all that is sophisticated in the romantic spirit to allow for its descent into rabblesome violence.

The mixing that results from cultural globalisation pollutes a comforting image of sameness. Our natural gag reflex must be suppressed in order to ensure that this mixing proceeds pacifically. One of America's greatest strengths, which was not properly exploited in the war on terror, is its capacity to swallow up foreigners rather than to gag, with the result that they soon consider themselves Americans. Terrorism in New York City is a dangerous gambit because of that city's truly cosmopolitan make-up. To attack New York is, in this way, to lash out at all mankind. But, instead of exporting its sophisticated capacity for cultural cohesion, America exported its revanchist grunt. Instead of the enlightened policies of a responsible, cosmopolitan, liberal democracy, America promulgated a primitive *lex talionis*. As a consequence, instead of alienating the terrorists who so indiscriminately attacked innocent civilians, America has alienated itself.

Hopefully, the inexorable intermixing of peoples will guarantee that theories of civilisational clash have a short life-span. We are confronted with each other and new others more frequently than ever before. Jeffrey Toobin is correct to think that 'the distinction between national security and domestic investigations

[58] S Rushdie, *The Satanic Verses* (Vintage, 1988) 392.

[59] N Ferguson, *The War of the World* (Allen Lane, 2006) xliv.

[60] GP Fletcher, *Romantics at war: glory and guilt in the age of terrorism* (Princeton University Press, 2002) 25.

is no longer meaningful'.[61] As the British terrorists of 7 July 2005 have proven, the war on terrorism has, at its root, principle, not the flimsy criteria of race or citizenship. We are fighting enemies within our societies and if we categorise the war, as Huntington and bin Laden do, as one of creed, we will nurture new enemies in our backyards.

It is in this light that Allott reflects that we must begin to think of ourselves as citizens of the world, because in 'a society which does not conceive of itself as society, social revolution is impossible'.[62] He made this observation in the context of his theory on international order. It is directly relevant to terrorism because terrorists are a scourge for all humanity. There is no reason why states cannot sign accords so that police and security forces the world over can share intelligence, pursue terrorists across borders, and pick apart terrorist networks. In fact, the only thing standing in the way of such fruitful collaboration in the last decade was a state that thought it could 'go it alone'. But the Bush administration is not synonymous with America, and America, perhaps of all states, has a remarkable capacity for self-correction. Indeed, the seeds of the global societal collaboration which I endorse can be found in some of the most captivating passages of US jurisprudence.

In 1866, David Davis J held that the US constitution 'is a law for rulers and people, equally in war and in peace, and covers with the shield of its protection all classes of men, at all times, and under all circumstances'.[63] These are of course, just words; their force depends on the backbone of officials and the preparedness of people to demand their rights. Anywhere that the United States purports to exert power *qua* administrator of justice, be it Cuba or Afghanistan, is a place where people can and should assert rights against the American government. Rights do not exist absent vigorous enforcement by their purported bearers.

Davis' comment must have more currency now than it did in 1866. As Ferguson suggests, racial distinctions, however tightly we cling to them, are becoming increasingly absurd in modern society. For instance, the number of mixed race couples in America quadrupled in the 1990s, to circa 1.5 million, and of every 20 children, one is of mixed origin.[64] This does not mean that racism will die out naturally. On the contrary, miscegenation can often portend mass ethnic slaughter, presumably because men inexplicably proud of their particular complexion worry about pollution of their 'type'. Eradication of the sort of racial distinctions that prevent international cooperation, then, is a fragile, fitful process and, I would argue, is more likely to proceed by the inculcation of empathy than the interbreeding of races. Otherwise, how is it that in Riga on the night of 1 July 1941, Jewish prisoners were loaded onto trucks and slaughtered in

61 Presidential Powers, 26 April 2006, Center for Law and Security at NYU School of Law.

62 P Allott, *Eunomia: new order for a new world* (Oxford University Press, 1990) 246.

63 *Ex parte Milligan* (1866) 71 US 4, 120–21.

64 N Ferguson, *The War of the World* (Allen Lane, 2006) xliv.

the woods 'by local Latvians who knew their victims by their first names'? Why did Ukrainians kill their own Polish wives?[65]

Fundamental to the growth of this empathy for one another is the development of an ability to diagnose our tendency to hate in others what we abhor in ourselves. As the Gestapo interrogator said to the Bolshevik prisoner:

> When we look one another in the face, we're neither of us looking at a face we hate – no we're gazing into a mirror … You may think you hate us, but what you really hate is yourselves – yourselves in us.[66]

This is a moral argument, but it can be cast in prudential terms. As we noted with Paine earlier, we should guard the liberty of our assumed enemies as we guard our own, because if we start encroaching on their freedoms we establish a precedent that can reach to ourselves. The Bush administration has made the terrible mistake of detaining, torturing and killing 'suspected' enemies, thereby imperiling good American soldiers in the field.

In World War II Warthegua, it was decreed that German citizens who had 'injured the ethnic interests of the Reich through relations with Poles' were to be 'transferred to a concentration camp'.[67] It is as if ethnic hatred is programmed to reveal its own pathological root of self-loathing. Arguments that this could not happen in the American context are presumptuous. On 17 October 2006, the President of the United States of America removed the right of habeas corpus for all citizens, so that Americans who were a supposed threat to national security could be detained on Presidential say-so. One man's whim is a thin thread from which to dangle the much-lauded freedom of the Western world.

The pathologies of counter-terror policies defined on ethnic lines were compounded by the tendencies of power. As a leader loses support and influence, he can be tempted avariciously to accumulate raw coercive power.[68] The expansion of executive discretion, the 'sabre-rattling' was a tell-tale sign that the Bush administration was losing political sway. It is useful now to investigate how this decline was predetermined by American identity and, looking back a little further, how that identity was generated.

Here, my focus is America and I want to rely on the work of Richard Slotnick, whose analysis of American mythology is insightful.[69] He begins with the prosaic assertion that popular myth informs political culture. Myths are fundamental to creating and sustaining nationhood. These myths are made up of images (of places and characters and of stories). The appearance of these elements in myths can cross over into policy because they have enormous power to generate our identity and, in particular, to affect our understanding of who is inside and

[65] *ibid*, 453.

[66] *ibid*, 505.

[67] *ibid*, 464.

[68] 'Presidential Powers', 26 April 2006, Center for Law and Security at NYU School of Law (Suzanne Spaulding).

[69] R Slotnick, *Gunfighter Nation* (University of Oklahoma Press, 1992).

outside the national group, the relationship between the individual and the state, and the role of the state, especially with respect to its enemies.

In America's nationhood, the original mythological struggle was simultaneously against the wilderness and its wild inhabitants (think of Native Indians) and marauding oppressive civilisation (think of the British). In this original myth, the American hero was a character who could use what he knew of both savagery and civilisation to fend them off, encapsulating in his character the American *via media*, or fusion of enemies presented as terrifying barbarism and oppressive government. In the industrial and immigration phase, the enemy was redefined as the urban savage, where again, the hero had access to their thoughts and ways, and was able to use this inside knowledge to suppress them. The hero is a vigilante cop or streetwise detective, standing on the border of law and disorder. He acts outside the law to defeat outlaws. After World War II, when the United States became a world power, American citizenship was tweaked to include new ethnicities. Consequently, the heroic figures were members of mixed race platoons, who would defend the United States and its utopic dream, against two enemies, the Japanese (represented as savage sameness) and Nazis (representing hyperorderly destructive sameness).

These myths are cumulative, contributing together to the America of today, but some elements feature throughout. They are what Slotnick calls the 'permanent heritage'. First, American story-telling favours a bias towards violent solution rather than negotiation or persuasion. Second, the violence, in order to be effective, is 'transgressive'; that is, the victorious hero is a white man who knows Indian ways, a representative of enlightenment who knows the dark side, a policeman who bends the rules, or a dark knight. The hero appropriates the villain's power, becoming what he fights. And he always has to act independently; he cannot succeed or save the world by toeing the line, filing warrants or abiding by the rules. Third, the conflicts involve ultimate stakes. They are Manichean. Fourth, in every genre, there is always an enemy of a different composition or complexion. Race remains a polarising factor in US culture. Finally, and most importantly, victory is not possible without this transgression: in the words of the Rumsfeld credo, 'the gloves must come off',[70] *il faut opérer en partisan partout oú il y a des partisans.*

Recently, Human Rights First have found that the number of torture scenes on television is significantly higher than it was five years ago and, fascinatingly, that the character who tortures is no longer the 'villain' but the 'good guy'. Torture is encoded as necessary, effective and patriotic.[71] The most successful amalgamation of this mythology is the popular television programme '24', which

[70] 'Rumsfeld "told officers to take the gloves off with Lindh"', *The Independent*, 10 June 2004, available at: www.independent.co.uk/news/world/americas/rumsfeld-told-officers-to-take-gloves-off-with-lindh-731644.html.

[71] Human Rights Watch, 'PrimeTime Torture' (available at: www.humanrightsfirst.org/us_law/etn/primetime/video_ptt.html).

has been called a 'referendum on torture'. But it made for a poor referendum for three reasons. First, its creator, Joel Surnow is a self-anointed 'right-wing nutjob';[72] second, liberals on the show are portrayed as naïve dupes, who fail to appreciate the magnitude of the threat; and third, the show's writers, who, before the sixth series, had never spoken to real interrogators, genuinely thought that torture worked.

How does all this relate to reality? Trained soldiers can, of course, under normal circumstances be relied upon to distinguish between reality and fiction. Part of the problem with the Bush administration was its insistence that we were facing a new enemy, and that the fight required abnormal measures. Tony Lagouranis, an Iraq veteran and interrogator, reports, in a chilling testimony, that, naturally, he was drilled in the Geneva Conventions and knew that when a prisoner of war was uncooperative they should not suffer any negative repercussions, that coercion was out of bounds.[73] However, when he arrived in Iraq, he received new rules of interrogation from the Pentagon, stating that the Conventions did not apply to Iraqi detainees. The prohibition on maltreatment was thrown out of the window, and the new protocol listed techniques which were acceptable forms of interrogation, including the usage of dogs, stress positions, hypothermia, isolation, sensory deprivation and overload – all banned by the pre-existing military code.

This was, of course, extremely dangerous advice, because the military had no training in the usage of such coercion. Worse still, Lagouranis relates how the most shocking feature of the Pentagon protocol was that it was open-ended and expressly stipulated that the interrogator have the freedom to be 'creative'. The world of fantasy conflict was thus allowed to surge into a real war, with disastrous results. He said that the things 'we conjured up' came directly from entertainment, including water-boarding, electrocution and mock-executions. He saw these things with his 'own eyes'.

Lagouranis explains that the military did not request the usage of torture; nor did the FBI. In experiments, the CIA had found it more likely to produce falsehood than helpful information. The staggeringly reckless instruction that military officers 'get creative' came from 'civilian leadership'. Importantly, Lagouranis is dismissive of the utility of torture, even in the ticking bomb situation. He claims that, yes, torture can successfully extract confessions (true or false) but it is always backward-looking. This cannot be described as intelligence, which must be forward-looking to avert disaster. In a ticking bomb situation, he explains, the detainee can, simply by furnishing the interrogator with a false location, send his captors on a wild goose chase, ensuring that the ticking bomb explodes, undiscovered and untouched.

[72] 'We're trafficking in fear', *The Guardian*, 22 January 2007, available at: www.guardian.co.uk/media/2007/jan/22/television.mondaymediasection.

[73] '24: Torture Televised', 21 March 2007, New York School of Law Center for Law and Security.

Slotnik's analysis and Lagouranis' testimony help us understand how American political life is perverted by its mythological heroes and villains, how fiction spilled over into the reality of the Iraq conflict, and how a constituency for torture silently amassed on the back of popular entertainment. But the role of fiction in generating American public ideals is perhaps less troubling than the fictions created by American officials. Reference has already been made to the falsehoods promulgated by the Bush administration.[74] Torture is perhaps the best example. On the occasion of the International Day in Support of Victims of Torture, on 26 June 2003, then President Bush claimed that 'the US is committed to the worldwide elimination of torture and we are leading this fight by example'. On the same day, William Schulz of Amnesty International, and 11 other organisations commented in a public letter that 'the welcome message that the Bush administration has sent today would be reinforced if it granted full access to independent human rights monitors to assure the world that this pledge is being fully redeemed in practice'.[75] The reader will remember that confirmation of just how fully that pledge was being fulfilled came shortly thereafter, when it was discovered that, five months after Bush's statement, Manadel al-Jamadi was tortured so brutally that he died in the US-run Abu Ghraib detention centre, his legs pulpified by the intensity of the beatings.

The Bush administration deceived the international community and the American people, many of whom still cannot accept that America tortures, but it also committed the worst perfidy of all by deceiving itself.[76] Such deception results in perverse doctrines. Richard Posner, one of the most respected judges and academics in American history, tells us that France, the United Kingdom and Israel have all recently resorted to the use of torture to extract information, yet none is a country that has descended into barbarism. He claims that

> civilized nations are able to employ uncivilized means, at least in situations of or closely resembling war, without becoming uncivilized in the process. I suspect this is particularly true when the torture is being administered by military personnel in a foreign country.[77]

Indeed, Posner's idea is not foreign to the British. Though the House of Lords used emphatic terms to denounce the use of torture to procure information, a Member of Parliament, David Davis, says he has seen 'compelling evidence' that the government outsourced torture.[78] I do not follow Posner's reasoning. Surely, a country that uses torture has no claim to civility, irrespective of the particular

[74] Center for Public Integrity, 'Report on Falsehood in the Bush Administration'.

[75] R Wilde, 'Legal "Black Hole"? Extraterritorial State Action and International Treaty Law on Civil and Political Rights' (2005) 26 *Michigan Journal of International Law* 739.

[76] F Dostoevsky, *The Brothers Karamazov* (Barnes and Noble, 1995, [1880]) 50.

[77] R Posner, 'Torture, Terrorism and Interrogation' in S Levinson (ed), *Torture: A collection* (Oxford University Press, 2004).

[78] 'MP claims UK outsourced torture', BBC News, 8 July 2009, available at: news.bbc.co.uk/2/hi/uk_news/8139622.stm.

henchman it chooses to mete out the torture, and irrespective of the location of the torture chamber. His suggestion that citizens of a country can be civilised if they endorse torture by military personnel in a foreign country is incoherent. Rather than being civilised, such citizens are not only cowards, because they want torture to be conducted out-of-sight and out-of-mind, but they are hypocrites too, because they attempt to preserve a veneer of civility at home whilst endorsing the worst imaginable brutality abroad. Hence, rather than finding a brilliant jurisprudential solution, were a democracy to adopt the Posnerian scheme, it could be charged with cowardice, hypocrisy and brutality to boot. Torturing abroad is *worse* than torturing at home because it implies an attempt to avoid accountability. So, having spent a life in American law, Posner counsels the sort of administrative impunity typical of tyranny and institutionalised criminality. Of course, a society *can* legalise torture (though by doing so, it might well precipitate the end of the rule of law), but contrary to Posner's nonsensical suggestion, a society can only be civilised if it criminalises torture and consistently punishes torturers.

Furthermore, in the context of the present war on 'terrorist-tyranny' and 'Islamic-fascists', fought, according to Bush, for 'human rights' and to 'liberate the people of Iraq' from an 'evil dictator' who had 'torture chambers', Posner's suggestion is especially odious. One would forgive Iraqis for scepticism about the benefits of American rule, for they simply replaced one set of torturers with another. Despite what Posner seems to think, torture does not magically become normatively laudable because it is ostensibly done in the name of democracy. It is still a form of punishment that no criminal could ever legally receive in the American justice system, and what is worse, it is administered before finding that the victim has committed any crime. Posner's theory that torture abroad is compatible with civilised liberal democracy at home is an uncommon feat of jurisprudential gymnastics.

Perhaps fear motivated this turn to tyranny, the academic attempt to scrabble desperately for justifications for the atrocities of Abu Ghraib and Guantánamo Bay. Herman Goering, Hitler's designated successor and commander of the *Luftwaffe*, argued that bringing the people to 'the bidding of the leaders' was easy. 'All you have to do is tell them they are being attacked and denounce the pacifists for lack of patriotism and exposing the country to danger. It works the same in any country'.[79] If we allow the spectre of oblivion at the hands of nuclear terrorists to dominate our horizon, inhibiting rational thought and suppressing our collective conscience, we will consign ourselves to ill-considered and immoral policies, run by governments for which a permanent state of exception becomes the rule.

[79] Quote from an interview in his prison cell in G Gilbert, *Nuremberg Diary* (Da Capo Press, 1995).

To avoid such a fate, we ought to consult our history books and, without drawing false analogies, use the written records of parliamentary wrangling and judicial review to our advantage, to prevent us from toppling in the future into the pitfalls of the past. I want to consider a single story from America and Britain's shared history, which illustrates the sort of public disposition, appreciation for civic duty, and relationship between necessity and legality I have been trying to describe.

Before recounting this tale, it is worth setting the scene. Richard Falkenrath does not like government to be criticised from armchairs. He argues, in defence of the Bush administration that the 'President and his policy makers do not have the luxury of academics and editorial writers of simply criticizing something and walking away'.[80] It is true that the role of the academic and the role of a political leader are very different. However, rather than 'walking away', there are lots of options for members of the Bush administration, for instance, admitting costly mistakes, apologising for serial falsehood, paying compensation to victims of misdirected American aggression, accepting responsibility for wasting time, blood and treasure in Iraq, resigning from politics, and submitting to international criminal jurisdiction. These actions, however, seem to be out of the question for the Bush administration which worked hard to ensure, not that its officials were accountable, but that they enjoy immunity from prosecution at least in the United States. For Rumsfeld, Yoo, Bybee and Gonzales, this means thinking twice about travelling to Germany, where they are wanted on war crimes charges.[81] It is a quirk of international law that the lawsuit originated with energetic constitutional lawyers in New York City, who chose Germany because its legal system provides for universal jurisdiction for war crimes. Even the complainants' lawyers readily admit that the likelihood of Rumsfeld et al appearing in a German court are dwindling. However, as well as marginalising the American officials, such suits serve to highlight the shortcomings of the international legal order. Until there is agreement on universally forbidden means (however lofty the purported goals), instances of international justice are doomed to be fitful, politicised and impotent.

That is the backdrop. The story I want to tell is of the Battle of New Orleans, or rather what happened in its aftermath. On 24 December 1814, the Treaty of Ghent officially ended the Anglo-American war. However, tragically, in their ignorance of peace the troops continued to fight into the New Year. In January 1815, General Andrew Jackson, 'Old Hickory', led an American army to a resounding victory against a numerically superior British force in the Battle of

[80] DS Hamilton, *Terrorism and international relations* (Calouste Gulbenkian Foundation; Center for Transatlantic Relations, Paul H Nitze School of Advanced International Studies, Johns Hopkins University, 2006) 192.

[81] '12 detainees sue Rumsfeld in Germany, citing abuse', *New York Times*, 14 November 2006, available at: www.nytimes.com/2006/11/15/world/europe/15german.html?_r=1&scp=3&sq=rumsfeld%20war%20crimes&st=cse.

New Orleans. Parenthetically, the battle seems to have been lost as much by the incompetent British attempt to traverse the terrain on the banks of the Mississippi as it was won by American strategy. Jackson did well out of it, going on to become the 7th President of the Union.

The interesting point for present purposes stems from what happened shortly after the battle. The victorious General, fearing a recrudescence of British hostilities, subjected New Orleans to martial law until 13 March. A state law-maker anonymously challenged this decision in a public letter to the press. Jackson compelled the release of his name and had him arrested for espionage. When a judge issued a writ of habeas corpus, Jackson had him arrested too, on a charge of 'exciting mutiny', and then, when a district attorney attempted to liberate the judge, Jackson had *him* interned too.

When Jackson belatedly heard of the Treaty of Ghent, he had his prisoners released. The District Attorney was not satisfied at the mere restoration of his liberty, and brought a charge of contempt of court against Jackson, which, in light not only of Jackson's pugnacity but also his own six-year stint on the bench of the Tennessee Supreme Court, was quite a bold move. Predictably, Jackson made a rousing speech, defending his actions by reference to necessity, but – and this is the crucial point – said he would 'submit cheerfully to the operation of the laws even when they punished actions taken to preserve them'.[82]

The coda to this story is that on 6 December 1844, Charles Ingersoll of Pennsylvania introduced a bill, which Congress approved, to refund to Jackson, with interest, the $1000 fine imposed on him 30 years earlier by the District Judge of Louisiana. Stephen Douglas, in his first major congressional address, denounced the decision of Louisiana's Dominick Hall J as 'unjust, irregular and illegal' and defended the handsome repayment of Jackson in colourful terms:

> Every unlawful act is not necessarily a contempt of court. Talk not to me about rules and forms in court, when the enemy's cannon are pointed at the door, and flames encircle the cupola! … I admire that elevation of soul which rises above all personal considerations, and, regardless of consequences, stakes life and honour and glory upon the issue, when the salvation of the country depends on the result.[83]

Douglas, in my view, is woefully wrong and on several counts. By elaborating these counts, I will, hopefully be able to demonstrate why I think this story is so important.

First, though these are mere factual quibbles, when Jackson began interning law-makers and banishing judges, no cannons were pointing at the courthouse door, and the cupola was not on fire. The war was over, though his martial rule endured.

[82] IB Wuerth, 'The President's Power to Detain "Enemy Combatants": Modern Lessons From Mr Madison's Forgotten War' (2003–04) 98 *Northwestern University Law Review* 1567, 1613.

[83] R Johannsen, *Stephen A Douglas* (University of Illinois Press, 1997) 129–30.

Second, like Douglas, I too admire those who make personal sacrifices for the public good. Such people are rightly regarded as heroes. The problem with the congressional repayment of the fine was that it retroactively stripped Jackson's submission to the laws of any heroic quality, by undoing his sacrifice.

Third, Hall J's judgment against Jackson was not unjust, or irregular, or illegal. Taking these in turn, it is unclear whether the decision was unjust. Jackson locked up respectable members of American society on charges of espionage merely because they questioned whether there was any enduring need for martial law. By any measure, that was an overreaction deserving of reprimand. Dissent is not treason, and critique is not mutiny. Next, it is hard to see the decision as irregular. On the contrary, after a period of significant unrest, involving the tearing up of social fabric, the fine can be seen as restoring regularity and repairing the material that holds us together. Jackson's actions, as Jackson admitted, were irregular. The judgment against him represented normal service resumed. Further, it is unclear how a tribunal's hearing, and a judge's solemn rendering of a verdict can possibly be described as illegal. Such things are the very stuff of law.

Fourthly, the President at the time of General Jackson's actions, James Madison, considered the rather overzealous ongoing defence of New Orleans justified, but not necessarily lawful. This approach, it is submitted, is infinitely preferable to the loose rhetoric of Mr Douglas. I would like to occupy a few lines explaining why.

Jackson's submission to legal punishment for breaking the laws of the legal order his transgressions were intended to protect was august. It does not follow from the proposition that he acted in a moral way that his actions were or must have been legal. Indeed, according to a sophisticated understanding of morality we can maintain two propositions. One, it was moral for Jackson to stay on guard, and exercise the extreme caution which informed the administrative detention of the lawmaker, judge and attorney. Two, it was moral for the judge to punish this act, when the purported crisis had passed. There is nothing odd about Jackson's actions being both necessary and illegal, moral and unlawful.

In order to explain this better, let us apply it to the nightmarish, fantastical and now infamous, ticking bomb scenario, which is said to justify torture. If a suspected terrorist in police custody admits having planted a bomb in a New York subway, but declines to give up its location, and a police officer, stricken with the thought of countless casualties, stamps viciously on the suspect's feet in order to ascertain the whereabouts of the device, that act might be described as morally preferable to letting numerous New Yorkers die. It might be called a necessary action, given the exigencies of the situation. However, the police officer has broken the law. It is perfectly consistent with the assertion that it was right for him to do so, for us to punish him after the event for an illegal act and for us to allow the suspected terrorist to seek compensation against the state.

In this way, legality survives necessity rather than being trumped by it. The police officer can 'cheerfully submit' to the laws, in the knowledge that society gratefully disapproves of his self-sacrifice. The rupture in the legal order caused by the pressures of necessity is repaired by the reparation of the suspect and the punishment of the police officer. If we allow necessity to trump legality, if we say, necessity knows no law the legal order becomes a slave to purported emergency. On the other hand, if we punish actions taken in dire straits, legality is preserved, respect for the law is ensured, and the integrity of the legal order is defended. It is precisely this integrity that is missing from Douglas' speech, Posner's suggestion that we delegate torture, and the British-American alliance today.

The greatest handicap in jurisprudential thought about law and terror, particularly in international law, is the fallacious presumption that the necessity of an action must entail its legality or, in other words, its legal permissibility or excusability. (Here, lawfulness and legal permissibility or excusability are intended to signify the same thing. Put simply, if something is not impermissible, it must be permissible.) On the contrary, it is entirely coherent to say, 'yes I had to do it, to preserve the state, save lives, fight terrorism and so forth, but it was illegal *and* I should be punished for it'. This is to sustain that my act was morally necessary but so is my punishment. This is not Draconian, radical or Rhadamanthine, nor is it new. Davis J expressed his rejection of necessity's law in the following terms, which resonate today:

> Time has proven the discernment of our ancestors … Those great and good men foresaw that troublous times would arise, when rulers and people would become restive under restraint, and seek by sharp and decisive measures to accomplish ends deemed just and proper; and that the principles of constitutional liberty would be in peril, unless established by irrepealable law… No doctrine involving more pernicious consequences, was ever invented by the wit of man than that any of its provisions can be suspended during any of the great exigencies of government … Such a doctrine leads directly to anarchy or despotism, but the theory of necessity on which it is based is false; for the government, within the Constitution, has all the powers granted to it, which are necessary to preserve its existence.[84]

Davis exhibits the sort of faith in the American constitutional system that Bush lacks. But how can restrictions on the executive power to respond in a crisis be useful? Remember the golf swing. An uncontrolled swing delivers less power than one with perfect form. Intelligent restrictions on governmental discretion to restrict the liberty of its citizens improve general security by fortifying the relationship between government and governed. They do so by ensuring that the governed are on the side of the government. Only this solidarity can truly secure a state.

Davis had an aversion to extra-legal space. He considered that American laws could cope in all situations and, conversely, that non- or extra-legal space is bound to accommodate tyranny. However, at any given time the law might be unclear. Indeed, it is in constant flux, as it warps to fit convention. This flux is

[84] *Ex parte Milligan* 71 US 2 (4 Wall) 121 (1866).

evident in the discursive practice of law and in the elaboration of law in the language and actions of officials, leaders and judges. That said, according to the theory espoused here, the law, though it might change and mutate, is constant. There simply are no black holes. Rather, there are unspoken rules that provide for the immunity of dungeon administrators. Guantánamo Bay did not exist in an airlock. To say it did is too comforting a conclusion for lawyers in a democracy. It allows them to avoid countenancing that torture chambers were tacitly approved of by a so-called civilised country. The barking dogs, frequent-flying, water-boarding and Palestinian-hanging which characterised American interrogative technique were *legal* measures. They must have been, for they went on largely unchecked and unpunished. Anything that is not illegal is, by definition, legal. And until those responsible are arraigned before a tribunal of collective repentance, Guantánamo will continue to enjoy lawful character. Depending on how society reacts, these acts might become illegal in the future or it might be determined that they were illegal at the time.

There is nothing in iniquity that is incompatible with law. Only squeamish theorists conclude that a military dictatorship cannot make laws, or that the Nazi regime did not legislate for the persecution of the Jews, or that the Bush administration did not rule that torture and assassination was legal. Such jurists, who assert that law is always right and true and kind and just – that it cannot contemplate torture or indefinite detention or indiscriminate killing – are like surgeons who faint at the sight of blood.

Above I mentioned that prior to the Iraq invasion, a violent, perverse fiction combining the most terrifying elements of tyranny and terrorism was allowed to refute the simple truth. Allott predicted something of the sort, casting an interesting light on religion.

> There is always the danger that the unreal reality of art may overwhelm the rest of the reality-made-by-consciousness and generate a world of fantasy, alienation, mental abnormality. In the art of mass entertainment, perfected in the twentieth century through the concentration and application of great quantities of social energy, there lies the danger of mass hallucination, a danger quite as great as the mass alienation which may be caused by religion.[85]

If modern entertainment represents an apotheosis of human beings, in preference to religious characters, are its idols ideal? And, are we not setting our sights a little low if we pander to those who spend their lives pandering to us? The essential point is that all of us live in a story in which our role is that of writer, narrator and protagonist. In that story, notions of the ideal form must be created with care, for the simple reason that man cannot be better than the ideal version of himself, and society 'cannot be better than its idea of itself'.[86] This point recalls the issue I touched upon earlier about the generation of the divine.

[85] P Allott, *Eunomia: new order for a new world* (Oxford University Press, 1990) 98.
[86] *ibid*, 298.

Irrespective of whether or not sublime form can exist independently of the human mind (whether it is an inner luminescence or external illumination), the retention of an imperfect idea of the perfect is crucial to our growth, as it resists earthly claims of perfect truth and justice.

The newspapers have a lead role in the creation of our world and our ideals. For present purposes (law generation in a liberal democracy), this means two things. First, they ought to be owned by diverse and independent actors. Second, they should be free of both undue governmental influence, and yet – and this requires governmental influence – immune to the totalising pressures of the market. Getting this balance wrong will result in a degeneration of the quality of what we read, and by extension, what we think, leading to the vicious circle of apathy. In America, the Bush war machine was fuelled by sensationalist, pro-government, nationalist reporting. Fortunately, this was counteracted by some intrepid, brave and incisive individual journalism.

The newspapers are a window to the world and, it has been argued here, that cultural aperture is vital to reducing the appeal of terrorism. The potentially microscopic nature of terrorist organisations and the massive, low-budget destructive power at their disposal are two very good reasons for an open society, where information flows freely, and where those with truculent natures feel at liberty to express themselves politically, not violently: first so that they can be assuaged by their more moderate contemporaries; and second, so that the government gives itself the chance to get wind of pyrotechnic plans before they explode. The sort of aperture described here will allow the public to defend *itself*, taking pressure off the government to deliver ambiguously defined undeliverables like security and freedom.

Another way for government to defend itself, and to preserve its power, by restraining that power is to invest in good relations with other states. John Ikenberry argues that: 'If American policy makers want to perpetuate America's preeminent position, they will need to continue to find ways to operate within international institutions, and by so doing restrain that power and make it acceptable to other states'.[87] The approach of the Bush administration was diametrically opposed to this advice. As Holmes observed,

> the federal executive … expanded its originally limited constitutional permission to repel surprise attacks, without Congressional approval, into an 'inherent power' to unleash military force in response to actual injuries or imagined threats to American interests, as the president unilaterally defines them, anywhere in the world.[88]

So, contrary to Kagan's assertion that America can 'go it alone' (probably an assertion whispered in the ear of many a tragic leader), according to the more grounded approach of Holmes or Ikenberry, power restrained is less offensive

[87] G Ikenberry, *After Victory* (Princeton Paperbacks, 2001) 258.

[88] S Holmes, *The Matador's Cape: America's Reckless Response to Terror* (Cambridge University Press, 2007) 295.

and therefore less likely to incite resentment or provoke attack. It has more chance of enduring. The latter theories certainly sound more plausible, and less like hubris. Furthermore, as we noted, Kagan asserts that Americans sought legitimacy for their actions abroad in their own parochial principles. Would it not be more fitting for a country intent on playing a 'grand role on the world stage' to pay heed to the interests and canvass the values of those for whom it purports to act? Listening to voices of dissent strengthens a democratic government, at home and abroad. By ignoring them, it prepares its own demise.

Our immediate task, then, is to reinvigorate democracy, and in so doing, rein in and reclaim economic and hegemonic monsters, so that they render easier not harder the distribution of abundant supply to desperate need. Intelligent investment is not in battlefield nuclear weaponry, but in facilitating world-over the provision of the simple stuff, vital and sufficient for human happiness. To do this, the British and Americans alike must turn their insides out, that is, rediscover themselves, and recall how to align the natural world with their needs and wants, without presumptuously taking from others. This may sound like a difficult and obscure project, but solace can be taken from the axiom that the human world is both prior to and ultimately beyond the control of governments. The choice is ours alone.

10

Legality and Brutality

The administration of law and force need never be at odds with the manner of a gentleman.[1]

BY CONSIDERING VARIOUS dynamics of the British-American attempt to fight terrorism, I have attempted to argue that the law is best thought of as coercion, approved prior to, subsequent to, or in the absence of, its exercise by power. It is hoped that if law is considered in this way, the tendency of our democratic societies, when faced with a significant threat, to descend into barbarism can be arrested. In the attempt to determine not what the laws are, but what the law is (in a liberal democracy) and how it comes about, the aim here was to suggest what the law ought to be, and how it ought to come about. The questions were: What constitutes law? And how ought law be constituted?

The context of our response to terrorism was chosen for this investigation, because it seems to challenge law; that is, terrorism has provoked something of an identity crisis (pardon the cliché) in Britain and America. This constitutional panic is, I argue, best viewed as an opportunity to reassess who we are, what our society is all about, and how that is expressed through our laws. As a consequence of this approach, much of this discussion – which invokes pragmatism, moral philosophy, psychology, history and theology – might not, on the surface, have seemed to be about law(s) at all. It was, however, at a deeper level, on the phenomenological plane always concerned with how law is generated and, secondarily, how it ought to be generated in a liberal democracy true to its deep ideals. Whether by omission or inclusion, our identity is encoded in our laws and, as a consequence, our identity can be made out from our laws, as our laws make out our identity.

At the outset, I suggest a hard-edged notion of law conjuring up notions of bailiffs, bullets and prison bars. Nevertheless, it is not as steely as it might initially appear. The power necessary for coercion to qualify as law comes from people, their reasons, instincts and emotions. Law might emanate from the silent acquiescence of an apathetic public, intoxicated and awestruck by military force

[1] This is a paraphrase of the *Times* correspondent's comment in Cape Town in 1901, where the British had herded women and children into concentration camps where one in three died of disease or as a result of poor sanitation. For the original, see N Ferguson, *The War of the World* (Allen Lane, 2006) 7.

or bent on revenge. It might radiate from the sheer numbers of people convinced by, and prepared to defend, an attractive-sounding philosophical proposition. As a result, the seemingly steely concept of law, though it makes room for the brutally oppressive laws of a dictator, also happily accommodates laws originating in our enchantment with aesthetic ideals, such as equality, opulence, liberty and justice.

It could be argued that I am defending a promiscuous breed of law, a harlot, who is just as comfortable in the court of cruel tyrants as she is in the service of benevolent prime ministers. Such criticism seems cheap. Though she might be a harlot, the species of law I am defending facilitates honesty, bravery and prudence. This can hopefully be demonstrated by reference to recent history.

By adopting this concept of law, we can be *honest* about the hollow nature of the promises made by America and Britain; in particular, by distinguishing law proper (administrative detention centres, extraordinary rendition, and other such invidious institutions) from political rhetoric and throwaway constitutional guarantees (prohibitions on torture, and bonds of fair treatment). With this concept, we can be *brave* enough to own the tyrannical methods we adopted, and to admit that, yes, torture, rather than being unlawful, was part of our law for a time. It is *prudent* for us to think of law in this way, not so we endorse these controversial means (as professed realists contend is necessary). On the contrary, an essentialist concept of law and its phenomenology helps us understand how such brutality surreptitiously stole into our strategy. The frank accommodation of iniquitous rules in the concept of law puts the burden on us to exert social power to ensure that such rules are not endorsed. Furthermore, it was argued that, contrary to received wisdom, we need not become monstrous to fight monsters; that morality and self-interest, military expediency and humanitarian considerations are in harmonious concert more often that might initially appear.

Here, it is worth pre-empting another possible (and I think flawed) rejoinder. It is claimed immediately above, that torture was *part of our law* for a time, and yet this seems inconsistent with the assertions made throughout the argument, that, apart from being of dubious utility and immoral, torture is *unlawful* (pursuant to various universally accepted rules of international law). Of course, superficially, torture cannot be both lawful and unlawful (and, for that matter, the ban on torture cannot be 'universally accepted' if it is still such a popular practice). But this rejoinder, this contention that there is contradiction in these pages, overlooks the function of 'power' in the definition of law suggested here, and misses the role of all of us as *vivus lapis*, as constituent elements of the law as written, spoken and applied.

As a result, the rejoinder, far from scoring a point against me, makes my point *for* me. I assert that if we fail to object to the practice of torture, if those tortured go unheard and torturers go unpunished, then torture is, in matter of fact, permissible and permitted. By claiming (as I enthusiastically do in the case of torture) that something ought to be illegal, depending on the cogency, appeal and energy of my claim, I add force to the proposition that it *really* is illegal, and therefore help to imbue the prohibition of torture with the character of law. Laws become laws in this way. The reason that this rejoinder fails is that our statements about what the law is cannot sensibly be separated from what the law becomes. From this position, I take the short step to arguing, as I did in the foregoing chapter, that we have a moral obligation to register our objections to pernicious governmental practices. By doing so, we exert the sort of social power that a norm needs before we can assume that it will be actively enforced and not simply honoured in the breach; tacitly affirmed by a society's silence.

No attempt will be made here to summarise the conclusions already reached. This has been a long discussion, because, more than merely furnishing a definition, I have tried to describe a certain disposition to the law. Here, in order to portray that disposition, it will perhaps suffice if I collect the quintessential messages of each chapter. I began by asserting that description is prescription. Thus, the categorisation of a conflict can affect the legal register applied to it, and by extension, can influence the outcome of the conflict itself. Words contain enormous potential: misdescription results in policy misfires, and yet, if our politicians can accurately describe conditions, we can expect them to legislate intelligently too.

The definition of law I proffer, though it accommodates international laws that can be enforced (however complex the machinery of enforcement), it excludes many international norms for the simple reason that they are not backed by force. However, international norms are valuable in their capacity as persuasive descriptions of moral aspirations, which generate the social power necessary to vouchsafe law. I have described some international rules, so-called soft laws, some human rights conventions and harmonising measures as guidelines; standing invitations to state self-limitation and betterment, which might in time mature into laws proper. I also reject the concept of legal plurality, understood here as the idea that many conflicting laws can contemporaneously apply to one situation. Though the true law might need to be discovered, there can only be one effective, enforceable rule for any given scenario. However, there is no dispute here with the proposition that there might be competing claims as to what that law is. This is law's dynamism, its capacity for change, its promise and its discursive nature. The ways in which we think, talk and act are also modes of law-making.

Images, like words, are immensely powerful, particularly given the ubiquity of modern media. Our laws and policies send messages that cannot be refuted by mere diplomatic platitudes. By insisting on a neutral definition of terrorism that focuses on *forbidden means* without concern for *ends*, there is a greater likelihood of international agreement. For what it is worth, the definition of terrorism suggested here, hopefully free of hypocrisy, baggage and confusion, reads: 'Terrorism is premeditated, politically motivated aggression perpetrated against a non-combatant or non-combatants, intended to influence an audience'.

Another aspect of the power of images is their ability to incarcerate our consciousness. It would seem that the quality of our laws depends on resisting the instinct to submit to the allures of brute force, and it is a strong instinct—leaders who commit genocide are more likely to remain in power than go to prison.[2] In the last seven years, British and American people largely failed to call for evidence, temperance and rationality, blinded or distracted as they were by the arresting aesthetics of military might and tempted by the alluring qualities of egomaniacal ideas like promoting democracy.

According to the definition of law preferred here, law is not drowned out by the drums of war: necessity does not trump legality. On the contrary, law is constant, though it might be unclear at any one time what the law is. Indeed, the kernel of crime in war and peacetime is the same—indiscriminating or excessive force. Furthermore, since military expediency and humanitarian considerations marry so happily, rules about the legitimate use of force can be drafted, on which all reasonable actors, military and civilian, can agree. I do believe that unreasonableness is at the roots of the tangled disputes on the definition of terrorism. Gains can be made by thinking about the legitimacy of force based on self-defence and proportionality, independently of the crude philosophical distinction between war and peace.

It was argued that liberty is empty of value and security is impossible, making neither concept a particularly helpful policy prop. Furthermore, when considered together it would seem wrong to assume that the sacrifice of liberty is necessary to ensure national security. On the contrary, the protection of people's liberties, both at home and abroad, is the state's best safeguard against insurrection and invasion. This might seem counter-intuitive but in our attempts to understand humans and human relations, and therefore in law- and policy-making too, our rationality can only take us so far. Particularly in our interactions with others, rational analyses must, at times, capitulate to emotional explanations: '*Es ist immer etwas Wahnsinn in der Liebe. Es ist aber immer auch etwas Vernunft im Wahnsinn*'. ('There is always madness in love. But there is always also reason in madness'.) An argument I repeated over and over was that moral action is no sacrifice, for it will, sooner or later, redound to our benefit. Conversely, laws based on ruthless self-interest tend to be self-defeating.

Rather than singing the praises of secularism, we ought to acknowledge and counteract the institutional intolerance of secret ballots by reinvigorating the adversarial traditions of democracy, and remembering the values informing our endorsement of this political system in the first place: equality, agency and solidarity. British and American citizens, accustomed to the structural selfishness of liberal democracy, have proved themselves capable of showing a flagrant disregard for the plight of others, making for laws and policies which, rather than securing order, provoke disorder, hatred and resentment. The greater our capacity for empathy, for understanding competing claims, the greater are the chances for efficient and peaceable administration of world affairs. Only an

[2] See generally S Power, *A Problem from Hell* (Basic Books, 2002).

empathetic, interpretive ability of individuals, stretching *beyond* sympathy for the liberal democratic ideal, can insulate our societies from flammable misunderstandings.

The desire for revenge, coupled with the almost belligerent refusal to comprehend the possible motivations for why we are hated led to self-defeating policies. In the context of Islamist terrorism, we are not facing an irrational, implacable, incomprehensible enemy. Rather, there is little, if anything, in other cultures that cannot be traced in our own, and, notwithstanding the uniqueness of persons, there is seldom an act of another that cannot be understood by a similar impulse in the self. Architects of torture and administrative detention seem to forget that we ought to treat others with respect and the proper decorum not only because it is right, but because, if we fail to do so, we create a precedent that might in an undistant future be applied to us. It was contended here that our efforts should be to create a world community of tolerant pluralism limited by a shared commitment to renounce the usage of certain means to push political agendas; where any version of the good can be propagated subject to limits on the acceptable modes of its propagation. It was suggested that this version of procedural pluralism could help forge a common human political and jurisprudential bond on the anvil of an international criminal law, which enjoins a wholesale repudiation of aggression and indiscriminating violence.

That jurisprudential bond can only be wrought by wrestling our own proclivities as well as accepting those of other cultures. The mere possibility that the coercive interrogation of detainees might have more to do with cathartic, revanchist perversion than the procurement of information useful to the counter-terrorist operation ought to alert us to the porosity of our constitutions to thuggery. I dealt with emotion herein because it is as much (if not more) of an energetic policy-maker as reason. Further, empathy is not exhausted by understanding another, but also includes understanding his understanding of you. When urges most base appear to drive law and policy, it is no wonder that regard for Britain and America has turned from reverence to revulsion in much of the Islamic world, which includes Britain and America. Better that we confront our darker inclinations lest they steal undetected into our legal order, resulting in institutionalised brutality inimical to the promises we make to ourselves, and causing the resentful, brooding umbrage that overspreads terrorism to dilate and darken.

Of course, brutality, putting our foot on the neck of our enemies and snapping it as a deterrent, has its visceral appeal, but these tactics are, in truth, traps. If we defile the liberal democratic order with measures more traditionally associated with the enemies we set out to fight, we leave nothing of ourselves worth defending. Similarly, the leaders of our society in politics and the media should resist the temptation to respond to terror by cynically suppressing our wisdom and ethical sensibilities. Our rulers should desire respect given freely, not the base raptures of a citizenry enslaved by the aesthetic arrest of terrifying force and fear of arbitrarily exercised power. This is the utility of an understanding of law that is candid about power's origins: it reveals that fidelity to laws backed by brutality is, in reality, a form of slavery; it is legality's collapse into barbarism and a far cry from the civility we are purporting to espouse in Afghanistan and Iraq.

The quality of law and policy in liberal democracies depends on the vitality of the public discourse informing decision-making. That discourse is thwarted by the perverse political mendacity pioneered by the Bush administration, jeopardised by the mere existence of torture, and undermined by the creation of administrative impunity for wayward officials. We know this from our experience of how democracies react to crises—we have archives crammed full of precious guidance in the form of legal, parliamentary and congressional records. To dispatch our time-honoured principles in a fight against any enemy, however ferocious, is to cast hard-earned wisdom to the wind, and install populist ignorance in its place.

But courage is needed for us to uphold the integrity of our laws, and with it, the respectability of our societies. We are animated narrators of the living history of our world. We are products and makers of the new international community. Our most insignificant sounding utterances and most prosaic of deeds and omissions constitute the laws. We imagine forms of the divine and our earthly attempts to emulate that form must be unrelenting but humbled by the knowledge that though we might strive for justice, it will never be up-thrown in our rickety, man-made institutional monuments. And yet, we constitute the divine and are a constituent part thereof. In Ivan Karamazov's delirious conversation with the devil, he chides Satan in the following terms: 'You just repeat what I am thinking. You are incapable of saying anything original'.[3] Dostoevsky's point is that, God or no God, Devil or no Devil, all good and evil on earth relies on manpower. Man's responsibility for everyman is inescapable.

Religion, be it Islam, Christianity or that of any other beneficent book, far from being inimical to democracy, can, in the discursive and humble mode I have described herein, remind us of the duty of self-betterment and the impossibility of self-perfection: it teaches ambition but tempers it with humility. Moreover, like law-making, prayer is a reflective activity, and by praying and legislating we imagine and aspire to a better version of ourselves. The claim that some issues cannot be legislated for, like torture, or targeted killings, or administrative detention, or war, is really just a confession to a lack of imagination or faith in ourselves.

Part of law's loyal instantiation of our inner selves can be seen in the pathologies of the economy. It was argued that, where suffrage is replaced by purchase, public values are destroyed. Where exchange value dominates the human mindset, the intrinsic value of human pleasures and freedoms is subjugated to trade. Governments must regulate markets before markets subordinate governments, but for this to happen, ordinary people must re-appraise their own

[3] F Dostoevsky, *The Brothers Karamazov* (Barnes and Noble, 1995, first published 1880).

choices, by re-evaluating the system that supports those choices. And this re-evaluation can begin with the acknowledgement that a trade based on global capitalism is not the loyal courtier of democracy, but Shakespeare's Iago, a hostile, scheming and unprincely pretender to its throne. The financial turmoil of the past year might not, in the long run, be a bad thing if it forces us to reconsider our relationship to credit.

Our economic interests have had a hand in creating a British-American foreign policy based on the idea that other societies must abide by rules to which neither the Americans nor the British consider themselves bound. But, despite the contrary conviction in some quarters of the American and British academy, a lawless hegemon should not and cannot create and sustain world order. In fact, the existence of a state with imperial pretensions, however well-camouflaged, is an obstacle to the peaceable administration of world affairs because its claims to impunity will be as intolerable to other states as an apparently all-powerful monarch was to the nascent American nation. Implied, symbolic assertions of untrammelled prerogative, such as were made in the global war on terror by means of rendition and targeted killings, invite insurrection and create insecurity for a sovereign. Conversely, power which admits of limits, including the sovereignty of other states, is more likely to endure. It should come as no surprise to former Prime Minister Gordon Brown that the overwhelming majority of serious threats to British security now emanate from or have links to Pakistan, for the Pakistani people have borne the brunt of poorly targeted CIA missile attacks.[4] But, rather than persuading America to stop its encroachments, which might increase British security, Brown elected to pour money into an unstable Pakistani administration, something the Americans have been doing, to no good effect, for decades.

It would appear that the same principle applies within the state. As I argued, just as a brutish golf swing, unrestricted by the strictures of technique, is unlikely to transfer its raw force into a powerful and accurate shot, capricious government, where power rudely exceeds pre-set constitutional parameters, is likely to be weak and ineffective. Furthermore, secrecy, deceit, and the expansion of administrative discretion are to be avoided, as tending to undermine the very powers they are designed to protect. In a liberal democracy, law and policy benefit from discourse, exposure, and a division of powers between the branches of government. Where these factors are absent, a liberal democracy hamstrings its own capacity for detection of errors and self-correction.

Furthermore, congressional or parliamentary reasoning and judicial morality have a symbiotic relationship with journalistic integrity, which itself derives from the ethical disposition of the public man. It is the adversarial interaction between the various organs of power in a democracy that ensures that laws and policies

[4] 'Pact targets terror link', *BBC Online*, 14 December 2008, available at: news.bbc.co.uk/2/hi/uk_news/7782125.stm.

are coherent, well thought out, durable, and in the public interest. When that interaction fails or falters due to judicial pusillanimity, congressional spinelessness or public apathy, liberal democracy, though retained in form, becomes substantially autocratic, replicating the central flaw in oppressive Middle Eastern regimes. The citizen is the first line of defence for a democracy against enemies without and within alike. As Jaspers had it, we are all responsible for the manner in which we are governed.

Our law is as much an instrument of justice as an axe is an instrument of forestry. Both can be wielded for other ends. Torture, though it might be inimical to the liberal democratic conception of legality, can comfortably be accommodated in a legal regime, though it might foretell the disintegration of that regime. But Britain and America can and ought do better. The quality of law depends entirely on the integrity of the people engaged in its administration, from the police officer to the president or prime minister, the soldier to the solicitor, the juror to the judge. Given the public's tendency to react to news of a threat with almost bovine torpor, the academy and the press must act as gadflies, stimulating the common man's ability to exercise his democratic right of critique. The law is our collective responsibility; it can be a testament to our civility, or an indictment of our depravity. Whatever the law is, our responsibility for its content is as inescapable as our responsibility for our conduct.

Being but a solemnisation of society's spoken or unspoken position on varied themes, it has been contended throughout that there is nothing inherently repugnant to law in egregious iniquity. Abu Ghraib, CIA black sites, and Guantánamo Bay are not legal black holes, per Johan Steyn. Rather, they are places that American society at large, tacitly or expressly, has chosen to ignore, with the regrettable consequence that there is an enduring absence of social will to punish official maltreatment of innocent civilians, maladministration which occurring in an American police station would attract serious disciplinary measures. Some brave reporters, courageous film-makers and stoic lawyers stood up against the seemingly overwhelming tide of American indifference which almost succeeded in washing away the indiscretions of the outgoing administration. The conclusion drawn here that law can effortlessly accommodate torture and other horrific practices does not lead us to the result that legality must hearken to necessity's demands. On the contrary, it has been argued that our understanding of the relationship between legality and necessity is enhanced by a realistic appraisal of the enforceability of norms.

If Davis J was wrong that a constitutional democracy has all the means necessary to defend herself, if it is truly necessary in circumstances of the greatest imaginable exigency—I doubt it ever will be—for a member of the executive to violate constitutional law in order to defend the legal order itself, the punishment of that official, when the crisis has passed, has several positive effects. First, it asserts that we are governed by impartial laws not whimsical men. Second, it repairs the rupture in the social fabric occasioned by official malversation, restoring the legal order to its previously untarnished condition. Third, it expresses a more sophisticated understanding of morality and law than the shriek bugling of necessity's supremacy, by asserting that, although it might have been morally correct for the official to transgress the rules of the legal order to protect that order, it is also morally correct to punish him for his transgression. Fourth, it expiates the official for his 'sin' against the legal order he was bound to uphold, restoring him to a state of moral equilibrium, and by imposing a sacrifice, converts a villain to a hero. Finally, it gives voice to society's remorse that it, through the transgressive, illegal act of the officer, departed from its promises to itself.

As Schmitt noted, he who thinks and fights like a partisan, becomes a partisan.[5] But it is neither right nor advantageous to succumb to the siren pathologies of indiscriminate violence. Rather, the most effective counter-terror strategy available is courageous adherence to the tenets of liberal democracy. Nothing terrorists can throw at America or the United Kingdom necessitates deviation from these venerable precepts. And yet, to date, we have proved ourselves just as unscrupulous as our despicable adversaries. Contrary to the assertions of the intellectual savages who argue that power stems from unprincipled ruthlessness, I say that brutality surfaces when political power is in jeopardy, and, uncurbed, portends its quietus.

Only once we summon the pluck to uphold our purported values will we deserve to speak of victory in this senseless, bloody and shameful war.

[5] C Schmitt, *The Theory of the Partisan: A Commentary/Remark on the Concept of the Political*, trans AC Goodson (Michigan State University Press, 2004 (Duncker & Humblot, [1963])).

Shall Prejudice, Priestcraft, Opinion, and Gold,
Every passion with interest alloyed,
Where Love ought to reign, fill the desolate void?
But the Avenger arises, the throne
Of selfishness totters—its groan
Shakes the nations—it falls, Love seizes the sway;
The sceptre it bears unresisted away.

Percy Bysshe Shelley, *The Complete Poetry of Percy Bysshe Shelley* (JHU Press, 2000) 106.

References

BOOKS

Agamben, G, *State of Exception* (University of Chicago Press, 2005).

Alexander, Y, *Combating terrorism: strategies of ten countries* (University of Michigan Press, 2002).

Allott, P, *Eunomia: new order for a new world* (Oxford University Press, 1990).

al-Tirmihdi, *Hadith Collection* (publication date unknown).

Arendt, H, *On Violence* (Harvest/HBJ, 1969).

de Beauvoir, S, *The ethics of ambiguity*, trans B Frechtman (Philosophical Library, 1949).

Benjamin, D and Simon, S, *The Age of Sacred Terror* (Random House, 2002).

Berman, P, *Terror and Liberalism* (WW Norton & Company, Inc, 2003).

Berns, W, *Making Patriots* (Chicago University Press, 2001).

Bianchi, A and Keller, A, *Counterterrorism: Democracy's Challenge* (Hart, 2009).

Blackstone, W, *Commentaries on the Laws of England* (University of Chicago Press, 1979).

Blokker, N and Schrijver, N, *The Security Council and the use of force: theory and reality—a need for change?* (Martinus Nijhoff Publishers, 2005).

Borradori, G, *Philosophy in a time of terror: dialogues with Jürgen Habermas and Jacques Derrida* (University of Chicago Press, 2003).

Brownlie, *Principles of public international law*, 3rd edn (Clarendon Press; Oxford University Press, 1979).

Burke, E, *Reflections on the revolution in France* (Yale University Press, 2003).

—— *A Philosophical Enquiry into the Origin of Our Ideas of the Sublime and Beautiful* (first published in 1757 (Oxford University Press, 1998 edition)).

Byers, M, *War law: international law and armed conflict* (Atlantic Books, 2005).

Byman D and Pollack, K, *Things Fall Apart* (Saban Centre, 2008).

Call, C, *Constructing Justice and Security After War* (United States Institute of Peace Press, 2008).

Camus and O'Brien, J, *The myth of Sisyphus* (Penguin, 1975).

Cannizzaro, E, Palchetti, P and Simma, B, *Customary international law on the use of force: a methodological approach* (Martinus Nijhoff, 2005).

Carson, C, *The Star Factory* (Arcade Publishing, 1998).

Cassese, A, *International law in a divided world* (New York, 1986).

—— *Terrorism, politics, and law: the Achille Lauro affair* (Princeton University Press, 1989).

—— *International law*, 2nd edn (Oxford University Press, 2005).

Chaucer, G, *The Canterbury Tales* (Various publishers, 14th Century).

Cheng, *International law: teaching and practice* (Stevens, 1982).

Cicero, MT, *On moral ends*, J Annas (ed) and R Woolf (trans) (Cambridge University Press, 2001).

—— *Selected Works*, trans M Grant (Penguin Classics, 1974).

Clarke, RA, *Against All Enemies: Inside America's War on Terror* (Free Press, 2004).

von Clausewitz, C and Pochhammer, B, *Vom Kriege* (Vier Falken Verlag, 1940).

Coady, T and O'Keefe, M (eds), *Terrorism and Justice: Moral Argument in a Threatened World* (Melbourne University Publishing, 2002).

Conforti, B and Francioni, F, *Enforcing international human rights in domestic courts* (Martinus Nijhoff, 1997).
Coker, C, *Ethics and War in the 21st Century* (Routledge, 2008).
Conrad, J, *Under Western Eyes* (Courier Dover Publications, 2003).
—— *Heart of Darkness* (Penguin Classics, 2007, [1899]).
—— *The Secret Agent* (Penguin Classics, 1990).
Dinstein, Y, *War, Aggression, and Self-defence* (Cambridge University Press, 2005).
Dostoevsky, F, *The Brothers Karamazov* (Barnes and Noble, 1995, [1880]).
Dreyfuss, R, *Devil's Game—How the United States helped unleash fundamentalist Islam* (Metropolitan Books, Henry Holt & Company, 2005).
Dudziak, M (ed), *September 11 in History: A Watershed Moment?* (Duke University Press, 2003).
Elster, J and Slagstad, R (eds), *Constitutionalism and democracy* (Cambridge University Press, 1988).
Feldman, *Formations of Violence* (Chicago University Press, 1991).
Ferguson, N, *The War of the World* (Allen Lane, 2006).
Fisk, R, *The Great War for Civilisation* (London, Fourth Estate, 2005).
Fletcher, GP, *Romantics at war: glory and guilt in the age of terrorism* (Princeton University Press, 2002).
Forbes, *The Afghan Wars* (Kessinger Publishing, 2004, [1892]).
Francioni, F (ed), *Access to Justice as a Human Right* (Oxford University Press, 2007).
Fried, *Modern liberty and the limits of government*, 1st edn (WW Norton & Co, 2007).
Friedman, G, *America's Secret War: Inside the Hidden Worldwide Struggle between America and its Enemies* (Doubleday, 2004).
Frost, RM, *Nuclear terrorism after 9/11* (New York, 2005).
Fukuyama, F, *America at the Crossroads: Democracy, Power, and the Neoconservative Legacy* (Yale University Press, 2006).
Fuller, LL, *The morality of law*, Rev ed (Yale University Press, 1977).
Gerges, FA, *The far enemy: why Jihad went global* (Cambridge University Press, 2005).
Gibbon, *The History of the Decline and Fall of the Roman Empire* (Alfred Knopf Incorporated, 1993).
Gilbert, G, *Nuremberg Diary* (Da Capo Press, 1995).
Gilbert, P, *New Terror New Wars* (Edinburgh University Press, 2003).
Goodrich, P, Barshack, L and Schuetz, A (eds), *Law, Text, Terror* (Glasshouse, 2006).
Gray, D, *International law and the use of force*, 2nd edn (Oxford University Press, 2004).
Guelke, *The Age of Terrorism* (Tuaris, 1995).
Habermas, J, *Faktizität und Geltung* (Suhrkamp, 1998).
Hamilton, S, *Terrorism and international relations* (Various, 2006).
Harris, J, *Cases and materials on international law*, 6th edn (Sweet & Maxwell, 2004).
Hegel, WF, Miller, AV and Findlay, JN, *Phenomenology of spirit* (Clarendon Press, 1977).
Heymann, PB, *Terrorism, Freedom and Security* (MIT Press, 2003).
Heymann, PB and Kayyem, JN, *Protecting liberty in an age of terror* (MIT Press, 2005).
Hirst, *The Gun and the Olive Branch* (Nation Books, 1977).
Hitler, A, *Mein Kampf* (Secker and Walberg, 1925).
Hobbes, T, *Leviathan* (Cambridge University Press, 1651).
Hobsbawm, EJ, *Age of extremes: the short twentieth century, 1914–1991* (Michael Joseph, 1994).
—— *Globalisation, democracy and terrorism* (Little Brown, 2007).
Holmes, S, *Passions and constraints: on the theory of liberal democracy* (University of Chicago Press, 1995).

—— *The Matador's Cape: America's Reckless Response to Terror* (Cambridge University Press, 2007).
Houen, A, *Terrorism and modern literature, from Joseph Conrad to Ciaran Carson* (Oxford University Press, 2002).
Huntington, SP, *The clash of civilizations and the remaking of world order* (Simon & Schuster, 1996).
Ignatieff, M, *The lesser evil: political ethics in an age of terror* (Edinburgh University Press, 2003).
Ikenberry, *After Victory* (Princeton Paperbacks, 2001).
Jansen, JG, *The Dual Nature of Islamic Fundamentalism* (Cornell University Press, 1997).
Jaspers, K, *The question of German guilt* (Greenwood Press, 1978).
Jenkins, *Will Terrorists Go Nuclear?* (Rand, 1976).
Jennings, R, *The Collected Writings of Sir Robert Jennings* (The Hague, 1998).
Johannsen, R, *Stephen A Douglas* (University of Illinois Press, 1997).
Johnson, *Nemesis: The Last Days of the American Republic* (Holt, 2008).
d Jouvenel, *On power: its nature and the history of its growth* (Beacon Press, 1962).
Kagan, R, *Of paradise and power: America and Europe in the new world order*, 1st edn (Alfred A Knopf: Distributed by Random House, 2003).
Kant, *Kritik der reinen Vernunft* (Hartnoch, 1781).
—— *Zum ewigen Frieden. Ein philosophischer Entwurf*, 1st edn (Unknown, 1795).
Keegan, *A history of warfare* (Pimlico, 1993).
Kennedy, *International Legal Structures* (Baden-Baden, 1987).
Koskenniemi, M, *From apology to utopia: the structure of international legal argument* (Finnish Lawyers' Publishing Co, 1989).
Kramer, MH, *In defense of legal positivism: law without trimmings* (Oxford University Press, 1999).
Kratochwil, *Rules, Norms and Decisions: On The Conditions of Practical and Legal Reasoning in International Relations and Domestic Affairs* (Cambridge University Press, 1989).
Kravchinsky, S and Stepniak, S, *Underground Russia* (C Scribner's Sons, 1883).
van Krieken, PJ *Terrorism and the international legal order: with special reference to the UN, the EU and cross-border aspects* (TMC Press, 2001).
Laursen, *Changing international law to meet new challenges: interpretation, modification and the use of force against terrorists* (Doctoral Thesis, European University Institute, Florence, 2006).
Laqueur, W, *No End to War: Terrorism in the 21st Century* (Continuum International, 2003).
Lawrence (ed), *Messages to the World: The Statements of Osama bin Laden* (Verso, 2005).
Legendre, P, *Sur la Question dogmatique en Occident* (Fayard, 1999).
—— *De la Société comme Texte* (Fayard, 2001).
Levinson, S (ed), *Torture: A collection* (Oxford University Press, 2004).
Locke, *Two treatises of government* (Cambridge University Press, 1988).
MacDonald, *Framing the Legal Within the Post-Foundational: International Law and Ethics after the Critical Challenge* (Doctoral Thesis, European University Institute, Florence, 2006).
Machiavelli, N, *The Prince*, trans G Bull (Penguin Classics, 2003).
Manning, *The Middle Parts of Fortune: Somme and Ancre* (Filiquarian Publishing, 2007).
Mansfield (ed), *His Own Words: A Translation of the Writings of Dr Ayman al Zawahiri* (TGL Publications, 2006).
McGrath, E, *Twilight of Atheism* (Rider, 2005).

McWhinney and McWhinney, E, *Aerial piracy and international terrorism: the illegal diversion of aircraft and international law*, 2nd, rev edn (M Nijhoff; Distributors for the US and Canada Kluwer Academic Publishers, 1987).
Meade, E, *The Siren* (White, 1898).
Mill, JS, *On Liberty* (Broadview Press, 1869).
—— *Considerations on Representative Government* (Kessinger Publishing, 2004).
Milton, J, *Complete Prose Works of John Milton* (Yale University Press, 1959).
de Montaigne, *The Complete Essays*, MA Screech (Penguin, 1991).
de Secondat Montesquieu, C, *The Spirit of the Laws*, trans T Nugent (Hafner, 1949).
Mornet, *Le Romanticisme en France au XVIIIe Siécle* (Ayer Publishing, 1971).
Dante Alighieri, *The Divine Comedy*, trans M Musa (Penguin Classics, 2003).
Nacos, *Mass-Mediated Terrorism* (Rowan and Littlefield, 2007).
Nickel, JW, *Making sense of human rights: philosophical reflections on the Universal Declaration of Human Rights*, 2nd edn (Blackwell Publishing, 2006).
Nietzsche, FW, *Thus Spoke Zarathustra*, trans RJ Hollingdale (Penguin Classics, 1961, [1883]).
—— *Beyond Good and Evil*, trans J Norman (Cambridge University Press, 2002).
—— *The gay science; with a prelude in rhymes and an appendix of songs*, trans WA Kaufmann, 1st edn (Vintage Books, 1974).
Nozick, R, *Anarchy, state, and Utopia* (Blackwell, 1975).
Nussbaum, C, *The Clash Within: Democracy, Religious Violence, and India's Future* (The Belknap Press, 2007).
O'Keefe, MP and Coady, CAJ, *Righteous violence: the ethics and politics of military intervention* (Melbourne University Press, 2005).
Oppenheim, L, Jennings, RY and Watts, A, *Oppenheim's international law. Uniform Title: International law*, 9th edn, Sir Robert Jennings and Sir Arthur Watts (eds) (Longmans, 1992).
Orwell, G, *1984* (Penguin Books, 1954 (Secker & Warburg, [1949])).
Pape, RA, *Dying to win: the strategic logic of suicide terrorism*, 1st edn (Random House, 2005).
Plato, *Gorgias*, trans W Hamilton (Penguin Books, 1960).
Power, S, *A Problem from Hell* (Basic Books, 2002).
Proudhon, P-J, *De la Justice dans la Révolution e dans l'Eglise* (1930 edn, [1858]).
—— *Philosophie du Progrés* (1946 edn, [1853]).
Randall, KC, *Federal courts and the international human rights paradigm* (Duke University Press, 1990).
Ricoeur, *Evil: A challenge to philosophy and theology*, trans J Bowden (Continuum, 2007).
Robertson, *Crimes against humanity: the struggle for global justice* (New Press, 2000).
Rockmore, T, Marsoobian, AT and Margolis, J (eds), *The Philosophical Challenge of September 11* (Blackwell Publishing, 2005).
Roy, *Power politics*, 2nd edn (South End Press, 2001).
Rubin and Rubin, JC, *Anti-American Terrorism and the Middle East* (Oxford University Press, 2002).
Rushdie, S, *The Satanic Verses* (Vintage, 1988).
—— *Imaginary Homelands* (Granta Books, 1991).
Sageman, M, *Understanding terror networks* (University of Pennsylvania Press, 2004).
Sartre, J-P, *Being and nothingness: a phenomenological essay on ontology*, trans HE Barnes (Washington Square Press: Pocket Books, 1992).
Scarry, *The Body in Pain* (Oxford University Press, 1985).

—— *Who Defended the Country? A New Democracy Forum on Authoritarian versus Democratic Approaches to National Defense on 9/11* (Beacon, 2003).

Scheuer, M, *Imperial Hubris* (Brassey's, 2004).

Schmitt, C, *The Theory of the Partisan: A Commentary/Remark on the Concept of the Political*, trans AC Goodson (Michigan State University Press, 2004 (Duncker & Humblot, [1963])).

Schwarzenberger, *The legality of nuclear weapons* (Stevens, 1958).

Scott, *Torture as tort: comparative perspectives on the development of transnational human rights litigation* (Hart, 2001).

Shaw, MN, *International law*, 5th edn (Cambridge University Press, 2003).

Sherry, M, *In the Shadow of War* (Yale University Press, 1995).

Shklar, N, *Ordinary Vices* (Harvard University Press, 1984).

Simpson, AWB, *In the highest degree odious: detention without trial in wartime Britain* (Oxford University Press, 1994).

Slotnick, R, *Gunfighter Nation* (University of Oklahoma Press, 1992).

Steiner and Alston, P, *International Human Rights in Context*, 2nd edn (Oxford University Press, 2000).

Sterba, JP (ed), *Terrorism and International Justice* (Oxford University Press, 2003).

Stone, *Perilous Times: Free Speech in Wartime From the Sedition Act of 1798 to the War on Terrorism* (WW Norton, 2004).

Strawson (ed), *Law after ground zero*, Repr with amendments ed (Glasshouse Press, 2004).

Suskind, R, *The One Percent Doctrine: Deep Inside America's Pursuit of its Enemies Since 9/11* (Simon and Schuster, 2006).

Taylor, *A Secular Age* (Harvard University Press, 2007).

Tickner, *The Spectacle of Women: Imagery of the Suffrage Campaign* (Chicago University Press, 1998).

Ullman, K and Wade, JP, *Shock and Awe* (NDU Press Book, 1996).

Walker, D, *The prevention of terrorism in British law* (Dover NH, 1986).

Weinberg, L and Pedahzur, A (eds), *Religious Fundamentalism and Political Extremism* (Frank Cass, 2004).

White, B, *Justice as Translation: An Essay in Cultural and Legal Criticism* (University of Chicago Press, 1994).

Wilkinson, P, *Terrorism versus democracy: the liberal state response* (Portland OR, 2001).

Woodward, *Bush at War* (Simon and Schuster, 2002).

Woodward, *State of Denial* (Simon and Schuster, 2006).

Žižek, *Welcome to the Desert of the Real* (Verso, 2002).

CHAPTERS IN BOOKS

'In re Yamashita, Decision of the United States Military Commission at Manila, 1945–46' in L Friedman (ed), *The Law of War: A Documentary History* (Random House, 1972).

Bodansky, D, 'Human Rights and Universal Jurisdiction' in M Gibney (ed), *World Justice? US Courts and International Human Rights* (Boulder, Colorado, 1991).

Cooper, R, 'The post-modern state' in M Leonard (ed), *Reordering the world: The long-term implications of September 11th* (Foreign Policy Centre, London, 2002).

Danner, 'Torture and Truth' in *Abu Ghraib—The Politics of Torture* (North Atlantic Books, 2004).

Ehrenreich, 'Feminism's Assumptions Upended' in *Abu Ghraib – The Politics of Torture* (North Atlantic Books, 2004).

Elster, E, 'Introduction' in J Elster and R Slagstad (eds), *Constitutionalism and democracy* (1993).

Foucault, M, 'Nietzsche, genealogy, history' in P Rabinow (ed), *The Foucault Reader* (New York, 1984).

—— 'On the Genealogy of Ethics: An Overview of Work in Progress' in P Rabinow (ed), *The Foucault Reader* (New York, 1984).

—— 'What is enlightenment?' in P Rabinow (ed), *Essential Works of Foucault* (New York, 1997).

—— 'The Ethics of Concern for the Self as a Practice of Freedom' in P Rabinow (ed), *The Essential Works of Michel Foucault* (New York, 1997).

Francioni, F, 'Balancing the Prohibition of Force with the Need to Protect Human Rights: A Methodological Approach' in E Cannizzaro and P Palchetti (eds), *Customary International Law on the Use of Force* (Martinus Nijhoff, 2005).

Genefke, S and Genefke, K, 'Medical Aspects of Torture' in A Cassese (ed), *The International Fight Against Torture* (1991).

Gray, 'Power and Vainglory' in *Abu Ghraib—The Politics of Torture* (North Atlantic Books, 2004).

Greenwood, C, 'Historical Development and Legal Basis' in D Fleck (ed), *The Handbook of Humanitarian Law in Armed Conflicts* (Oxford University Press, 1995).

Habermas, J, 'The Postnational Constellation and the Future of Democracy' in Habermas (ed), *The Postnational Constellation* (Polity Press, 2001).

Higgins, R, 'The Identity of International Law' in B Cheng (ed), *International Law, Teaching and Practice* (London, 1982).

—— 'The General International Law of Terrorism' in R Higgins and M Flory (eds), *International Law and Terrorism* (London, 1997).

Holmes, S, 'Precommitment and the paradox of democracy' in J Elster and R Slagstad (eds), *Constitutionalism and democracy* (1993).

—— 'The Curious Debate' in K Greenberg (ed), *The Torture Debate in America* (Cambridge University Press, 2005).

Jenkins, B, 'Will Terrorists Go Nuclear: A Reappraisal' in HW Kushner (ed), *The Future of Terrorism* (1998).

Kratochwil, F, 'Of Law and Human Action: A Jurisprudential Plea for a World Order Perspective in International Law' in R Falk, F Kratochwil and S Mendlowitz (eds), *International Law: A Contemporary Perspective* (Boulder CO, 1985).

Lawrence, TE, 'The Science of Guerrilla Warfare' in *Encyclopedia Britannica* (1957 edn).

Matlin, D, 'Abu Ghraib: The Surround' in *Abu Ghraib—The Politics of Torture* (North Atlantic Books, 2004).

Smith, A, 'Of the Sense of Duty' in *The Theory of Moral Sentiments* (1853).

Tully, J, 'On Law, Democracy and Imperialism' in S Tierney and E Christodoulidis (eds), *Political Theory and Public Law* (Ashgate, 2007).

Vaneigem, R, 'Basic Banalities II' in K Knabb (ed), *Situationist International Anthology* (2007).

Walker, N, 'The Reframing of Law's Imperial Frame' in S Tierney and E Christodoulidis (eds), *Political Theory and Public Law* (2007).

Yoo, J, 'Memorandum for Alberto R Gonzales Counsel to the President' in KJ Greenberg and JL Dratel (eds), *The Torture Papers: The Road to Abu Ghraib* (2005).

JOURNAL ARTICLES

Abtahi, H, 'The Protection of Cultural Property in Times of Armed Conflict: The Practice of the International Criminal Tribunal for the Former Yugoslavia' (2001) 14 *Harvard Human Rights Journal* 1.

Allott, P, 'Reconstituting Humanity—New International Law' (1992) 3 *European Journal of International Law* 219.

—— 'Thinking Another World: 'This Cannot Be How the World Was Meant to Be' (Review Essay Symposium on Phillip Allott's Eunomia and Health of Nations)' (2005) 16 *European Journal of International Law* 255.

Bamford, B, 'The United Kingdom's "War Against Terrorism"' (2004) 16:4 *Terrorism and Political Violence* 737.

Bianchi, A 'Ferrini v Federal Republic of Germany' (2005) 99 *American Journal of International Law* 242.

Bos, M, 'The Recognised Manifestations of International Law, A New Theory of Sources' (1977) 20 *German Yearbook of International Law* 74.

Bradley and Goldsmith, J, 'Customary International Law as Federal Common Law: A Critique of the Modern Position' (1997) 110 *Harvard Law Review* 815.

—— 'The Current Illegitimacy of International Human Rights Litigation' (1997) 66 *Fordham Law Review* 319.

Brose, K, 'Voelkervertragsrecht und Voelkergewohnheitsrecht Bemerkungen zum Urteil des Internationalen Gerichtshofes zu den miltaerischen und paramilitaerischen Aktivitaeten der USA in und gegen Nikaragua' (1987) 36(6) *Staat und Recht* 471.

Brown, RS, 'The House of Lords Ruling on Torture: A and Others v Secretary of State for the Home Department' (2006) 15 *Italian Yearbook of International Law* 153.

Byford, G, 'The Wrong War' (2002) 81(4) *Foreign Affairs* 34.

Campbell, '"Wars on Terror" and vicarious hegemons: The UK, International Law and the Northern Ireland Conflict' (2005) 54 *International and Comparative Law Quarterly* 321.

Caplan, L, 'State Immunity, Human Rights and Jus Cogens' (2003) 97 *American Journal of International Law* 741.

Cassese, 'The International Community's "Legal" Response to Terrorism' (1989) 38 *International and Comparative Law Quarterly* 589.

—— 'The Marten's Clause: Half a Loaf or Simply Pie in the Sky?' (2000) 11(1) *European Journal of International Law* 187.

Crawford, J, 'International Law and Foreign Sovereigns' (1983) 54 *British Yearbook of International Law*

Czaplinsky, W, 'Sources of International Law in the Nicaragua Case' (1989) 38 *International and Comparative Law Quarterly* 151.

Dworkin, R, 'Is there a right to pornography' (1981) 1 *Oxford Journal of Legal Studies* 177.

—— 'Terror and the Attack on Civil Liberties' *New York Review of Books* 6 November 2003.

Dyzenhaus, 'An Unfortunate Outburst of Anglo-Saxon Parochialism' (2005) 68(4) *Michigan Law Review* 673.

Elliott, M, 'United Kingdom: Detention without trial and the "war on terror"' (2006) 4(3) *I-CON* 553.

—— 'The 'War on Terror' and the United Kingdom's Constitution' (2007) *European Journal of Legal Studies*, available at www.ejls.eu.

Evans, 'Aircraft Hijacking: What is to be done?' (1972) 66(4) *American Journal of International Law* 819.

Falk, R, 'Nuremberg: Past, Present and Future' (1971) 80 *Yale Law Journal* 1501.
Fallows, J, 'Declaring Victory' (2006) September *The Atlantic Monthly*
Farer, TJ, 'Beyond the Charter Frame: Unilateralism or Condominium?' (2002) 96(2) *American Journal of International Law* 359.
Fletcher, 'The Right to Life' (1997) 13 *Georgia Law Review*
Fox, 'State Immunity and the International Crime of Torture' (2006) 2 *European Human Rights Law Review* 142.
Francioni, F, 'Of War, Humanity and Justice: International Law after Kosovo' (2000) 4 *Max Planck Yearbook of UN Law* 107.
Franck, T, 'Terrorism and the Right of Self-Defense' (2001) 95(4) *American Journal of International Law* 839.
Fromkin, D, 'The Strategy of Terrorism' (1975) July *Foreign Affairs* 345.
Fullinwider, R, 'Terrorism, Innocence and War' (2001) 21(4) *Philosophy and Public Policy Quarterly* 9.
Gardiner, R, 'UN Convention on State Immunity: Form and Function' (2006) 55 *International and Comparative Law Quarterly* 407.
Golove, D and Holmes, S, 'Terrorism and Accountability: Why Checks and Balances Apply Even in "The War on Terrorism"' (2004) 2 *New York University Review of Law and Security* 2.
Guillaume, 'Terrorism and International Law' (2004) 53 *International and Comparative Law Quarterly* 537.
Hall, K, 'UN Convention on State Immunity: The Need for a Human Rights Protocol' (2006) 55 *International and Comparative Law Quarterly* 411
Hargrove, 'The Nicaragua Judgment and the Future of the Law of Force and Self-defense' (1987) 81 *American Journal of International Law* 135
Hickman, T, 'Between Human Rights and the Rule of Law: Indefinite Detention and the Derogation Model of Constitutionalism' (2005) 68(4) *Michigan Law Review* 655.
Hiebert, 'Parliamentary Review of Terrorism Measures' (2005) 68(4) *Michigan Law Review* 676.
Holmes, S, 'In Case of Emergency: Misunderstanding Tradeoffs in the War on Terror' (2009) 97 *California Law Review* 303.
Huskisson, D, 'The Air Bridge Denial Program and the Shootdown of Civil Aircraft under International Law' (2005) 56 *Air Force Law Review* 109, 145.
Investigation, 'Excerpts from Report of ICAO Fact-Finding Investigation Pusuant to Decision of ICAO Council of July 14, 1988' (1988) 83 *American Journal of International Law* 332.
Johnson, C, The Arithmetic of America's Military Bases Abroad' (2004) *History News Network* available at: hnn.us/articles/3097.html.
Jowell, J, Judicial Deference, Servility, Civility or Institutional Capacity?' (2003) *Public Law* 592.
King, D, When an Empire is not an Empire: The US Case' (2006) 41 *Government and Opposition* 163.
Kirkpatrick, JJ, 'Dictatorships and Double Standards: Rationalism and Reason in Politics' (1979) *Commentary*
Koh, H, 'Transnational Public Law Litigation' (1991) 100 *Yale Law Journal* 2347.
Koskenniemi, M, The Pull of the Mainstream' (1990) 88 *Michigan Law Review* 1946.
——, 'The Lady Doth Protest Too Much' (2002) 65 *Michigan Law Review* 159.

Kramer, M, 'The Perils of Counterinsurgency—Russia's War in Chechnya' (2004) 29 *International Security* 4.
Kratochwil, F, 'The Force of Prescriptions' (1984) 38 *International Organization* 685.
Krauthammer, 'In Defense of Democratic Realism' (2004) Fall *The National Interest*
Krepinevich, J, 'How to win in Iraq' (2005) September/October 2005 *Foreign Affairs*
L'Heureux-Dubé, 'The Importance of Dialogue: Globalisation and the International Impact of the Rehnquist Court' (1998) 32 *Texas Law Journal* 15.
Leigh, M, 'Denial of Liability: Ex Gratia compensation on a humanitarian basis' (1989) 83 *American Journal of International Law* 319.
Levie, H, 'The History of the Law of War on Land' (2000) 838 *International Review of the Red Cross* 339.
Locke, J, 'A letter concerning toleration' (1689)
Lowe, V, '"Clear and Present Danger": Responses to Terrorism' (2005) 54 *International and Comparative Law Quarterly* 185.
Lowenfeld, 'Looking Back and Looking Ahead' (1989) 83(2) *American Journal of International Law* 336.
Maier, H, 'Ex Gratia Payments and the Iranian Airline Tragedy' (1989) 83 *American Journal of International Law* 325.
Marks, S, 'Torture and the Jurisdictional Immunity of Foreign States' (1997) *Cambridge Law Journal* 8.
McBride, J, 'Protecting Life: A Positive Obligation to Help' (1999) 24 *European Law Review Human Rights Survey* 43.
McGregor, L, 'State Immunity and Jus Cogens' (2006) 55 *International and Comparative Law Quarterly* 437.
Murphy, L,'A Proposal on International Legal Responses to Terrorism' (1991) 2 *Touro Journal of Transnational Law* 67.
Nickel, JW, 'Due Process Rights and Terrorist Emergencies' (2007) 1 *European Journal of Legal Studies*, available at www.ejls.eu.
Orakhelashvili, A, State Immunity and International Public Order' (2002) 45 *German Yearbook of International Law* 227.
Pape, RA, 'The Strategic Logic of Suicide Terrorism' (2003) 97(3) *American Political Science Review* 344.
Paust, JJ, 'Judicial Power to Determine the Status and Rights of Persons Detained Without Trial' (2003) 44(2) *Harvard Law Review* 503.
Poole, T, 'Harnessing the Power of the Past? Lord Hoffman and the Belmarsh Detainees Case' (2005) 32 *Journal of Law and Society* 534.
Rosenfeld, M, 'Habermas's Call for Cosmopolitan Constitutional Patriotism in an Age of Global Terror: A Pluralist Appraisal' (2007) 14(2) *Constellations* 159.
Schachter, O, International Law: The Right of States to Use Armed Force' (1984) 82 *Michigan Law Review* 1620.
Scheffler, S, 'Is Terrorism Morally Distinctive?' (2006) 14:1 *Journal of Political Philosophy* 1.
Scheuerman, WE, 'Survey Article: Emergency Powers and the Rule of Law after 9/11' (2006) 14:1 *Journal of Political Philosophy* 61.
—— 'Carl Schmitt and the Road to Abu Ghraib' (2006) 13(1) *Constellations* 108.
Schmitt, M, 'Bellum Americanum Revisited: US National Security and the Jus ad Bellum' (2003) 176 *Michigan Law Review* 364.
Sealing, K, 'State Sponsors of Terrorism' (2003) 38 *Texas International Law Journal* 119.
Simpson, WB, 'Shooting Felons' (2005) 32 *Journal of Law and Society* 241.

Sofaer, A, Terrorism and the Law' (1986) 64 *Foreign Affairs* 901.
Steyn, J, 'Guantanamo Bay: The Legal Blackhole' (2004) 53 *International and Comparative Law Quarterly* 1.
Tamanaha, Z, 'Understanding Legal Pluralism' (2007) 29 *Sydney Law Review*
Thomas, J, Emergency and Anti-Terrorist Powers 9/11: USA and UK' (2003) 26 *Fordham International Law Journal* 1193.
Ticehurst, R, The Martens Clause and the Laws of Armed Conflict' (1997) 317 *International Review of the Red Cross* 125.
Tierney, S, Determining the State of Exception: What Role for Parliament and the Courts?' (2005) 68(4) *Michigan Law Review* 668.
Travalio, G, Terrorism, International Law, and the Use of Military Force' (2000) 18 *Wisconsin International Law Journal* 145.
Waldron, J, 'Security and Liberty: The Image of Balance' (2003) 11 *Journal of Political Philosophy* 191.
—— 'Torture and Positive Law: Jurisprudence for the White House' (2005) 105 *Columbia Law Review* 1681.
Watkin, K, 'Controlling the Use of Force: A Role for Human Rights Norms in Contemporary Armed Conflict' (2004) 98 *American Journal of International Law* 1.
de Wet, 'The Prohibition of Torture as an International Norm of jus cogens and its Implications for National and Customary Law' (2004) 15 *European Journal of International Law* 97.
JB White, 'Thinking About Our Language' (1986–87) 96 *Yale Law Journal* 1960.
—— 'What Can a Lawyer Learn From Literature? (Review of *Law and Literature: A Misunderstood Relation* by Richard Posner)' (1988–89) 102 *Harvard Law Review* 2014.
Wilde, R, Legal "Black Hole"? Extraterritorial State Action and International Treaty Law on Civil and Political Rights' (2005) 26 *Michigan Journal of International Law* 739.
Wuerth, B, 'The President's Power to Detain "Enemy Combatants": Modern Lessons From Mr Madison's Forgotten War' (2003–04) 98 *Northwestern University Law Review* 1567.
Zedner, L, 'Securing Liberty in the Face of Terror: Reflections from Criminal Justice' (2005) 32(4) *Journal of Law and Society* 507.

CONFERENCE PROCEEDINGS, LECTURES, AND PUBLIC STATEMENTS

Annan, K, 'Democracy: An International Issue' (2001) 19 June 2001, Oxford University.
Iraq, Iran, and Beyond, 24 January 2007, Center of Law and Security at NYU School of Law.
Presidential Powers, 26 April 2006, Center for Law and Security at NYU School of Law.
Power Politics: Iran, Saudi Arabia and Leadership in the Muslim World, 16 January 2008, Center on Law and Security at NYU School of Law.
'24: Torture Televised', 21 March 2007, New York School of Law Center for Law and Security.
P Allott, 'Lecture', at Rome, The Pontifical Academy of the Social Sciences, XIII Plenary Session (2007).
W Arthur, at The Hague Lectures, The Legal Position in International Law of Heads of State, Heads of Government and Foreign Ministers (1994-III 247 *Recueil des Cours*).

GW Bush speaking with President Chirac, 6 November 2001, White House.

GW Bush Discusses Global War on Terror, 29 September 2006, Wardman Park Marriott Hotel, Washington DC.

GW Bush, discussing terrorism with Columbia President (The Oval Office 2002).

GW Bush and G Brown, at 5th Anniversary of Operation Iraqi Freedom (2008).

L Lloyd, at the French Institute in London, 'The State's Reaction to Terrorism' (14 November 2006).

Chairman of the CAT, Meeting with the UK Delegation, CAT/C/SR. 354, 18 November 1998.

WJ Clinton, Statement, 20 August 1998.

J Kerry, 140 Congressional Rec 8256, 1 July 1994.

D Rumsfeld, Remarks, Town Hall Meeting, Des Moines, Iowa, 7 September 2004.

NEWSPAPER REPORTS

'Dick Cheney Rules', *New York Times*, 3 June 2007 available at: www.nytimes.com/2007/06/03/opinion/03sun2.html?scp=1&sq=cheney%20rules&st=cse.

'MP claims UK outsourced torture', BBC News, 8 July 2009, available at: news.bbc.co.uk/2/hi/uk_news/8139622.stm.

'Bush calls for Saddam Execution', BBC News, 17 December 2003, available at: news.bbc.co.uk/2/hi/americas/3326311.stm.

'We're trafficking in fear', *The Guardian*, 22 January 2007, available at: www.guardian.co.uk/media/2007/jan/22/television.mondaymediasection.

'Language skills an urgent need in changing threat landscape', *Federal Times*, 22 February, 2007, available at: www.federaltimes.com/index.php?S=2562275.

'Drones kill dozens in Pakistan', *BBC Online*, 8 July 2009, available at: news.bbc.co.uk/2/hi/south_asia/8139739.stm.

'45 minutes', BBC News, 13 October 2004, available at: news.bbc.co.uk/2/hi/uk_news/politics/3466005.stm.

'Canada puts US on torture list', BBC, 18 January 2008, available at: news.bbc.co.uk/2/hi/americas/7195276.stm.

'UK Nuclear Plans', BBC, 4 December 2006, available at: news.bbc.co.uk/2/hi/uk_news/politics/6205174.stm.

'After the War: Nuclear Fuel', *New York Times*, 24 July 2008 available at: query.nytimes.com/gst/fullpage.html?res=9D01E6DA163BF932A15755C0A9659C8B63&n=Top/Reference/Times%20Topics/Subjects/I/International%20Relations&scp=5&sq=al%20tuwaitha&st=cse.

'US kills Afghans in Strike'', BBC News Online, 13 July 2008, available at news.bbc.co.uk/2/hi/south_asia/7504607.stm.

'Officials: Missiles kill nine in Pakistan', *Washington Post*, 14 August 2008, available at: www.washingtonpost.com/wp-dyn/content/article/2008/08/13/AR2008081300469_2.html.

'Pakistan shuns CIA build up sought by US', *New York Times*, 27 January 2008, available at: www.nytimes.com/2008/01/27/world/asia/27pakistan.html?scp=2&sq=predator%20cia&st=cse.

'New Incidents Heighten Tensions Among British Muslims', *New York Times*, 23 July 2005, available at www.nytimes.com/2005/07/23/international/europe/23muslims.html?_r=1&scp=1&sq=racially%20motivated%20attack%20muslim&st=cse&oref=slogin.

'The New Berlin Wall', *New York Times*, 4 December 2005, available at: www.nytimes.com/2005/12/04/magazine/04berlin.html?scp=3&sq=racially%20motivated%20attack%20muslim&st=cse.

'Video of London Suicide Bomber Released', *The Times*, 6 July 2006, available at: www.timesonline.co.uk/tol/news/uk/article683824.ece.

'Inside a 9/11 Mastermind's Interrogation', *New York Times*, 22 June 2008, available at: www.nytimes.com/2008/06/22/washington/22ksm.html.

'9/11 Suspects Arraigned at Guantánamo Hearing', *New York Times*, available at: www.nytimes.com/2008/06/05/washington/05cnd-gitmo.html?_r=1&scp=2&sq=mohammmed%20arraigned&st=cse&oref=slogin.

'After the Attacks', *New York Times*, 13 September 2001, available at: query.nytimes.com/gst/fullpage.html?res=9A0DE0D61338F930A2575AC0A9679C8B63&scp=31&sq=taliban%209/11&st=cse.

'Legal case against God dismissed', *BBC News Online*, 16 October 2008, at: news.bbc.co.uk/2/hi/americas/7673591.stm.

'Airstrike kills eight militants in Pakistan', *New York Times*, 24 October 2008, available at: www.nytimes.com/2008/10/24/world/asia/24pstan.html?_r=1&scp=3&sq=pakistan&st=cse&oref=slogin.

'Israel could kidnap Ahmadinejad', BBC Online, 8 September 2008, available at: news.bbc.co.uk/2/hi/middle_east/7605852.stm.

'Three die in Guantánamo Suicide Pact', *Sunday Times*, 11 June 2006, available at: www.timesonline.co.uk/tol/news/world/article673738.ece.

'Are British troops at breaking point in Iraq?' *The Independent*, 18 October 2005, available at: www.independent.co.uk/news/world/middle-east/are-british-troops-at-breaking-point-in-iraq-511404.html.

'Three found guilty in August 2006 UK Liquid Explosives Plot', Transport Security Administration, 8 September 2008, available at: www.tsa.gov/press/happenings/terror_plot_hearing.shtm.

'US Ideology Takes a Knock', BBC Newsnight, 30 September 2008, available at: news.bbc.co.uk/2/hi/programmes/newsnight/7645438.stm.

'Taliban dog pen', *The Daily Telegraph*, 2 September 2008, available at: www.news.com.au/dailytelegraph/story/0,22049,24286455–5006009,00.html.

'Taleban suspects held in dog pen', BBC Online, 2 September 2008, available at: news.bbc.co.uk/2/hi/south_asia/7593434.stm.

'Olympians will salute you, Brown tells troops', *The Times*, 22 August 2008, available at: www.timesonline.co.uk/tol/news/politics/article4578623.ece

'Taleban reveal arms suppliers', BBC Online, 18 September 2008, available at: news.bbc.co.uk/2/hi/south_asia/7622335.stm.

'US air raid kills Iraq civilians', *BBC News Online*, 19 September 2008, available at: news.bbc.co.uk/2/hi/middle_east/7625167.stm.

'Defeat is not yet inevitable', *Independent*, 8 October 2008, 24 & 26.

'We can't defeat Taleban', *The Times*, 6 October 2008, available at: www.timesonline.co.uk/tol/news/world/asia/article4887927.ece.

New York Times, 7 September 1983, A10 col 2, col 4.

'US must act first to battle terror', *New York Times*, 2 June 2002, available at: query.nytimes.com/gst/fullpage.html?res=9904E4DC123AF931A35755C0A9649C8B63.

'UK Troop Deaths in Iraq', BBC, available at: news.bbc.co.uk/2/hi/uk_news/3847051.stm.

'Press Deaths in Iraq', Committee to Protect the Press, available at: www.cpj.org/.

'New Blackwater Range', *Guantánamo Bay Gazette*, 18 July 2008.

Barry, D, 'Preaching the gospel of Sept 11 to visitors', *New York Times*, 21 March 2003, available at: query.nytimes.com/gst/fullpage.html?res=9A00EFDE1E31F932A15750C0A9659C8B63.

Barstow, D, 'Security firm says its workers were lured into Iraqi ambush', *New York Times*, 27 October 2008, available at: query.nytimes.com/gst/fullpage.html?res=9C0DE4DB1238F93AA35757C0A9629C8B63&scp=2&sq=fallujah%20contractor%20mutilate&st=cse.

Baudrillard, J, L'esprit du terrorisme', *Le Monde*, 1 November 2001, available at: www.egs.edu/faculty/baudrillard/baudrillard-the-spirit-of-terrorism-french.html.

Beard, M, *London Review of Books*, 4 October 2001.

Bergen, P, 'War of Error', *The New Republic*, 22 October 2007.

Bremer, P, 'How I didn't dismantle Iraq's Army', *New York Times*, 6 September 2007, available at: www.nytimes.com/2007/09/06/opinion/06bremer.html.Burns, J, 'The Struggle for Iraq', *New York Times*, 27 April 2004, available at: query.nytimes.com/gst/fullpage.html?res=990CE0D9113AF934A15757C0A9629C8B63&scp=1&sq=fallujah%20US%20bomb%20mosque%202004&st=cse.

Buruma, I, Extremism: the loser's revenge', *The Guardian*, Saturday 25 February, at: www.guardian.co.uk/world/2006/feb/25/terrorism.comment.

Bush, GW, 'President discusses War on Terror at National Endowment for Democracy', White House Press Release, 6 October 2005, available at: www.whitehouse.gov/news/releases/2005/10/20051006–3.html.

Chomsky, N, '9/11: Not since the war of 1812', available at: www.scribd.com/doc/93592/Noam-Chomsky-Not-Since-The-War-of-1812?ga_related_doc=1.

Cloud, D, 'Colleagues say CIA Analyst played by the rules', *New York Times*, 26 April 2006, available at: www.nytimes.com/2006/04/23/washington/23mccarthy.html?_r=1&oref=slogin.

Fallaci, O, 'La Rabbia e L'Orgoglio', *Corriere della Sera*, 15 September 2006.

Ferguson, N, 'The Empire that Dares not Speak its Name', *Sunday Times*, 13 April 2003.

Gerges, F, 'The Ultimate Terrorist: Myth or Reality', *Beirut Daily Star*, 12 March 2001.

Glaberson, W, 'Evidence Faulted in Detainee Case', *New York Times*, 1 July 2008, at: www.nytimes.com/2008/07/01/washington/01gitmo.html?_r=1&scp=3&sq=muslim%20guantanamo%202008&st=cse&oref=slogin.

Gordon, M, 'Why Falluja remains a crossroads', *New York Times*, 9 April 2004, available at: www.nytimes.com/2004/04/09/international/middleeast/09FALL.html?ex=1217044800&en=67c0114a875b3f0f&ei=5070.

Gourevitch, P and Morris, E, 'The woman behind the camera at Abu Ghraib', *New Yorker*, 24 March 2008, available at: www.newyorker.com/reporting/2008/03/24/080324fa_fact_gourevitch?printable=trueHamid, M, 'Why do they hate us?' *Washington Post*, 22 July 2007, available at: www.washingtonpost.com/wp-dyn/content/article/2007/07/20/AR2007072001806.html.

Hedges, S, 'US Columbia to Resume Air Patrols; Anti-Drug Flights Halted in '01 after Missionary's death', *Chicago Tribune*, 20 August,

Kennan, GF, 'Where Do You Stand on Communism?' *New York Times Magazine*, 27 May 1951.
Lawson, M, 'A wing and a prayer just isn't enough', *The Guardian*, Saturday, 6 October, 2001, online.
Lewis, A, Guantánamo's Long Shadow', *New York Times*, 21 June 2005, available at: www.nytimes.com/2005/06/21/opinion/21lewis.html?_r=1&th&emc=th&oref=slogin.
Lewis, W, 'A Super Krupp—Or War's End', *Blast* 2, 16.
LEXISLibrary, 'Security Council Condemns Use of Weapons Against Civil Aircraft', *Federal News Service*, 31 July, 1996.
Lyall, S, *New York Times*, 9 December 2005.
Milbank, D, 'Cheney Authorized Shooting Down Planes', *Washington Post*, Friday, 18 June 2004, A01.
Milne, S, *London Times*, 21 September 2001.
Mir, H, 'Interview with Osama bin Laden, "Muslims Have the Right to Attack America"', *The Observer*, 11 November 2001.
Pfaff, W, 'The Truth about Torture', *The American Conservative*, 14 February 2005.
Rajeev, R, 'Saudi 'Torture' Victims lose their right to sue', *The Times-online*, 15 June 2006.
Said, E, 'Islam and the West are Inadequate Banners', *The Observer*, 16 September 2001.
Schmitt, E, '3 in 82nd Airborne Say Beating Iraqi Prisoners Was Routine', *New York Times*, 24 September 2005, available at: www.nytimes.com/2005/09/24/politics/24abuse.html?scp=1&sq=fallujah%2082nd%20airborne&st=cse.
—— 'Exception Sought in Detainee Abuse Ban', *New York Times*, 25 October 2005, Late Edition, A.
—— 'Marines Battle Guerrillas in Streets of Falluja', *New York Times*, 27 October 2008, available at: query.nytimes.com/gst/fullpage.html?res=9501E1DB1238F93AA35757C0A9629C8B63&sec=&spon=&&scp=5&sq=fallujah%20contractor%20mutilate&st=cse.
Suskind, R, 'The Untold Story of an Al Qaeda Plot to Attack the Subway', *Time*, 19 June 2006, available at: www.time.com/time/magazine/article/0,9171,1205478,00.html?cnn=yes.

OFFICIAL REPORTS

UNHCR Global Trends Report, available at: www.unhcr.org/4a375c426.html.
Report on Homicide Trends, US Department of Justice, Bureau for Crime Statistics, available at: www.ojp.usdoj.gov/bjs/homicide/homtrnd.htm.
International Commission on Intervention and State Sovereignty, 'Responsibility to Protect' (2001).
Independent Police Complaints Commission, 'Investigation into the shooting of Jean Charles de Menezes' (2005).
The Iraq Study Group Report (Vintage, 2006).
'Eighteenth JCHR Report: Review of Counter-Terrorism Powers' (Session 2003–2004, HL 158/HC 713).
Committee Against Torture, 'Consideration of reports submitted by states parties under Article 19 of the Convention CAT/C/USA/CO/2' (18 May 2006).

High Level Panel 'Report on Threats Challenges and Change (A59/565)' (2 December 2004).

Human Rights Watch, 'PrimeTime Torture' (available at: www.humanrightsfirst.org/us_law/etn/primetime/video_ptt.html).

British Government, 'September Dossier' (September 2002).

Committee Against Torture, '34th Session, Consideration of Article 19 Reports, CAT/C/CO/CAN'.

'The National Security Strategy of the United States' (March 2006).

Center for Public Integrity, 'Report on Falsehood in the Bush Administration' (2008).

Foreign Affairs Select Committee, 'Foreign Affairs Ninth Report' (20 July 2008).

CAT, 'Summary Record of the Second Part (Public) of the 646th Meeting, 6 May 2005, Cat/C/SR. 646/Add.1'.

PCR Committee, London, Stationery Office, 'Antiterrorism, Crime and Security Act 2001 Review: Report' (2003).

ICRC, 'Commentary on the Protocol Additional to the Geneva Conventions of 12 August 1949, and relating to the Protection of Victims of International Armed Conflicts (Protocol I), 8 June 1977'.

P Kooijmans, United Nations Commission on Human Rights 'Resolution 1992/32, UN Doc E/CN. 4/1987/13'.

Taguba, 'US Army Report on Conditions in Detention' (2004, available at: ww.npr.org/iraq/2004/prison_abuse_report.pdf).

Human Rights Watch, 'Leadership Failure: Firsthand Accounts of Torture of Iraqi Detainees by the US Army's 82nd Airborne Division' (25 September 2005).

Preventing torture: a study of the European Convention for the Prevention of Torture and Inhuman or Degrading Treatment or Punishment available at: www.loc.gov/catdir/enhancements/fy0603/98024190-d.html.

INTERNATIONAL MATERIALS AND DOMESTIC STATUTES

Protocol Additional to the Geneva Conventions of the 12th of August 1949, and Relating to the Protection of Victims of International Armed Conflicts, 1977.

Universal Declaration of Human Rights, GA Res 217A(III), UN Doc A/810 1948, 71.

Geneva Convention relative to the treatment of Prisoners of War, 1949.

Rome Statute of the International Criminal Court, 1998.

Geneva Convention Relative to the Protection of Civilian Persons in Time of War, 1949.

Draft Articles on Responsibility of States for Internationally Wrongful Acts 2001.

Convention on International Civil Aviation, 1944.

Charter of the United Nations, 1945.

European Convention on Human Rights, 1950.

Vienna Convention on the Law of Treaties, 1969.

European Convention on State Immunity, 1972.

Convention against Torture and Other Cruel, Inhuman or Degrading Treatment or Punishment, 1984.

UK Human Rights Act, 1998.

The Anti-Terrorism, Crime and Security Act, 2001.

American Service Members Protection Act, 2002.

The Uniting and Strengthening America by Providing Appropriate Tools Required to Intercept and Obstruct Terrorism Act, 2001.

ELECTRONIC MATERIAL

'War On Iraq Was Illegal, Say Top Lawyers', available at: www.globalpolicy.org/component/content/article/167/35770.html.

Nari Jibon available at: www.siu.edu/~narijibon/DADV.htm.

D Rumsfeld, 'Request for authorization of counter-resistance techniques from William J Haynes II, General Counsel' (27 November 2002) available at: www.defenselink.mil/news/Jun2004/d20040622doc5.pdf.

C Horner, 'How and Where to Apply Shock and Awe' available at: www.shockandawe.com/index1.htm.

CASES

McCann v United Kingdom Series A No 324 (1995) 21 EHRR 97.

Nicaragua v United States of America [1986] ICJ Rep 103.

Case Concerning the Gabcikovo-Nagymaros Project [1997] ICJ Rep 7.

Case Concerning Iranian Oil Platforms, Iran v United States [2003] ICJ Rep 161.

Case Concerning the Aerial Incident of 27 July, 1955, Preliminary Objections [1959] ICJ Rep 127, 130.

Khashiyev and Akayeva v Russia (Application Nos 57942/00 and 57945/00) (2005) 42 EHRR 20.

Bubbins v United Kingdom (Application No 50196/99) (1999) 41 EHRR 458.

Nachova v Bulgaria (Application Nos 43577/97 and 43579/98).

Makaratzis v Greece (Application No 50385/99).

United States v Manuel Antonio Noriega 808 F Supp 791 (SD Fla 1992).

Ergi v Turkey (Application No 23818/94).

A (Children) [2000] WL 1274054 CA (Civ Div).

Jones v Kingdom of Saudi Arabia [2004] EWCA Civ 1394.

Jones v Kingdom of Saudi Arabia [2006] UKHL 26.

Prosecutor v Anto Furundzija (1998) Case No IT-95–17/1.

El-Masri v US (Fourth Circuit Opinion, 2 March 2007).

Brown v United States of America (1814) 12 US 110.

Emperor of Austria v Day & Kossuth (1861) 30 LJ Ch 690; 2 Giff 628.

Ex parte Milligan (1866) 71 US 4.

Hilton v Guyot (1895) 159 US 113.

Garcia and Garza (Mexico) v United States of America (1926) 4 RIAA 585; 21 *American Journal of International Law* 581.

Case concerning the SS 'Lotus' (1927) PCIJ Series A, No 10.

Oppenheimer v Louis Rosenthal & Co [1937] 1 All ER 23.

Judgment of the Nuremberg International Military Tribunal (1947) 41 *AJIL* 172.

Youngstown Sheet & Tube v Sawyer (1952) 103 F Supp 569, affirmed.

Rahimtoola v Nizam of Hyderabad [1958] AC 379.

Baker v Carr (1962) 369 US 186.

Attorney General of Israel v Eichmann (1962) 36 ILR 277.
Banco Nacional de Cuba v Sabbatino (1964) 376 US 398.
North Sea Continental Shelf Cases [1969] ICJ Rep 42.
Barcelona Traction, Light and Power Company Ltd [1970] ICJ Rep 3.
Oppenheimer v Cattermole [1976] AC 249.
Trendtex Trading Corp Ltd v Central Bank of Nigeria [1977] 2 WLR 356.
Ireland v United Kingdom [1978] 2 EHRR 25.
Airey v Ireland [1979] 2 EHRR 305.
Filártiga v Peña-Irala (1980) 630 F 2d 876 (CA, 2 Cir).
Case concerning United States Diplomatic and Consular Staff in Tehran [1980] ICJ Rep 3.
Smith Kline & French Laboratories Ltd v Bloch [1983] 2 All ER 72.
I Congreso del Partido [1983] 1 AC 260.
Marsh v Chambers (1983) 463 US 783.
Hannoch Tel-Oren v Libyan Arab Republic (1984) 726 F2d 774.
Spiliada Maritime Corporation v Cansulex Ltd [1987] 1 AC 460.
Velasquez Rodrizuez Inter-American Court of Human Rights, 29 July 1988, Series C no 4.
Godinez Cruz Inter-American Court of Human Rights, 20 January 1989, Series C, no 5.
Trajano v Marcos 878 F 2d 1439 (9th Cir 1989).
Mary M v City of Los Angeles (1991) 814 P 2d 1341 (California Supreme Court).
Brind and others v Home Secretary [1991] All ER 720.
In re Estate of Ferdinand Ed Marcos (1992) 978 F 2d 493, 497 (9th Cir 1992), cert denied, 113 S Ct 2960 (1993).
Saudi Arabia v Nelson (1993) 113 S Ct 1471.
Hunt v T&N plc [1993] 4 SCR 289.
Prinz v Federal Republic of Germany (1994) 307 US App DC 102.
Tolofson v Jensen [1994] 3 SCR 1022.
Fayed v United Kingdom (1994) Series A 294-B, Judgment of 21 September 1994.
R v Brown [1994] 2 All ER 75.
Neira Alegria et al, Inter-American Court of Human Rights, 19 January 1995, Series C, no 21.
Prosecutor v Tadic, Decision on Jurisdiction (Appeals Chamber), Judgment of 2 October 1995 (1995) 105 ILR 453.
Loizidou v Turkey (Preliminary Objections) Series A, No 310 (1995) 20 EHRR 99.
Case C-120/94 *Commission v Greece (The FYROM case)* Opinion of AG Jacobs [1996] ECR I-1513.
Case C-84/95 *Bosphorous v Minister for Transport, Energy and Communications, Ireland and the Attorney General* [1996] ECR I-3953.
Legality of the Threat or Use of Nuclear Weapons, Request for an Advisory Opinion by the United Nations General Assembly (1996) 110 ILR 163.
Al-Adsani v Government of Kuwait (1996) 107 ILR 536 (CA).
Al-Adsani v United Kingdom (Application No 35763/97) 21 November 2001, ECHR 2001-XI.
Prosecutor v Erdemovic, Sentencing Judgment (1996) 108 ILR 180.
Controller and Auditor General v Sir Ronald Davidson [1996] NZLR 278.
Mohammed v Bank of Kuwait [1996] 1 WLR 1483.
Case C-124/95 *Centro-Com v HM Treasury and Bank of England* [1997] ECR I-81.
Propend Finance v Alan Sing and Commissioner of the Australian Federal Police (1997) 111 ILR 611.
Osman v United Kingdom (Application No 23452/94) (1998) 29 EHRR 245.

R v Bow Street Metropolitan Stipendiary Magistrate, Ex p Pinochet Ugarte (No 1) (1998) 37 ILM 1302.

Connelly v RTZ Corporation PLC [1998] AC 854 (HL).

R v Bow Street Metropolitan Stipendiary Magistrate and others, ex parte Pinochet Ugarte (No 3) [1999] 2 All ER 97.

Matthews v United Kingdom (Application No 24833/94), 18 February 1999 (Grand Chamber) ECHR 1999-I.

Mamatkulov and Askarov v Turkey (Application Nos 46827/99 and 46951/99) 4 February 2005 (Grand Chamber) ECHR 2005-I.

Public Committee Against Torture in Israel v State of Israel (1999) HCJ 5100/94, 53(4) PD 817.

Public Committee against Torture in Israel and Palestinian Society for the Protection of Human Rights and the Environment v Government of Israel et al (2006) HCJ 769/02.

Zoran Kupreskic et al (Case No IT-95–16-T) (2000) ICTY, Trial Chamber II, decision of 14 January 2000.

Prefecture of Voiotia v Federal Republic of Germany (Aerios Pagos) Case No 11/2000.

Holland v Lampen-Wolfe [2000] 1 WLR 1573.

McElhinney v Ireland and UK (App No 31253/96) 21 November 2001, ECHR 2001-XI.

SEGI and Gestoras Pro-Amnistia v Germany and Others (Application Nos 6422/02 and 9916/02) 23 May 2002, ECHR 2002-V.

Strugar and others (Decision on Defence preliminary motion challenging jurisdiction) [2002] ICTY Appeals Chamber, decision of 7 June 2002.

Federal Republic of Germany v Miltiadis Margellos Case 6/17–9-2002 (Decision of the Greek Special Supreme Court).

Bouzari v Iran [2002] OJ No 1624 (Ontario Superior Court of Justice).

Case Concerning the Arrest Warrant of 11 April 2000 (Democratic Republic of Congo v Belgium) (2002) www.icj-cijorg/icjwww/idocket/iCOBE/iCOBEframehtm.

John Doe I v Unocal Corporation 395 F 3d 932 (9th Cir 2002).

Prosecutor v Naletilic and Martinovic, ICTY (2003) Case No IT-98–34-T.

Ferrini v Repubblica Federale di Germania Cass March 11, 2004 (Sez Un), (2004) 87 *Rivista di Diritto Internazionale* 589.

Sosa v Alvarez-Machain [2004] US Sup Ct 03–339.

Rasul et al v Bush, President of the United States et al 542 US 466 (2004).

Hamdi et al v Rumsfeld, Secretary of Defense, et al No 03–6696, 542 US 692 (2004)

A v Secretary of State for the Home Department [2004] UKHL 56.

Case T-306/01, *Ahmed Ali Yusuf and Al Barakaat International Foundation v European Council and Commission* [2005] ECR II-3533.

Case T-315/01, *Yassin Abdullah Kadi v European Council and Commission* [2005] ECR II-3649.

A (FC) and others (FC) (Appellants) v Secretary of State for the Home Department (Respondent) [2005] UKHL 71.

Bosphorus Hava Yollari Turizm ve Ticaret Anonim Sirket (Bosphorus Airways) v Ireland (Application No 45036/98) 30 June 2005.

Die Luftsicherheitsgesetzentscheidung, BVerfG, 1 BVR 357/05 vom 15.2.2006.

Prosecutor v Milošević ICTY (2007) Case No IT-98–29/1-T.

Boumediene et al v Bush, President of the United States; Al Odah v United States Nos 06–1195 and 06–1196, 553 US 723 (2008).

Ex parte Merryman 17 F Cas 144 (1861) (Circuit Court, D Maryland).

Saadi v Italy (Application No 37201/06) 28 February 2008, ECHR.

Index